Hacking The LSAT

Full Explanations For LSATs 29-38

or

Explanations For "The Next Ten Actual Official LSATs"

Volume II: LSATs 34-38

Graeme Blake

ISBN 13: 978-0-9881279-1-3
ISBN 10: 0-9881279-1-1

Testimonials

Self-study is my preferred way to prep, but I often felt myself missing a few questions each test. Especially for Logic Games, I wanted to see those key inferences which I just couldn't seem to spot on my own. That's where *Hacking The LSAT* came in. These solutions have been a tremendous help for my prep, and in training myself to think the way an experienced test taker would.

- Spencer B.

Graeme paraphrases the question in plain terms, and walks through each step in obtaining the right answer in a very logical way. This book uses the same techniques as other guides, but its so much more consistent and concise! By the time you read through all the tests, you've gradually developed your eye for the questions. Using this book is a great way to test your mastery of techniques!

- Sara L.

Graeme's explanations have the most logical and understandable layout I've seen in an LSAT prep book. The explanations are straightforward and easy to understand, to the point where they make you smack your forehead and say 'of course!

- Michelle V.

"Graeme is someone who clearly demonstrates not only LSAT mastery, but the ability to explain it in a compelling manner. This book is an excellent addition to whatever arsenal you're amassing to tackle the LSAT."

- J.Y. Ping, 7Sage LSAT, www.7Sage.com

I did not go through every single answer but rather used the explanations to see if they could explain why my answer was wrong and the other correct. I thought the breakdown of "Type", "Conclusion", "Reasoning" and "Analysis" was extremely useful in simplifying the question. As for quality of the explanations I'd give them a 10 out of 10.

- Christian F.

LSAT PrepTests come with answer keys, but it isn't sufficient to know whether or not you picked the credited choice to any given question. The key to making significant gains on this test is understanding the logic underlying the questions.

This is where Graeme's explanations really shine. You may wonder whether your reasoning for a specific question is sound. For the particularly challenging questions, you may be at a complete loss as to how they should be approached.

Having these questions explained by Graeme who scored a 177 on the test is akin to hiring an elite tutor at a fraction of the price. These straightforward explanations will help you improve your performance and, more fundamentally, enhance your overall grasp of the test content.

- Morley Tatro, Cambridge LSAT, www.cambridgelsat.com

Through his conversational tone, helpful introductions, and general recommendations and tips, Graeme Blake has created an enormously helpful companion volume to *The Next Ten Actual Official LSATs*. He strikes a nice balance between providing the clarity and basic explanation of the questions that is needed for a beginner and describing the more complicated techniques that are necessary for a more advanced student.

Even though the subject matter can be quite dry, Graeme succeeds in making his explanations fun and lighthearted. This is crucial: studying for the LSAT is a daunting and arduous task. By injecting some humor and keeping a casual tone, the painful process of mastering the LSAT becomes a little less painful.

When you use *Hacking The LSAT* in your studying, you will feel like you have a fun and knowledgeable tutor guiding you along the way.

- Law Schuelke, LSAT Tutor, www.lawLSAT.com

Graeme's explanations are clear, concise and extremely helpful. They've seriously helped me increase my understanding of the LSAT material!

- Jason H.

Graeme book brings a different view to demystifying the LSAT. The book not only explains the right and wrong answers, but teaches you how to read the reading comprehension and the logical reasoning questions. His technique to set up the games rule by rule help me not making any fatal mistakes in the set up. The strategies he teaches can be useful for someone starting as much as for someone wanting to perfect his strategies. Without his help my LSAT score would have been average, he brought my understanding of the LSAT and my score to a higher level even if english is not my mother tongue.

- Patrick Du.

This book is a must buy for any who are looking to pass or improve their LSAT, I highly recommend it.

- Patrick Da.

This book was really useful to help me understand the questions that I had more difficulty on. When I was not sure as to why the answer to a certain question was that one, the explanations helped me understand where and why I missed the right answer in the first place. I recommend this book to anyone who would like to better understand the mistakes they make.

- Pamela G.

Graeme's book is filled with thoughtful and helpful suggestions on how to strategize for the LSAT test. It is well-organized and provides concise explanations and is definitely a good companion for LSAT preparation.

- Lydia L.

The explanations are amazing, great job. I can hear your voice in my head as I read through the text.

- Shawn M.

Hacking the LSAT, especially the logic games sections, was extremely helpful to my LSAT preparation.

The one downside to self study is that sometimes we do not know why we got a question wrong and thus find it hard to move forward. Graeme's book fixes that; it offers explanations and allows you to see where you went wrong. This is an extremely helpful tool and I'd recommend it to anybody that's looking for an additional study supplement.

- Joseph C.

Regardless of how well you're scoring on the LSAT, this book is very helpful. I used it for LR and RC. It breaks down and analyzes each question without the distraction of classification and complicated methods you'll find in some strategy books. Instead of using step-by-step procedures for each question, the analyses focus on using basic critical thinking skills and common sense that point your intuition in the right direction. Even for questions you're getting right, it still helps reinforce the correct thought process. A must-have companion for reviewing prep tests.

- Christine Y.

Take a thorough mastery of the test, an easygoing demeanor, and a genuine desire to help, and you've got a solid resource for fine-tuning your approach when you're tirelessly plowing through test after test. Written from the perspective of a test-taker, this book should help guide your entire thought process for each question, start to finish.

- Yoni Stratievsky, Harvard Ready, www.harvardready.com

This LSAT guide is the best tool I could have when preparing for the LSAT. Not only does Graeme do a great job of explaining the sections as a whole, he also offers brilliant explanations for each question. He takes the time to explain why an answer is wrong, which is far more helpful when trying to form a studying pattern.

- Amelia F.

Table Of Contents

Introduction

The LSAT is a hard test.

The only people who write the LSAT are smart people who did well in University. The LSAT takes the very best students, and forces them to compete.

If the test's difficulty shocked you, this is why. The LSAT is a test designed to be hard for smart people.

That's the bad news. But there's hope. The LSAT is a *standardized* test. It has patterns. It can be learned.

To get better, you have to review your mistakes. Many students write tests and move on, without fully understanding their mistakes.

This is understandable. The LSAC doesn't publish official explanations for most tests. It's hard to be sure why you were wrong.

That's where this book comes in. It's a companion for *The Next Ten Actual Official LSATs*. (LSATs 29-38)

This book lets you see where you went wrong. It has a full walk through of each question and of every answer choice. You can use this book to fix your mistakes, and make sure you understand *everything*.

By getting this book, you've shown that you're serious about beating this test. I sincerely hope it helps you get the score you want.

There are a few things that I'd like to highlight.

Logical Reasoning: It can be hard to identify conclusions. You don't get feedback on whether you identified the conclusion correctly.

This book gives you that feedback. I've identified the conclusion and the reasoning for each argument. Try to find these on your own beforehand, and make sure they match mine.

Logic Games: Do the game on your own before looking at my explanation. You can't think about a game unless you're familiar with the rules. Once you read my explanations, draw my diagrams yourself on a sheet of paper. You'll understand them much better by recopying them.

Reading Comprehension: You should form a mental map of the passage. This helps you locate details quickly when needed. Make a 1-2 line summary of each paragraph (it can be a mental summary).

I've written my own summaries for each passage. They show the minimum amount of information that you should know after reading a passage, without looking back.

Always do these three things:

1. Know the point of the passage.
2. Understand the passage, in broad terms. Reread anything you don't understand.
3. Know where to find details. That's the point of the paragraph summaries. I usually do mine in my head, and they're shorter than what I've written.

If you do these three things, you can answer most Reading Comprehension questions with ease.

Other Resources

This is volume II of my explanations for *The Next Ten Actual Official LSATs*.

This volume covers LSATs 34-38. If you don't already have it, volume I covers LSATs 29-33.

This book assumes some basic familiarity with LSAT concepts such as formal logic. There wasn't space to add more general tips - this book is already pretty big.

If you need introductory help, check out www.lsathacks.com or www.reddit.com/r/LSAT, where I'm the moderator.

Good luck!

Graeme

p.s. I'm a real person, and I want to know how the LSAT goes and what you think of this book. Send me an email at graeme@lsathacks.com!

p.p.s. If you like this book, please let everyone know by leaving an Amazon review. I'd really appreciate it!

How To Use This Book

The word "Hacking" in the title is meant in the sense used by the tech world and Lifehacker: "solving a problem" or "finding a better way".

The LSAT can be beaten, but you need a good method. My goal is for you to use this book to understand your mistakes and master the test.

This book is *not* a replacement for practicing LSAT questions on your own.

You have to try the questions by yourself first. When you review, try to see why you were wrong *before* you look at my explanations.

Active review will teach you to fix your own mistakes. The explanations are there for when you have difficulty solving on a question on your own.

When you *do* use the explanations, have the question on hand. These explanations are not meant to be read alone. You should use them to help you think about the questions more deeply.

Most of the logical reasoning explanations are pretty straightforward. Necessary assumption questions are often an exception, so I want to give you some guidance to help you interpret the explanations.

The easiest way to test the right answer on a necessary assumption question is to "negate" it.

You negate a statement by making it false, in the slightest possible way. For example, the negation of "The Yankees will win all their games" is "The Yankees will *not* win all their games (they will lose at least one)."

You *don't* have to say that the Yankees will lose *every* game. That goes too far.

If the negation of an answer choice proves the conclusion wrong, then that answer is *necessary* to the argument, and it's the correct answer.

Often, I negate the answer choices when explaining necessary assumption questions, so just keep in mind why they're negated.

Logic games also deserve special mention.

Diagramming is a special symbolic language that you have to get comfortable with to succeed.

If you just *look* at my diagrams without making them yourself, you may find it hard to follow along. You can only learn a language by using it yourself.

So you will learn *much* more if you draw the diagrams on your own. Once you've seen how I do a setup, try to do it again by yourself.

With constant practice, you *will* get better at diagramming, and soon it will come naturally.

But you must try on your own. Draw the diagrams.

Note that when you draw your own diagrams, you don't have to copy every detail from mine. For example, I often leave off the numbers when I do linear games. I've included them in the book, because they make it easier for you to follow along.

But under timed conditions, I leave out many details so that I can draw diagrams faster. If you practice making drawings with fewer details, they become just as easy to understand.

Keep diagrams as minimal as possible.

If you simply don't *like* the way I draw a certain rule type, then you can substitute in your own style of diagram. Lots of people succeed using different styles of drawing.

Just make sure your replacement is easy to draw consistently, and that the logical effect is the same. I've chosen these diagrams because they are clear, they're easy to draw, and they *keep you from forgetting rules*.

Short Guide to Logical Reasoning

LR Question Types

Must be True: The correct answer is true.

Most Strongly Supported: The correct answer is probably true.

Strengthen/Weaken: The answer is correct if it even slightly strengthens/weakens the argument.

Parallel Reasoning: The correct answer will mirror the argument's structure exactly. It is often useful to diagram these questions (but not always).

Sufficient Assumption: The correct answer will prove the conclusion. It's often useful to diagram sufficient assumption questions. For example:

The conclusion is: $A \rightarrow D$

There is a gap between premises and conclusion:

$A \quad B \rightarrow C \rightarrow D$ **missing link:** $A \rightarrow B$ or $\cancel{B} \rightarrow \cancel{A}$

$A \rightarrow B \rightarrow C \quad D$ **missing link:** $C \rightarrow D$ or $\cancel{D} \rightarrow \cancel{C}$

$A \rightarrow B \quad C \rightarrow D$ **missing link:** $B \rightarrow C$ or $\cancel{C} \rightarrow \cancel{B}$

The right answer will provide the missing link.

Necessary Assumption: The correct answer will be essential to the argument's conclusion. Use the negation technique: If the correct answer is false (negated), then the argument falls apart.
The negation of hot is "not hot" rather than cold.

Point at Issue: Point at Issue questions require two things. 1. The two speakers must express an opinion on something. 2. They must disagree about it.

Flawed Reasoning: The correct answer will be a description of a reasoning error made in the argument. It will often be worded very abstractly.

Practice understanding the answers, right and wrong. Flawed Reasoning answers are very abstract, but they all mean something. Think of examples to make them concrete and easier to understand.

Basic Logic

Take the phrase: "All cats have tails."

"Cats" is the sufficient condition. Knowing that something is a cat is "sufficient" for us to say that it has a tail. "Tails" is a necessary condition, because you can't be a cat without a tail. You can draw this sentence as $C \rightarrow T$

The **contrapositive** is a correct logical deduction, and reads "anything without a tail is not a cat." You can draw this as $\cancel{T} \rightarrow \cancel{C}$. Notice that the terms are reversed, and negated.

Incorrect Reversal: "Anything with a tail is a cat." This is a common logical error on the LSAT.

$T \rightarrow C$ (Wrong! Dogs have tails and aren't cats.)

Incorrect Negation: "If it is not a cat, it doesn't have a tail." This is another common error.

$\cancel{C} \rightarrow \cancel{T}$ (Wrong! Dogs aren't cats, but have tails.)

General Advice: Always remember what you are looking for on each question. The correct answer on a strengthen question would be incorrect on a weaken question.

Watch out for subtle shifts in emphasis between the stimulus and the incorrect answer choices. An example would be the difference between "how things are" and "how things should be."

Justify your answers. If you're tempted to choose an answer choice that says something like the sentence below, then be sure you can fill in the blank:

Answer Choice Says: "The politician attacked his opponents' characters",

Fill In The Blank: "The politician said _____ about his opponents' characters."

If you cannot say what the attack was, you can't pick that answer. This applies to many things. You must be able to show that the stimulus supports your idea.

A Few Logic Games Tips

Rule 1: When following along with my explanations....draw the diagrams yourself, too!

This book will be much more useful if you try the games by yourself first. You must think through games on your own, and no book will do that for you. You must have your mind in a game to solve it.

Use the explanations when you find a game you can't understand on your own, or when you want to know how to solve a game more efficiently.

Some of the solutions may seem impossible to get on your own. It's a matter of practice. When you learn how to solve one game efficiently, solving other games becomes easier too.

Try to do the following when you solve games:

Work With What Is Definite: Focus on what must be true. Don't figure out every possibility.

Draw Your Deductions: Unsuccessful students often make the same deductions as successful students. But the unsuccessful students forget their deductions, 15 seconds later! I watch this happen.

Draw your deductions, or you'll forget them. Don't be arrogant and think this doesn't happen to you. It would happen to *me* if I didn't draw my deductions.

Draw Clear Diagrams: Many students waste time looking back and forth between confusing pictures. They've done everything right, but can't figure out their own drawings!

You should be able to figure out your drawings 3 weeks later. If you can't, then they aren't clear enough. I'm serious: look back at your old drawings. Can you understand them? If not, you need a more consistent, cleaner system.

Draw Local Rules: When a question gives you a new rule (a local rule), draw it. Then look for deductions by combining the new rule with your existing rules. Then double-check what you're being asked and see if your deduction is the right answer. This works 90% of the time for local rule questions. And it's fast.

If you don't think you have time to draw diagrams for each question, practice drawing them faster. It's a learnable skill, and it pays off.

Try To Eliminate a Few Easy Answer Choices First: You'll see examples in the explanations that show how certain deductions will quickly get rid of 1-3 answer choices on many questions. This saves time for harder answer choices and it frees up mental space.

You don't have to try the answer choices in order, without thinking about them first.

Split Games Into Two Scenarios When Appropriate: If a rule only allows something to be one of two ways (e.g. F is in 1 or 7), then draw two diagrams: one with F in 1, and one with F in 7. This leads to extra deductions surprisingly often. And it always makes the game easier to visualize.

Combine Rules To Make Deductions: Look for variables that appear in multiple rules. These can often be combined. Sometimes there are no deductions, but it's a crime not to look for them.

Reread The Rules: Once you've made your diagram, reread the rules. This lets you catch any mistakes, which are fatal. It doesn't take very long, and it helps you get more familiar with the rules.

Draw Rules Directly On The Diagram: Mental space is limited. Three rules are much harder to remember than two. When possible, draw rules on the diagram so you don't have to remember them.

Memorize Your Rules: You should memorize every rule you can't draw on the diagram. It doesn't take long, you'll go faster, and you'll make fewer mistakes. Try it, it's not that hard.

If you spend 30 seconds doing this, you'll often save a minute by going through the game faster.

You should also make a numbered list of rules that aren't on the diagram, in case you need to check them.

Test 34
Section I - Reading Comprehension
Passage 1 - Authoritarian Rulers
Questions 1-6

Paragraph Summaries

1. Authoritarian rulers tend to reform only when they see society will force them out of power otherwise.
2. Three changes can cause this. The first is changing values that lead to a demand for freedom.
3. The second factor is shifting economic interests.
4. The third factor is the formation of independent groups that can challenge the dictator.
5. If a dictator is successful at making reforms, then often this creates even more pressure for change. Smart authoritarian rulers will eventually make democratic changes.

Analysis

The passage is a neutral discussion of what causes authoritarian rulers to implement reforms, and what happens when authoritarian rulers do reform. The authoritarian rulers are motivated by preserving their own power.

The author doesn't say whether he likes or dislikes dictators. But he thinks most of them will face societal changes that force them to make democratic reforms (lines 50-60).

This passage clearly illustrates the difference between positive arguments ("what will happen") and normative arguments ("what should happen"). This argument is positive; it doesn't tell us what we should do or hope for.

Question 1

DISCUSSION: The passage is t a descriptive argument. It tells us what will happen, and why.

It doesn't tell us what *should* happen. All we know is that authoritarian rulers will often be forced to make democratic reforms because of changes in society.

_____

A. Actually, most authoritarian rulers only make changes when threatened. (lines 6-7)
B. The article is about how authoritarian rulers make changes to *preserve* power. The passage never said that dictators are doomed to fail. They just might have to make democratic changes.
C. There was no talk of success being short lived. Lines 54-56 mention stability. This stability gives citizens time to think about democracy.
D. The passage implies that authoritarian rulers can keep holding power, if they implement some level of democratic reforms (lines 59-60).
E. **CORRECT.** The first paragraph tells us that authoritarian rulers only make reforms when compelled. Authoritarian rule inevitably causes changes in society that in turn force the dictator to make changes of his own.

Question 2

DISCUSSION: The passage's author seems to believe that authoritarian governments will inevitably be pushed towards the democratic changes mention in lines 59-60. And if authoritarian governments don't make changes, then they will lose power (lines 5-7).

A. The first paragraph implies that the democratic changes are real. If the changes were just superficial then it's unlikely that the rulers could hold onto power. Society demands real change.
B. The motives of authoritarian rulers are clear: keep power. The passage says changes in *society* are what lead to the end of authoritarian rule.
C. **CORRECT.** The author seems certain that most authoritarian societies will change in the ways he describes (lines 50-52). That will force authoritarian rulers to make the changes described in lines 59-60.
D. We tend to dislike authoritarian rulers. But the author doesn't say what they think of them. So be careful about bringing in *unwarranted* outside assumptions. Not everyone dislikes dictators.
E. Lines 50-52 show that the author believes most authoritarian societies will undergo the changes mentioned, and force democratic change.

Question 3

DISCUSSION: In short, the passage says that changes in society force political change. It discusses different types of societal change, and the inevitability of change.

A. The article isn't encouraging anyone to dissent. It's predicting people *will* dissent, but that's different from saying they *should* dissent.
B. Name me one specific human right abuse mentioned. (there are none). This answer is playing on our association of authoritarian societies with human rights violations. They are mentioned as a cause of dissatisfaction in lines 21-22, but that's all.
C. What strategy is given for a democratic coalition? (hint: none. This is a nonsense answer).
D. **CORRECT.** The passage discusses the reasons authoritarian rulers make changes. That's all.
E. This ignores the non-economic reasons citizens may demand change.

Question 4

DISCUSSION: The intro mentions the reasons why a dictator might be forced to change. The three reasons are described. The final paragraph talks about how likely these changes are.

Take this part by part. For example, the first sentence in the last three answers isn't as good as the first sentence in the first two answers. And the final sentence in the first answer is bad. That told me I should focus on seeing whether B matches, and it did.

_____

A. There are no alternative causes rejected in the final paragraph.
B. CORRECT. The phenomenon is "political change in authoritarian societies", the causes are "societal changes". The next three paragraphs explain each cause in more detail. And the final paragraph does expand on the relationship and confirm it.
C. There is no cause preferred over the others.
D. Democratic change isn't _compared_ to societal change. The argument is saying societal change _leads to_ democratic change.
E. Same as D. There is no comparison being made.

Question 5

DISCUSSION: Inference questions are sometimes hard. Narrow them down to a couple of answers, they try to see which can be supported based on the passage. You can usually find a specific line to support the right answer.

_____

A. The first paragraph says most authoritarian rulers only change when they _have_ to. If _could_ still be true that some change even if not pressured, but we've got no evidence for that, and plenty of evidence to counter it.
B. The passage seems to imply that citizens get more dissatisfied as time goes on. See lines 8-12 and 54-56.
C. Lines 53-56 show that economic success can make a government _weaker_, because it gives citizens time to think about other values, such as democracy.
D. CORRECT. That's why rulers are forced to make changes (we're told they make changes to hold on to power, lines 5-7). If leaders could hold on to power without making changes, then most would make no changes.
E. Line 12 says that citizens don't like concentration of power either.

Question 6

DISCUSSION: Authoritarian rulers seem to like power. Democratic reforms cost them power, but allow them to hold on to at least some influence. That's better than nothing.

_____

A. We have no evidence the rulers care about the health of the nation. As far as we know, they only care about themselves.
B. If rulers believed this, then they would always make democratic reforms. Instead, they only reform when they're forced to.
C. Same as B.
D. Rulers only seem to care about the economy if it helps them keep power.
E. CORRECT. By giving up a bit of power in the short term, rulers can hold onto at least some power in the long term.

Passage 2 - The Blues
Questions 7-12

Paragraph Summaries

1. Contrary to popular belief, the blues aren't just songs of sadness. They share much with African-American "spirituals".
2. The blues and spirituals can both be linked to West African religious practices. These aimed to turn sadness into elation.
3. Likewise, the blues attempts to transform sad experiences into something positive and artistic.

Analysis

This is a hard passage. It delves deep into the origins and purpose of the blues. They aren't just sad songs, despite what people might believe. They have a lot in common with African-American religious music (spirituals). Both the blues and spirituals seem to have descended from West African religious rites.

The purpose of all of these practices is to turn negative experiences into something positive.

Question 7

DISCUSSION: Support the right answer using the passage. There's never much else to say on specific detail questions. But if you don't check the passage for your answer, you're pretty much guessing.

A. The author said the blues have some similarities to organized religion. But that's different from saying they *are* organized religion.
B. The author doesn't mention modern forms of the blues.
C. The author doesn't mention other types of African American folk art, apart from spirituals. This answer is too general for our limited evidence.
D. Hard to say. There could be other ways the blues produces tension.
E. **CORRECT.** Lines 9-12 and 29-30 make this clear: the blues aims to transform the listeners' sadness into something better.

Question 8

DISCUSSION: Eliminate the wrong answers using specific lines. If you didn't have time, then you should practice making a map of the information in the passage (i.e. paragraph summaries). And learn to skim for information faster.

Rereading to find information is the most important skill for Reading Comprehension.

A. Lines 26-27.
B. Lines 29-30.
C. Lines 30-33
D. Lines 29-30.
E. **CORRECT.** This is never mentioned. The blues and spirituals have similar aims, but different forms. The blues are described as "secular" (non-religious) in lines 13-14.

Question 9

DISCUSSION: You'll want to read lines 19-20 as well. Line 19 refers to the aesthetic that's part of African-American culture.

A. Differing cultures? These lines refer to something *within* African-American culture.
B. All music? That's way too broad. This is only referring to spirituals and the blues.
C. **CORRECT.** The experiences belonged to the whole African-American community. The experiences helped lead to both the blues and spirituals.
D. Huh? This gibberish is just designed to confuse you. "Irreconcilable dichotomies" would mean that something was split into two opposing parts. That's not the blues and spirituals; they are similar.
E. This is too narrow. The cultural aesthetic could have arisen from all aspects of African-American culture, not just from folk music.

Question 10

DISCUSSION: The second paragraph discussed the links between spirituals and the blues, and showed how they both likely descended from West African religious practices.

_____

A. CORRECT. They both originated from West African religious practices.
B. Ecstasy is mentioned, but it's a small part of the whole paragraph.
C. This ignores spirituals, which were a major focus of the paragraph.
D. This ignores spirituals.
E. This is too vague. The paragraph was specific to the blues, spirituals, and the West African religious practices which led to them both.

Question 11

DISCUSSION: Read backwards from line 39 and you'll see that it's telling us how we should understand the word ecstasy.

The word has several different meanings, and the author is says we should use one of them in particular: standing out from yourself.

_____

A. We're not told what the standard meaning of the word ecstasy is. We're just told to understand it according to a rare meaning.
B. CORRECT. We're supposed to understand ecstasy according to this etymological meaning. See 37-39.
C. Blues performances aren't mentioned *anywhere* near line 39. The passage is talking about West Africa at that point.
D. In line 31 the passage says the blues can be linked to the practices referred to in line 39. So the passage suggests they are *similar*.
E. Same as C. This section of the passage talks about West African rites, not the blues.

Question 12

DISCUSSION: A *lot* of people get this wrong. Take it part by part to eliminate some answers. Then, match up your 2-3 best choices with the passage to be sure they really do work, or to eliminate them.

_____

A. This doesn't work, because the blues and spirituals are quite similar, once we get past appearances.
B. The blues and spirituals are not *subtly* different. They seem *very* different to most people, so much so that many fail to realize they are alike.
C. Most people choose this answer. The blues are *conventionally* misunderstood. So people who don't know much about the blues misunderstand them. But *experts* have presumably long understood how the blues are linked to spirituals and West Africa. There's been no new discovery that prompted the author to write this passage.

Botanists are experts, and we shouldn't expect them to be ignorant. They're only changing their minds because of a recent discovery. There was no recent discovery in the passage.
D. This gets it backwards. The *two* forms (spirituals and blues) evolved from *one* older form.
E. CORRECT. Many people think the blues and spirituals are different, but they're really similar. This is probably because they both come from West African religious rituals.

Passage 3 - Was Lamarck Right?
Questions 13-18

Paragraph Summaries

1. Scientists thought Lamarck was wrong because they couldn't find genetic evidence for his theory. Lamarck's thought disuse or use of an organ would be passed on to an animal's children.
2. If you remove a cell wall from a bacteria, it will pass that on to its children without any genetic changes.
3. Other examples: heating fly eggs will overcome poor genes. And bacteria can spread genes horizontally (meaning from one to another, not from parents to child).
4. Some organisms can inherit genes horizontally, even between species. This may show Lamarck was right and that acquired characteristics can be inherited.

Analysis

The scientific language in this passage might throw you off. It's crucial to reread anything you're not clear on. It takes more time, but it allows you to approach the questions with confidence.

The main theme of the passage is that organisms can acquire some characteristic without having inherited them genetically from their parents.

You don't need to know all of the examples. You can refer back to the passage if needed. But you should understand vertical transmission (a parent giving genes to a child at birth) and horizontal transmission (one organism passing on a trait to another, not at birth).

Question 13

DISCUSSION: As with all specific detail questions, you should support the right answer with the passage. This prevents many mistakes.

A. Scientists don't believe that a *parent* using an organ will affect the *child's* organ. But it's common knowledge that using an organ in *your own* body will affect that organ.
B. The passage suggests this is true, so scientists probably believe it.
C. Scientists likely *never* believed this, so it's unlikely to be something they *no longer* believe. "No longer" implies they used to believe it.
D. This is something scientists *do* believe.
E. **CORRECT.** Now we know that some genes are transmitted horizontally instead of vertically (lines 46-50).

Question 14

DISCUSSION: This is mentioned in lines 15-22. If you take away a bacterium's cell wall, it will pass that lack of walls on to it's offspring.

_____

A. Lines 26-27 make clear that CO2 vulnerability *was* genetic.
B. Same as A.
C. CORRECT. See lines 15-22. Removing a bacterium's cell wall changes how its genes interact.
D. Close, but it's the *absence* of cell walls that we know can be passed on.
E. Plasmids are mentioned around line 35. This is an example of horizontal *gene transmission.*

Question 15

DISCUSSION: The last paragraph summarizes and clarifies the info on horizontal transmission. It also suggests the discoveries may support Lamarck.

_____

A. What modification? If you can't answer this question, you can't pick this answer choice.
B. Lines 56-58 say that Lamarck *might* be proven correct. There's no certainty.
C. What would be the significance? We're never told.
D. What words did the passage use to criticize scientists? If you can't find any, then there's no reason to choose this answer choice.
E. CORRECT. The recent discoveries show how Lamarck's hypothesis could work. Scientists had previously rejected it, because they could find no genetic mechanism to explain his theory.

Question 16

DISCUSSION: Lamarck's hypothesis is described in lines 1-6. You should reread those lines. He said that the way a parents uses an organ will affect how the child's organ works.

For example: I start running marathons, and because of that my future children are born as good endurance runners.

_____

A. This doesn't say whether a parent's usage of antlers affects the child's antlers.
B. CORRECT. An animal uses an organ in one way, and that affects the organs of future animals.
C. This has nothing to do with potatoes transmitting traits to future potatoes.
D. This doesn't tell us whether the *children* of those lions tend to be worse at directions, even if they're raised in the wild.
E. This is very tempting. Can you think of another reason why wild dogs might be more wild? The dogs bred for hunting are likely being raised by humans, and this probably makes them less wild. It may have nothing to do with genetics.

Question 17

DISCUSSION: This is a tricky question. There's only one place in the passage where the significance of acquired characteristics is mentioned: lines 37-38. Horizontal acquisition and subsequent inheritance of acquired characteristics seems to have sped up evolution.

The rest of the answers are designed to confuse you. They mix terms from the passage to say things that the passage never said.

_____

A. Not even true. Lines 40-45 show that photosynthesis may have *developed* faster thanks to horizontal transmission. But nothing talks about the speed of photosynthesis itself.
B. So, how does the passage say inheriting acquired characteristics helps explain natural selection? If you can't answer, then this answer isn't right.
C. Non-genetic inherited changes are only discussed in paragraph 2 (bacterial cell walls). This *is* an acquired characteristic, but the passage doesn't say whether it's important that a bacterium can inherit a lack of cell walls.
D. **CORRECT.** Lines 39-40 say that bacteria that inherited acquired characteristics might have sped up the development of photosynthesis.
E. Many things can be changed or stopped in experiments. This isn't significant.

Question 18

DISCUSSION: Scientists were able to make cell walls disappear without removing genes. They just changed how genes interacted.

_____

A. We're not told if it's possible to reverse the loss of cell walls.
B. This might be true, but in paragraph 2 no gene was introduced. The change was done without removing or adding any genes.
C. **CORRECT.** One bacterium lost its cell wall, then passed that on to its offspring. In the end, many bacteria were without cell walls.
D. We're never told if it's possible to prevent the further loss of cell walls.
E. We're not told if horizontal transmission is possible. This was an example of vertical transmission, from parent bacterium to child bacteria.

Passage 4 - Refugees
Questions 19-26

Paragraph Summaries

1. Women fall under the social group category if they apply as a refugee under UN rules.
2. The original rules did not mention social groups. They were added under the UN *Convention* as a catch-all for refugees who did not qualify under any other category.
3. UN documents such as the *Handbook* support a broad reading of "social group"
4. The UNHCR's broad position will probably help make national laws broader as well.

Analysis

The passage's author seems to agree that women ought to be included as refugees, and that the social group category is a decent way to do that. Though they don't say that explicitly.

Instead, the passage is a neutral discussion of how women can qualify as refugees, and how they came to be included in the category of "social group".

(If a women if being persecuted because of her race or religion, she can apply under those categories instead, of course. "Social group" is for women who are persecuted *because* they are women.)

Question 19

DISCUSSION: This question requires a bit of work. I had to double check to make sure the right answer was supported by the passage. You should too. If you go based on gut feeling, you *might* get it. But you might also fall into one of LSAC's traps.

In particular, note that the *Handbook* and the *Convention* are different.

_____

A. Lines 53-55 suggest the UNHCR manual will have a broad impact on national laws. But will *that* improve the status of women? Sometimes a law can have good intentions but little practical effect.
B. Nope. "Explicit" means they say it directly. But the *Convention* doesn't mention women directly (see lines 9-10). Instead, women can use the category of "social group".
C. Lines 28-33 say that the *Convention* is intentionally vague. It's doubtful the document specifically mentions women anywhere.
D. **CORRECT.** Lines 28-33 show that the drafters intentionally made "social group" a vague category. It was intended to let anyone in who might not otherwise qualify. And lines 39-41 show that the *Handbook* uses a broad interpretation.
E. The *Handbook* says this (lines 37-39). But we're not told how the *Convention* describes social groups.

Question 20

DISCUSSION: The drafters were intentionally vague. So they probably thought there was an advantage to vagueness.

———————

A. Maybe? Or maybe they wanted to give countries a broad enough law that they could work everything out themselves.
B. Lines 19-23 say that the IRO document didn't mention social groups. They probably also didn't mention women. So by including social groups, the *Convention* probably broke with tradition by allowing the inclusion of women, indirectly.
C. **CORRECT.** If the drafters thought they could list every category, then they probably wouldn't have included "social group" as a separate category. They could just have listed each group directly and have been done with it.
D. Hard to say. There are other reasons for being vague, apart from not caring. They may have thought that countries would reject the *Convention* if it explicitly protected women.
E. Same as D. There are other reasons for not listing something directly.

Question 21

DISCUSSION: All the answers talk about a woman, so that doesn't help narrow things down. Remember that "social group" is for someone who doesn't fall under the categories listed in lines 6-8.

We're looking for someone being persecuted *because* she is a woman.

———————

A. This person isn't facing discrimination because she is poor. She may not even be facing discrimination (unequal treatment). Maybe almost everyone is poor and starving in that country.
B. Racial discrimination is explicitly prohibited, so there's no reason for this women to apply under "social group".
C. Religious discrimination is explicitly prohibited, see lines 6-8.
D. **CORRECT.** She is facing persecution for being part of a social group. Because she is a woman and is standing up for herself, she faces discrimination.
E. Political discrimination is explicitly prohibited, see lines 6-8.

Question 22

DISCUSSION: There's nothing to say here except that you should really read lines 37-40. They say "social group" is described in broad terms, and the meaning is expansive.

———————

A. There's nothing specific about the definition. It's up to us to interpret "similar habits".
B. There's nothing obscure about the definition. Everyone generally understands what habits are and what social status is.
C. Exhaustive would mean the definition covered every situation. That's not the case: the definition is general and not very descriptive.
D. **CORRECT.** The definition could apply to many situations; it is very flexible and speaks in broad terms.
E. Comprehensive would mean that every specific situation is covered. That's not the case, the definition is vague.

Question 23

DISCUSSION: The IRO is mentioned on lines 21-23. We know that they didn't include "social group" in their definition.

The passage's author never says outright that they think social groups should be protected. But they seem to implicitly agree that social groups deserve protection. So A is fairly well supported.

This is only a "most strongly supported" question, not a "must be true".

––––––––––––

A. CORRECT. The author *seems* to like the fact that the "social group" category exists. So they would think that the IRO should have included social groups.

B. Doubtful. The IRO document didn't mention social groups, so it probably didn't mention women either.

C. This is true of the *Convention*, but not the IRO.

D. Same as C. The IRO document didn't mention social groups.

E. Who knows? Maybe the IRO document was just a toothless piece of paper.

Question 24

DISCUSSION: The author uses "lynchpin" to mean that being persecuted is the most important factor when deciding whether someone is a refugee.

––––––––––––

A. We have no idea whether countries agree on what persecution is. The passage doesn't mention this..

B. We have no idea why the document was created. Was it to protect refugees, or was it for some other, political reason?

C. As with A, we're not told what countries think about the word persecution. Maybe they had to be dragged kicking and screaming into agreeing.

D. We don't know why people have to leave their homes (they could leave for poverty without being persecuted, for example). We do know they'll only be accepted as refugees if they are persecuted.

E. CORRECT. If you're not persecuted, it's doubtful that you'll qualify as a refugee. This question was testing whether you knew what to look for, or whether you would waste time thinking about A-D.

Question 25

DISCUSSION: In lines 55-58, the passage suggests that the UNHRC document will influence national laws. They may start protecting social groups too.

A. We're not given example of many terms used in UN documents. We only have evidence for one term: "social group".

B. National asylum laws are mentioned only once. It's suggested that those laws are influenced by UN documents, and not the other way around.

C. **CORRECT.** This is why the UNHCR's broad interpretation is significant. Countries look to the UNHCR when interpreting their own refugee laws.

D. This goes too far. The UNHCR document isn't official law. There's no reason that a UNHCR interpretation *must* influence national laws.

E. If the UNHCR document influences national laws, then why would the terms in national laws be in direct opposition to the UNCHR's interpretations? Of course, it's *possible* some countries have conflicting laws, but we have no evidence to support this.

Question 26

DISCUSSION: The main point of the passage is to discuss the history of the term "social group" and how it can be used to protect women.

A. **CORRECT.** The whole passage discusses the history and usage of the term "social group".

B. What circumstances led to the creation of the *Convention*? We're never told.

C. Which document? And which terms? There's only one interpretation of "social group" given: a broad interpretation. And there are multiple documents mentioned, so this answer choice hardly covers the entire passage.

D. What is being disputed? We're not told of any debate. And there's no solution given to any problem. We already have a solution for how to protect women refugees: they can be classed as part of a social group.

E. No! The passage seems to *agree* that it's proper to interpret social group broadly.

Test 34
Section II - Logical Reasoning

Question 1

QUESTION TYPE: Flawed Reasoning

CONCLUSION: Professionals don't have to pay attention to R's book.

REASONING: R is a jerk. He also calls people names.

ANALYSIS: This argument is nothing but an ad hominem attack. It doesn't address whether any of the information in R's book has value.

Ironically, the argument mostly accuses R of making ad hominem attacks.

―――――――――――――

A. CORRECT. The whole stimulus is just a character attack against R. But the author hasn't shown that R is in any way scientifically incompetent.
B. This is a problem with *R's book,* not R. The author's doesn't say whether R himself had funding.
C. The stimulus doesn't even mention a scientific theory.
D. It's quite possible for a reviewer to verify what R actually said about other scientists. It also shouldn't be hard to find out if R is arrogant or nasty.
E. This is a different error. The stimulus implied that R's work wasn't worthy of merit because his findings about bias likely weren't true.

Question 2

QUESTION TYPE: Sufficient Assumption

CONCLUSION: The city should buy new subway cars.

REASONING: It makes economic sense to have a good subway system. The city should always do what makes good economic sense.

ANALYSIS: The author hasn't shown that the city needs new cars to have an efficient subway system. If we did need them to make the system efficient, then it would make economic sense to buy them.

―――――――――――――

A. This doesn't tell us whether we need to invest in subway cars to invest in the subway system. Maybe we could build tunnels instead.
B. Careful: this doesn't say "new" subway cars. It says cost-effective subway cars. Maybe we already have those and don't need more.
C. This could just mean that new subway cars are less of a bad investment than buying some other things. It doesn't actually say that buying them makes good economic sense.
D. Great! But does it make good economic sense to buy new subway cars? I can afford lots of inexpensive things that would be really, really stupid to buy. Mmm, imagine what I could do with 2,000 pez dispensers.
E. CORRECT. We need the cars to make the system effective. And an effective subway system makes good economic sense. And we should *always* do things that make good economic sense.

Question 3

QUESTION TYPE: Flawed Reasoning

CONCLUSION: Our customers would rather not eat potatoes.

REASONING: I gave our vegetarian customers a choice of dishes. No one ordered the potato dish with *cheese*.

ANALYSIS: This is an awful argument. There are several alternate explanations:

1. The customers didn't want to eat cheese. This could be because of taste or because it is an animal product (they're vegetarians)
2. The potato dish isn't very good.
3. One of the other dishes is incredibly good.
4. The customers like to eat potatoes at home (they're easy to cook) but prefer to eat something fancier when they go out.

I could go on all day. The manager needs way more evidence, because his evidence is consistent with many alternate explanations.

A. An example of this error would be if you have a car accident and lose your job, and you assume it must be because someone is scheming against you. It could just be an unfortunate coincidence. In any case, the manager only mentioned one event.
B. There's no inconsistency: it's *possible* that the customers don't like potatoes. It just isn't certain.
C. This would be if people said they don't like potatoes and yet many people ordered potatoes. That didn't happen.
D. This would be like saying: Ghosts must exist because most people believe in ghosts. That didn't happen here.
E. CORRECT. There are many other possible reasons that could explain why no vegetarians order potatoes with cheese.

Question 4

QUESTION TYPE: Most Strongly Supported

FACTS: 4-6 week old children can be comforted by the sound of their mothers' voices, while the voices of others do nothing (assuming that mothers are the main caregivers)

ANALYSIS: This supports the idea that infants have formed a bond with their mothers.

They recognize their mother's voice and realize that their mother will help them.

A. Not quite. The babies might recognize the voices of other people. The problem is that the other voices don't comfort the babies.
B. Hard to say. At 4-6 weeks old the baby will have already recognized many things. We don't know what the first thing they recognized was.
C. CORRECT. Babies stop crying because they think their mother will come help them.
D. Not necessarily. Someone else might help the baby. The baby won't know that help is on the way, just by hearing the voice. But the baby might stop crying once they've been helped.
E. Hard to say. Discomfort is probably best relieved by the mother actually helping her baby.

Question 5

QUESTION TYPE: Paradox

FACTS: Computers have helped elementary school students with math, helped a little with science and haven't helped at all with reading and writing.

ANALYSIS: We need to either find an advantage for math or a disadvantage for reading when using a computer. Anything that doesn't distinguish between subjects is irrelevant. Answer B gives us an advantage for math.

_____

A. This doesn't explain anything. We want to know why arithmetic worked well on computers and reading didn't.

B. **CORRECT.** This gives us a reason why arithmetic works particularly well, compared to the other subjects.

C. We're talking about classrooms where the technology *was* used. It doesn't matter what happened in classrooms where the teachers didn't use it.

D. This explains why computers might be used. It doesn't explain why reading couldn't be taught well using a computer.

E. This makes the situation even more puzzling. Reading lessons didn't go well despite the fact that there were more of them.

Question 6

QUESTION TYPE: Parallel Reasoning

CONCLUSION: It's incoherent to think that it is a good idea to behave irrationally in pursuit of a worthy goal.

REASONING: The goal would be even better served if you behaved rationally.

ANALYSIS: This isn't a good argument. The author hasn't shown that rational behavior is more likely to achieve the goal than irrational behavior. Acting crazy works, sometimes.

The argument is circular. The conclusion is that acting irrationally is dumb. The evidence is that it is dumb to act irrationally. They're the same thing.

This argument *sounds* like a good argument. But that's only because we tend to believe that irrational actions are inferior to rational actions. But the fact that something is justified does not make it rational. The right answer also *sounds* good. It's hard to see how an accident can be intentional.

_____

A. This just states the obvious: it isn't good for officers of the law to commit crimes. There isn't any circular reasoning.

B. **CORRECT.** This is a bad argument, and it parallels the stimulus. It's perfectly possible to plan to spill water accidentally. I could create a situation where I am likely to spill water, but without knowing *when* and *how* the spill would happen. So it would be an accident.
The argument's premise is the same as its conclusion (spilling water intentionally isn't an accident.)

C. This is a bad argument, but it isn't circular. The conclusion is about how to live the good life. The evidence is about whether neighbors see that we live the good life. Those are different things.

D. This is a bad argument. It hasn't shown that self-diagnosis requires good medicine. Maybe a doctor can diagnose something even if it is bad medicine. But this isn't circular reasoning.

E. This is a bad argument. It hasn't established that merely by owning both animals we are placing the goldfish at the cat's disposal. Most people keep fish in fish tanks, sealed away from cats. But this argument isn't circular.

Question 7

QUESTION TYPE: Paradox

FACTS: An act is worthy of praise only when you have to overcome powerful temptations. Yet sometimes an act can be worthy of praise if it is performed out of habit.

ANALYSIS: Sometimes building a habit means you have to overcome powerful temptations. That would be enough to make it praise-worthy.

Most of the wrong answers don't mention habits.

A. CORRECT. This shows that performing those good actions out of habit did require overcoming powerful temptation (in the past.)
B. This doesn't help explain anything about habits.
C. This doesn't tell us anything about habits or temptation.
D. That means it's hard for us to tell if someone else did something praiseworthy. But they themselves could know since they would know if they had been tempted. Interesting as all of this is, it tells us nothing about habits.
E. This tells us how often people perform good deeds. But it doesn't tell us how an action performed out of habit can be praiseworthy.

Question 8

QUESTION TYPE: Method of Reasoning

CONCLUSION: The pilot concludes that the conservationist is being misleading.

REASONING: Most of the collisions have happened in the past couple of years. And the number of birds is increasing steadily.

ANALYSIS: The pilot makes a good point. His method of argument is to provide context. The recent increase in collisions sounds worrisome. Now the conservationist's argument seems misleading.

A. CORRECT. The pilot added context. The conservationist should have mentioned that the number of collisions has increased markedly in the past couple of years.
B. The pilot didn't say *why* he thought the conservationist was being misleading.
C. The pilot is talking about this particular situation involving bird collisions. He isn't making a statement about whether all situations, everywhere, always become more dangerous. That's sort of extreme.
D. The pilot only made a comment about the *effects* of the wildlife reserve. He didn't mention its morality or why it existed.
E. The pilot agrees that the figures were accurate. But he thinks that the way the conservationist presented them was misleading.

Question 9

QUESTION TYPE: Flawed Reasoning

CONCLUSION: It was the difference in methods that caused the two reports to find different results.

REASONING: There is no reasoning given to support the conclusion.

ANALYSIS: This is a very bad argument. Different methods shouldn't automatically lead to different results. If the methods are accurate then it is quite possible for different methods to find the same result.

Suppose we want to find out what time the movie is playing. I call the theatre. You check the internet. Your friend checks the paper schedule he picked up at the theatre. All three methods should find the same result.

A difference in method doesn't explain anything.

A. The stimulus did clearly distinguish between the two reports. It even noted that they got different results.
B. The purpose of the investigation is not mentioned. But the doesn't doesn't say anything to indicate that he thinks the method of an investigation is the same thing as a purpose.
C. It's actually possible that both studies used a terrible method.
D. **CORRECT.** There is no reason that different methods should automatically lead to different results.
E. The studies looked at the average workweek *in the same period*. Lots of changes surely occurred, there's no reason to focus on economic conditions. If both studies were properly conducted they would have found the same change in hours worked.

Question 10

QUESTION TYPE: Sufficient Assumption

CONCLUSION: The school is violating its charter.

REASONING: The charter says the schools needs to have some students with special educational needs. But there are no children with learning disabilities.

ANALYSIS: This is a bad argument because it doesn't make clear that all students with special educational needs have a learning disability. The school might have students with special educational needs even if none of them have a learning disability.

We could show that all special needs students have a learning disability. Then the lack of students with a learning disability means that there are also no special education students.

A. Not quite. This leaves open the possibility that there is a student who has special educational needs but doesn't have a learning disability.
B. The stimulus already tells us that no students with learning disabilities are enrolled. This is just repetition.
C. This tells us what we should do: it's a value judgment. But the stimulus is making a statement of fact: there are *currently* no special needs students enrolled.
D. **CORRECT.** Every special needs student has a learning disability. Since there are no students with learning disabilities then there must be no students with special educational needs.
E. This doesn't tell us whether or the charter actually is being violated.

Question 11

QUESTION TYPE: Weaken

CONCLUSION: The psychologists are wrong that deep empathy would be the best way to understand someone else.

REASONING: Deep empathy is impossible. So if the psychologists were right there would be no way to understand anyone. But we can understand people.

ANALYSIS: This argument makes a simple error. The psychologists said the *best* way to understand someone would be deep empathy. They didn't say it was the *only* way.

_____

A. Deep empathy is pretty clear: a complete grasp of someone else's motivations and feelings.
B. The only thing the argument denies is that deep empathy is possible. And the argument never claimed that deep empathy was possible.
C. **CORRECT.** The psychologists only said it would be the best way ("would be" doesn't necessarily mean the psychologists thought it was possible.) The argument misunderstood them and thought they meant deep empathy was the only way.
D. Actually the argument is *denying* the claim of the psychologists. And the argument gives (flawed) evidence for its own claim.
E. This doesn't matter. The argument is about disproving the claim. The stimulus didn't say how many psychologists believed it.

Question 12

QUESTION TYPE: Weaken

CONCLUSION: Synethesiacs have senses that do not respect the usual five boundaries.

REASONING: Some people taste a banana and *claim* they taste blue or see a color and *say* that it has a smell.

ANALYSIS: I'm surprised this question exists. Normally the LSAT is pretty politically correct. But in this case we weaken the conclusion by showing that synesthesiacs are crazy people and we can't trust what they claim to see or smell.

Seriously.

I've got a friend who is synesthesiac. She's pretty smart and seems to understand the words she uses. What a weird question, especially since the LSAT is usually very sensitive to minority groups.

_____

A. **CORRECT.** This means that when a synesthesiac said they taste purple, they really meant to say "tastes sweet!" or something like that. If synesthesiacs can't use or understand words then it's hard for us to trust them when they say they have different senses than we do.
B. This *strengthens* the argument.
C. This would support the idea that there is a condition called synesthesia and that synesthesiacs' senses are different from ours.
D. This supports the idea that the phenomenon exists worldwide.
E. This suggest that synesthesiacs really do have certain senses that are different than normal. It's possible to use drugs to shut off the other senses. E.g. anesthetics turn off the sense of touch/feeling.

Question 13

QUESTION TYPE: Necessary Assumption

CONCLUSION: Laissez faire economics isn't completely accurate.

REASONING: Laissez-faire says that an increase in the minimum wage will lower the number of minimum wage jobs. But the recent increase in the minimum wage did not lower minimum wage jobs in the restaurant industry.

ANALYSIS: This is a really bad argument. Its only evidence is that minimum wage jobs did not decline in *one* out of thousands of industries. And the author hasn't shown that restaurant jobs are representative of all minimum wage jobs.

So it could be that minimum wage jobs actually did decline in other industries.

A. The conclusion did not claim that laissez-faire is completely wrong. The argument just said that it isn't right about this single prediction.
B. **CORRECT.** If the restaurant industry was not representative then there could have been many minimum wage jobs lost in other industries.
C. Even if a study hypothetically did find that one business reduced jobs, that does not prove much. Another business could have increased jobs at the same time. The argument is claiming that *on average* no jobs will be lost, across the entire economy.
D. Actually the argument is assuming that the fast food restaurants *did* increase salaries to comply with the new, higher minimum wage. Otherwise, there would be no temptation to fire workers.
E. This is tempting but the argument is restricted to *minimum wage* jobs. It doesn't hurt the argument if other jobs were lost as long as minimum wage jobs did not decline.

Question 14

QUESTION TYPE: Strengthen

CONCLUSION: We don't have to listen to their boring claim.

REASONING: Some people say that discovery or invention is self-expression. But everything we do is self-expression, in a trivial sense.

ANALYSIS: The argument has succeeded in showing that the claim is uninteresting. It then concludes we don't have to pay attention.

That isn't always true. If your house is on fire it is "trivial" to figure out that you will be hurt if you don't try to escape. Not an intellectually interesting claim. But you should definitely listen to that advice, even though it is trivial!

The correct answer strengthens the argument by showing that we don't have to listen to trivial things.

A. We already know that this particular claim is uninteresting. The argument says so. It doesn't help much to know that every other trivial claim is uninteresting, too.
B. It doesn't matter what most people do. "Most people" can be wrong.
C. **CORRECT.** This claim is trivial; therefore it too is unworthy of serious consideration.
D. This would support the idea that the claim could be restated in a more interesting way. But it doesn't affect the immediate conclusion that we don't have to bother paying attention to their boring, dull claim. Yawn.
E. It doesn't really matter if every claim is trivial. We're trying to support the idea that we don't have to pay attention to this particular trivial claim.

Question 15

QUESTION TYPE: Main Point

CONCLUSION: The sorts of differences in lens resolution typically advertised are irrelevant for practical photography.

REASONING: Modern lenses are so good that they project much more detail than can be reproduced in a developed image. The advertised differences in lens resolution don't make a difference.

ANALYSIS: This is a good argument. The main point is that all lenses are so good that it doesn't matter which one you pick.

———————————

A. The argument has *not* said what camera manufacturers "should" do. It just makes a factual claim about the relevance of camera advertisements for the purposes of practical photography.
B. Not quite. The argument only mentions that difference in lens resolution are irrelevant. There might be other relevant difference (e.g. flash quality, zoom distance, etc.)
C. **CORRECT.** All of the lenses are so good that it hardly matter which one you choose. So the advertised differences don't matter.
D. The manufacturers might be right to advertise lens differences. Consumers might be fooled and pay extra for a camera with a high lens resolution (even though it does not benefit them.)
E. The argument doesn't even mention different types of film. It just says that *any* lens produces more detail than *all* types of film can display.

Question 16

QUESTION TYPE: Necessary Assumption

CONCLUSION: The sorts of differences in lens resolution typically advertised are irrelevant for practical photography.

REASONING: Modern lenses are so good that they project much more detail than can be reproduced in a developed image. The advertised differences in lens resolution don't make a difference.

ANALYSIS: The argument is assuming that there are no effects of increased resolution apart from the amount of detail projected onto film.

———————————

A. This is hard to understand, but it's saying that the argument is assuming that resolution is not an important part of camera quality. The argument actually assumes the opposite. Resolution is very important, but all cameras now have such good resolution that the *differences* are meaningless.
B. **CORRECT.** If differences in resolution *do* make film's deficiencies worse then it is important to know what the resolution of a camera is.
C. This shouldn't matter because the stimulus says that resolutions project *far* more detail than film can capture. So even a significant impact seems unlikely to have an effect.
D. Who cares? The resolution projects so much detail that it's irrelevant if and how we can hit the maximum. The pictures will all look the same.
E. It seems likely that there are other factors that affect picture quality. But that wouldn't hurt the argument that differences in *one* factor, lens resolution, are irrelevant.

Question 17

QUESTION TYPE: Weaken

CONCLUSION: Human lifespan could not be extended through caloric restriction.

REASONING: Restricting lab animals' diet just brings their calorie consumption back to the levels they ate in the wild. It is their normal lifespan that is being restored.

ANALYSIS: This isn't a great argument. Humans no longer live in the wild and we tend to eat large amounts of calories. So caloric restriction might boost our lifespan back to natural levels.

––––––––––––––––

A. **CORRECT.** This would mean that we are like lab animals. We would benefit from eating smaller amounts of calories as it would restore us to our natural diet.
B. This doesn't tell us whether or not calories affect lifespan. *Both* groups ate low-calorie. Percentage of fat was the only difference.
C. If some experiments not based on lab animals *do* produce worthwhile ideas...how does that weaken the idea that this experiment based on lab animals *doesn't* have a worthwhile idea?
D. "Some" is always pretty vague. This could mean 3 people out of 2 million. This doesn't weaken the idea that on average, low-calorie diets will not increase lifespan.
E. As in D, "some" is a very, very vague term. It could mean that worms life longer on low calories but that humans don't.

Question 18

QUESTION TYPE: Main Point

CONCLUSION: Radical environmentalists are useful even though they are generally wrong.

REASONING: Radical environmentalists cause the public to fear disaster. This allows environmental progress.

ANALYSIS: This is a plausible argument. We'd need a bit more information to evaluate it. But the main point is that radicals serve a purpose even if their ideas are wrong.

––––––––––––––––

A. This goes too far. The argument didn't claim that most progress was due to radicals. It just argued that radicals made progress possible. They are a necessary condition but most of the credit could belong elsewhere.
B. **CORRECT.** Radicals make us fear disaster and cause us to take action. They are useful.
C. This also goes too far. We might not want the public to be extremely fearful and paranoid. All sorts of weird things might happen.
D. Not quite. Radical environmentalists *do* put forward untenable positions. But they themselves might not realize that they will never succeed and that their actions only serve to make the public do the right thing. People don't always understand their own impact on a system.
E. This is true, sometimes, according to the stimulus. But the main point is that these positions can spur the public on to approve more moderate reforms.

Question 19

QUESTION TYPE: Most Strongly Supported

FACTS:

1. People should avoid calcium carbonate in doses large than 0.5 grams.
2. It neutralizes stomach acids.
3. But above a set dose it increases calcium in the blood and hurts the kidneys.
4. And if you have half a gram you could trigger gastrin, a hormone that causes acid secretion.

ANALYSIS: Many people find answer choice D, the correct answer, confusing. The stimulus is written to make it sound as though if you take more than half a gram of calcium carbonate you will increase the amount of stomach acid in your system.

That could be true, but it doesn't have to be. We're not told how much stomach acid gastrin produces. It could be a very small amount. We're also not told how much acid is neutralized by calcium carbonate. It could be a very large amount.

So if you took a gram of calcium carbonate then all we know is that some acid will be neutralized and some extra acid will be produced. But we don't know if the total amount of acid will go up or down.

———————————

A. We don't know how much stomach acid gastrin produces. It could be a very, very small amount. Direct neutralization might be most effective… but we risk hurting our kidneys.
B. This is had to say…there are a lot of factors that could affect the kidneys. If people who avoid antacids are also much more likely to drink then maybe their kidneys will be worse off.
C. This is very tempting. But we don't know how much stomach acid is produced when we secrete gastrin. It could be a very, very tiny amount. If you ate ten pounds of calcium carbonate it might neutralize all of your stomach acid.
D. **CORRECT.** The calcium carbonate directly neutralizes stomach acid. But it also triggers gastrin and so it indirectly contributes to the production of stomach acid too.
E. It's the other way around. Calcium in the blood impairs kidney function.

Question 20

QUESTION TYPE: Principle – Strengthen

ARGUMENTS: Chan argues that the literature department should only study literary works and that it should avoid studying advertisements.

Professor Wigmore isn't sure if ads are literary works. But he is sure that they influence society because people can't figure out their true messages. The literature department trains people to understand what they read. Therefore it should train people to understand ads.

ANALYSIS: Sure, the literature department teaches students to understand texts. But there are a lot of texts that we don't study in literature classes. Wigmore's argument needs help to show that ads should be studied as literature.

The right answer gives us a specific reason to study ads: they can harm society and literature classes should study any text that can harm society.

———————————

A. This would actually ruin Professor Wigmore's argument. He wanted to study ads only because people can't figure them out.
B. Ads do affect people's thoughts and actions but we don't know if they are subtly constructed. So this can't help.
C. *All* of the literature department's courses already teach students critical skills. This ads nothing.
D. **CORRECT.** Ads are texts that can affect society, and presumably they can therefore harm it. So students must be taught how to understand ads.
E. This weakens Wigmore's argument. He's arguing that teachers shouldn't be able to choose: they must have a course that teaches ads.

Question 21

QUESTION TYPE: Necessary Assumption

ARGUMENTS: Chan argues that the literature department should only study literary works and that it should avoid studying advertisements.

Professor Wigmore isn't sure if ads are literary works. But he is sure that they influence society because people can't figure out their true messages. The literature department trains people to understand what they read. Therefore it should train people to understand ads.

ANALYSIS: Wigmore is assuming that the literature department has broad responsibilities. If it doesn't (and can only study true literature) then his argument might be wrong.

A. Professor Wigmore isn't arguing that ads are literary works. So it's irrelevant what qualities literary works have.
B. Actually Wigmore assumes that courses *could* teach both true literature and ads.
C. If students also learned how to write essays (a new skill,) that would not harm Wigmore's argument. He only needs to assume that students don't learn how to figure out ads from the course as it's currently taught.
D. If visual ads did hurt society then Wigmore would probably feel it was even more important to study ads.
E. **CORRECT.** If the literary department *is* limited to teaching true literary work then Wigmore might be wrong. He admits that ads might not be true literary works.

Question 22

QUESTION TYPE: Role in Argument

CONCLUSION: The critics are wrong to say that capital punishment was not an essential part of the labor discipline of British capitalism.

REASONING: The critics point out that fewer people were executed after industrialization. But the critics forget that capitalism preceded industrialization by several centuries.

ANALYSIS: The sociologist makes an important distinction: capitalism predated industrialization. So it's quite possible that capital punishment was essential even though the use of execution declined over time.

The point of making the distinction was to show that the critics' evidence was inappropriate.

A. The sociologist was arguing against the critics. *The critics* were the ones arguing against this claim. The sociologist's evidence actually provides some support to the idea that capital punishment was a part of capitalist labor discipline.
B. Same as A. This is the same answer choice except its worded a bit more strongly ("direct contradiction" instead of "some evidence against")
C. This goes too far. The sociologist doesn't say that the claim is definitely right. He just points out that the critics used bad logic in attacking the claim.
D. The sociologist attacked the critics. He did not support them. E.g. "such a criticism overlooks…"
E. **CORRECT.** The sociologist uses this fact to show that the critics are making a bad argument.

Question 23

QUESTION TYPE: Must be True

FACTS:

1. If a monster is horrific then it is threatening.
2. If a monster is physically dangerous then it is threatening.
3. Even a non-dangerous (benign) monster that inspires revulsion is horrific (and therefore threatening)

ANALYSIS: We can combine terms to get the following:

Revulsion → horrific → threatening

Not threatening → not horrific, nor physically dangerous, nor something that inspires revulsion.

Note: Most of the second sentence is fluff. On similar questions, learn to cut out the stuff at the start and only focus on the sufficient-necessary relationships (or terms like some, most, etc.)

———————————

A. This gets it backwards. Horrific is always threatening but threatening doesn't have to be horrific.
B. This is an incorrect negation. There are other ways to be horrific apart from inspiring revulsion.
C. The only way we could conclude that a monster doesn't inspire horror is if the monster wasn't threatening. Otherwise we simply don't know what might cause a monster to be horrific.
D. As with C, the only way we can be sure that a monster isn't revolting is if it is also not horrific. We know *nothing* about a monster that is psychologically threatening.
E. **CORRECT.** Any monster that inspires revulsion is also horrific. And any horrific monster is threatening.

Question 24

QUESTION TYPE: Flawed Parallel Reasoning

CONCLUSION: The defendant maliciously caused harm.

REASONING: Malice is intent to cause harm. The defendant intended to put the snow on the sidewalk.

ANALYSIS: The lawyer is confused. Sure, the defendant had intent: the intent to move snow. But the lawyer hasn't shown the defendant meant to hurt anybody.

We generally only have intent for the things we mean to do, or for anything that we're sure will happen as a result of our actions. If the defendant didn't know that the snow would hurt the plaintiff then we can hardly blame the defendant.

———————————

A. This is a good argument.
B. **CORRECT.** This is a bad argument and it parallels the stimulus. Bruce wanted to eat mincemeat pie. The fact that he wanted to eat mincemeat pie didn't mean that Bruce wanted to eat poison...he didn't know it was there!
C. This is a good argument, assuming that we denigrate someone if we denigrate their wine choices.
D. This is a bad argument. The correct conclusion would have been "unbeknownst to her she has lunch with someone *generally thought* to be an industrial spy." But this doesn't parallel the flaw about intent.
E. This is a good argument. The car was a stolen car even if Edwina didn't know.

Question 25

QUESTION TYPE: Weaken

CONCLUSION: Wood-burning stoves are more dangerous that open fireplaces.

REASONING: Their smoke travels more slowly and therefore leaves behind more creosote. Creosote can clog up a chimney or burn inside of it.

ANALYSIS: This argument makes a common error: it lists *one* relevant difference and then makes a final judgment. We know one disadvantage of stoves. But it could be that fireplaces have other disadvantages that make them even more dangerous.

The correct answer lists one such disadvantage.

A. This sounds tempting but it doesn't do much. The stimulus is talking about how dangerous the stoves are on average. It could be that the most efficient stove costs $1,000,000 and nobody owns one. That won't affect the average stove.
B. This makes sense - if you don't use your stove, how can it produce creosote. But this affects both fireplaces and stoves.
C. **CORRECT.** This shows a reason that fireplaces are dangerous. It might outweigh the creosote danger and it weakens the argument.
D. That doesn't matter since we know that stoves produce more creosote.
E. But *if* they used them, which type would be more dangerous? This doesn't let us conclude that fireplaces are as dangerous as stoves.

Test 34
Section III - Logical Reasoning

Question 1

QUESTION TYPE: Principle - Must be True

PRINCIPLE: Fewer options lead to better patient adherence to a doctor's orders.

ANALYSIS: It's important not to ready anything extra into this. The principle did not say that additional options are confusing, or similar, or difficult to explain, or hard to imagine or anything else. It just said there are more of them, period.

A. We don't have any indication that patients become confused when they get more advice. They might understand it but simply not do anything about it.

B. It might be that there is always a clear difference between the options even when there are a lot of them.

C. **CORRECT.** Varies inversely means: when the choices go up, compliance goes down. That's exactly what the principle says.

D. If I tell you that you will die, you should be able to vividly imagine the consequences whether I give you two options or twenty.

E. There's no reason to think that a doctor couldn't be as clear about five options as they are about two options.

Question 2

QUESTION TYPE: Paradox - Exception

FACTS: Some psychologists study animals in order to understand the structure and development of the human personality.

ANALYSIS: The correct answer is backwards. It talks about understanding animals. We're trying to figure out how animal experiments help us understand *humans*.

A. This means that animals provide the easiest way to study human instincts.

B. Humans might make for better experiments, but it's illegal. Therefore psychologists experiment on animals as a second best option.

C. Similar to B. Human experiments might be better but animal experiments are cheaper.

D. **CORRECT.** This is backwards. We're trying to model the personality of *humans*, not animals.

E. Animals let us think of things to test in human experiments.

Question 3

QUESTION TYPE: Necessary Assumption

CONCLUSION: Most of the world's bananas are not really threatened by Sigatoka disease

REASONING: Sigatoka disease can be prevented using a fungicide. The fungicides are only suitable for bananas plantations away from where humans live. Fortunately most large plantations are in locations where the fungicides can be used safely.

ANALYSIS: This argument sounds good. But it didn't say most *bananas* are grown where the fungicide can be used. It said most large banana *plantations* are located in those areas.

If most bananas are grown in small groves where we can't use the fungicide then we are in trouble.

A. This would be helpful for the future, but for now the fungicide should keep most bananas safe.
B. CORRECT. If this isn't true then it could be that most bananas grow in areas where we can't use the fungicide.
C. It doesn't really matter how fast the disease spreads as long as we can kill it with fungicides.
D. The conclusion is specifically about the threat from Sigatoka disease. Other diseases don't matter.
E. It doesn't matter whether or not the trees have been exposed as long as the fungicide can do its job.

Question 4

QUESTION TYPE: Flawed Reasoning

CONCLUSION: The vast majority of high school students want to graduate. The dropout rate can't be blamed on a lack of motivation.

REASONING: A single survey of 1000 high school students from a mid-sized city found that 89% want to graduate.

ANALYSIS: This survey may not be representative. There could be big differences between those three high schools and high schools in other cities. Or between those high schools and rural high schools.

A. 89% of pretty clearly an overwhelming majority. Only 11% said no, at most.
B. The conclusions don't conflict: students want to graduate and the reason the drop out rate is so high is not because students don't want to graduate.
C. The argument says "*if*...the dropout rate...is high." It's open to the possibility that it isn't high.
D. Nope. The argument is claiming that some *other* reason explains the alleged dropout rate. Maybe they need to get a job to help pay the bills.
E. CORRECT. There can be massive differences between cities. The survey should have looked at students nationwide.

Question 5

QUESTION TYPE: Necessary Assumption

CONCLUSION: Reliance on movies and electronic media are destroying democracy.

REASONING: Democracy need bonds of mutual trust. Bonds of trust are made and strengthened only by participation in organized civic groups outside the family.

ANALYSIS: This is the argument from *Bowling Alone*. It's assuming that electronic media are causing us to join fewer civic groups.

———————

A. This is too strong. It's only necessary that reliance on such media makes people less likely to form bonds of trust. It doesn't have to be impossible.
B. Even if they could, they would have a problem if no one joined their organizations because they were all watching TV.
C. The argument would still work if newspapers were merely neutral for democracy.
D. **CORRECT.** If people are just as likely to participate in groups even if they rely on electronic media then the argument falls apart.
E. The argument would not be affected if people who relied on electronic media were just as close to their families as people who didn't.

Question 6

QUESTION TYPE: Weaken

CONCLUSION: We can't use standard archaeological techniques to date prehistoric paintings made on limestone.

REASONING: Standard archaeological techniques can't date anything that has any minerals containing carbon. We can't collect samples of paintings made on limestone without removing some limestone. Limestone is a mineral containing carbon.

ANALYSIS: All of our samples will have carbon. But the right answer tells us we can remove the carbon from those samples in the lab.

———————

A. According to the argument, all of those techniques will contain limestone and thus the samples will be worthless.
B. **CORRECT.** This would do it. The samples contain limestone, but we can remove it. Then we could date the paint samples.
C. We're not trying to date the *limestone*. We're trying to date the paint. The limestone is certainly much older.
D. This strengthens the argument. The argument is discussing techniques for dating vegetable matter: none of them work if there is carbon. This answer choice rules out the possibility of dating any other materials in the paint.
E. That's nice. But *any* carbon means we can't date the sample.

Question 7

QUESTION TYPE: Point at Issue

ARGUMENTS: Dr. Jones thinks that telecare will help rural patients, at least. Specialists in urban centers can examine them from a great distance.

Dr. Carabella thinks that telemedicine will eventually cause doctors to leave rural areas since examinations will no longer have to be done in person. Even urban care will eventually be affected.

ANALYSIS: The two doctors pretty clearly disagree on whether telecare will help rural patients.

A. They both seem to agree on this. Carabella agreed that rural patients would initially receive better care from specialists.
B. Dr. Jones doesn't express a clear opinion on whether telecare will be extended to urban areas.
C. Dr. Jones thinks it will be widely adopted (and beneficial.) Dr. Carabella also seems to think that telecare will eventually be widely adopted (and harmful.)
D. This depends. They don't really say anything about the patients who need it most. Jones thinks urban patients will still be seen personally. And Carabella does think rare cases (the most important?) will have personal examinations.
E. **CORRECT.** Jones is pretty clear that telecare will benefit rural patients. Carabella thinks it will hurt *all* patients.

Question 8

QUESTION TYPE: Method of Reasoning

ARGUMENTS: Dr. Jones thinks that telecare will help rural patients, at least. Specialists in urban centers can examine them from a great distance.

Dr. Carabella thinks that telemedicine will eventually cause doctors to leave rural areas since examinations will no longer have to be done in person. Even urban care will eventually be affected.

ANALYSIS: Carabella goes further then Jones and asks him to consider what the world would look like if people really used Telecare to its full extent.

A. No. This would be, for example, if a doctor proved that a weight loss drug was really just eliminating muscle and not fat.
B. **CORRECT.** Carabella agrees with Jones that the early stages will help. But then they describe the future consequences that will occur if Telecare is adopted.
C. Carabella didn't do that. They disagreed with Jones, respectfully.
D. This sounds tempting, but statistics describe the present or the past. We have no statistics for the future: we don't know what the future will be like.
E. What term would that be? Don't pick this type of answer choice unless you can pinpoint where Carabella says that Jones misused a word.

Question 9

QUESTION TYPE: Necessary Assumption

CONCLUSION: There are no parallel lines in our universe, if those physicists are right.

REASONING: The non-Euclidean system of geometry with the most empirical verification (real world proof) is seen by some physicists think it accurately describes our universe.

Euclidean geometry can have parallel lines.

ANALYSIS: The argument didn't tell us whether or not the non-Euclidean system can have parallel lines. A necessary assumption is that they cannot.

A. **CORRECT.** If there are parallel lines in the system then this argument is wrong.
B. This just tells us that more physicists think the system is correct. But that doesn't tell us whether or not our universe has parallel lines or what the geometry system is like. So this isn't necessary.
C. This would be a *sufficient* assumption. But it's only necessary that the particular non-Euclidean system in question has no parallel lines.
D. This isn't necessary. The argument was describing what would be true *if* the physicists were correct. It was *not* arguing that the physicists were necessarily correct.
E. It doesn't matter how many physicists think the system is correct. The argument isn't claiming that the system is correct. Instead, it's telling us what would be true *if* the system were correct.

Question 10

QUESTION TYPE: Flawed Reasoning/Necessary Assumption

CONCLUSION: We can only find happiness in small political units like villages.

REASONING: We're not intellectually well suited to live in large, bureaucratic societies.

ANALYSIS: This is a bad argument because there isn't necessarily any link between being intellectually suited for a society and being happy.

A. **CORRECT.** It might be possible to be happy even if you aren't intellectually well suited for something.
B. They didn't assume this. They just said that those places offer us our best chance to be happy. It doesn't mean the purpose of those places is to make us happy.
C. Nay. They just said that we can't be happy in any society that does happen to be both bureaucratic and large.
D. Actually the argument is doubtful that we can find happiness even in such places. It said "if at all."
E. The argument didn't claim that we would be willing to go there. The philosopher just pointed out that we would never be happy if we stayed in our current society.

Question 11

QUESTION TYPE: Necessary Assumption

CONCLUSION: More and more people will have degenerative brain disorders once we start living longer.

REASONING: We'll be able to transplant all organs except for the brain. And there are many, many nerves in our body.

ANALYSIS: The argument is assuming that transplants are the only way to cure brain disorders.

The math on this question may be confusing so I'll give an example. Suppose you have 100 old people. Normally 50 die of a heart attack, 40 die of some kind of cancer and 10 die from a degenerative brain disorder.

But...now that we can save people with transplants, fewer people will die of heart attacks and cancer. Eventually all 100 of the old people would die of degenerative brain disease, since it is the only thing we can't fix with a transplant.

_____

A. Not true. The argument is only assuming that we'll be able to save people from more and more diseases *except* for degenerative brain disorders. So they will become more frequent as people stop dying from other things.
B. It doesn't matter how many transplants people need as long as we can successfully do them and keep people alive.
C. **CORRECT.** If we could cure all degenerative disorders without transplants then we could save people from that disease too. Degenerative disorder might cause an even smaller proportion of deaths.
D. It doesn't really matter what the percentage is now as long as it can increase in the future.
E. It doesn't matter how much is being spend as long as:
   i. we're able to do lots of transplants and **ii.** We can't cure brain disorders.

Question 12

QUESTION TYPE: Complete the Argument

ARGUMENTS: The politician says he will not compromise in order to work together with his opponents. The city's founding fathers warned against compromising the city's principles.

The critic points out that the politician is misusing a key term. The logical completion is compromise.

ANALYSIS: In the first sense, compromise means "giving up something to get something you want." In the second sense it means "betray." The founding fathers were not warning people against working together. That's silly.

_____

A. The use of betray was clear: be a traitor to the city.
B. Common was clear: That which we share.
C. **CORRECT.** Compromise was not clear: The opponents were talking about working together. The leaders accused them of wanting to betray the city.
D. "Principles" is clear: ideals.
E. "Opponents" is clear: People you are working against.

Question 13

QUESTION TYPE: Must be True

FACTS:

1. Some insects die after they reproduce.
2. Others may live for years.
3. Some of the insects that live for years help to benefit the ecosystem. Bees are an example.

ANALYSIS: Pretty much all we can say is that some bees don't die shortly after reproducing.

A. We have no idea what the "goal" of insect populations is. Maybe survival of the individual is the goal but they are really, really bad at it.
B. Who knows? We're only told that some insects that live a while benefit the ecosystem. But it could also be true that insects that die young benefit the ecosystem. We're not told that they don't.
C. This we don't know. We only know they live well beyond the survival of the next generation has been secured. But bees might not live even beyond the onset of the next generation. It's a different concept.
D. **CORRECT.** Because if all bees that reproduced died shortly afterwards then bees would belong to the first group and not the second.
E. Maybe? We only know that "many" insects die soon after reproducing. It might not be most of them.

Question 14

QUESTION TYPE: Role in Argument

CONCLUSION: Voters often reelect politicians whose behavior they dislike.

REASONING: A lot of voters say they don't like government intervention. But then they don't reelect inactive politicians. But an active politician is one who supports a lot of intervention.

ANALYSIS: This is a good argument. If voters truly wanted to stop intervention then they should elect the laziest politicians they can find.

The claim that voters tend not to reelect inactive politicians is just a premise that supports the conclusion. It is an example of how they people vote.

A. We don't actually know why voters don't reelect inactive politicians.
B. **CORRECT.** It's just a simple premise supporting the conclusion.
C. It is the next sentence that describes a politician's activity. The phrase in the question stem is about *inactivity*.
D. This describes the first sentence.
E. The argument does not say that people's beliefs *never* match their behavior. That's pretty extreme.

Question 15

QUESTION TYPE: Point at Issue

ARGUMENTS: Lea argues that contemporary art is big business and no longer has any creativity or spontaneity. This can be seen by visiting an art gallery.

Susan thinks that some art is still creative. We can see this in smaller independent galleries.

ANALYSIS: They disagree on whether you can find creative work. Susan doesn't actually say if she thinks art is big business or not.

_____

A. Susan seems to agree that large galleries aren't creative.
B. Lea says no. Susan doesn't express a clear opinion. She only said most *smaller* galleries have creative work. She didn't say what percent of galleries in total have uncreative work.
C. You might be tempted to pick this because Susan said "I disagree." But Susan's evidence shows that she was disagreeing about whether you can find creative work in galleries. Susan might agree that modern art is generally now big business.
D. **CORRECT.** Lea says any gallery will lack creative work. Susan says it's easy to find it in smaller galleries.
E. Susan doesn't say if she thinks are has become less about self-expression.

Question 16

QUESTION TYPE: Principle - Strengthen

CONCLUSION: It was morally wrong for the company to change its mind and sue.

REASONING: The company had signed a contract that said it would not sue. But then it did sue and it won the case.

ANALYSIS: There's a big difference between a moral right and a legal right. Here the company was apparently correct, legally, despite the contract. But they may have been morally wrong.

We're trying to conclude "morally wrong." That means that the right answer has to have morally wrong as a necessary condition. So something like "If X $\rightarrow$ morally wrong"

Answers that have the form of "If morally wrong $\rightarrow$ then X" are not good, because they just tell us what happens *if* we know that something is wrong.

We're trying to *conclude* that something is morally wrong, so it has to be a necessary condition.

_____

A. This only allows us to say when something *isn't* morally wrong. Morally wrong is just a sufficient condition that tells us that if something *is* morally wrong then the other side broke the deal. We need morally wrong as a necessary condition.
B. This does have morally wrong as a necessary condition...but the contractor *was* able to make restitution. They just have to pay them some money.
C. This is saying that the company induced the contractor to screw up (that's what they're being penalized for.) But we have no evidence the company caused the contractor to screw up.
D. This again tells us that something is morally wrong *only if*. We need to know that something is morally wrong *if*.
E. **CORRECT.** The company did promise to forego compensation in case of a problem. And they are suing because of an action performed in the context of that promise. This tells us it is therefore immoral to seek compensation for that action.

Question 17

QUESTION TYPE: Necessary Assumption

CONCLUSION: The fact that animals can signal to each other with sounds and gestures does not prove that they can use language.

REASONING: We don't know if animals can use sounds or gestures to refer to concrete objects or abstract ideas.

ANALYSIS: The argument assumes that a language can only refer to concrete objects or abstract ideas.

A. It's only necessary that animal don't know how to *communicate* those ideas.
B. It doesn't matter if an animal can entertain (think about) abstract ideas. It only matters if they can communicate those ideas to other animals.
C. This is tempting, but it isn't necessary. The key is that the zoologist said we can't *prove* that animals use language. So animals could be referring to abstract ideas. We just can't prove that they are.
D. **CORRECT.** If a system of sounds or gestures could be a language even without reference to objects or abstract ideas then maybe we could prove that animals can use language.
E. The argument would be stronger if this weren't true, since the argument claims we can't prove if any animals can use a language.

Question 18

QUESTION TYPE: Weaken

ARGUMENT: The older a person, the more likely they are to be disabled. In East Wendell fewer old people get disability benefits compared to younger people. The explanation is that the percentage of jobs offering a disability benefit has increased recently.

ANALYSIS: There isn't really any reasoning given in favor of the solution. On these sorts of questions we simply have to look for an alternate explanation to explain the facts.

A. This is sort of vague. How long ago did this improvement start? How big is the impact: are the people still disabled? Does it change overall population disability rates? Without more precise info we can't use this to weaken or strengthen the argument. It's useless.
B. This is also very vague. Some could be 1-3% of people. We need *detail* to weaken an argument.
C. Great! When did this happen? How much longer do we live? Does it affect disability rates? This doesn't let us do anything.
D. This tells us how much money people get. We're interested in the *percentage* of people receiving money.
E. **CORRECT.** This is a strong alternate explanation. Most disability plans simply stop at age 65. That explains why fewer people in the older age groups have disability plans.

Question 19

QUESTION TYPE: Most Strongly Supported

FACTS:

1. Rhodopsin molecules register light by changing shape.
2. Rhoposin sometimes changes shape because of molecular motion even when they are not struck by light.
3. The warmer the retinas the more motion there is.

ANALYSIS: We can reasonably conclude that there is more error when the retina is warmer.

———————————

A. We have no clue what determines retina temperature. It isn't mentioned.
B. **CORRECT.** This is hard to understand. Humans are an animal with a body temperature that does not match our surroundings. We always stay around 98.6 degrees.

Reptiles tend to match their surroundings. So if it is warm then they get warm. And presumably their retinas get warm. This causes more molecular motion and therefore causes the Rhoposin to get errors.
So animals that shift their body temperature to match their surroundings will have more errors when it is warm because their retinas warm up. When it is cold their retinas cool and they have fewer errors.
C. We only know that their error rate from molecular motion increases. But Rhodopsin still might be just as fast at dealing with light from photons.
D. We have no idea. The stimulus doesn't even mention surface area. More light might get in but presumably the animals have more Rhodopsin as well.
E. There might be more. We aren't told if Rhodopsin is alone or if there are other pigments.

Question 20

QUESTION TYPE: Weaken

CONCLUSION: The society as a body metaphor promotes authoritarian repression. It is more authoritarian than the metaphor of society as a family.

REASONING: Political usefulness determines how popular metaphors are. The metaphor of society as a body is very popular in authoritarian societies. It implies a connection between society working well and having a government as its head.

ANALYSIS: It's important to note that the conclusion is comparing the society as a body metaphor to other metaphors. That's all.

It isn't talking about how common metaphors or, or what metaphors are used elsewhere, etc.

The best way to weaken it is to show that another metaphor is more popular in authoritarian societies. Answer choice A does this.

———————————

A. **CORRECT.** If the society as a family metaphor is equally popular then it must be equally useful to authoritarian governments. This contradicts the conclusion that the society as a body metaphor is the most useful metaphor for authoritarians.
B. This strengthens the argument slightly by showing that political metaphors are real and common. But it doesn't tell us anything specific to authoritarian societies.
C. We would expect the metaphor to occasionally be used elsewhere. That's fine as long as it tends to be more common in authoritarian societies.
D. So? We're mainly concerned with whether the body or the family metaphor is more useful to authoritarian governments.
E. This slightly strengthens the argument by showing that the metaphor is not so popular in countries that are not authoritarian.

Question 21

QUESTION TYPE: Strengthen

CONCLUSION: Incomes must have risen faster than the price of food.

REASONING: People used to spend a larger percentage of their income on food.

ANALYSIS: This sounds like a good argument, but there are some nuances. For instance, people might be spending their food money differently. If you eat out less then you will spend less on food even though the price of food did not fall.

Also, the quantity of food might change. The right answer keeps things equal by telling us that food types and food quantity haven't changed in 30 years.

––––––––––––––––

A. This isn't determinative. If you eat the same amount of food as normal, but you eat it in a restaurant, then you will spend a *lot* more money. Maybe people just eat at restaurants less and spend less money for that reason.
B. We don't know if healthier food costs more or less. This doesn't help much. And if we're eating less then maybe *that* is why we spend less on food.
C. **CORRECT.** This holds everything equal. We purchase almost exactly what we did 30 years ago except we spend less.
D. This doesn't tell us how fast the price of food has risen. If anything it indicates that people might have had to cut back on food spending (and quantities) to afford everything else that was rising in price.
E. This indicates that *single* people may have changed their spending habits but prices probably stayed the same. Families are much more likely to be representative of food habits than single people since they count for more people.

Question 22

QUESTION TYPE: Must be False

FACTS:

1. Viruses can help humans.
2. For example, some viruses kill more-complex microorganisms that can sometimes hurt humans.
3. Viruses have very simple structures. Even small alterations can make them very deadly.
4. Random mutations big enough to make viruses deadly often happen. So any virus could easily become dangerous to humans.

ANALYSIS: The right answer is based on the second point.

––––––––––––––––

A. This could happen. It's easy for the helpful viruses to become deadly and the deadly viruses to become helpful through mutation.
B. This could happen. We aren't told how likely it is that more complex organisms mutate.
C. This could be. We only know that *some* of those micro-organisms are deadly to humans.
D. This could be true. Those viruses could kill deadly micro-organisms, for example.
E. **CORRECT.** This *cannot* be true. We know that at least some viruses help humans by killing more complex micro-organisms. It's the second sentence.

Question 23

QUESTION TYPE: Flawed Parallel Reasoning

CONCLUSION: Non-industrial societies must tend to be unified.

REASONING: When societies use money to measure value, they fragment into isolated social units. But non-industrial societies do not use money as the main measure of value.

ANALYSIS: This is an incorrect negation. The premise is "money → fragment"

We can't conclude that not using money leads to not fragmenting. There could be many different reasons why a society might fragment. The right answer will have an incorrect negation.

_____

A. This is a good argument. The argument isn't saying that jackals and wolves *can* interbreed. It just points out that the premise by itself doesn't prove that they can't.
B. This makes the mistake of assuming that what must be true on average must be true of every individual. Places further north *tend* to have fewer species. But exceptions are possible and Siberia might have more species than the desert does. But this isn't an incorrect negation.
C. This argument saves itself by saying "probably." It's still not good because it provides no evidence that arthropods are all like insects. But it isn't a terrible argument.
D. **CORRECT.** Poets → metaphors is the premise. The conclusion is an incorrect negation. There could be people apart from poets who use metaphors (such as journalists.)
E. This is a bad argument because it confuses what tends to be true with what is always true. A pencil might be more troublesome than a computer. But there is no incorrect negation.

Question 24

QUESTION TYPE: Strengthen

CONCLUSION: The opossums are going extinct because of non-native predators rather than from a lack of food.

REASONING: 75% of opossums released from captivity were eaten by foxes.

ANALYSIS: This is a bad argument. The opossums were living in captivity. They may not have had a chance to learn how to survive amongst predators. *Wild* opossums might not get eaten by foxes often and lack of food might be a bigger problem for them.

_____

A. This doesn't help, since the conclusion is that *non-native* predators are threatening the opossum. The conclusion would be stronger (slightly) if there were more non-native predators.
B. All that matters is that the foxes adapted well enough to eat opossums. The fact that some other species adapted better does not strengthen the argument.
C. This doesn't affect the fact that it was foxes that killed the opossums once they were released. We have no indication that food was an issue for these opossums.
D. This doesn't matter. The conclusion was that non-native *predators* were harming the opossum. The opossums weren't dying from lack of food. They were dying because foxes ate them.
E. **CORRECT.** This eliminates the possibility that the opossums raised in captivity were simply unprepared to deal with predators.

Question 25

QUESTION TYPE: Parallel Reasoning

ARGUMENTS: Jordan points out that business will be damned if they do and damned if they don't.

Terry points out a way that environmental controls could be implemented without harming any particular business. Terry offers a solution.

ANALYSIS: Structure is very important here. Jordan is pessimistic and shows how things we go wrong either way. If the companies help the environment then they will be hurt. But if then don't help the environment then there will be lots of pollution.

Terry is a problem solver. He says that if consumers demand change then we can help the environment without causing problems.

So the structure is: Jordan is whiny. You can't have good without bad. Terry shows us how we can have a good thing without a bad thing.

A. **CORRECT.** Jordan's part is good: something bad happens either way. Terry offers a solution to one of the problems.
B. Here Jordan describes how something can be *good* either way. And Terry just argues with his evidence.
C. Jordan does point out that taxes and social reform are mutually exclusive. Terry doesn't offer a solution. He just tells us what will happen if we don't do anything.
D. Here Terry is just warning about a possible bad consequence.
E. Here Terry is just telling us which of two bad options we should choose.

Question 26

QUESTION TYPE: Role in Argument

CONCLUSION: The increase in crime coverage is because the public is more interested in crime stories. It is not because there is more crime.

REASONING: The media pays close attention to the tastes and interests of the public when it decides what to cover.

ANALYSIS: The argument presents an alternate explanation for why crime coverage is increasing.

It's because people are more interested in crime. I disagree slightly with the correct answer, E.

I think the fact that people are more interested in crime is just part of the larger conclusion: there is more crime coverage because of this increased interest, not because there is more crime.

But E is still the best choice. The increased interest in crime is an alternate explanation.

The "after all" indicates that the statement right before is the conclusion.

A. I found this very tempting. But it mis-states the conclusion. We have no idea how much crime coverage is justified. All we know is that there is more coverage than ten years ago - but maybe there wasn't enough crime coverage then!
B. Actually, no evidence was given for the claim that the media decide to cover stories based on interest. The LSAT usually doesn't have to give evidence for its premises.
C. I think the LSAT is trying to impress us by using the word "counterexample". This is nonsense. The stimulus never attempts to disprove the idea that crime coverage has increased - it tries to explain this fact.
D. Crime coverage has increased. We're not told whether the crime rate has increased.
E. **CORRECT.** If you ignore my caveat in the Analysis section, this is pretty straightforward. The increased public interest in crime explains the increase in coverage.

Test 34
Section IV - Logic Games
Game 1 – Supermarket Aisles
Questions 1-7

Setup

This is a linear game. There's nothing particularly devious about it, but there are a lot of rules to keep track of. Make sure to have them all clear in your head before moving on to the questions: it will pay off.

We can arrange this with the regular setup of horizontal slots (drawn belowo, except there are nine instead of seven. It's important to note that each clerk can only go twice, at most. That means that four clerks will go twice and one (Olga, first rule) will go once.

Rule 1

There's no single best way to represent the first rule. I prefer to simply memorize it. You can draw something like this if it helps you:

O = 1

(That's the letter O, not a zero, in case I offended any mathematicians)

You could also make a list of variables, as follows: JJ, MM, KK, LL, O

The method doesn't really matter, as long as it achieves the goal: don't let yourself forget that O only appears once.

Rules 2 and 3

You should draw the next two rules directly onto your diagram. There's no chance of forgetting that way. Kurt is placed second, and you can draw M with a line through it underneath the first slot to show that Manny can't go there.

Rule 4

J can't go beside itself. You can draw this as a box with a line through it.

(**Also:** This should tip you off that other variables *can* go beside themselves, in case you weren't sure)

Rule 5

This is the kind of rule I like: it helps pin down variables. You already knew one K has to go in the second slot. Now you know the second K is wedged in between *both* Mannys. That takes out two variables at once.

Here's how you can draw this rule. The box indicates the three variables have to be beside each other, in that order:

$$\boxed{\text{MKM}}$$

We know that this MKM bloc can't go in slots 1-3 because M can't go in slot one.

Rule 6

This is another great rule type. It split the game into two scenarios: one where Larissa is on the left and one where Larissa is on the right. If a game is split into two scenarios, you should almost always draw both. Usually that lets you make additional deductions, and it always helps you visualize the game and draw local rules.

In this game, the two scenarios don't add as much as they usually do, but they're still useful.

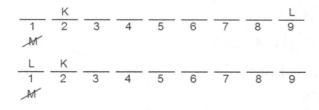

Rule 7

Another good rule. Olga has to come after Kurt. We can combine this with rule five to see that Olga also has to come after Manny.

As long as there is at least one L after O, everything's fine.

Main Diagram

Bringing everything together, we get the following:

Before Moving On To The Questions

It's always a good idea to review your rules, and commit any to memory that aren't clearly captured in the diagram.

- Olga only goes once.
- O has to go before *one* of the Ls.

Also try to see which variables are the most restrictive. We can see that the block of MKM-O-L is five variables long. That's hard to fit in. Visualize where this block can go (though *don't* waste time drawing every single place it could go.)

Know the rules. Success on this game depends on being able to make scenarios quickly and accurately.

Lastly, you should always look for random or flexible variables. L and J are the most flexible variables. They're the only two with a "spare" placement. Manny and Kurt are tied up together, and Olga can only go once.

Fast sketches are very important for this game. Practice making sketches quickly and accurately (even if the lines aren't straight and you'll move confidently through the game section. I've drawn neat little computer diagrams, but I normally solve logic games with drawings that look like they were drawn by a kindergartner.

Question 1

For this question, you must remember that each person can only go two times, at most. It turns out that Larissa is the only person who can go twice. **C** is **CORRECT.**

Jill: Rule four says Jill can't go twice.
Kurt: Kurt is wedged between Manny, so he can't.
Manny: Manny has Kurt stuck between him.
Olga: Olga can only go once.

The following scenario proves that Larissa can go consecutively:

J	K	M	K	M	O	J	L	L
1	2	3	4	5	6	7	8	9

M̶

Question 2

This right answer has two clerks that *both* can't go in slot five. Manny is in three answer choices. If we can eliminate him, then we can eliminate answers **A, C** and **D.**

J	K	M	K	M	J	O	L	L
1	2	3	4	5	6	7	8	9

M̶

Voila. Manny can definitely go in slot five.

Next we see that Olga is in both **B** and **E.** So Olga must be part of the right answer. That means we only have to test whether K or L can go in slot five.

J	K	L	M	K	M	J	O	L
1	2	3	4	5	6	7	8	9

M̶

Kurt fits easily.

E is **CORRECT.**

This next diagrams shows why Larissa can't go in slot five. We need four spots to fit MKM-O in front of L. There are only three spaces in the second case, and only two spaces in the first.

| | | M | K | M | O | | | |
L	K			L				
1	2	3	4	5	6	7	8	9

M̶

| | | | | M | K | M | O | |
	K			L				L
1	2	3	4	5	6	7	8	9

M̶

O can't go in slot five for the same reason. There's not enough space to fit MKM in front.

Question 3

Want to go faster on this type of question? Check which variables are in multiple answer choices. Jill and Larissa are in *every* answer choice! Clearly they can both go in slot three.

That leaves Olga, Manny and Kurt to test. Olga definitely doesn't fit in slot three.
She needs MKM in front of her.

L	K	O						
1	2	3	4	5	6	7	8	9

M̶

MKM — O — L

Kurt doesn't fit either. We already figured out in the first question that Kurt can't go beside himself. There's no space for Manny.

	K	K						L
1	2	3	4	5	6	7	8	9

M̶

So it's only Jill, Larissa and Manny who can go in slot three. **B is CORRECT.**

Question 4

Aisles three and five are in every answer choice. You don't have to test those.

A is wrong because it says Manny can be in the first slot. The third rule says that can never happen.

B is wrong because it says Manny can be in the ninth slot. That leaves no room for Olga to come after Manny.

So you have to see if Manny can go in 4, 6 and 7. Turns out he can go in all of those places, so **D** is **CORRECT.** Here are a couple of diagrams that prove he can go in those spots:

L	K	J	M	K	M	O	L	J
1	2	3	4	5	6	7	8	9

M̶

J	K	L	J	M	K	M	O	L
1	2	3	4	5	6	7	8	9

M̶

Question 5

You need to put Larissa's aisles as far apart as possible. That means putting Larissa's non-end aisle at one off of the end (the 6th rule says Larissa can't go in both end slots).

So Larissa goes either in 1 and 8, or 2 and 9. But, Larissa can't go in 2, since Kurt is there. So we need to put Larissa in slots 1 and 8.

MKM-O all have to come before Larissa. So we *have* to put a J in slot nine: there's nothing else left to go after L. We get the following diagram:

MKM — O,J

L	K						L	J
1	2	3	4	5	6	7	8	9

M̶

I drew the remaining variables above the diagram, separated by a comma to show that the J could go before or after (or in between) the other variables. M can't go directly before L in slot 7 because then there would be no space for O.

Turns out **A** is **CORRECT.** This diagram proves it:

L	K	M	K	M	J	O	L	J
1	2	3	4	5	6	7	8	9

M̶

B is out because Manny can't be in seven. There's no room for Olga.

C and **D** are gone because one J *has* to come in spot nine (after O, and in an odd numbered spot.)

E is out because both L and J have to come after Olga.

Question 6

Always draw local rules. On this question I drew both scenarios, and then put J in slot three. There's no immediate further deduction (there usually is on most games), but this still makes it easier to visualize.

I went through the answer choices, and visualized whether they seemed restrictive. You should do a quick pass through each answer choice before trying them seriously...sometimes E is correct, and you don't want to waste a lot of time on A-C without at least glancing at E.

Look at what happens when I try to put O in six in both of those diagrams. It's clear there's no space for MKM in front of O:

L	K	J			O			
1	2	3	4	5	6	7	8	9

M̶

	K	J			O			L
1	2	3	4	5	6	7	8	9

M̶

Done! **E** is **CORRECT.**

Students underestimate how much time they spend thinking about questions. It's usually a lot quicker to make a simple sketch and then pencil in a scenario that tests each answer choice (start with one that seems more restrictive, such as O.) You're also less likely to make a mistake when you put your thoughts on paper.

You can disprove the other answer choices by making a couple of quick sketches. The first sketch below eliminates answer choices **A, B** and **C.** The second eliminates **D.**

L	K	J	L	M	K	M	O	J
1	2	3	4	5	6	7	8	9

M̶

L	K	J	M	K	M	O	L	J
1	2	3	4	5	6	7	8	9

M̶

Question 7

A new rule! Don't think about it: draw it, then think about it.

L	K							L
1	2	3	4	5	6	7	8	9

M̶

It can pay off to scan the answer choices to see which one to try first. We saw in the last question it can sometimes be tricky to stick O in slot six. We couldn't do it there, and it turns out we can't do it here, either. **B** is **CORRECT.**

Why? Take a look.

L	K	M	K	M	O	J	J	L
1	2	3	4	5	6	7	8	9

M̶

The two Js are side by side. Normally we could put L between them, but L is stuck on both ends and can't help.

The following scenario proves answer choices **A** and **E** wrong. O and L can be beside each other, and J can go in 3.

L	K	J	M	K	M	J	O	L
1	2	3	4	5	6	7	8	9

M̶

And this scenario proves answer choices **C** and **D** wrong.

L	K	M	K	M	J	O	J	L
1	2	3	4	5	6	7	8	9

M̶

Game 2 – Philosophy Lectures
Questions 8-12

Setup

This is another linear game, but it plays out differently from most linear games. We're trying to determine the lecture topic for each of five days. The topics can't repeat. This is the major limiting factor.

There are five lecturers. Each can only lecture about certain philosophers. They lecture in order, one each day for five days. We can draw the speakers horizontally. Underneath we can put the possible lecture topics they can cover.

1	2	3	4	5
K	K	M	M	N
L	L	N	N	O
M	M			P
	N			

Take a look at 3 and 4. They don't have many options: only M or N. If 3 lectures about M, then 4 can only speak about N, and vice-versa.

This means that 3 and 4 *have* to talk about M. No one else can lecture about M and N!
So 1 and 2 can only lecture about K and L. 5 can only lecture about O or P.

It doesn't matter which of 1 and 2 lectures about K or L. The speakers are quite interchangeable. It's the same for 3 and 4. The key to the game simply lies in knowing what each speaker's (limited) options are. This next diagram shows which topics each speaker can lecture about.

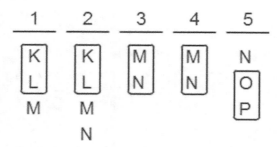

There's nothing else to do. This diagram will let us answer every question with ease.

Question 8

Speakers 1 and 2 can't lecture about M. That gets rid of **A** and **B**.

Speakers 2 and 5 can't lecture about N. That gets rid of **C** and **D**.

But there's nothing to stop speaker 5 from lecturing on Ockham. **E** is **CORRECT.**

Question 9

Alphabetical order...don't feel bad if you had to recite the alphabet to answer this one (I did!) It's better to feel silly than to be wrong.

K-L-M-N is the only alphabetical order for the first four speakers. Then five can lecture about either O or P, since both letters come after N. That gives us two options, so **A** is **CORRECT.**

Question 10

Think about who we have to pin down. We need to know who lectures about one of either M and N, one of the pair K and L, and we also need to know who 5 lectures on.

Answer **C** lets us do that. **C** is **CORRECT.** If we know when M is lectured about (for example, on day 3) then we know N must be lectured about on the other day (day 4.)

If we know where half of a pair goes, then we can also say where the other half goes.

This type of question can take a long time, without the right method. So before wading through the answers on this type of question, ask yourself which variables you need to pin down.

A and **B** don't let us choose between O and P.

D and **E** don't let us know when to place K and L.

Question 11

This new rule about British and German philosophers doesn't really change anything. It's just LSAC's way of disguising what they are asking. The wrong answer violates the master diagram, reproduced below:

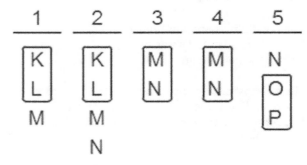

German = K and N
British = L, M and O

Take a minute to memorize who is German and British before starting.

A could be true because L can be first and M can be fourth. (first and fourth British)

B could be true because K can be first and N can be fourth. (First and Fourth German)

C could be true because L could be second and M could be third. (Second and Third British)

D is **CORRECT.** There's only one German philosopher split between 3 and 4: Nietzsche. They can't both lecture about a German.

E is wrong because M could go fourth and O could go fifth. (Fourth and Fifth British)

Question 12

This new rule changes *everything*. The limiting factor on the game was that 3 and 4 had to lecture about M and N. So nobody else could ever lecture about M and N. But now that 3 can lecture about S, then (for example) 4 could lecture about N. That lets 1 or 2 lecture about M.

The possibilities are now quite open. Do *not* try to figure them all out, it's wasted effort. Just try to get a feel for the new situation.

Since almost anything can happen, the only good way to violate a rule is to have 3 *not* lecture about S. If 3 doesn't use the new option, then the game will work as before.

The new diagram looks like this. There are virtually no restrictions as long as 3 *does* choose S.

1	2	3	4	5
K	K	M	M	N
L	L	N	N	O
M	M	S		P
	N			

A could work, because 3 could lecture about S. (All of the wrong answers will have this same dull explanation.)

B *doesn't* work because if 3 lectures about N then 4 must lecture about M. So 2 can't lecture about M. **B** is **CORRECT.**

C doesn't work, because 3 could lecture about S. That frees up M and N to be used elsewhere.

D doesn't work, because 3 could lecture about S. That frees up N to go in 5.

E doesn't work, because 3 could lecture about S. That frees up N to go in 2.

Game 3 – Train Station
Questions 13-18

Setup

This is another linear game. They're my favorite type. I like this game in particular because the game can be split into two clear scenarios that let you deduce a lot.

The seven trains arrive one at a time. This is the same seven-slotted setup you'll find on so many logic games.

The first rule immediately lets us split this into two scenarios. You should *always* draw two scenarios when a rule this clearly divides the game.

$$\underset{1}{\rule{1.5em}{0.4pt}}\quad \underset{2}{\rule{1.5em}{0.4pt}}\quad \underset{3}{\rule{1.5em}{0.4pt}}\quad \overset{Y}{\underset{4}{\rule{1.5em}{0.4pt}}}\quad \underset{5}{\rule{1.5em}{0.4pt}}\quad \underset{6}{\rule{1.5em}{0.4pt}}\quad \underset{7}{\rule{1.5em}{0.4pt}}$$

$$\underset{1}{\rule{1.5em}{0.4pt}}\quad \underset{2}{\rule{1.5em}{0.4pt}}\quad \underset{3}{\rule{1.5em}{0.4pt}}\quad \overset{W}{\underset{4}{\rule{1.5em}{0.4pt}}}\quad \underset{5}{\rule{1.5em}{0.4pt}}\quad \underset{6}{\rule{1.5em}{0.4pt}}\quad \underset{7}{\rule{1.5em}{0.4pt}}$$

You might wonder why you should make two separate diagrams. The rule itself is obvious, and it seems like a lot of work to make more drawings.

Well, it lets you more easily visualize the game. And there are usually many deductions unique to each diagram. The second rule has different effects in each scenario.

$$\overset{\textstyle W-S-Y}{\underset{\ }{}}$$
$$\underset{1}{\rule{1.5em}{0.4pt}}\quad \underset{2}{\rule{1.5em}{0.4pt}}\quad \underset{3}{\rule{1.5em}{0.4pt}}\quad \overset{Y}{\underset{4}{\rule{1.5em}{0.4pt}}}\quad \underset{5}{\rule{1.5em}{0.4pt}}\quad \underset{6}{\rule{1.5em}{0.4pt}}\quad \underset{7}{\rule{1.5em}{0.4pt}}$$

$$\overset{\textstyle W-S-Y}{}$$
$$\underset{1}{\rule{1.5em}{0.4pt}}\quad \underset{2}{\rule{1.5em}{0.4pt}}\quad \underset{3}{\rule{1.5em}{0.4pt}}\quad \overset{W}{\underset{4}{\rule{1.5em}{0.4pt}}}\quad \underset{5}{\rule{1.5em}{0.4pt}}\quad \underset{6}{\rule{1.5em}{0.4pt}}\quad \underset{7}{\rule{1.5em}{0.4pt}}$$

In the first scenario, the W-S-Y ordering goes before 4. In the second scenario, it goes after 4.

The next rule is just straightforward sequencing.

But it becomes a bit more interesting when we add in the fact that T can't go beside V. Here's how I draw that type of rule:

Pretend that box is a suitcase. Imagine you can pick it up by the handle and flip it around. You can't have either TV or VT.

So T and V come after R and they can't come beside each other.

Q is our only random variable: it has no rules attached to it.

Putting It All Together

You should never move onto the questions without at least trying to combine rules. It's true that on some games there aren't many deductions. But on many games you can make some very important deductions that strictly limit what can be true.

This game is like that.

Take a look at our first scenario:

```
         W— S— Y
                  Y
   ___  ___  ___  ___  ___  ___  ___
    1    2    3    4    5    6    7
```

Where can you put R, T and V? R has to go before them.

If you put R in 5, then T and V will be in 6 and 7... *beside* each other. That doesn't work. And there's no space for T or V to go before Y.

You need to put T and V in 5 and 7. R will go in front of Y somewhere, along with W and S. And there's only one spot left for Q, in slot 6.

The end result looks like this:

```
   R,W— S
   ___  ___  ___  ___  ___  ___  ___
    1    2    3   Y    V/T   Q   T/V
                  4    5    6    7
```

I placed the first three variables overhead to indicate that they go in the first three slots, but I don't know where. I use the comma between R and W-S to indicate that R is in the same region as W and S, but I have no idea where it is in relation to them.

We know the first three variables are before Y, and W is before S. That's all.

You don't have to draw R, "W --S " the same way I did. It makes sense to me, but you might think of some other method that makes more sense for you.

But make sure you represent it *somehow*. If you don't draw a deduction, there's a good chance you'll forget it. Even *I* forget if I don't draw my deductions.)

The T/V and V/T mean that one of them goes in 5 and the other goes in 7.

The second scenario is similarly restricted. Take a look and try to think about where you can put R, T and V. Remember, R goes before V and T, and V and T aren't beside each other:

```
         W— S— Y
                  W
   ___  ___  ___  ___  ___  ___  ___
    1    2    3    4    5    6    7
```

Did you figure it out? There is only one space free after W, and one of T/V has to go there.

If you put R, T and V in spots 1-2-3, T and V will be beside each other. So one of T/V goes with S-Y after W.

That leaves R, the other V/T and Q to go before W. It looks like this.

```
   R— V/T,Q                S— Y , T/V
   ___  ___  ___  ___  ___  ___  ___
    1    2    3   W    5    6    7
                  4
```

The variables are placed overhead to indicate which region they go in. The commas show that Q can go before or after (or in between) R-V/T.

Master Diagram

Scenario 1

R,W — S

Y   V/T   Q   T/V

___ ___ ___ ___ ___ ___ ___
1   2   3   4   5   6   7

Scenario 2

R — V/T,Q   S— Y , T/V

               W

___ ___ ___ ___ ___ ___ ___
1   2   3   4   5   6   7

The entire game reduces to these two little diagrams. Neat.

Study them well before trying the questions. And make sure to think a little about how the variables can be placed (without drawing all of the possibilities). It's important to understand the possibilities your diagrams represent.

The explanations for this game are a lot more mechanical than for some games. That's because once you understand the two scenarios, this is a very easy game. If you're still a little confused by them, try to draw them on your own using the rules, and go over my set-up again.

Question 13

For the first question, I like to start with an easy rule such as "Y or W must be 4ᵗʰ." Check each answer choice to see if it violates the rule.

(Don't use your scenarios for the first question. Rules are faster.)

D has Sunnyvale 4ᵗʰ. Wrong.

Next, let's try R before T and V. You can also check if T and V are beside each other at the same time.

A has T and V beside each other. It's out.

E has T before R. Oops.

Two answers left. I had to look at my rules again, because I forgot the other rule. I didn't look at the answer choices, that would have been a waste of time. Don't waste time.

The other rule is that S is between W and Y. **B** violates that rule.

C is **CORRECT.**

Question 14

This is a local rule question. The first step is to check which scenario we are in. The first scenario is the only one that allows us to put W before R. And we have to put W in slot 1, because S also has to go after W.

$$\underset{1}{\underline{W}} \quad \underset{2}{\underline{}} \quad \overset{R,S}{\underset{3}{\underline{}}} \quad \underset{4}{\underline{Y}} \quad \underset{5}{\underline{V/T}} \quad \underset{6}{\underline{Q}} \quad \underset{7}{\underline{T/V}}$$

You have two ways to place R and S. R can be second and S third, or vice versa.

There are also two ways to place T and V. T in 5 and V in 7, or vice-versa.

2 possibilities times 2 possibilities equals 4 possibilities. **A is CORRECT.**

The math works, but if you don't believe me, try drawing out the possibilities. It will save you from making a mistake:

RS TV
RS VT
SR TV
SR VT

Such a drawing doesn't take long. It's the best way to solve this if your math teacher never taught you how to calculate permutations.

Question 15

This must be true question is testing for a general deduction we should have made. The more "must be true" questions you see that don't involve a local rule, the more likely it is that you should have made deductions during the setup.

A could be true, but it doesn't have to be. In the *last* question, we figured out W could be first.

B is disproved by the first scenario, when Q is in slot 6.

C is disproved by question 14, just like **A**. R *can* go first, but it doesn't have to. W can go first in scenario 1, and Q can go first in scenario 2.

D is disproved by scenario 1, where V has to arrive *after* the York.

E is **CORRECT.** W is before S and S is before the Y. This answer choice is a reward for getting through the others.

Sometimes the LSAC makes the correct answer easy, but puts it at the end. It can pay to go quickly through the answers you're not certain you can disprove. Don't eliminate them, but looking through all the answers lets you check if LSAC has hidden an easy answer choice right at the end.

Question 16

I'm reproducing the scenarios so you don't have to look back to the setup.

Scenario 1

R,W — S

			Y	V/T	Q	T/V
1	2	3	4	5	6	7

Scenario 2

R — V/T,Q   S — Y , T/V

			W			
1	2	3	4	5	6	7

This general question shows that the LSAC expected us to make deductions in our general setup.

A is wrong because in both scenarios Q and S are on opposite sides and can't go beside each other.

B is **CORRECT.** In scenario 1 S could be 2 and R could be 3. We saw this could be true in question 14. Try to remember what you've done on previous questions.

C is wrong because in scenario R always has to come *before* T.

D is wrong because in both scenarios Q and S are on opposite sides.

E is wrong because in scenario 1 Q and W are on opposite sides and in scenario 2 Q is *before* W.

Question 17

One train between W and Y. That could only be S, because S has to be somewhere between them in all scenarios.

This new rule is pretty restrictive. Here are the diagrams:

R	W	S	Y	V/T	Q	T/V
1	2	3	4	5	6	7

R — V/T,Q

			W	S	Y	T/V
1	2	3	4	5	6	7

A can't work, S has to be 3 or 6.

B is no good, because the sixth train is either Q or Y.

C can't be true. R is in 1 in the first scenario and in the second scenario R has to go before V/T, so it is second at the latest.

D can't be true because S is either 3 or 5.

E is **CORRECT.** In the first scenario, R *has* to go first. In the second scenario, R could be first, in front of V/T and Q.

Question 18

This questions puts Q before R...that can only be the second scenario.

R — V/T,Q   S— Y , T/V

                          W

____ ____ ____ ____ ____ ____ ____
 1   2   3   4   5   6   7

Q now has to be in front of both V/T and R, so Q must be first.

The question is asking us where W must arrive. In the second scenario, W arrives fourth. **C** is **CORRECT.**

Game 4 – Doctors at Their Clinics
Questions 19-24

Setup

This is a grouping game. Every doctor is at one of two clinics. This means you can treat the game as an in-out grouping game, like the birds in the forest game from test 33. "You're either in or out" is the same as "you're either at S or R".

We're going to draw all the rules, then recombine them into two chains of sufficient and necessary conditions. This will let us figure out a *lot*.

The first two rules can be easily confused if you don't read them carefully. LSAC placed the sufficient condition second. The first rule would mean the same thing if it read:

"If Juarez is at Souderton, Kudrow is at Randsborough."

Always focus on words such as "if" "only if" etc. Word order doesn't always change much. Like Yoda be.

Here are the rules drawn out. The subscripts indicate the clinics:

$$J_s \longrightarrow K_r$$

$$J_r \longrightarrow O_s$$

$$L_s \longrightarrow N_r \text{ and } P_r$$

$$N_r \longrightarrow O_r$$

$$P_r \longrightarrow K_s \text{ and } O_s$$

When you've finished drawing the rules on this sort of game, look back over the game's written rules to make sure you haven't made any mistakes. I *always* do. Any mistake is a disaster, especially when you're combining rules.

I've also drawn the contrapositives below. Remember that you have to change "and" to "or." For example, since L being at S requires *both* N and P to be at R then *either* one of them being at S is sufficient to show that L must be at R.

In a two group game, the negation of L being at S is L being at R. There's no need to put a line through the variables. There are only two groups, so if you aren't at one then you must be at the other.

$$K_s \longrightarrow J_r$$

$$O_r \longrightarrow J_s$$

$$P_s \text{ or } N_s \longrightarrow L_r$$

$$O_s \longrightarrow N_s$$

$$K_r \text{ or } O_r \longrightarrow P_s$$

Now it's time for a game of mix and match. If the same variable is both a necessary and a sufficient condition for two separate statements, you can join the two. It's like lego!

For example, Or leads to Js. And Js leads to Kr. So we get:

$$O_r \longrightarrow J_s \longrightarrow K_r$$

For in-out or two group games, it's often the case you can connect *everything*. So let's build on that and see if we can fit all of the variables.

For example, Nr leads to Or.

$$N_r \longrightarrow O_r \longrightarrow J_s \longrightarrow K_r$$

Next, Kr leads to Ps. And Ps leads to Lr. Done!

$$N_r \longrightarrow O_r \longrightarrow J_s \longrightarrow K_r \longrightarrow P_s \longrightarrow L_r$$

(Note: we also know Or leads directly to Ps. You can draw that separately if you want, but it's not necessary since Or leads to Ps indirectly through Kr.)

Now we can take the contrapositive. Be very careful when you do this, you don't want to misinterpret your AND/OR statements. I always reread my rules once I've drawn a contrapositive chain, to make sure I didn't make a mistake.

I start with Ls leads to Pr. Then Pr leads to Ks. Ks leads to Jr.

$$L_s \longrightarrow P_r \longrightarrow K_s \longrightarrow J_r$$

Next, Jr leads to Os, and Os leads to Ns.

$$L_s \longrightarrow P_r \longrightarrow K_s \longrightarrow J_r \longrightarrow O_s \longrightarrow N_s$$

(I took a shortcut. Pr leads to both Ks and Os. I didn't draw Pr --> Os, because Ks leads to Os.)

Lastly, Ns leads to Lr.

$$L_s \longrightarrow P_r \longrightarrow K_s$$
$$\searrow J_r \longrightarrow O_s \longrightarrow N_s \longrightarrow L_r$$

(I've added the curve only because the diagram was too big for the page otherwise)

Huh? Yes, you read that diagram right. Ls leads to Lr.

Obviously, that doesn't work, L can't be in two places at once. A hidden deduction is that L always *has* to be at R.

This is very weird, since they gave us a rule that tells us what happens if L is at S. But it's true: L can't ever be at S.

If you're not convinced, here's a diagram of what happens when we take the Ls rule and combine it with other rules:

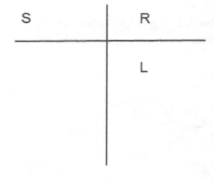

Clearly, we can't have Ps and Pr at the same time. L has to be in R.

And we're done! Combining rules really is just like lego. Or dominoes.

We can set up the deduction about L in a table.

S	R
	L

There's a bit more we can add. Consider these rules:

$$J_s \longrightarrow K_r \quad K_s \longrightarrow J_r$$

$$J_r \longrightarrow O_s \quad O_r \longrightarrow J_s$$

If J is at S, K is at R, and vice versa. J and K can't both be at S; one of them has to be at R.

Both *could* be in R. This may look confusing. Try putting J in R.

Jr is the *necessary condition* in the rule above. Knowing that J is in R can't tell us *anything* about K. You can only read the diagrams left to right, not backwards.

This is the most confusing relationship on in-out grouping games, so make sure you understand it. *

O and J have a similar relationship. One has to be in S. You can add both relationships to the table.

```
      S    |    R
_____|_____
           |
     O\J   |    L
           |    J\K
           |
           |
           |
           |
```

* Here's an example of the "at least one" relationship. If you're a parent, you have a boy or a girl. You could also have both. So we no that if someone is a parent, and:

no boy --> girl
no girl --> boy

Parents always have at least one, and maybe both.

Whenever the suffiicient condition is negated, and the necessary condition is positive, you must have at least one, and *could have both*.

Master Diagram

$$N_r \longrightarrow O_r \longrightarrow J_s \longrightarrow K_r \longrightarrow P_s \longrightarrow L_r$$

$$P_r \longrightarrow K_s \longrightarrow J_r \longrightarrow O_s \longrightarrow N_s \longrightarrow L_r$$

```
      S    |    R
_____|_____
           |
     O\J   |    L
           |    J\K
           |
           |
           |
```

Question 19

Use the rules one by one to eliminate answers.

C is out, because L can't go in S. Ok, this wasn't a rule, this was a deduction from our diagram.

If J is in S, then K is in R. So **A** is wrong.

B doesn't violate any rules. **B** is **CORRECT.**

D is wrong because Pr leads to Ks. (You need to consider which variables go in R)

E is wrong because Jr leads to Os.

Question 20

If Palermo is at Randsburough, then we know everything. This scenario was one of our diagrams from the setup. See how easy these are once you get the diagram right.

$$P_r \longrightarrow K_s \longrightarrow J_r \longrightarrow O_s \longrightarrow N_s \longrightarrow L_r$$

A is **CORRECT.** Juarez has to be at Randsborough. All of the other answers always have to be *false,* based on this diagram.

Question 21

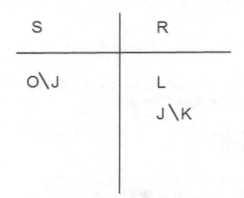

We need to find the lowest number at Souderton. Let's start with the diagram above. We definitely need one of O or J at S.

This eliminate **A.** We can't have zero people at S.

Let's try the diagrams. If we put P in R, then K, O and N are at S. Three people are at S. So **E** is wrong.

$$P_r \longrightarrow K_s \longrightarrow J_r \longrightarrow O_s \longrightarrow N_s \longrightarrow L_r$$

Let's see if we can do better, and try Nr instead. That only causes 2 people to be in S.

$$N_r \longrightarrow O_r \longrightarrow J_s \longrightarrow K_r \longrightarrow P_s \longrightarrow L_r$$

We can't get that number any lower. J has to be at S, because one of O/J has to be there. And if we moved P into R, we'd be in the scenario from the first diagram.

C is **CORRECT.** Two is the lowest number of doctors we can have at S.

Question 22

Nance and Onawa must be kept apart. That means N has to go in S. Why? Look what happens if we put them in R.

$$N_r \longrightarrow O_r \longrightarrow J_s \longrightarrow K_r \longrightarrow P_s \longrightarrow L_r$$

O goes in R! So Ns, Or is how we set this up.

(Just start from Or on the top diagram and move right, and start from Ns on the lower diagram and move right)

$$P_r \longrightarrow K_s \longrightarrow J_r \longrightarrow O_s \longrightarrow N_s \longrightarrow L_r$$

So what can we deduce? Ns just leads to Lr, which we knew already. Or leads to Js and Kr.

We can see that P must be in S. If P were in R, then O would be in S.

So: R = L, K, O
S = P, N, J,

This answers our question; J must be at S. **A** is **CORRECT.**

Local rule questions are that simple. Draw the local rule, make deductions, check if those deductions give you the right answer.

Question 23

This question isn't too hard either. We need two doctors who can't both be at Randsborough.

So just look to see where one of the doctors listed is a sufficient condition for the other doctor to be at S. Scan the diagrams left to right. For example, for **A,** look for Jr and Kr.

Kr leads to nothing, so that's fine. And Jr doesn't lead to anything involving K. So there's no obvious reason these two couldn't be at R together.

Try it yourself. Look for Jr and Pr. See if either of them being at R causes the other doctor to be at S.

(It doesn't. Pr leads to Jr. So those two can definitely be together at R.)

E is **CORRECT.** P at R leads to N at S.

$$P_r \longrightarrow K_s \longrightarrow J_r \longrightarrow O_s \longrightarrow N_s \longrightarrow L_r$$

Question 24

What happens if K is at S? It's this diagram, starting from K.

$$P_r \longrightarrow K_s \longrightarrow J_r \longrightarrow O_s \longrightarrow N_s \longrightarrow L_r$$

Our deductions are: Jr, Os, Ns and Lr.

We don't know anything about P, they could go in either clinic. You can only go right to left on the diagrams, not left to right).

Now that we've made a few deductions, we should check if they give us the right answer. They do; **B** says N has to be at S.

B is CORRECT.

A and **C** must be false, and **D** and **E** are just things that could be true.

Local rule questions are often dead simple. If your diagram is correct, there's no need to second guess it. The LSAC is rewarding you with easy points for figuring out how everything fits together.

Test 35
Section I - Logical Reasoning

Question 1

QUESTION TYPE: Main Conclusion

CONCLUSION: Operatic Stage directions can be reflected in music.

REASONING: Mozart's operas contain scenes where the music sounds like stage directions.

ANALYSIS: The question stem reads a lot like a "role in argument" question stem. But it's actually asking us to figure out what the conclusion is.

The argument argues against the conclusion that an opera's stage directions are never reflected in music. They give an example from Mozart to show that changes of scenery can be reflected in the music. Then they conclude that other stage directions can therefore be reflected as well.

It's an ok argument. They've correctly proven that stage directions (changes of scenery) *can* be reflected in music. But they don't have much evidence for the conclusion that other types of operatic directions can be reflected as well.

_____

A. The stimulus says that a change of scenery is the most basic stage direction. But it doesn't say it's the stage direction most frequently reflected in music. It just says it *can* be reflected in music.
B. The whole argument argues that stage directions *can* be reflected in music. Mozart's operas are an example.
C. The argument goes further than this. Stage directions are reflected *in* the music.
D. **CORRECT.** This is the last sentence. Mozart's stage directions were just an example of a wider phenomenon, according to the author.
E. We only know this is true for Mozart's change of scene music. We don't know if it's true for all operatic stage directions.

Question 2

QUESTION TYPE: Principle – Strengthen

CONCLUSION: The generalization is a scientific law.

REASONING: The generalization has never been falsified. It hasn't been conclusively verified either.

ANALYSIS: Technically we can't prove whether any theory is true. We can only prove a theory false. But we still need to accept some theories in order to work with them.

So we use the standard the lecturer described. If a theory hasn't been disproved and often has made successful predictions then we call it a law. But we must remember that some laws could be disproved.

The correct answer tells us when to conclude that something is a law. A and B only let us say when something *isn't* a law. C and E are too broad.

_____

A. This tells us a necessary condition for a scientific law. We need a sufficient condition.
B. This tells us when *not* to say something is a scientific law. We need to conclude that something *is* a scientific law.
C. We don't actually know if the second law of thermodynamics is true universally.
D. **CORRECT.** We have tested this law as far as current science allows. That lets us correctly conclude that it is a law.
E. This goes too far. It says that anything that we think is a law will be a law. But the lecturer implies that some laws could be proven false.

Question 3

QUESTION TYPE: Main Conclusion

CONCLUSION: The theory that more women get Alzheimer's because they live longer may be wrong.

REASONING: It might instead be due to a lack of estrogen due to menopause. Men end up fine because testosterone gets converted to estrogen and men keep a steady supply of testosterone into old age.

ANALYSIS: The argument's author hedges his bets. New evidence shows that the old theory *may* be wrong. We don't know anything for sure.

————————————

A. CORRECT. The theory isn't certain to be wrong but new evidence is compelling.

B. This is true, but it isn't the main point. The argument was trying to explain why we get Alzheimer's.

C. We're not even sure if this is true. It might be that there has to be some combination of menopause + old age for Alzheimer's to occur.

D. This is true, but it isn't the main point. This is just information that supports the idea that the old theory may be wrong.

E. This isn't even true. Testosterone wouldn't be necessary if men could be given estrogen, for example.

Question 4

QUESTION TYPE: Strengthen

ARGUMENTS: P argues that children will need computer skills. So we should teach children about computers from an early age and eventually teach them programming languages.

Q argues that things change so fast that the children's computer knowledge would become obsolete by the time the children enter the workforce.

ANALYSIS: We're trying to support P. The right answer shows that skills learned on obsolete technologies will transfer to new technologies.

————————————

A. This answer sounds very good. But P is talking about giving children skills for *tomorrow's* world. P wants to give children training now so that they can adapt to the world once they graduate. P doesn't necessarily think the children will need computer skills *before* then. This answer choice talks about adapting to *today's* world.

B. This wouldn't address Q's point that the technology the children did learn to use would become obsolete. And if children will adapt then do we really have to bother teaching them?

C. CORRECT. This is a sensible reply. Children gain general computer skills through technology training, even if that technology eventually becomes obsolete. These general skills will let them work with any new computer.

D. Analogies can't prove anything. Just because people don't have to relearn to drive doesn't mean that people won't have to relearn how to use new computers. Computers are very different from cars.

E. This doesn't change the fact that the technology we teach the children during school will become obsolete by the time they graduate.

Question 5

QUESTION TYPE: Method of Reasoning

ARGUMENTS: The proponent argues that irradiation leaves no radiation behind. And while it does destroy nutrients it doesn't destroy any more nutrients than cooking does. The advantage to irradiation is that it prevents spoiling and also kills salmonella.

The opponent points out that irradiation could kill the smelly bacteria that warn us of botulism. But botulism would survive. We could get very, very sick. Also, it's easy to kill both salmonella and botulism using a chemical dip.

ANALYSIS: It's hard to say who is right. We don't know how common botulism is or how useful shelf life extension is.

The opponent's argument addresses only the bacterial part of the proponent's argument. They point out there is an alternative that has the same benefits as the proponent's proposal, but none of the drawbacks. A chemical dip would avoid the botulism problem and clear up unwanted bacteria.

———————————

A. There's no ambiguity. The opponent just points out that the proponent doesn't address the botulism problem.
B. There isn't a self-contradiction. The problem is that the opponent's new information about botulism makes irradiation look like a bad idea.
C. Actually the opponent seems to think the chemical dip has no risks.
D. Both speakers are focused on consumer safety. There's no shift in perspective.
E. **CORRECT.** The opponent's proposal seems like a good alternative. The advantage of a chemical dip is killing smelly bacteria. The chemical dip also kills salmonella, which avoids the disadvantage of irradiation.

Question 6

QUESTION TYPE: Flawed Reasoning

ARGUMENTS: The proponent argues that irradiation leaves no radiation behind. And while it does destroy nutrients it doesn't destroy any more nutrients than cooking does. The advantage to irradiation is that it prevents spoiling and also kills salmonella.

The opponent points out that it could kill the smelly bacteria that warn us of botulism. But botulism would survive. We could get very, very sick. Also, it's easy to kill both salmonella and botulism using a chemical dip.

ANALYSIS: The proponent says we don't lose any more nutrients than we do in cooking. But we still have to cook the food. So now we're losing the nutrients twice: once from irradiation and a second time from cooking.

There could be a 20% loss during irradiation and a further 20% loss during cooking, for example. That's not good.

The correct answer has to be about vitamins, in the irradiated food. A and E aren't about vitamins. C and D don't say anything about vitamins in *food*.

———————————

A. This answer choice has nothing to do with vitamins. And this situation isn't even a huge problem: presumably the food lasts longer than it would have without irradiation. All food spoils eventually.
B. **CORRECT.** Vitamins are lost during irradiation, whether we cook the food or eat it raw.
C. Yes, vitamin loss and safety are separate issues. But this doesn't tell us anything about the proponent's reasoning on vitamin loss.
D. Pills have nothing to do with the issue of how much vitamin loss irradiation causes in foods.
E. This answer choice has nothing to do with vitamins. And it's not really a bad thing that irradiation helps sellers as long as it doesn't hurt consumers.

Question 7

QUESTION TYPE: Principle - Parallel Reasoning

PRINCIPLE: Audio recordings of authors reading their books have caused a large drop in print sales.

ANALYSIS: A new book product has cut into sales of another type of book product.

The right answer will have a similar pattern: A new X is introduced and takes away sales from other types of X. And the seller of X gains and loses.

_____

A. Machines are taking away from labor. But those are *different* things. The stimulus had two versions of the *same* product.
B. This shows that one product has *increased* sales of another, different product.
C. **CORRECT.** A new brand of soft drink has cut into the market for soft drinks. Those are the same type of product.
D. This is just a little story about how to motivate a child. Work cut into daydreaming, but they're hardly the same thing.
E. This doesn't even show if one program takes away from the other.

Question 8

QUESTION TYPE: Weaken

CONCLUSION: The proposal to stop putting sewage into the harbor is pointless.

REASONING: Lobsters (eaten by humans) get gill disease when sewage is dumped in their water. But most lobsters don't live long enough to be harmed by the disease.

ANALYSIS: This is one of the worst arguments I've seen on the LSAT, but it's also very clever. So clever that many people don't even see what's wrong with it. The lobsters aren't harmed, so what's the issue, they ask?

Would you like to eat lobster contaminated by sewage and that have gill disease?

Just because the *lobsters* aren't harmed doesn't meant that there is no point to preventing gill disease. We eat them! Blech.

Further, the conclusion is really, really broad: the proposal is *pointless*. But the only evidence is about lobsters. There might be some benefit to cleaning the harbor, apart from healthier lobster. Maybe some fish will get less sick, maybe we can swim in the harbor, maybe the town will smell better, etc. There could be many other benefits that show the proposal is not "pointless."

_____

A. The proposal was only talking about redirecting sewage. Other contaminants are irrelevant since no one was proposing to clean them up.
B. That's nice. But we don't know why lobsters live longer in oceans and we have no evidence that it is due to lack of sewage.
C. This would *strengthen* the argument. Sewage doesn't seem to harm lobster breeding.
D. This doesn't really affect anything since the lobsters don't get sick from the gill disease.
E. **CORRECT.** This gives us a good reason to prevent gill disease: we get sick if we eat polluted lobster. So the proposal has a point: it could make us healthier.

Question 9

QUESTION TYPE: Role in Argument

CONCLUSION: It is not necessarily divorce that causes psychological problems amongst children of divorced parents.

REASONING: It is equally likely that the children simply learn bad habits from their dysfunctional parents. It is these bad habits that both increase the likelihood of divorce and cause children to have psychological problems.

ANALYSIS: This is a reasonable argument. It could be that divorce causes psychological problems but it's just as reasonable that dysfunctional behavior both leads to divorce and teaches children bad habits that lead to have psychological problems.

The sentence in question is a fact the author attempts to explain.

A. The conclusion is that it would be a mistake to think that divorce is definitely the cause of children's psychological problems.
B. The argument tries to *explain* the fact that children of divorced parents have more problems. It doesn't argue with the fact that they do have more problems.
C. Actually the argument argues against the claim that divorce itself is harmful. Kids would still be harmed even if dysfunctional parents stayed together.
D. It's the other way around. Certain behaviors are responsible for divorce *and* could also explain that children of divorced parents tend to have psychological problems.
E. **CORRECT.** The author says that there is more than one possible explanation for this finding. It could be divorce or it could be poor learned behaviors that cause psychological problems.

Question 10

QUESTION TYPE: Paradox - Exception

PARADOX: Marathon runners who train 90 minutes a day do better than those who train 120 minutes (2 hours) per day. Marathons take over two hours to run for even the most experienced runners.

ANALYSIS: All of the wrong answers explain how running a long time makes things harder. The right answer mentions that long training makes it *easier* to run different race lengths.

The word easier should be a big tip off. We're trying to explain why those who train more do *worse*.

A. This could be it. Those who train longer get sick from pollution and underperform.
B. **CORRECT.** This actually shows that longer training makes things *easier*. Runners who train longer could run a marathon or a shorter race: longer training allows them to adjust between both.
C. This shows that those who train longer are more likely to disable themselves.
D. You *need* motivation to finish a marathon. This could explain why those runners who trained longer did worse.
E. This also works. If you train too long then you will wreck your energy reserves.

Question 11

QUESTION TYPE: Method of Reasoning

CONCLUSION: The studies that showed bilingual children have smaller vocabularies were flawed.

REASONING: Bilingual children often know a word in only one of their two languages. The tests were only given in one language.

ANALYSIS: This is a good argument, assuming that we can say a child knows a word if they know it in one but not both of their languages.

The argument proceeds by showing an error in the in the studies: the vocabulary tests were unilingual.

_____

A. The argument hasn't said bilingualism is an advantage. It just concluded against the idea that bilingualism had been shown to be a disadvantage.
B. There was no inconsistency. There was just an error in how the tests were done. An inconsistency is a contradiction, and not all errors are contradictions.
C. Not all vocabulary tests are flawed. Dual-use tests can adequately measure a bilingual child's vocabulary.
D. The studies found *disadvantages* to bilingualism. This answer choice got that wrong: it says *advantages*.
E. **CORRECT.** The methodological error was that the vocabulary tests were only in one language.

Question 12

QUESTION TYPE: Most Strongly Supported

FACTS:

1. Gene splicing can create farm animals we don't fully understand.
2. We can use gene splicing to create animals with good genes.
3. But the animals might also get bad genes. The bad genes would be subtle and we wouldn't notice.

ANALYSIS: We can't combine these facts. But they support the idea that there are pros and cons to gene splicing and we should be careful how we use it.

_____

A. This stimulus only supports the idea that at least some toxin production is genetically controlled.
B. **CORRECT.** There are advantages to gene splicing, but there are also disadvantages. And it is hard to detect the disadvantages.
C. Actually gene splicing *is* effective at producing new varieties of animals. It's just that these varieties might come with side effects and unforeseen consequences.
D. We only know that *some* varieties *might* develop cancer. This statement is way too strong.
E. We have no idea. Maybe we'll never overcome the unforeseen consequences of gene splicing.

Question 13

QUESTION TYPE: Weaken

CONCLUSION: We continue to hold onto acquired beliefs even when there is no longer any evidence to support them.

REASONING: A psychological experiment was conducted. People were give statements that caused them to believe something new. Then they were told that the statement was wrong. But most people still thought their new belief was true.

ANALYSIS: This argument sounds good, but it doesn't explain why the subjects held onto their beliefs. The right answer choice explains that they had new evidence. This contradicts the conclusion that they had *no* evidence.

_____

A. Not quite. If doesn't matter if the beliefs were true or not. What matters is whether the subjects had any evidence they were true. The conclusion was that people hang on to beliefs even if *they* don't have any evidence.
B. This actually supports the journal by providing a reason for the observed behavior. People can't keep track of whether all their beliefs are supported by facts.
C. This could explain why the subjects were led to form new beliefs. But it doesn't change the fact that people kept believing even when told that the statement was false.
D. **CORRECT.** This means that it would be wrong to say that the subjects held on to their beliefs without evidence. They had acquired new evidence to support the beliefs.
E. This makes it even more puzzling that the subjects held onto their beliefs so strongly.

Question 14

QUESTION TYPE: Necessary Assumption

CONCLUSION: Novelists cannot become great if they remain in academia.

REASONING: Schools help teach observation and analysis. But you can't intuitively understand the emotions of everyday life unless you leave academia.

ANALYSIS: The argument is assuming that novelists must understand the emotions of everyday life.

An interesting psychological note is that answers A and C contain the word impartial. Many people think academics are biased and so they associate leaving academia with impartiality. These two answer choices are much more tempting if you bring in this outside assumption about academics. The stimulus doesn't mention impartiality: it's completely irrelevant to the question.

Most LSAT questions use these types of triggers for outside assumptions. When you get a question wrong, see if you can spot outside assumptions you used that went beyond the stimulus.

_____

A. The stimulus does *not* mention impartiality. This is completely off-base.
B. The stimulus just said that observation and analysis are useful to novelists. They aren't necessarily essential. These qualities come from academia.
C. It isn't necessary that participation in life always makes novelists great. It's only necessary that novelists *need* to participate in life if they are going to be great (i.e. it has to be a necessary condition but not necessarily a sufficient condition.)
D. **CORRECT.** If novelists don't need to grasp everyday emotions then maybe they can remain in academia.
E. This is not right because it's not just "knowledge" that novelists get by leaving academia. They could get "an intuitive grasp" of the emotions of everyday life. That's something more profound than knowledge.

Question 15

QUESTION TYPE: Strengthen - Exception

CONCLUSION: We should be skeptical about the magazine's conclusion.

REASONING: The sample is unrepresentative (it's a financial magazine: readers are likely interested in finances) and the question is biased ("the *joy* of earning money)

ANALYSIS: The correct answer makes a comparison to an irrelevant issue: social issues. The magazine was only comparing politics to finances. It didn't claim finances were more important than any other issue.

_____

A. This does *slightly* strengthen the statistician's argument. Demonstrating that someone is a frequent liar is more than just an ad hominem attack. We *should* be skeptical of a liar who generated all of the evidence supporting their argument.
B. This supports the idea that *this* survey could be wrong, too.
C. This shows that this survey doesn't have the final word on this issue: other surveys disagree.
D. This survey *was* biased and unrepresentative. So we have reason to be skeptical.
E. **CORRECT.** The conclusion is only about whether politics or finances are most important. Social issues aren't relevant to that comparison. The magazine didn't claim that finances are the most important issue. They're just more important than politics.

Question 16

QUESTION TYPE: Main Conclusion

CONCLUSION: The Antarctic ice sheet must have temporarily melted three million years ago.

REASONING: Some fossils were found in Antarctica that previously were only found on the sea floor. The fossils were three million years old.

ANALYSIS: This is a bad argument. It's possible that the ice melted. Or it's possible that the fossils were from an animal that could live both on land and in the ocean (e.g. maybe some kind of bird.)

The fossils had only been found on the ocean floor, but that doesn't mean they *couldn't* be found anywhere else.

So while melting ice is a possible explanation, it isn't the only explanation.

The main conclusion is that the available evidence is wrong and the ice sheet melted three million years ago. The last sentence supports the conclusion by showing how the fossils got to Antarctica.

_____

A. Close, but not quite. We don't know how many people agree with the stimulus on this issue.
B. The stimulus disagrees with this answer choice. If this were true then the stimulus' conclusion might not be true - this answer provides an alternate explanation for the discovery of the fossils.
C. **CORRECT.** The stimulus argues that the ice disappeared three million years ago, temporarily.
D. This is just supporting evidence. It explains how the ice sheet could have melted.
E. This sounds tempting but the argument wasn't claiming that those were the *only* ways the ice sheet could have melted. The main point was that it did melt. We know it did because sea fossils were found.

Question 17

QUESTION TYPE: Flawed Reasoning

CONCLUSION: The Antarctic ice sheet must have temporarily melted three million years ago.

REASONING: Some fossils were found in Antarctica that previously were only found on the sea floor. The fossils were three million years old.

ANALYSIS: This is a bad argument. It's possible that the ice melted. Or it's possible that the fossils were from an animal that could live both on land and in the ocean (e.g. maybe some kind of bird.) The fossils had only been found on the ocean floor, but that doesn't mean they *couldn't* be found anywhere else.

So while melting ice is a possible explanation, it isn't the only possible explanation.

A. The argument doesn't mention public opinion or popular belief as to whether Antarctica melted. We have no idea what people think.
B. The argument did not claim that volcanic activity and climactic warming could not have happened together.
C. The argument didn't claim to know the cause for certain. The last sentence shows that the author isn't sure of the cause. The melting could have been due to warming or volcanoes. The author's only conclusion is that the ice sheet *did* melt.
D. The claim is pretty specific: there was temporary melting, in Antarctica, three million years ago.
E. **CORRECT.** The inconsistency is that fossils that were previously found only in the ocean were found on land. The resolution (explanation) given in the stimulus is that Antarctica must have been underwater once. But it could also be true that the animal that left the fossils lived both on land and on water.

Question 18

QUESTION TYPE: Necessary Assumption

CONCLUSION: Human consumption patterns will have to change.

REASONING: We rely on non-renewable resources such as metal ore. We'll either have to stop using those resources or replace them with renewable resources.

ANALYSIS: This argument sounds good. The right answer presents a third option that wrecks the argument: we can constantly shift between non-renewable resources.

A. This isn't necessary, we have another option: "doing without" the resources.
B. **CORRECT.** The argument presents two options: doing without or replacement with renewables. Its assuming this third option is unavailable (replacement with *non*-renewables)
C. Same as A. If a non-renewable resource is exhausted then we still have the option of doing without.
D. The author would be fine with consumption increasing in the *near* future. He's arguing that things must *eventually* change, in the long run.
E. The argument is arguing that we *could* do without non-renewable resources.

Question 19

QUESTION TYPE: Most Strongly Supported

FACTS:

1. Lathyrism is caused by eating a legume.
2. It affects many domestic animals.
3. We can't seem to infect rats with Lathyrism by making them eat the legume.

ANALYSIS: It's a reasonable conclusion that rats are generally immune to Lathyrism.

_____

A. The physiology of rats doesn't have to be *radically* different. Even slight differences can often make a species immune to a disease.
B. It actually sounds like the rats ate *more* legumes. The scientists were trying hard to give them the disease.
C. **CORRECT.** Rats seem to be less susceptible than some domestic animals.
D. We have no idea about other wild animals apart from rats. Maybe other wild animals are even more susceptible that domestic animals.
E. Hard to say. We could probably infect a domestic animal in a lab.

Question 20

QUESTION TYPE: Sufficient Assumption

CONCLUSION: Almost anyone can be an expert.

REASONING: There are no official rules for being an expert. Anyone is an expert if they can convince some people that they have qualifications in an area.

ANALYSIS: We don't know if almost anyone can actually convince people of their expertise. If they could then this would be a good argument.

_____

A. **CORRECT.** If this is true, then those people ("almost anyone") can be experts.
B. The conclusion is that almost anyone can be an expert. It doesn't matter what people can do once they are experts.
C. This would weaken the argument that almost anyone can be an expert. Not everyone has qualifications.
D. This doesn't even have to be true, based on the stimulus. Convincing people was a sufficient condition but not a necessary condition. This doesn't help show that almost anybody can be an expert.
E. "Some" people could be as few as 2-3. This doesn't let us conclude that almost anyone can become an expert.

Question 21

QUESTION TYPE: Paradox

FACTS: A tired patient only slept 4-6 hours. This worsened their exhaustion, but doctors did not tell them to sleep more.

ANALYSIS: We can be pretty sure that the patient should sleep more. So we must explain the doctors' advice.

The correct answer tells us that telling the patient to sleep might cause them to sleep less.

A. The patient doesn't really care about awakening: they feel tired and want to sleep.
B. But the other hours are still important: that's why the patient's low total sleep was contributing to their fatigue.
C. That's good for them. But this particular patient needs more sleep.
D. We have no idea whether this patient has nightmares. And the last hour of sleep wasn't mentioned. This is completely irrelevant.
E. **CORRECT.** If you tell the patient to sleep more, then maybe they will worry and sleep less.

Question 22

QUESTION TYPE: Sufficient Assumption

CONCLUSION: P → not H

REASONING: C → T̶ and P → T. These can be joined to form P → T → C̶

ANALYSIS: This question is truly worth drawing. We have to get from P to not H. Notice that *nothing* is connected to H. So the only way we can get there is through T and C̶. Here's what we have so far:

P → T → C̶   ???? H̶

Just put an arrow in place of the question marks and we get our conclusion: P → T → C̶ → H̶

So the right answer has to be either "C̶ → H̶" or the contrapositive of that: "H → C"

A. This doesn't work. We can't connect it up to our diagram to reach the conclusion. If no H were T, this would have worked.
B. **CORRECT.** See the diagrams above.
C. This doesn't help us connect anything to H. The right answer will always have to mention the disconnected term.
D. This tells us that if you are C then you are not H. That doesn't help, because Ps are *not* Cs.
E. This still leaves us without any connection to H.

Question 23

QUESTION TYPE: Weaken

CONCLUSION: The statisticians are wrong.

REASONING: Their plan would mean we would have fewer and fewer beliefs. But we need many beliefs to survive.

ANALYSIS: The argument assumes that the statisticians thought people should actually try their plan or that people could survive using their plans.

The statisticians didn't say that. They just said their plan was "the surest way to increase the overall correctness" of one's beliefs. The plan might kill you but that doesn't mean it isn't the best way to be sure your beliefs are correct.

A. **CORRECT.** Likewise, I could say that the best way to get warm is to jump into a fire. You'll be badly hurt, but that doesn't change the fact that it would be very effective at making you warmer. The statisticians might be correct even though their idea will hurt you.

B. The statisticians are *very* clear: accept no new beliefs.

C. This is fine. But the statisticians would say that the surest way to make either set more correct would be to eliminate beliefs without adding any.

D. The argument didn't say we should accept beliefs that we know are false. The argument seemed to be saying that we should accept new beliefs that we think are true. If we only reject beliefs then eventually we won't have enough.

E. The argument didn't say that beliefs have to be correct. But if one followed the statisticians' plan then one would eventually get rid of all incorrect beliefs and be left with too small a number.

Question 24

QUESTION TYPE: Flawed Parallel Reasoning

CONCLUSION: The same mastermind must have been behind every single case of political unrest.

REASONING: The police have found that at least one person organized each individual case of political unrest.

ANALYSIS: The police have shown that each event had an organizer. But that doesn't mean that every event had the *same* organizer.

This is a really strange argument.

A. I haven't run through the math to be sure about this argument. We'd at least have to know if Chicago used all possible numbers. In any case, this doesn't repeat the "single cause" flaw from the stimulus.

B. This is a bad argument because it ignores the fact that two numbers can have the same area code. But this error assumes that everything must be different. The stimulus assumed that everything had to be the same.

C. **CORRECT.** This is an odd argument and it matches the structure. Every citizen has a number so they must all have the same number. What a funny idea: there's no reason citizens couldn't have different numbers.

D. This is a terrible argument. It ignores the fact that many insignificant events can count as a significant event if you add them together. But this is not like the "single cause" flaw from the stimulus.

E. This is actually a good argument. It didn't say that every moment has been followed by a later moment *so far*. It just said it will always happen. So Vlad is immortal.

Question 25

QUESTION TYPE: Paradox

CONCLUSION: A cologne company did worse when it switched from general circulation magazines to a sports magazine with a male readership.

ANALYSIS: Presumably the company switched because it thought the sports magazine would help it sell more cologne. And men are the target market, so it would seem to make sense to advertise in a magazine that men read.

The correct answer explains that women often buy cologne for men. So the company accidentally cut itself off from many customers.

———————————

A. This tells us absolutely nothing. It just tells us the company never advertised on TV. We've learned nothing new about magazines.
B. This tells us that it was a bad idea to leave those magazines, as they would have increased sales. But it doesn't explain why sales shrank: presumably the company switched because it thought the sports magazines would work at least as well.
C. Some men still wore the cologne, even if most don't. Otherwise the product wouldn't exist. So this doesn't explain it.
D. **CORRECT.** Women often buy cologne. Women read the general circulation magazines but they don't read the male sports magazines. So the company cut itself off from many customers.
E. This doesn't tell us if the company used athletes in their ads in either magazine category. It also doesn't tell us if the ads featuring athletes work. This tells us nothing.

Question 26

QUESTION TYPE: Agreement – Most Strongly Supported

ARGUMENTS: Kim argues that the growing population is taking up lots of land for food production and cities. Nature is threatened.

Hampton thinks that technology will allow us to feed the increased world population without using more land for agriculture.

ANALYSIS: They both agree that the population will grow. They also think that it is good to restrict the amount of land devoted to agriculture.

The wrong answers can all be eliminated because Hampton would disagree. They all mention that overpopulation will cause problems. But we can be fairly sure that Hampton thinks technology might solve *all* problems related to overpopulation.

This question asks which statement is most strongly supported. So it doesn't matter that the correct answer (B) is not 100% established by the stimulus.

———————————

A. Hampton doesn't think there is a problem, so it's not clear why he would agree to this.
B. **CORRECT.** Hampton definitely supports technology. And Kim probably would support this technology as well. There's no obvious downside and it would help preserve nature by limiting the land needed for agriculture.
C. Hampton probably doesn't think this is a problem: technology will save us.
D. Hampton disagrees, because technology will fix things.
E. Hampton disagrees, because technology will fix things.

Test 35
Section II - Reading Comprehension
Passage 1 - Revolutionary Memoirs
Questions 1-6

Paragraph Summaries

1. Few women wrote memoirs of the French Revolution. Those who did were upper class. This was for social and political reasons.
2. Were the memoirs accurate? For objective events, we can compare memoirs. For subjective, personal events, we must look to other factors.
3. Bertholet studied the memoirs. While many women conformed to female roles, other showed individual acts of feminism.

Analysis

This passage is a neutral summary of some information about women who wrote about the French Revolution. The passage *seems* to favor the perspective of women who supported the revolution or who wrote from a feminist perspective. However, the author doesn't openly give their point of view.

Question 1

DISCUSSION: The main idea is in paragraphs 2 and 3. The memoirs can be reliable, if we cross-check them against other accounts, and make sure they are internally consistent.

_____

A. The passage doesn't say why only 80 memoirs out of 1000 were written by women. Maybe there was intolerance, but maybe there was another reason why few women wrote memoirs.

B. The passage goes beyond this. Lines 23-25 show that we can check the biographies against other accounts and confirm whether they are objectively accurate.

C. **CORRECT.** This covers paragraphs 2-3, and they are the heart of the passage. The first paragraph merely gives some context; the theme of the biographers being upper class wasn't developed. So it doesn't matter that this answer doesn't mention the first paragraph.s

D. This contradicts the second paragraph. Lines 23-25 show that we can corroborate the biographies with other evidence to show whether they are accurate.

E. The women's movement was mentioned in lines 58-59, but we're not told *why* it occurred and whether it had anything to do with the subjects discussed in the biographies.

84

Question 2

DISCUSSION: We're not told anything about male memoirs. But lines 3-5 say that most female memoirs were from the upper class. It seems likely that this was true of men's memoirs as well. Upper class men could read and write, and the same political pressures described in lines 11-15 would apply to men as well.

_____

A. The men's memoirs might not talk about women at all.
B. Same as A. We're not told whether men's memoirs mention women.
C. Maybe? It's more likely that some memoirs were suppressed and therefore _never written_ or _never published_. The question is only referring to published memoirs. If you're published, you're usually not suppressed.
D. CORRECT. This was true of the memoirs written by women, so it's probably true of men's memoirs as well.
E. Why should male biographers be lower class? The _opposite_ was true for women, and we're not given any reason why male biographers would be from the lower classes.

Question 3

DISCUSSION: Lines 45-50 mention Villirouet, but we have to read a bit earlier to get the context. While most of the memoirs fit female social roles, lines 40-45 say that there were many important acts by women. Villirouet is an example.

_____

A. We're not told that Villirouet's social status had anything to do with her role. Maybe a well-educated poor woman could have done everything she did.
B. How so? Villirouet _did_ publish a biography of her life during the French Revolution. She demonstrates the opposite point, if anything: women _could_ publish biographies.
C. We're not told that Villirouet's upper class position biased her biography.
D. CORRECT. Line 45 says "for example". This shows that Villirouet is mentioned in lines 45-50 to demonstrate the claims made just before.
E. We're not told whether republican memoirs have a different theme from Villirouet's.

Question 4

DISCUSSION: Lines 11-15. There was political pressure from the King to only publish biographies that supported the monarchy.

I couldn't find much to say about the wrong answers. They aren't in the passage. They show why it's important to find what you're looking for in the passage *before* looking at the answers. The LSAT is very good at tricking you if you don't.

It isn't always possible to find the answer in the passage first, but this question asks for a very specific detail.

A. **CORRECT.** Republicans could get in trouble if they praised the revolution.
B. This isn't said anywhere. Make sure you can support answers using the passage.
C. This might have been true, but it's not mentioned anywhere.
D. We're not told what republicans wanted. All we know is that they risked trouble if they published memoirs.
E. Find me a line that mentions republicans' professions. (it doesn't exist)

Question 5

DISCUSSION: The historians doubted that the memoirs were fully accurate. Their reason was that the memoirs were written long after the revolution.

A. The historians only complained that the biographies were written long after the revolution. We have no idea whether the historians thought royalists were more accurate than republicans.
B. This is the same as A. The historians didn't mention whether they preferred royalist or republican memoirs. They may think they're all flawed, because they were written long after the revolution.
C. **CORRECT.** This is supported by lines 17-18. The historians think the memoirs are unreliable.
D. The historians thought the memoirs were *inaccurate*. Maybe they thought *some* memoirs were unbiased, but we have no evidence for that.
E. This sounds good...but there's no reason the historians need to argue that the accounts were *unverifiable*. Verification of the facts could show that the memoirs were inaccurate and unreliable.

Question 6

DISCUSSION: Lines 28-34 describe the criteria that the authors use to judge if a subjective memoir is reliable: Is the text internally consistent? Does it match accounts of the author? Or is the text full of biased justifications?

A. **CORRECT.** This is stated on lines 30-31.
B. There's no way to prove anything for sure: we're talking about an author's subjective, personal experience. We can only show that the account is *plausible* (possible).
C. There's no need for this. The scholars are deciding how to verify a memoir *now*.
D. This isn't mentioned. A partisan account can still be relatively accurate.
E. Why should we care whether a certain view of the past is preserved? The scholars only seem interested in truth.

Passage 2 - Romare Bearden
Questions 7-14

Paragraph Summaries

1. The two triumphs of Romare Bearden: innovative painting techniques, and exploration of the African-American experience.
2. Description of Bearden's style.
3. How Bearden depicted the struggles of African Americans during the depression. He used innovative techniques to show individual suffering.
4. How Bearden showed the happy side of the African-American experience.

Analysis

This passage praises and describes Bearden's work. The concepts aren't too hard compared to other passages. But that doesn't make this type of passage easy. Questions 12 and 13 are both exception questions; they demand a mastery of the passage's structure and an ability to quickly find details.

Most of the questions ask about specific details. So it's very important to make a good map of the passage. That way you can quickly find anything you need to know. By "map of the passage" I mean the sort of information I listed in the paragraph summaries above. Not all details from the passage are there, but the summaries make it easy to know where to look for details.

If you know to look for a detail in paragraph 3, it's must faster than having to search the entire passage.

Question 7

DISCUSSION: The main idea is that Bearden was innovative in two ways. He created new artistic styles, and he portrayed African Americans in all of their subtleties.

Many of the wrong answers aren't even true.

_____

A. It's true that Bearden was relatively unique in painting joyful scenes of *African-Americans* during the depression. But other painters may have painted happy scenes of non-African-Americans.
B. **CORRECT.** This captures Bearden's two successes, mentioned in the first paragraph: he was stylistically innovative (lines 4-5), and he showed many sides of the African-American experience (lines 5-7). Paragraph 2 details his stylistic innovations, and paragraphs 3-4 show the variety of his art.
C. Not quite. Bearden worked hard to show the realities of African American life. There was no competition between his stylistic innovations and painting reality. Lines 34-38 give an example where stylistic innovations helped Bearden show reality through a new use of color.
D. This ignores half of Bearden's importance: he also tried to show the varied reality of African-American life.
E. We're not told whether Bearden is famous, or why.

Question 8

DISCUSSION: Bearden's techniques are discussed in paragraph 2. Lines 12-14 seem important: Bearden showed that ordinary subjects could be transformed thanks to effective technique.

———————————

A. Bearden did call attention to human suffering, but we're not told whether this was thanks to his techniques. He might have focussed on suffering even if his techniques were entirely conventional.
B. The passage does not mention any links between Bearden and other painters. Not once. This is a nonsense answer, with no support from the passage. If you picked it, it shows that you must practice finding a line in the passage to support your answer.
C. **CORRECT.** Lines 12-14 say this directly. You should never look at the answers unless you first reread the relevant part of the passage. Then you'll usually know what you're looking for.
D. Photography is only mentioned once, on line 48. We're told that Bearden's painting *opposed* the conventions of photography. This answer choice is designed to make you hallucinate; it's nonsense. (I'm being serious: many LSAT wrong answers mingle words in an attempt to create false associations and misleading images)
E. Line 50 tells us Bearden did exactly the opposite: he emphasized poetry.

Question 9

DISCUSSION: Bearden went further than protest painting and showed the sufferings of individuals. This implies that protest painting focussed on showing groups.

Most of the wrong answers describe things that are true about Bearden. The question asks about his paintings. This question is easy if you reread lines 25-30 and think about them, but hard if you don't.

———————————

A. **CORRECT.** Bearden painted individual scenes, and his paintings were different from protest poetry. General scenes are the opposite of individual scenes.
B. Bearden painted people alone, in nonspecific scenes (Bearden didn't do protest painting). (lines 29-31)
C. Bearden challenged traditional technique. It's implied that protest painting was more conventional.
D. This is tricky. We know that protest painters showed African-Americans who suffered in Harlem during the great depression. But in paragraph 4 we're told that the African-American experience included more than suffering. The protest painters seem to have only focussed on the miserable aspects of African-American experience.
E. This is true of *Bearden. He* focussed on individuals, the protest painters didn't.

Question 10

DISCUSSION: Bearden's two dominant traits were:

1. Stylistic innovations.
2. Painting the African-American experience in all of its individual complexity.

Bearden used innovative styles to show how African-Americans lived during the depression.

———————

A. This is contradicted by line 50: Bearden focussed on poetry.
B. **CORRECT.** Lines 35-40 show this is true. Bearden used color to show the pain that resulted from the policies in place during the Great Depression.
C. We're not told whether Bearden thought subject matter was more important than style. He seemed to use style to support subject matter. (lines 38-40)
D. Bearden *did* show injustice. See paragraph 2: he showed African-Americans who suffered because of the great depression.
E. Bearden opposed those techniques. See lines 46-48.

Question 11

DISCUSSION: From lines 45-50, it sounds like journalism and photography didn't do a very good job of showing the full character of African-American life during the depression. They showed the bad side of things, but Bearden showed scenes of happiness as well as misery.

———————

A. There may have been innovation in showing us the dreary side of life in Harlem (e.g. new camera angles, new lighting effects, etc.), but that doesn't change the fact that journalism generally gave a cliched view of Harlem.
B. Hard to say. We know *painters* generally didn't show individual suffering; that was mentioned in paragraph 3. But journalists might have. The main problem was that journalists' view were *one-sided*.
C. Lines 45-48 suggest that journalism and photography probably *did* deal in platitudes. They simplified things, and platitudes are simplifications.
D. **CORRECT.** *Bearden* showed African-American life in all of its fullness, unlike journalists and photographers, who only dealt in simple cliches. (lines 46-48)
E. Lines 47-48 say that journalists and photographers *did* muddle the picture of everyday life. The passage *directly* contradicts this answer.

Question 12

DISCUSSION: You should be able to eliminate the wrong answers by finding them in the passage. If that takes too long, then practice - you'll get faster. Locating information in the passage is *the* skill that lets you succeed on reading comp.

———————

A. **CORRECT.** We're not told anything about Bearden's past.
B. His contributions were paintings that showed individuals' perspectives (lines 28-29) and lines 45-46 show that Bearden revealed new aspects of the African-American experience.
C. Lines 29 tells us that Bearden painted individual suffering. Lines 41-44 tell us he painted happy scenes too.
D. Lines 35-37 mention Bearden's use of color and how it made his works more powerful.
E. Line 37 tells us that Bearden wanted his colors (in those paintings) to suggest sadness.

Question 13

DISCUSSION: My advice from question 12 applies here. You should be able to eliminate most or all of the wrong answers by referring to the passage.

Only lines 29-35 mention human figures. This question is testing whether you can find, read and understand those lines.

———————

A. Lines 24-25 say that Bearden painted hardship. Lines 29 tells us he painted individuals. Individual is a synonym for particular. So he examined particular cases of human hardship in his paintings.
B. Lines 30-33 tells us that Bearden used people to suggest elements that lay outside of his painting.
C. Line 34 says that the human figures mentioned in line 30 were part of Bearden's artwork.
D. **CORRECT.** This isn't mentioned anywhere. Bearden's paintings show sad or happy scenes, but it's not clear if it is the human figures that produce the emotional effect.
E. This is line 30-31. They say it directly.

Question 14

DISCUSSION: The author suggests that Bearden's techniques helped Bearden get his message across. For example, Bearden's colors give us a sense of the tragedy of the Depression. (lines 34-40)

———————

A. **CORRECT.** The author thinks that Bearden's techniques helped him convey his message. And the author likes Bearden's message.
B. The author *liked* the complexity of Bearden's paintings. See line 54-58.
C. If Bearden's techniques were innovative, then it's not clear they were traditional. Bearden may have used techniques from outside the African-American experience to show it in all of it's depth. (Or maybe not...but the passage isn't clear on where Bearden got his techniques, which is why this answer is wrong.)
D. On the contrary, Bearden's techniques seem to have enhanced his message. See lines 34-40.
E. We don't know. Bearden's techniques may have been appropriate during the depression, but they may not be appropriate now. Or maybe only *Bearden* could successfully use his techniques.

Passage 3 - Philosophy of Biology

Questions 15-20

Paragraph Summaries	Analysis

Paragraph Summaries

1. Philosophers are more comfortable with physics than with biology. Physics is more certain. Biology may depend on how history previously unfolded

2. Some biologists have tried to use universal laws. But other biologists say that may be no universal laws for biology, and that it may depend on randomness.

3. Statement one: All planets move in ellipses. This statement is true of all planets that do or could exist. Everyone agrees on how to interpret this kind of statement.

4. Statement two: every swan is white. The two camps disagree on this. The rigid thinkers believe this means every swan must be white, as a law of nature. The non-determinists think the swans could have been white due to historical accident. And maybe there are swans that aren't white that we haven't discovered yet.

Analysis

It's difficult to understand this passage without knowing what contingency means. That's unusual, normally you can work around the meanings of difficult words in RC passages.

Contingency in this case means that the world is the way it is only because of the random events of history. If history had unfolded differently, biology would be different, but not physics.

The determinists would say swans are white because whiteness provided an evolutionary advantage. The laws of evolution determined their color.

The non-determinists believe that the color of the swans might be due to an accident of history. Some swans happened to be white, *and* also happened to be successful, for other reasons. Their children became white, and so all swans became white, because of a historical accident.

That's what contingency means. One thing happens, which causes another. The second only happened because of the first, so it was sort of a coincidence that it happened at all. It's happening was *contingent* on the first thing happening.

So, you growing up in your hometown was contingent on your parents moving there. It wasn't necessarily due to the laws of the universe conspiring to have you grow up where you grew up. That would be the non-determinist argument, in any case.

Non-determinists also point out that all swans might not be white. Our only evidence is that every swan we've seen is white. But what about the swans we haven't seen yet?

Incidentally, in Australia swans are black. The non-determinists win this argument.

Question 15

DISCUSSION: The article contrasts two sides. There are philosophers and determinist biologists. They believe science must obey universal laws of nature. Non-determinist biologists oppose them. They think that many things in life and science are determined by historical coincidence.

A. The article only tells us that *some* biologists want universal laws (lines 16-17). So this isn't even true, necessarily. It certainly isn't the main point.

B. CORRECT. *Philosophers* seem to think that science needs universal laws. Who know where they got that idea, since many biologists disagree with them. Non-determinists and determinists disagree with each other on universal laws (in the last two paragraphs).

C. We're told what *philosophers* have traditionally believed, but we don't know what most biologists have tended to believe. This is the reverse of answer choice A.

D. We don't know whether biologists tend to be determinist or non-determinist. We only know that some are (lines 16-17) and some aren't (lines 25-28)

E. This is completely off base. We don't know if 'many' biologists disagree with philosophers. We only know that "some" do (lines 25-28). And we know at least some biologists do agree with philosophers (lines 16-17).

Question 16

DISCUSSION: Line 21 gives us one example of the type of universal law that determinist biologists are trying to discover.

A. Not so. *Determinists* might think that this drives biology, but the author of the passage seems to disagree with the determinists.

B. What uncertainty? The determinists are laying down a very certain rule. They say *all* life must struggle to survive.

C. The main cause of controversy between the (two) schools of thought is whether there are universal laws for biology. Line 21 just gives us *one* example of such a law. Its the question of whether universal laws exist that is the main cause of controversy.

D. CORRECT. Examples help us understand difficult concepts. Lines 20-25 give us examples to help clarify what determinists believe.

E. No. Lines 21 is talking about determinists. They don't think historical contingency should be part of biological science.

Question 17

DISCUSSION: The determinists think that biology must follow universal laws. If something happened, then it must have been because of some law of nature. It couldn't have been a random coincidence.

_____

A. The determinists don't like the idea of chance. They want there to be laws that cause everything.
B. Line 23 says thats determinists think that DNA changes at the same speed, always. This seems to go against that, even though DNA and physical characteristics aren't quite the same thing.
C. The determinists don't like this either. If we can just figure out the laws, then we should be able to figure everything out.
D. Is the process a universal law, or a random process of historical contingency? There's no way to know if determinists would agree with this idea.
E. **CORRECT.** The determinists like things to be the unavoidable result of eternal laws.

Question 18

DISCUSSION: The first paragraph tells us that the philosophers think that science should follow universal laws. The philosophers like physics. This implies that the philosophers think the laws of physics are correct universal laws.

_____

A. The laws of history are imprecise and uncertain. Everything depends on circumstance. Physics is different: the laws are universal.
B. The first few lines tell us that physics is preferred because it *is* certain.
C. **CORRECT.** Lines 36-41 tell us that this is true. The laws of planetary motion apply not only to all existing planets, but to all planets that could exist.
D. 'Particular' is the opposite of universal, and the laws of physics are universal. (Line 7)
E. The laws of physics are contrasted with things that rely on historical contingency in lines 1-7.

Question 19

DISCUSSION: Lines 14-16 are the key. They say that determinist scientists agree with philosophers that science needs universal laws. Physics uses many universal laws.

———————————

A. No one in the entire passage mentions ideas being understood by non-scientists. Indeed, the passage itself is hard to understand. This is totally unrelated.

B. We're only told that *philosophers* respect physicists. We don't know if scientists do. Pay close attention to words; this answer choice is a well laid trap.

C. **CORRECT.** Lines 14-16 say this directly. Some biologists (determinists) agree with physicists that science needs universal laws. So they're trying to find biology's universal laws.

D. This is nonsense. Why should biologists want to apply the laws of planetary motion to biology? The determinists are interested in the *idea* of universal laws, but that doesn't mean they want to apply the laws of physics to biology. They want to find *biology's* universal laws.

E. "All" scientific projects? That's an extreme statement. We're not told what biological determinists think about chemistry, or geology, or other sciences. Maybe they think *those* sciences are misguided and they don't want to copy them.

Question 20

DISCUSSION: Philosophers like physics because philosophers seem to have gotten it into their heads that science requires universal laws. Physics uses universal laws, so philosophers think physics is superior to biology. (Biology doesn't use many universal laws).

———————————

A. Some biologists disagree with the philosophers: they don't think biology *should* have universal laws. It's not simply that the laws are harder to discover. These biologists say there are none to discover. That annoys the philosophers.

B. The philosophers don't seem to care what the public thinks. The public is never mentioned. Philosophers care mainly about universal laws. See lines 3-7.

C. Universities and research institutes are never mentioned. We're not told whether they prefer physics to biology, or vice-versa.

D. We're not told anything about the personal or professional lives of these philosophers of science. Maybe they aren't even teachers.

E. **CORRECT.** Physicists study planets and other phenomena that can be explained using universal laws. Biology is hard to explain using universal laws. Philosophers like universal laws, so they like physics.

Passage 4 - Ronald Dworkin
Questions 21-26

Paragraph Summaries

1. Dworkin is worried. Judges (rightly) reject natural law. But that doesn't mean they should use legal positivism.
2. Legal positivists say judges should only figure out whether there is a consensus on what the law says.
3. Dworkin argues the law has an internal logic, separate from morality. There doesn't have to be a consensus for a legal interpretation to work. An interpretation only needs to be consistent with the law's internal logic.

Analysis

This is a confusing passage. Do *not* try the questions on this sort of passage without rereading it and attempting to understand it. You should have at least a rough idea of the differences between natural law, legal positivism and Dworkin's theory.

Natural Law: Judges can find the meaning of the law by using their sense of morals. Natural law may disagree with the actual written law.

Legal Positivism: Law and morals are different. People might disagree about what the law means. Judges' role is to interpret whether there is a consensus about the meaning of the law.

Dworkin's Theory: Dworkin says that there is an internal logic to the law. A legal interpretation can be fine as long as it is consistent with this logic. There is no need for consensus on a single, correct interpretation.

There are some terms you don't need to know. For example: "legal fact of the matter". It's never explained, but that's alright. No question requires you to know what it means or even to understand it, as long as you can guess that it seems like something important to have.

Question 21

DISCUSSION: The main point is to present Dworkin's theory. He thinks that natural law (moral intuitions) and positivism (consensus) are both wrong. His theory is that judges should use the law's internal logic.

A. Natural law isn't the middle ground. *Dworkin's* theory is the middle ground. (Lines 33-34)
B. **CORRECT.** This just says that Dworkin disagrees with legal positivism and natural law. Judges should follow Dworkin's theory instead, and rely on the internal logic of the law.
C. This is directly contradicted by lines 43-44. Dworkin thinks that both morality and consensus are less important than the logic of the law.
D. Not even close; Dworkin's theory is quite different. Neither of the other two theories mentioned the logic of law, and that's the main part of Dworkin's theory.
E. This is a nonsense answer. It ties together some key terms from the passage, but doesn't have anything to do with what Dworkin proposed. In any case, lines 43-44 contradict this answer. They show that Dworkin doesn't think judges should let moral intuition be the most important factor.

Question 22

DISCUSSION: The second paragraph is a neutral presentation of the ideas of legal positivism. There's no judgment given. That comes in the third paragraph, when we're told why Dworkin disagrees with legal positivism.

_____

A. We're never told whether anybody likes legal positivism. All we know is that Dworkin doesn't like it.
B. An evaluation would involve calling the theory good, bad, or making some sort of value judgment. But the second paragraph is just some information about positivism, presented neutrally.
C. We're never told how judges achieve consensus. It's all a little fuzzy.
D. **CORRECT.** One clue is the use of the word "holds" in line 13. To hold something is to argue something. Paragraph 2 just presents legal positivism's arguments.
E. There's nothing in paragraph 2 that says positivism is good or bad.

Question 23

DISCUSSION: The author is fairly neutral, but seems to agree with Dworkin. They present Dworkin's criticisms of the other two legal theories, and the author never criticizes Dworkin. The author seems quite certain in everything they say; they don't hedge their opinions.

Later in the passage, the author is explicit in agreeing with Dworkin. See line 45, for example. They say Dworkin has spotted a mistake the positivists make.

_____

A. **CORRECT.** The author never disagrees with Dworkin, and they agree with Dworkin explicitly in the final paragraph. See line 45 and lines 49-53.
B. Find me a single word of caution or criticism, and you can choose this answer choice. If you can't find a word of criticism, then why choose this answer? Dworkin's theory is presented in paragraph 3, and it's never criticized.
C. Same as B. Dworkin's theory is explained in paragraph 3, without criticism. And in paragraph 4, the author _agrees_ with Dworkin.
D. Lines 45 and lines 49-53 disprove this. The author agrees with Dworkin's critiques, and they don't say anything about originality.
E. The author makes no prediction on which theory will win. In lines 1-2 they do argue that Dworkin is afraid positivism will win, as opposed to Dworkin's theory. There's no support for this answer.

Question 24

DISCUSSION: Dworkin has at least two goals. The first is given in lines 1-5. He provides an alternative to judges who think they only have two choices (natural law or legal positivism).

Second, Dworkin is providing cover for lawyers and judges. Lines 27-29 tell us that the way judges actually work is different from how legal positivism or natural law predicts they will work. The judges are wrong, according to those theories. So Dworkin provides a theory to explain their behavior: they are following the internal logic of the law.

A. Name *one* legal interpretation by a judge that Dworkin discusses.
   You can't, there are none....This is simply nonsense strung together using terms from the passage. The LSAT does this frequently, to catch those who don't know what they're looking for.
B. Dworkin doesn't say that consensus has *no* place in the law. That's a pretty strong statement. "Social consensus" might be important to the internal logic of the law.
C. Same as B, this goes too far. Lines 41-42 even say that Dworkin sees a role for moral intuition in legal decision making.
D. Lines 45-48 contradict this. Dworkin thinks the internal logic of the law is more important even than what the original drafters of a law thought.
E. **CORRECT.** Lines 27-29 support this. Positivism contradicts the actual observed behavior of judges, so it isn't a very good theory. A theory should explain results from the real world. Dworkin offers us such an explanation.

Question 25

DISCUSSION: You should be able to support the right answer using something Dworkin said.

A. This is something a positivist might say. Lines 23-24 tell us that positivists think there is no fact of the matter if there is no consensus. Yet lines 29-30 tell us judges often believe there is a fact of the matter even without consensus.
B. Who knows? In line 48 we see that Dworkin doesn't care much for the original intent of legislators. He mainly cares about the internal logic of the law.
C. It's not clear that it's *easier* for a judge to use legal positivism. Natural law lets them decide based on their own moral sense of right and wrong. Legal positivism makes them search for consensus, which seems difficult.
D. Another nonsense answer. Dworkin talked about the internal logic of *the* law, not of *a* law. And Dworkin doesn't seem to think consensus is very important.
E. **CORRECT.** Legal positivists think there is no role for moral intuition in the law (lines 13-14). Lines 39-41 shows that Dworkin thinks moral intuition can sometimes be appropriate.

Question 26

DISCUSSION: Legal positivists think that law and morality must be kept apart (lines 13-14). They think that consensus about the meaning of the law is the most important thing (Lines 23-26).

A. See lines 13-14. Positivists think the law has no place for morals.

B. Lines 17-20 show that legal positivists think disagreement could be legitimate if it were about the underlying convention. And a disagreement about convention might be because of a disagreement over the law's meaning.

C. This is something *Dworkin* might say. He was concerned with the meaning of the law.

D. **CORRECT.** In lines 14-16 the positivists say that the law's meaning depends on convention. If there is a consensus that the law means "X", then positivists would argue the law really does mean "X". (Non-positivists would argue that a consensus could simply be wrong).

E. Positivists think that morals have nothing to do with the law (lines 13-14). So they wouldn't think moral conviction has anything to do with the fact of the matter.

Test 35
Section III - Logic Games
Game 1 – Geologists and Radiobiologists
Questions 1-5

Setup

This is an in/out game. Many students find it difficult. I think it tests an incredibly important skill: how well and how quickly you can use a diagram.

Note that this is not like the in-out games from tests 33 and 34. The diagram is completely different.

This is actually a very simple game. We've got to pick four astronauts. Two are experienced, and two aren't. Two of them need to be radiobiologists, and two have to be geologists. Lastly, either P or L or both have to be included.

That's it.

Here's my drawing that explains everything. Now, your first impression might be "huh?", but give it a chance. It will let you solve everything *very* quickly:

E : [F] J K L

Ɇ : [M] N [P] [T]   [ ] = G

It's just a list of the experienced and inexperienced astronauts. I've put a box around those that are geographers. Those that are radiobiologists aren't highlighted.

I've seen people use this vertically, or put another symbol around the radiobiologists, or make any number of stylistic changes. That's fine. Draw it in a way that makes sense to you. But make sure you understand the logic. Here are the rules.

- You need two people from each row. (E/not E)
- You need two people with a box, and two people without a box.
- You need to include either P or L.

Study the diagram well. I'm going to reproduce it with each question.

The questions are mostly local rules. For instance, question two tells you that F and P are included. They both have a box, so they're geologists. So look at your diagram: who else do you need?

You'll need N (an inexperienced radiobiologist) and one of J/K/L (experienced radiobiologists.) That's answer choice A. Done.

So the steps are:

1. Check who the local rule selects.
2. Look at the diagram, and count how many astronauts of each type that gives you.
3. Figure out which other types you need to fill your quotas (experienced vs. inexperienced, R vs. G, do we have L or P?)
4. Figure out which of the remaining astronauts therefore have to go, and who else *could* go. It won't be very many.
5. Check what the question is asking for, and choose the right answer.
6. Score perfectly on this game!

Question 1

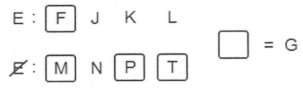

A doesn't have P or L

B has three geologists: F, M and P.

C has too many geologists: F, M, P

D is **CORRECT.** It has two from each group, and L is included.

E has too many radiobiologists. K, L and N.

Question 2

The local rule says we have F and P. We're missing two radiobiologists, one of whom has to be inexperienced, and one of whom should be experienced. We need N + one of J/K/L.

A is **CORRECT.**

All of the other answer choices must is *false*. For **B,** we already have enough geologists. **C** would give us three experienced astronauts. **D** and **E** would give us three experienced astronauts and three inexperienced astronauts, respectively.

Question 3

F and J. Those are our experienced astronauts. We need one inexperienced radiobiologist and one inexperienced geologist. And we need P, because we don't have L.

So that means we need P (geologist) and therefore N as well (radiobiologist). **D** is **CORRECT.**

We can't choose K (answer **A**) because we already have two experienced astronauts. Same for L (answer **B**) M can't be selected, because P has to be the inexperienced geologist since we don't have L (answer **C**) Same for T (Answer **E**)

Question 4

E : F J K L
⧸E : M N P T
= G

M and T are two inexperienced geologists. That means we need two experienced radiobiologists. And we also need L, because we don't have P.

So we need L, and could have either J or K.

B is **CORRECT.** J could be chosen but doesn't have to be.

We *can't* choose F (answer **A**). We *have* to choose L (answer **C**). We can't choose N, because we already have enough inexperienced astronauts (answer **D.**) Same for P (answer **E**).

Question 5

E : [F] J K L

[ ] = G

E̸ : [M] N [P] [T]

If N is selected, then the we'll have to pick a geologist to be the other inexperienced astronaut. We can pick either M, P or T.

That means we need one geologist and one radiobiologist from the experienced astronauts. F is the only geologist, so **A** is **CORRECT.**

J, L, M and T all could be selected (answer choices B-D), but none of them have to be.

Game 2 – New Cars
Questions 6-12

Setup

This is a grouping game. We have to match features to cars: the cars either have a feature or they don't. We can make *many* deductions by combining rules.

The first question is whether to set this up vertically or horizontally. I find a vertical diagram best, but you can draw it differently if you prefer.

If you read through the rules, you'll see that the cars are the base units, and you have to decide which features they have. Each car has at least one option.

Here's how I drew it. Each car has three possibilities: P, L or S, so I drew three spaces by each car.

```
T  ____  ____  ____
V  ____  ____  ____
W  ____  ____  ____
X  ____  ____  ____
Y  ____  ____  ____
Z  ____  ____  ____
```

The first two rules are simple. They just tell us which options V and W have.

```
T  ____  ____  ____
V   P     S    ____
W   P     L    ____
X  ____  ____  ____
Y  ____  ____  ____
Z  ____  ____  ____
```

At this point, we're not told those are the *only* options V and W have. As far as we know, those cars could have a third feature.

The next rule is more restrictive. Y doesn't have any option that W has. Since W already has two options, that means Y must have the third: S.

```
T  ____  ____  ____
V   P     S    ____
W   P     L    |
X  ____  ____  ____
Y   S    |
Z  ____  ____  ____
```

Further, now W *can't* have S. If W did have S then it would have an option in common with Y. So Y can only have one option, and W can only have two. I've drawn a vertical line to indicate that they can't have any more.

V's lack of vertical line means it can have 2 or 3 options.

The next rule is also quite informative. X has a larger number of options than W. Since W has 2, X must therefore have all 3 options.

```
T  ____  ____  ____
V   P     S    ____
W   P     L    |
X   P     S     L   |
Y   S    |
Z  ____  ____  ____
```

The next rules says that V and Z have exactly one option in common. Z can't have three options, otherwise it would share *two* with V.

```
T  ____  ____  ____
V   P     S    ____
W   P     L    |
X   P     S     L   |
Y   S    |
Z  ____  ____  |
```

The last rule almost completely locks down the game. Z has more options than T. That means Z *must* have two options, since T has to have at least one.

That means Z has L, and one of P/S. We also know V can't have L, because Z and V only share one option.

We don't know which option T has, but it can only have one, since Z has more options.

```
T  ____  |
V   P     S    |
W   P     L    |
X   P     S     L   |
Y   S    |
Z  P\S    L    |
```

Wow. There isn't much to decide here, is there? The *only* options are whether Z has P or S, and which option T has.

Question 6

Just count from the Main Diagram. We don't know about T and Z, but we know *exactly* which options the other four cars have.

C is the **CORRECT.**

Whenever you see a question like this, it's a strong sign you should have made many deductions in your setup.

Question 7

A can't be true. At most Z, X, W and T can have leather interiors. **A** is **CORRECT.**

B can be true since Z, Y, X, V and T could all have sunroofs.

C can be true because Z, X, W and T can have leather interiors.

D can be true since, Z, Y, X and V can all have power windows.

E can be true since Z, Y, X, V and T can all have sunroofs (but T and Z don't have to). So we can have four sunroofs, but we don't have to.

Question 8

For this question, if you have leather you also have power windows. This tells us two things. Z has power windows, and T *doesn't* have leather, because it has no space to also have power windows. Here's the local diagram:

```
T   P\S  |
V    P      S   |
W    P      L   |
X    P      L      S   |
Y    S   |
Z    P      L   |
```

For **A**, T can have power windows. The only thing T can't have is L, because that would force T to have P as well.

B can be true. The only thing T can't have is L, because that would force T to have P as well.

C could be true. Z, X, W and V have power windows and T could have a sunroof.

D *has* to be true, since every car with L needs P

E can't be true. The fact that Z has L tells us that Z also needs to have P instead of S for its second feature. **E** is **CORRECT.**

Question 9

```
T  __P__|
               |
V  __P__ __S__|
                   |
W  __P__ __L__|
                   |
X  __P__ __L__ __S__|
Y  __S__|
           |
Z  __S__ __L__|
```

For Z to have options in common with all cars apart from T, it must have S, because S is Y's only option. The local diagram is drawn above.

Since Z now has S and L, then T must have P so that T and Z have no option in common.

A must be *true*.

B must be *true*.

C must be *true*. X, W, V and T all have P.

D must be false. Only Z, X and W have L. T can't, because T needs P. **D** is **CORRECT.**

E must be true. Z, X, V and T all have S.

Question 10

No car has exactly the same options for this question. Let's look at the two things we can actually change.

T must have L or P, so that it doesn't have the same option as Y.

Z must have S, so that it doesn't have the same options as W.

```
T  _P\L_|
V  __P__ __S__|
                   |
W  __P__ __L__|
                   |
X  __P__ __L__ __S__|
Y  __S__|
           |
Z  __S__ __L__|
```

A could be true, if T has L.

B could be true, if T has P. Then X, W, V and T would all have P.

C cannot be true. Z, Y, X and V all have sunroofs. **C** is **CORRECT.**

D *has* to be true. Z, Y, X and V all have sunroofs and T can't have a sunroof.

E could be true if T has L. Then Z, X, W and T would all have L.

Question 11

T   L |

V   P   S |

W   P   L |

X   P   L   S |

Y   S |

Z   P   L |

Four cars have P and four have L.

T is the only car that can have an extra L. That leaves Z as the only car that can have an extra P.

So T: L
And Z: P and L

A is true. T has L and V has P and S.

B is true. T has L and Y has S.

C is true. T has L and so does Z.

D is false. Z has P and L, and so does W. **D** is **CORRECT.**

E is true. Y has S and Z has P and L.

Question 12

You have to look back at your rules here and make sure which rules involve X. It turns out only one does.

So now X has the same options as W: P and L. X *could* also have S, but it no longer has to.

T   ___ |

V   P   S |

W   P   L |

X   P   L   ___

Y   S |

Z   P\S   L |

A could be true, if T has S and X doesn't have a third option.

B could be true, if X doesn't have a third option.

C could be true, if X does have S, a third option.

D must be false. X and Z always have options in common. **D** is **CORRECT.**

E could be true, if Z has P.

107

Game 3 – Opera Seating
Questions 13-17

Setup

Time for a night at the opera. But where to sit? There are five people and six seats. And everybody has to sit beside someone. So the seats in the middle can't be empty. It's not much fun to go to the opera and sit all by yourself.

Here's the setup plus the first rule:

G ____ ____ ____

H ____ ____ ____ T,U
     1   2   3

Two horizontal rows of three seats. T and U have to be in row H, so I've drawn them beside it.

The next rule tells us that T comes after S and U. T and U are in row H. We *don't* know which row S is in; it could be in row G. We also don't know whether U or S comes first.

The third rule tells us that R needs either Q or S in the same row.

R ⟶ Q or S

And the last rule tells us R is in seat two. We can combine this with the other rules to figure out that R must be in the second seat of row G.

R needs at least one other variable with it: Q or S. So there must be space for two variables in R's row.

But row H only has space for *one* variable: T and U are already there.

So R is in seat 2 of row G.

G ____ R ____

H ____ ____ ____ U — T
    1   2   3

I've added a line between U and T to indicate that T goes first.

At this point, you might think we're done. Not so fast! We still get to do my very favorite thing: split the setup into two scenarios.

Always be on the lookout for this. It can be tricky to develop an intuition for it. The place to start is to look at the most restricted variables. In this case, U and S must go before T. There aren't many ways to do that.

If U and S both go in row H, then we get this scenario:

G ____ R ____ Q

H U\S U\S T
   1   2   3

It doesn't matter where Q goes.

If we put S in row G, then it can't go in the third spot. It wouldn't be before T. It can only go in the first spot. (U can't go in row G, because of the first rule)

Here's what we get:

G _S_ _R_ ____

H ____ ____ ____ U — T ^{Q}
   1   2   3

I placed Q in the middle to show that it could be either in row G or H.

The rule about R having to be with Q or S is superfluous. Every correct scenario automatically takes care of that.

There's only one more thing to remember about this scenario: the second seat in row H always has to be full. The first rule says that everyone sits beside someone else.

If it helps you remember, draw U/T/Q in there to show that *somebody* has to fill that seat.

And that's it. There's no other way to place S, so there's really only two scenarios in this game!

Main Diagram

Scenario 1

G ____ _R_ ____ Q

H _U\S_ _U\S_ _T_
    1   2   3

Scenario 2

G _S_ _R_ ____

H ____ ____ ____ U — T ^{Q}
   1   2   3

Question 13

The first two questions are general questions. No local rules, no sifting through five lists of possible setups.

When you see that, it means that the LSAC *really* expected you to make a lot of deductions. It's a strong sign to take another look at your diagrams to see if you missed something.

A could be true, in the second scenario. We could have U and T in 1 and 2, and Q in seat 3 of H. **A** is **CORRECT.**

B can *never* be true. Then the poor people in H1 and H3 wouldn't have anyone beside them.

C can't be true, because S always has to be before T.

D is wrong because T can't be in 1. He needs S and U to the left of him.

E is wrong because U has to be in front of T.

Question 14

R can't be in H, because R is always with Q or S. And there aren't two free spots for them in H, because T and U are there. So **A** is wrong.

S can be in row H in the first scenario. **B** is **CORRECT.**

C is wrong because in the first scenario S and Q are in different rows. In the second scenario Q and S can both be in row G but they are separated by R.

D is wrong because R can't fit into row H, because he needs Q or S along with him.

E is wrong for the same reason **D** is.

Question 15

If T is in 2, then U must be in H1. S has to go in G1 to be numbered lower than T. Q can go in either row.

$$
\begin{array}{c}
\text{G} \underline{\quad\text{S}\quad} \underline{\quad\text{R}\quad} \underline{\qquad} \\[4pt]
\text{H} \underline{\quad\text{U}\quad} \underline{\quad\text{T}\quad} \underline{\qquad} \ \text{Q} \\[2pt]
\phantom{\text{H}}\ \ 1 \qquad 2 \qquad 3
\end{array}
$$

A is wrong because Q is always in seat 3.

B is wrong because U is always in 1.

C could be false. Q could sit in row H rather than beside Robert. **C** is **CORRECT.**

D is wrong. S has to be beside R because it's the only way for S to be in a lower numbered row than T.

E is wrong because U has to go directly before T.

Question 16

The scenario from question 15 proves that G3 and H3 can be empty. **E** is the only answer that has those two spots listed. **E is CORRECT.**

Using past scenarios can really help speed you up on this type of question.

Another trick is to use limiting factors. If you find that H3 can be empty, then any answer without H3 is wrong.

Here are some scenarios that prove the other spots can be empty.

Scenario 1 proves that G1 could be empty. Q can go in the third spot.

$$G \underline{} \quad \underset{}{R} \quad \underline{} \quad Q$$

$$H \quad \underset{1}{\underline{U \backslash S}} \quad \underset{2}{\underline{U \backslash S}} \quad \underset{3}{\underline{T}}$$

This next scenario proves that H1 can be empty

$$G \quad \underset{}{\underline{S}} \quad \underset{}{\underline{R}} \quad \underset{}{\underline{Q}}$$

$$H \quad \underset{1}{\underline{}} \quad \underset{2}{\underline{U}} \quad \underset{3}{\underline{T}}$$

Question 17

Scenario 1 proves that U and S can sit in H2.

$$G \underline{} \quad \underset{}{R} \quad \underline{} \quad Q$$

$$H \quad \underset{1}{\underline{U \backslash S}} \quad \underset{2}{\underline{U \backslash S}} \quad \underset{3}{\underline{T}}$$

The scenario from question 15 shows that T can sit there.

$$G \quad \underset{}{\underline{S}} \quad \underset{}{\underline{R}} \quad \underline{}$$

$$H \quad \underset{1}{\underline{U}} \quad \underset{2}{\underline{T}} \quad \underset{3}{\underline{}} \quad Q$$

And the diagram below shows that Q can go there. It's based on scenario 2.

$$G \quad \underset{}{\underline{S}} \quad \underset{}{\underline{R}} \quad \underline{}$$

$$H \quad \underset{1}{\underline{U}} \quad \underset{2}{\underline{Q}} \quad \underset{3}{\underline{T}}$$

E is CORRECT.

Game 4 – Hiring Professors
Questions 18-23

Setup

This is a normal linear game in disguise. It has seven spaces, one after each other. Except this game calls them 1989-1995.

The only other thing that makes this game different is that more than one professor can be hired in each year.

We can draw the layout and the first rule like this:

		R		M		
89	90	91	92	93	94	95

The second rules tells us that M, O and T can't be beside each other or hired in the same year. We could draw this a few different ways. I choose to put the variables underneath the spaces where they can't go, and put lines through them.

We don't know where O and T might go, so I drew the box with a suitcase handle to show that they can't go beside each other, in either order.

(Note: a smarter method would have been to read through all the rules first, and notice you can put O directly in 1990)

The next rule tells you that N and R have a specialty in common. That means that N can't go in 1990, 1991 or 1992.

The next rule lets you place N in 1989. The rule says that P and S come before M but after N.

$$N \text{ -- } P, S \text{ -- } M$$

The only place N could go is 1989.

Why? 1989, 90, 91 and 92 are the only spots before M, and you already know you can't put N in 90, 91 and 92.

The next rule lets you solve almost everything. O was hired in 1990, and S can't go beside O. So S can't go in 89, 90 or 91. Since S has to go before M, S must therefore go in 1992.

And what about T? We know T can't go in 92, 93 and 94. Now that O is in 1990, T can't go in 89, 90 or 91, because O and T can't go beside each other. So T has to go in 1995.

N	O	R	S	M		T
89	90	91	92	93	94	95

The *only* person left to place is P! P can go in 1990, 1991 or 1992, because P has to go between N and M.

As you can see, there's no huge trick to getting this kind of diagram set up. All I've done is looked at each rule, and asked if I could make any deductions by combining the rule with the previous rules. Look for variables in common, and think about which variables are most restricted. The LSAT is expecting people to make these types of diagrams.

A big factor in the questions will be whether P ends up sharing a specialty with any professors.

Main Diagram

N	O	R	S	M		T
89	90	91	92	93	94	95

P is the only uncertain variable. It's between N and M:

N – P – M

If you're unsure about this diagram, draw it on your own, following the setup.

Question 18

If we look at our main diagram and count, we see that N, O and R *have* to have been hired in 1989-91. And P *could* have been hired in 89-91, so we can include P as well. **C is CORRECT.**

We can see from the diagram that S, M and T all have to be after 1991.

Question 19

If only one professor was hired in 1991 then P was hired in another year: either 1990 or 1992.

A could be true, if P was hired in 1990. Then P wouldn't be beside M. **A is CORRECT.**

B can *never* be true, even without the local rule. R and S are always beside each other.

C is wrong. One year after Orozco is 1991, and we know only one professor can be hired that year. R is already there.

D is wrong. No professor can ever be hired in 1994.

E is wrong. P can never be hired in 1993. Only M can be hired that year.

Question 20

N	O	R	S	M		T
89	90	91	92	93	94	95

N – P – M

A must be true, from the diagram. N is always in 1989.

B could be true. P can be hired anytime between 90-92

C could be true. P can be hired anytime between 90-92

D *must* be true, from the diagram. S is always hired in 1992.

E must be false. T can't be hired in 1994 because T and M share a specialty. **E is CORRECT.**

Question 21

A doesn't have to be true, since O could be hired in the same year as P: 1990.

B doesn't have to be true, if P was hired in 1992.

C can't be true. R is always in 1991 and S is always in 1992, *after* R.

D must be true. R is in 1991 and S is in 1992. **D** is **CORRECT.**

E can't be true. M is in 1993 and S is in 1992.

Question 22

N	O	R	S	M		T
89	90	91	92	93	94	95
S̸	S̸	S̸	Ø	Ø	Ø	
P̸	P̸	P̸	P̸	P̸	P̸	

N – P – M

I reproduced the diagram above. For this question, two professors are hired in 1992. P is the only professor left to place, so now they *have* to go in 1992 with S.

This lets us conclude that P doesn't share a specialty with R, S or M.

A could be true and is therefore **CORRECT.** Neither O nor T are beside P if P is in 1992.

B must be false. P is beside M.

C must be false. P was the only professor left to place and we had to put them in 1992.

D must be false. P can never go in 1993.

E must be false. P has to be hired in 1992, since they are the only professor we had left to place.

Question 23

If P and M share a specialty then P must not be in 1992.

So P is in 1991 or 1990. That means P is beside O, and therefore P can't share a specialty with O.

A doesn't have to be true since P could go in 1991.

B could be false, because P could also go in 1990.

C could be false, because P could go in 1991 along with R.

D *must* be false. We can never have more than one year with two professors (the year with P.)

E must be true: P can't go in 1992 and therefore P is hired before S. **E** is **CORRECT.**

Test 35
Section IV - Logical Reasoning

Question 1

QUESTION TYPE: Most Strongly Supported - Exception

FACTS:

1. Geometric illustrations help students learn geometry by making it more intuitive.
2. This makes it easier for them to calculate by manipulating symbols.
3. Algebra could be made easier with illustrations, too.
4. This is true even though the deepest mathematical understanding is abstract.

ANALYSIS: On these questions it's best to narrow it down to 2-3 answer choices and then refer back to the stimulus to disprove the more difficult wrong answers. Every wrong answer will always be disproved by a specific part of the stimulus.

A. The final stage of mathematical understanding is abstract.
B. **CORRECT.** The stimulus doesn't support this. It doesn't mention any people who can manipulate symbols but don't understand math.
C. True. Illustrations help make geometry intuitive.
D. The stimulus said that "teachers use" illustrations for geometry. This implies that the practice is widespread.
E. Symbols could be effectively used in each case.

Question 2

QUESTION TYPE: Role in Argument

CONCLUSION: It's not likely that bureaucracies will be simplified.

REASONING: Bureaucracies are good at resisting change.

ANALYSIS: The word "thus" usually indicates a conclusion. The second sentence is the conclusion, and the claim in the first sentence supports it.

A. **CORRECT.** It supports the conclusion by giving us a reason that bureaucracies are unlikely to change.
B. No. Dissatisfaction doesn't affect whether or not bureaucracies are designed to resist change.
C. The stimulus didn't even say that bureaucratic systems are becoming more complex. It said that dissatisfaction is growing – that's different.
D. The stimulus didn't say if it would be good or bad to weaken complex bureaucracies. It just said that it isn't likely to happen.
E. This gets it backwards.

Question 3

QUESTION TYPE: Most Strongly Supported

FACTS:

1. We use gesture and tone of voice when speaking to show what we mean.
2. Writers can't use this method.
3. So they need to rely on style (the arrangement of words and sentences) to make meaning clear.

ANALYSIS: We're told that writers can't use speech to convey intended meaning. And we know that readers see a writer's intention from how the writer's style.

If the reader gets an accurate impression of the writer's intention, then it's strongly supported that writing style is a decent guide to intended meaning.

———————————

A. We have no evidence that this is the *primary* function of style. Conveying meaning is just one function.
B. **CORRECT.** This seems true, otherwise how could readers detect intention from writing style?
C. We have no idea which is easier. There are different methods used and we don't know how effective they are.
D. This is possible, but we have no evidence for it.
E. The stimulus doesn't even mention the idea of aesthetic value.

Question 4

QUESTION TYPE: Paradox

PARADOX: Three divisions with 25% of the workforce were cut. But the number of employees is only down 15%, despite no new hiring.

ANALYSIS: This is a rare math question. It sounds like the company kept some of the employees from the divisions it cut.

Answers A, C and E don't even talk about the number of employees.

———————————

A. This shows that it might have been a mistake to eliminate the divisions. But it doesn't explain anything about the number of employees.
B. This makes it even harder to explain the situation. There was no new influx of workers.
C. This explains the method by which some employees left. It doesn't affect how many of them left.
D. **CORRECT.** The company cut the divisions but it didn't cut all of the employees.
E. This explains how the company still managed to get its work done. But it doesn't affect the number of employees.

Question 5

QUESTION TYPE: Weaken

CONCLUSION: The BT bacterial toxins are better than chemical pesticides for pest control.

REASONING: The toxins only harm the insects in question. They don't harm birds or the insects that prey upon the pest insects.

ANALYSIS: The correct answer shows how BT toxins have a disadvantage against chemical toxins. The wrong answers mostly show limitations of BT toxins. These don't help, because they are limitations that likely also affect chemical pesticides.

———————

A. This could be bad, if the chemical insecticides kill beneficial insects.
B. That's fine. The stimulus argues that the toxins should be used in combination. It always says BT *toxins,* plural.
C. This doesn't matter. We have no evidence that chemical insecticides would harm weeds.
D. **CORRECT.** The BT toxins could work better at first but then slowly become ineffective.
E. So? The stimulus didn't claim that BT toxins will fix every problem.

Question 6

QUESTION TYPE: Flawed Parallel Reasoning

CONCLUSION: We don't need to take population control measures.

REASONING: The current increase in population has been accompanied by economic growth.

ANALYSIS: This is a bad argument. It doesn't show us that population *caused* the increase in economic growth. Perhaps we would be even richer without population growth. And there is also no guarantee that growth will continue in the future.

The structure is the following: There is no reason to worry about the problem, because presently the problem is accompanied by the solution.

———————

A. This isn't claiming there is no problem: magazine subscribers really will pay higher rates.
B. **CORRECT.** We don't know if sales are increasing *because* of the aggressive behavior. It might be a coincidence: perhaps sales would be higher if the manager weren't such a jerk. And there's no guarantee that sales will keep increasing in the future.
C. This argument does provide a possible solution, and there's no reason to think that the solution wouldn't keep working in the future.
D. This doesn't claim that there is no problem. It just urges caution.
E. This doesn't claim that there is no problem. Price increases are real, but fortunately they may stop soon.

Question 7

QUESTION TYPE: Flawed Reasoning

CONCLUSION: Mr. Smith is guilty of assaulting Mr. Jackson.

REASONING: Ms. Lopez testified that Mr. Smith is violent. Mr. Smith never disagreed.

ANALYSIS: There are a couple of problems. First, even if Ms. Lopez is correct, we don't have any evidence that Smith assaulted Jackson. Lots of people have violent tempers yet do not assault people.

Second, we don't know if Ms. Lopez was telling the truth or correct that Smith generally has a violent temper. He may just have been angry with her on one occasion.

A witness isn't obliged to refute testimony. Silence doesn't prove guilt.

_____

A. If Lopez was telling the truth, then Smith's behavior was beyond aggressive. Shouting loud threats is pretty close to actual violence.
B. The attorney didn't mention any testimony by Smith.
C. **CORRECT.** Lopez could simply be lying. We don't have anyone to confirm Lopez's testimony.
D. The attorney didn't mention whether Lopez was also loud and aggressive, or not.
E. Having a violent character is definitely *associated* with committing violent crimes. People with a violent character are probably more likely to be violent. It's only true that having a violent character isn't a *guarantee* that any particular aggressive person will commit violent crimes.

Question 8

QUESTION TYPE: Flawed Reasoning

CONCLUSION: The belief that old people are dumber and more forgetful is false.

REASONING: Old people did just as well as 30 year olds at playing a card game designed to test perception and memory.

ANALYSIS: Card games usually aren't the most demanding tests of our mental abilities. The argument is assuming that they are.

_____

A. This isn't a problem, since the conclusion is restricted to perception and memory.
B. Actually, the argument fails to consider the possibility that card games are *not* the most difficult cognitive tasks.
C. This shouldn't matter, as long as we're able to measure perception and memory accurately. We can measure something without fully understanding it.
D. The argument wasn't trying to explain why people think that older people are slow and forgetful.
E. **CORRECT.** The stimulus didn't say how much perception and memory were required to succeed at the card game.

Question 9

QUESTION TYPE: Main Conclusion

CONCLUSION: Some acts of altruism cannot be said to be moral acts.

REASONING: We have a natural tendency to be altruistic. But only acts that are intended to fit within a moral code (i.e. they aren't just the result of a natural tendency) can be moral.

ANALYSIS: This is a good argument, if we accept its premises. Moral behavior excludes acts that are merely based on instinctive tendencies.

A-C talk about what moral acts require. But the stimulus didn't say anything about this except that moral acts must be consciously designed to follow a moral code.

_____

A. The argument hasn't said what moral codes do or do not allow.
B. The argument hasn't said what motivates moral behavior.
C. The argument has said *nothing* about moral behavior, except that it must be behavior consciously intended to comply with a moral code.
D. CORRECT. Some are just instinctive, and therefore they weren't consciously intended to fit within a moral code.
E. Actually, the argument says that altruism is often based on a natural tendency: the opposite of reason.

Question 10

QUESTION TYPE: Strengthen

CONCLUSION: Alzheimer's may be caused by a virus.

REASONING: Blood from Alzheimer's patients was injected into rats. The rats developed symptoms of Creutzfeld-Jacob disease, another degenerative neurological disorder. Creutzfeld-Jacob disease is caused by a virus.

ANALYSIS: The fact that the rats got sick implies that something in the human blood (perhaps a virus) caused them to get sick. But they got a different disease.

This doesn't help show that Alzheimer's is caused by a virus unless the two diseases are related. Answer choice D says they are the same disease.

_____

A. This would weaken the argument that Alzheimer's is caused by a virus in humans.
B. It doesn't really matter what the symptoms are. The main point is that the disease is caused by a degeneration of brain tissue, just like Alzheimer's.
C. This also weakens the argument. We'd like to think that the disease is caused by a virus in both species.
D. CORRECT. If the diseases aren't the same then it isn't clear how rats getting Creutzfeld-Jacob disease shows that *Alzheimer's* is caused by a virus. Just because the diseases are both neurological disorders, that doesn't mean they have the same causes.
E. This doesn't help much, because the sick rats were injected with *human* blood, not rat blood.

Question 11

QUESTION TYPE: Principle - Strengthen

CONCLUSION: The approach is flawed. [The approach is to say that an object discussed by science is real only if the most powerful explanatory theories in science say the object is real.]

REASONING: Most scientific theories describe things that are only theoretical.

ANALYSIS: This is dense and hard to understand. I'll use an example:

A scientific theory with powerful explanatory power (it explains things well) might posit (say) that stars exist, and that some subatomic particles exist. We can prove that stars exist in the real world, but we have no non-theoretical proof for many subatomic particles.

According to the principle in the first sentence, we should designate both stars and all subatomic particles as real because a powerful theory says they are real. But the argument implies that it is not appropriate to say that all subatomic particles are real, because our only evidence for some of them is theoretical.

The argument doesn't show why we should be skeptical of objects that are only theoretical.

––––––––––––––––

A. This *weakens* the argument. The argument claims that not all entities described by science are real.
B. **CORRECT.** The argument is implying that theoretical objects aren't exactly real, even if our best theories support their existence.
C. This goes too far. An example would be: I have a theory that birds have wings. But I shouldn't talk about any actual birds unless they make my theory even better at explaining the fact that birds have wings. According to this answer choice it's no longer enough if my theory fully supports the existence of an object. That object must also support my theory.
D. The argument isn't talking about what scientific theories should do. It's about what we should consider to be real, based on scientific theories.
E. Not quite. The argument goes beyond this and implies that theoretical objects should not be considered real, even if they are backed by powerful theories.

Question 12

QUESTION TYPE: Paradox

PARADOX: Doctors recommend that pregnant women eat well. But most babies born to women who ate well still develop at least one health problem in their first year.

ANALYSIS: Healthy eating is not necessarily a complete cure. If the babies of women who ate healthy are *less* sick then this would explain the paradox.

It could be that most babies born to women who didn't eat well had *even more* health problems.

––––––––––––––––

A. This makes things even more confusing. The women are constantly eating healthy yet the babies get sick.
B. This doesn't explain much. It's talking about *late* childhood rather than the first year.
C. **CORRECT.** Women who don't eat nutritious diets have children that are even sicker. Eating healthy is not a complete cure but it helps.
D. This just tells us something about medical problems. It doesn't explain why children get sick.
E. This just tells us something about how often doctors reaffirm their recommendations. It doesn't explain why children still get sick despite the recommendations.

Question 13

QUESTION TYPE: Flawed Reasoning

CONCLUSION: The law against jaywalking has no purpose.

REASONING: Many people break the jaywalking law. And those who always obey the law would not cross at red lights even if there were no law. A law has no useful purpose unless it deters the behavior it prohibits.

ANALYSIS: The argument mentions two kinds of people: those who always break the law and those who never break the law.

The correct answer introduces a third kind of person: those who only break the law sometimes. It's possible that the law deters them.

_____

A. The argument is talking about pedestrians. It's irrelevant what drivers do.
B. Law is used consistently throughout. It means a legal prohibition.
C. The argument didn't say that a law definitely would serve a useful purpose if people obeyed it because they were deterred. It just claimed that there would definitely *not* be a useful purpose if people *didn't* obey it.
D. **CORRECT.** The argument ignores the middle ground between people who always jaywalk and people who never jaywalk.
E. The argument is not talking about danger. It's only talking about whether or not people obey the law.

Question 14

QUESTION TYPE: Sufficient Assumption

CONCLUSION: Marian Anderson did not take success for granted.

REASONING: Anderson had to struggle early in life. Anyone who struggles early must keep a good perspective on the world.

ANALYSIS: The argument is missing a link between struggling early and keeping a good perspective on the world.

If we diagram what we have so far, we get:

Struggle early in life → keep a good perspective on the world

If we say that everyone who keeps a good perspective will not take success for granted then we can get our conclusion:

Struggle early → good perspective → not take success for granted.

_____

A. This would disprove the argument. The stimulus argues that Marian Anderson (who succeeded) did *not* take success for granted.
B. **CORRECT.** We can then say: Struggle Early → good perspective → doesn't take success for granted.
C. This doesn't tell us how these people deal with success.
D. This tells us that struggling early in life is a *necessary* condition. We need a *sufficient* condition for not taking success for granted.
E. Same as D. This makes a good perspective a *necessary* condition. The right answer shows that it is a *sufficient* condition.

Question 15

QUESTION TYPE: Role in Argument

CONCLUSION: It is not realistic to imagine that cloning could produce an army of exact duplicates.

REASONING: Clones must be raised and educated. They will end up different. It's more realistic to imagine that the wealthy will use clones as an organ bank.

ANALYSIS: The argument is not claiming that there are no problems with cloning. It's only pointing out that fears of armies of identical clones are silly. The fact that adult clones will not be identical supports this conclusion.

A. Not quite. There are still some valid ethical concerns about cloning. For instance, the wealthy could use clones as organ banks. It's just that fears of an army of identical clones are groundless.
B. The argument said that clones *could* be produced. They just wouldn't form an identical army.
C. The argument didn't claim that only the wealthy could make clones. It just mentioned the wealthy in order to show one possible use for clones.
D. No. The wealthy can use clones as organ banks whether or not adult clones will be identical to the originals. It's only the idea of making a clone army that doesn't work if clones will not be identical.
E. **CORRECT.** There are still other valid fears about cloning. But a scary army of identical clones is impossible.

Question 16

QUESTION TYPE: Necessary Assumption

CONCLUSION: It's not likely that publicity campaigns for endangered species will help solve the most important environmental problems.

REASONING: It's easy to make people want to save large mammals. It's very hard to make people care about soil microorganisms.

ANALYSIS: The argument is assuming that the most important environmental problems depend on doing more than saving the largest mammal species.

A. **CORRECT.** If all of the most important environmental problems just involve large mammals then maybe publicity campaigns will work.
B. It doesn't matter what feelings microorganisms have. It only matters whether or not we can convince people to save them.
C. This is irrelevant. The argument was claiming that publicity campaigns won't work. It would be sad if they were the most effective way, but that's all.
D. It isn't necessary that this is always the case. People might pay attention to environmental problems that threatened them directly, for example. That wouldn't weaken the argument.
E. The argument wouldn't be weakened if an organism could be environmentally significant despite not affecting large ecosystems or agriculture.

Question 17

QUESTION TYPE: Weaken - Exception

CONCLUSION: If a nation wants to maintain its way of life then it should not allow its highest tax bracket to take more than 30% of income.

REASONING: High tax on income → negative incentive for tech innovation → fall behind in international arms race.

Strategically disadvantageous position → lose their voice in world affairs.

ANALYSIS: This long winded argument sounds impressive, but the politician makes many unsupported assumptions. He doesn't show that many of his premises are necessarily connected.

I drew the premises separately above. There's no link between falling behind in the arms race and losing your voice in world affairs.

There's also no evidence that 30% is too high. We know too high is bad, but not how high "too high" is.

A. The politician provides no evidence that 30% is too high.
B. Here we see that reduced monetary incentives won't do very much to lower innovation. They will lower it a little, but probably not by much.
C. Right. The politician provided no evidence that there is a strategic loss if a country falls behind in the arms race.
D. The argument assumed that there was a connection between these two things, but there may be no connection.
E. **CORRECT.** This doesn't matter. The argument says that strategically disadvantageous positions are bad whether they were caused by foolishness or historical accident.

Question 18

QUESTION TYPE: Flawed Reasoning

CONCLUSION: The activities of the scientific community as a whole are directed towards enhancing the status of that community. They only further truth as a side effect.

REASONING: Individual scientists are mostly interested in enhancing their own status. Individual scientists only further the pursuit of truth as a side effect.

ANALYSIS: This argument assumes that the whole (the scientific community) is just the sum of its parts (the individual scientists). But it's possible that the scientific community as a whole is directed at the pursuit of truth even if all individual scientists are merely trying to further their own interests.

A. The stimulus didn't say that every scientist is self-interested. It just said that most are and as a result the whole community was mainly self-interested.
B. **CORRECT.** The scientific community isn't necessarily the same as individual scientists.
C. The argument said that the truth might be advanced but that it would be only incidental (an unintended side-effect.)
D. Self-interested is clear: mainly looking out for one's own interests.
E. The cause was the fact that most scientists are self-interested. The effect was that the entire scientific community was therefore self-interested. The stimulus didn't add any new information about the cause.

Question 19

QUESTION TYPE: Sufficient Assumption

CONCLUSION: It is false to say that writing formal poetry is a politically conservative act.

REASONING: Some progressive feminists write formal poetry.

ANALYSIS: Just because someone is a progressive feminist does not mean that none of their actions are conservative. The two poets mentioned could be progressive *except* when they write formal poetry. They would be committing a conservative act when writing poetry.

It's similar to the idea that a pacifist is capable of committing a violent act, or a villain is capable of committing a kind act. The nature of the act doesn't necessarily affect who they are.

All of the wrong answers ignore the fact that the conclusion is about whether the *act* of writing a formal poem is politically conservative.

———————————

A. This talks about *being* a political conservative. The stimulus talks about committing a politically conservative act. Different things.
B. Same as A. You can commit an act that is politically conservative even if you aren't a political conservative.
C. CORRECT. Because the two poets are progressive, then none of their acts are politically conservative. Therefore, writing formal poetry can't be a conservative act.
D. The stimulus didn't say if formal poetry had to be politically conservative. Writing formal poetry was claimed to be a politically conservative act, even if the poems themselves weren't really conservative.
E. The stimulus did not talk about the consequences of poems. It was addressing the question of whether a writing a formal poem necessarily had to be a politically conservative act.

Question 20

QUESTION TYPE: Weaken

CONCLUSION: The first Eurasian settlers in North America came from a more distant part of Eurasia.

REASONING: A skeleton of a mastodon that became extinct at the height of the ice age was found with a projectile inside of it. The projectile is dissimilar to all projectiles found so far in the part of Eurasia closest to North America.

ANALYSIS: By showing that there is no evidence of the projectiles in near Eurasia the stimulus is implying that there is some evidence the projectiles existed in far Eurasia.

The correct answer choice tells us that the projectiles haven't been found in far Eurasia either.

Therefore it is equally likely the people came from either place. We have no evidence that would favor one part of Eurasia over another.

———————————

A. CORRECT. The argument's only evidence was that the projectile wasn't found in any near part of Eurasia. This tells us that the projectile is unknown in *all* of Eurasia. So we have no idea where it comes from, and it could well come from the near part of Eurasia.
B. So? The settlers might have been nomadic within their region, or they might have traveled further. This tells us nothing, and it gives us no information about what kind of projectiles they used.
C. This shows that the projectile was not completely unique. It slightly strengthens the argument. If the projectile were unique then we wouldn't expect it to be found anywhere else.
D. This strengthens the argument by showing that many artifacts have been linked to far Eurasia.
E. This strengthens the argument by showing that people were more likely to live in far Eurasia.

Question 21

QUESTION TYPE: Most Strongly Supported

ANALYSIS: In plain English, this says that labor saving technology can sometimes eliminate an entire category of jobs.

That will undermine the values of society. The reason is because the values of society depend on the prestige given to different social roles (categories of jobs.)

If a social role disappears then that eliminates the prestige attached to that role as well.

The right answer may not seem directly related to this, but it does follow. It says that if a society's values can't change, then that society won't let technology eliminate economic roles. Eliminating economic roles changes a society's values.

_____

A. There could be other things that undermine a society apart from technology. Famine, for example, has undermined many societies.
B. We only know *labor-saving* technology is likely to undermine a system.
C. **CORRECT.** In plain English, this says: if it is *impossible* to change the values of a social system then technology won't be able to get rid of any social roles. [If you get rid of social roles then you change the values of society. So you can't get rid of them if you can't change the values.]
D. Not necessarily true. There may be many roles that are highly valued in a technologically advanced society. It just could be the case that technology more frequently eliminates roles.
E. We only know this is true if the technology is *labor-saving*.

Question 22

QUESTION TYPE: Must be False

FACTS:
1. Gamma interferon (one of the body's defenses against viruses) made multiple sclerosis patients much worse.
2. Multiple sclerosis acts by having white blood cells attack the myelin sheath that protects nerve fibers.
3. The unsuccessful gamma interferon tests led to a drug that can treat multiple sclerosis.

ANALYSIS: From the sounds of things, the researchers made a drug that lowers levels of gamma interferon.

They realized that gamma interferon made the patients' MS much worse. So why not invent a drug to reduce gamma interferon?

_____

A. **CORRECT.** This is highly unlikely. Gamma interferon made the multiple sclerosis *much* worse. And MS acts by using myelin-destroying compounds from the white blood cells.
B. This is possible. It seems likely that gamma interferon produced more white blood cells in the MS patients.
C. This is quite consistent with the stimulus. It could be gamma interferon that causes the symptoms.
D. This would explain why the anti-viral treatment did not work.
E. This would explain why the experiments led researchers to a successful drug. They realized that gamma interferon was hurting MS patients.

Question 23

QUESTION TYPE: Parallel Reasoning

CONCLUSION: The air is thinner in Mexico City than in Panama City.

REASONING: Air is thinner at higher altitudes. Mexico City is higher than Panama City.

ANALYSIS: This is a good argument. Air is always thinner at higher altitudes. It goes from sufficient to necessary, like answer choice D. Answer choice E goes from necessary to sufficient.

A. This is a bad argument. We get wiser as we get older. But this doesn't tell us how wise we are to start with. A 70 year that started with little wisdom might be less wise than a 27 year old who started with a lot of wisdom.
B. This is a bad argument because it doesn't tell us who beat their eggs whites the longest.
C. This is a bad argument. It goes from statistics about the general population to a specific marathon runner, Charles. Charles might be slower even if marathon runners are faster on average.
D. **CORRECT.** This is a good argument. Any tree that is older than another will have more rings, so Lou's tree must have more rings.
E. This is a bad argument. It confuses necessary conditions and sufficient conditions. Bigger vocabulary makes a language harder but a harder language won't necessarily have a bigger vocabulary.

Question 24

QUESTION TYPE: Flawed Reasoning

CONCLUSION: Lowering cholesterol levels reduces the risk of heart disease

REASONING: People with heart disease often have high cholesterol. Pravastatin lowered heart disease risk and also lowered cholesterol.

ANALYSIS: This is a bad argument. It could be that Pravastatin lowers heart disease risk for some other reason, and that it is only a coincidence that it lowers cholesterol as well.

Similarly, the mere fact that heart disease patients have high cholesterol does not mean that cholesterol causes heart disease. It could be that some third factor causes both heart disease *and* also often causes high cholesterol.

A. The argument didn't say whether it was a good idea to take Pravastatin. It just claimed that the Pravastatin study helped show that cholesterol caused heart disease. Pravastatin could have horrible side effects.
B. **CORRECT.** We have no evidence that Pravastatin reduced heart disease *because* it lowered cholesterol. Lowered cholesterol could have just been a side effect.
C. The argument relied on past findings *and* the study. There's nothing wrong with that.
D. The conclusion is about heart disease. There's no reason the conclusion has to focus on Pravastatin. That was just evidence.
E. That's irrelevant. The study was big enough that it can be used for results. It doesn't matter who else is using Pravastatin.

Question 25

QUESTION TYPE: Method of Reasoning

CONCLUSION: Stephen concludes that we should not strip the frescos down to the original fresco work.

REASONING: Stephen points out that Michelangelo may have added details to the frescos himself after the paint had dried from the original fresco work.

ANALYSIS: Zachary is assuming that Michelangelo never added more than a single coat of paint to the fresco. Stephen implies that Michelangelo might have added an extra coat of paint.

———————————————

A. **CORRECT.** Zachary is assuming that Michelangelo only painted the first layer. But Stephen points out that painters commonly added extra layers.
B. Stephen didn't redefine any words. His answer is only a sentence long and talks about when painters redid work.
C. Stephen doesn't explicitly draw a conclusion. Instead he merely implies that Zachary is wrong.
D. Stephen didn't say straight out that Zachary was wrong. Instead, he added new information that changed how we should view Zachary's idea.
E. Zachary's conclusion is consistent with his own premises. But Stephen adds a new premise which casts doubt on Zachary's conclusion.

Question 26

QUESTION TYPE: Most Strongly Supported

CONCLUSION: Stephen concludes that we should not strip the frescos down to the original fresco work.

REASONING: Stephen points out that Michelangelo may have added details to the frescos himself after the paint had dried from the original fresco work.

ANALYSIS: Stephen's main point is that if we go down to the original fresco then we might miss some of Michelangelo's added layers.

———————————————

A. Actually, Stephen thinks that we could work down to the original fresco work. But the problem is that we might remove some of Michelangelo's additional fresco work if we did that.
B. **CORRECT.** We would likely strip away some of the layers added by Michelangelo.
C. Who knows? Michelangelo may have considered any additions he made to be the most important part of the fresco.
D. Stephan doesn't even talk about the other painters. There is no support for this idea.
E. Stephen doesn't say anything about Michelangelo specifically. Instead, he only talks about painters from that era. Maybe Michelangelo *never* added to his frescos.

Test 36
Section I - Logical Reasoning

Question 1

QUESTION TYPE: Method of Reasoning

CONCLUSION: Ruth concludes that it's possible for a company to succeed by completely changing its business after bankruptcy.

REASONING: Joanna said that it could never happen. But Ruth provided an example of one company that succeeded.

ANALYSIS: Ruth uses a counterexample. A single counter-example is enough to disprove a sufficient-necessary statement.

If I say: "All dogs are brown," then you can prove me by wrong by pointing to a single dog that is black.

A. **CORRECT.** Kelton Company is a counterexample that disproves Joanna's claim.
B. No. Ruth disagrees with Joanna that the phenomenon even exists.
C. An analogy is different than a counterexample. An analogy is when you prove one argument by showing that the argument works in a parallel situation. Ruth's evidence instead simply contradicts Joanna's argument.
D. There's no ambiguity, Joanna is clear: She doesn't think a company can succeed by changing its business. Ruth disagrees.
E. Ruth didn't say that it is *always* a good idea to change direction and *never* a good idea to produce the same goods. She just said that it *can* be a good idea to switch.

Question 2

QUESTION TYPE: Weaken

CONCLUSION: Juicers are not worth the money.

REASONING: We have no evidence that there are benefits from drinking juice separated from its pulp.

ANALYSIS: The nutritionist is ignoring the possibility that people might be more likely to drink carrot juice versus eating a carrot. Always doing something that is half-effective is better than never doing something that is 100% effective.

A. **CORRECT.** If this is true then juicers could let people consume more nutrients than if people ate solid foods.
B. This *supports* the argument that juicers are a bad idea.
C. This doesn't mean that buying a juicer still wouldn't be a stupid idea. Just because you can afford something, doesn't mean you should buy it.
D. This just shows that the nutritionist has experience with juicers. It doesn't affect the argument or show any bias.
E. This shows that we should eat real food rather than taking pills. But what does that have to do with juice?

Question 3

QUESTION TYPE: Necessary Assumption

CONCLUSION: Mikkeli argues that he could not have plagiarized Halden's book.

REASONING: The book was published in a foreign language that Mikkeli does not speak. And no one ever published a review of Halden's book.

ANALYSIS: Mikkeli's defense assumes that there is no other way he could have learned about the book.

A. It's possible to meet someone without stealing all of their ideas.
B. It doesn't matter if the book became popular in Norway as long as it didn't become popular in Sweden, where Mikkeli lived.
C. CORRECT. If some Norwegian friend told Mikkeli the book's story then Mikkeli could have plagiarized it based on those details.
D. This would help Mikkeli but it isn't necessary.
E. Even if Mikkeli could read Old Icelandic that doesn't necessarily mean he could read Norwegian.

Question 4

QUESTION TYPE: Most Strongly Supported

FACTS: Anti-depressants tend to cause weight gain. Dieting can help, but it's virtually inevitable that you'll gain some weight.

ANALYSIS: It seems very obvious, but the stimulus supports the idea that people will likely gain weight if they take antidepressants.

A. Hard to say. It might be more important to prevent depression even if the patient will gain weight.
B. This is sort of like A. Treating depression might be even more important than weight gain for those patients.
C. CORRECT. The entire stimulus supports the idea that some people will likely gain weight.
D. We have no idea what causes the weight gain. If they gain it as a result of a pill then it's unlikely diet is the main cause.
E. We have no idea. Maybe there are some patients who could not safely diet.

Question 5

QUESTION TYPE: Must be False

COMPANY POLICY: An employee must be impartial in everything they do. Family should not be favored.

ANALYSIS: There is a difference between impartiality and the *appearance* of impartiality. In the real world, company policies often forbid the appearance of impartiality. But this question talks about impartiality itself.

For example, we often think that impartiality means we should never give a job to a family member. But it makes sense to hire a family member who is the best candidate.

The reason that companies often have policies against employing family members is to avoid the *appearance* of impartiality. But those policies could actually be a violation of impartiality if the family member really is the best candidate.

———————

A. CORRECT. This goes too far. The company policy supports the idea that you should hire the best, impartially, even if they are family. Not hiring qualified family members violates the impartiality policy.
B. This is fine. The employee treated their mother just like everyone else.
C. This could be fine, if those family members perform well and don't deserve to be fired.
D. This would be ok if every employee were treated similarly. It might be bad management, but it would be impartial.
E. This could be fine, if the family member deserved it.

Question 6

QUESTION TYPE: Main Point

CONCLUSION: It could be that stress causes both acne and the desire to eat chocolate.

REASONING: Studies show that stress causes hormonal changes that cause acne. And people who are stressed eat more chocolate.

ANALYSIS: This is a good argument. The evidence isn't very definite, but neither is the conclusion. It does seem possible that stress is the cause of both eating chocolate and acne.

———————

A. This goes too far. The argument only says it is *likely* that common wisdom has mistaken an effect for a cause.
B. This gets it backwards. Stress likely leads to the desire to eat chocolate.
C. No. Chocolate is a *result* of stress.
D. CORRECT. This isn't certain, but there is good evidence to support it.
E. This is true, but it isn't the main point. The main point is that stress likely causes both chocolate eating *and* acne.

Question 7

QUESTION TYPE: Method of Reasoning

CONCLUSION: It could be that stress causes both acne and the desire to eat chocolate.

REASONING: Studies show that stress causes hormonal changes that cause acne. And people who are stressed eat more chocolate.

ANALYSIS: This is a good argument. The evidence isn't very definite, but neither is the conclusion. It does seem possible that stress is the cause of both eating chocolate and acne.

The method of reasoning is to show that there is a plausible alternative explanation, backed by scientific studies.

––––––––––––––––

A. There is *no* evidence for the position being challenged apart from the fact that there is a correlation between acne and eating chocolate. The stimulus agreed that happens.
B. **CORRECT.** The argument's evidence supports the fact that stress causes both chocolate eating and acne: that's why they happen at the same time.
C. No. Science has no "superior authority." The argument uses evidence from science to make a case, but it doesn't dismiss anything out of hand. It even admits the common explanation might be right.
D. No. The stimulus even agrees that chocolate and acne go together. It just has an alternate explanation for the reason why.
E. The position being criticized did not suppose that causes always preceded effects. And the stimulus' alternate explanation says that stress (the cause) does precede its effects!

Question 8

QUESTION TYPE: Weaken

CONCLUSION: There is no equal time obligation for scientific disputes.

REASONING: An equal time obligation only exists for social disputes.

ANALYSIS: The argument is assuming that a scientific dispute can never also be a social dispute.

––––––––––––––––

A. This would *strengthen* the argument.
B. "Often" doesn't tell us how often. Maybe this is still only true for social issues and not scientific issues.
C. Great! But this tells us nothing about what to do with *scientific* issues.
D. **CORRECT.** This shows that these scientific disputes are similar to social disputes. Therefore both sides may deserve equal time.
E. That's one way to solve the problem. But it doesn't tell us what to do if a network *does* decide to broadcast a scientific issue.

Question 9

QUESTION TYPE: Paradox

PARADOX: Raisins have more iron per calorie than grapes do. But raisins are just dried grapes. Grapes lose water when they are turned into raisins. Some sugar is caramelized, but nothing is added.

ANALYSIS: We only care about how much iron is in the grapes and raisins, and why.

We don't care about how often we can eat them (answer D), or what we eat with them (answers E) or how many of them we have to eat to get the same number of calories (answer A) or how fast we can absorb the iron (answer C.)

Always think about what you're looking for, before looking at the answers.

————————————

A. This would explain why raisins have more iron per *gram*. But the stimulus is talking about calories, so it doesn't matter how dense grapes are.
B. CORRECT. Raisins lose some calories from caramelization. If iron stays the same, then there will be relatively more of it since the remaining calories shrank.
C. It doesn't matter how fast we can absorb iron. This has nothing to do with how much iron is in raisins.
D. This doesn't tell us how much iron is in grapes or raisins.
E. This has no effect on how much iron is in grapes or raisins.

Question 10

QUESTION TYPE: Weaken

CONCLUSION: Cortell can't write superior quality articles.

REASONING: Cortell must have plagiarized any superior quality articles he submitted.

ANALYSIS: This is a circular argument. It argues that Cortell can't write superior quality articles because Cortell can't write superior quality articles.

There's no evidence that Cortell plagiarized.

————————————

A. The argument didn't ignore counterevidence. It did mention that Cortell produced superior articles, but explained them away by saying they were plagiarized.
B. Actually, the article looks at all articles produced by Cortell and concludes they are either of average quality or plagiarized.
C. CORRECT. This is another way of saying circular reasoning.
D. Name me *one* expert mentioned in the stimulus. This answer choice didn't happen.
E. Actually, the stimulus infers limits on ability from a generalized pattern of not producing good work + (alleged) plagiarism.

Question 11

QUESTION TYPE: Must be True

Diagram:

Sale item → store credit but no refund.

Home appliances, gardening tools and some construction tools are on sale. Therefore they can be returned for store credit but not for a refund.

ANALYSIS: We don't know anything about products that aren't on sale. Stick to what we know.

A. We don't know. There might be other reasons that other items can't be returned.
B. We don't know *anything* about items *not* on sale.
C. We don't know. Maybe all construction tools are returnable. We only know some construction tools aren't eligible for a full refund.
D. **CORRECT.** All gardening equipment is on sale so none of it can be returned for a refund.
E. We only know that *some* construction tools are on sale. The ones that aren't on sale might be returnable for a refund.

Question 12

QUESTION TYPE: Weaken

CONCLUSION: Government benefits sometimes are raised too high compared to the true increase in the cost of goods and services.

REASONING: The consumer price index is used to measure changes in the cost of *retail* goods. But the consumer price index doesn't take into account technological innovations that reduce the cost of *producing* goods.

ANALYSIS: This is a subtle question. The cost of production of a product can be very different from its retail price. We should care about the price people pay in the store (retail price).

We only know how technology affects production costs. We have no idea how this affects retail prices, so it's irrelevant information.

A. If the consumer price index didn't change then it's still possible that costs fell due to technology. In that case, benefits should have shrunk.
B. It doesn't matter which goods are included as long as the CPI accurately reflects changes in retail goods.
C. What does this matter? The CPI is designed to measure general changes that affect the population *on average*. Obviously some people will be affected more than others if the things they buy rise more or less in price.
D. Actually, the CPI measures the past and the government benefits are changed to reflect past changes. The future is not relevant.
E. **CORRECT.** The CPI measures *retail* prices. Technology affects the cost of *producing* things but we don't know if it affects retail prices.

Question 13

QUESTION TYPE: Paradox

PARADOX: The astronomers couldn't see the comet breaking into pieces until 2 months after seeing the bright lights that showed it had broken into pieces.

ANALYSIS: We need to explain why the astronomers saw light before the comet broke up. There's nothing in the stimulus that provides an obvious answer. Instead, you have to consider each answer choice and ask how it affects the stimulus.

The correct answer tells us that the break of the comet occurs only after it starts releasing the dust that causes increased brightness.

A. This is even more confusing, because it means the comet broke up even before it grew brighter. When it light up we ought to have seen it was broken.
B. This explains why comets light up but it doesn't explain why we couldn't observe the breakup.
C. **CORRECT.** This shows that gas and dust can start increasing the comet's light even before it breaks up. This explains the delay between the light and the breakup.
D. This makes it even stranger that the breakup wasn't observed. The comet became easier to see.
E. This explains why the comet broke but it doesn't explain why we didn't see it.

Question 14

QUESTION TYPE: Must be True

CONCLUSION:
1. If Slater wins, then McGuiness will be appointed.
2. Even though Yerxes is more qualified.
3. Slater will win unless the polls are completely wrong.

ANALYSIS: This shows that if the polls are right, McGuiness will be appointed even though Yerxes is more qualified.

Note that McGuiness could still be appointed, even is Slater doesn't win. Slater winning is a sufficient condition, not a necessary condition.

A. Who knows? Maybe McGuiness will be appointed no matter who wins.
B. Not quite. We know that McGuiness will be appointed *if* the polls are correct. But he might be appointed even if someone else wins the election.
C. No. Yerxes might not be appointed even if Slater loses.
D. We don't know that *both* of these things are true. We only know that at least one of them is. McGuiness could be an inexperienced architect, for instance.
E. **CORRECT.** If the polls are right then Slater wins and he'll appointed McGuiness, who is less qualified than Yerxes.

Question 15

QUESTION TYPE: Principle - Strengthen

CONCLUSION: It isn't always a good idea to buy advanced technological tools.

REASONING: The argument gives a couple of examples where people who trained with low tech methods did just as well as people who used high tech methods.

ANALYSIS: The engineers and military personnel are just given as examples. They aren't important to the argument except as illustrations of how people can learn without expensive tools.

The right answer tells us not to invest in expensive tools if less expensive tools work just as well.

———————————

A. This doesn't matter. Engineers and military personnel were just used as examples. The argument could equally have mentioned circus trainers and scuba divers who used non-advanced educational tools.
B. This doesn't matter: both methods produced equally knowledgeable personnel.
C. Same as A. The two groups were only given as examples. And we're trying to say that spending lots of money *isn't* always justified.
D. **CORRECT.** This gets "If you invest → no other tools" and the contrapositive "if other tools → don't invest" In this case, we had less expensive tools that were equally effective. So it was correct not to invest.
E. This doesn't help. Excluding expensive materials reduces variety.

Question 16

QUESTION TYPE: Most Strongly Supported

CONCLUSION:
1. Growth, unemployment and inflation are important economic indicators.
2. A bunch of countries have good economies but are small.
3. All of the countries listed in the stimulus have populations seven million or smaller.

ANALYSIS: We're not given *any* information on what effect population has on a country's economy. Most of the wrong answers talk about this.

———————————

A. Too strong. Maybe those countries would have even better economies if they had larger populations.
B. We don't know *anything* about countries with populations larger than 7 million. Maybe they all have terrible economies.
C. **CORRECT.** Many of the countries listed in the stimulus have viable economies but populations smaller than 7 million. So a small country can have a good economy.
D. It's hard to say. We only have a few scattered examples of small countries, all of which are successful. But we don't know if size had anything to do with it.
E. We have *zero* information on what effect population has.

Question 17

QUESTION TYPE: Principle – Parallel Reasoning

PRINCIPLE: You should go backwards from the crime when writing a detective story. Write details to match to crime.

ANALYSIS: This principle tells us to start from the end/main event, and then go backwards.

A. This isn't quite it. Only the people who decide where they are going and then plan are following the principle from the stimulus.
B. This principle should have told us to imagine our ideal garden and then work to make it.
C. This just tells us that architecture takes a lot of work and involves many factors. It doesn't say where to start.
D. This doesn't tell us where to start.
E. **CORRECT.** Start from the end (where the shot goes), and then work backwards to positioning.

Question 18

QUESTION TYPE: Sufficient Assumption

CONCLUSION: Moderate exercise lowers the risk of blood clots.

REASONING: If a recent study is correct....etc. a chain of reasoning is presented that exercise lowers blood clots.

ANALYSIS: This is almost a trick question. The argument presents the following chain of reasoning:

Lower cholesterol → less hardening arteries → lower risk of arterial blockage.

And then it tells us that a study shows that exercise lowers cholesterol, *if* the data are correct. That information would let us reach our conclusion, if we knew the study was accurate. But the study might be wrong!

The right answer simply tells us the data are correct.

A. It doesn't matter what the study investigated. It's only important to know what the results let us prove.
B. This doesn't help us prove that *exercise* is a way to prevent clots.
C. This doesn't help us establish that exercise can help with cholesterol. (we're not sure if the study is correct)
D. **CORRECT.** If the study is correct then everything else falls into place.
E. We already know this is true.

Question 19

QUESTION TYPE: Flawed Reasoning

CONCLUSION: The "patriotism" in Arton's work was ironic.

REASONING: Conditions in Arton's country were bad when she wrote her poetry.

ANALYSIS: The argument doesn't take into account the possibility that people may not always feel the same way about what's going on in their country.

Arton might have loved her country when writing her poetry, even if others were upset at the time.

_____

A. The argument didn't say if unemployment causes crime. And that is irrelevant to the question of whether Arton was patriotic.
B. Not quite. The argument is assuming that patriotism is impossible for a serious writer *living in a country going through hard times*.
C. **CORRECT.** Arton may have been patriotic even if most of her fellow citizens weren't.
D. This is a relevant point, but C is better. We don't know if Arton prospered, and individual prosperity might not be enough to make someone optimistic if their country was in danger.
E. These are clearly different things and the argument didn't mix them up. The point of mentioning irony was to show that Arton couldn't possible have been seriously patriotic when morale was so low.

Question 20

QUESTION TYPE: Necessary Assumption

CONCLUSION: The legal system doesn't guarantee justice.

REASONING: Citizens lack knowledge of how to create a system that deters crime. And citizens must be capable of criticizing anyone who determines the punishment of criminals.

ANALYSIS: The argument is assuming that we have to understand something before we can criticize it. That is rarely the case.

_____

A. It doesn't matter how citizens view justice. It only matters whether they are able to criticize those who punish criminals.
B. This has nothing to do with citizens.
C. That may be. But another important concern is whether citizens can criticize the system.
D. The stimulus doesn't mention a concern for punishment. It just talks about whether citizens can criticize those who determine punishments. That isn't the same thing as a "concern" for punishment.
E. **CORRECT.** If citizens can criticize experts even without understanding, then the legal system might be just.

Question 21

QUESTION TYPE: Flawed Parallel Reasoning

CONCLUSION: The reproduction of the painting will not be an accurate reproduction of *the painting*.

REASONING: The painting was not an accurate reproduction of *Rosati*.

ANALYSIS: This argument confuses reproducing Rosati and reproducing the flawed portrait of Rosati. It's perfectly possible to copy a flawed portrait well. The painting would still not be a good portrait of Rosati but it would be a good reproduction of the flawed portrait.

Both the stimulus and the right answer compare irrelevant qualities. It's possible to copy any portrait or recording, whether the original is good or bad.

————————————

A. **CORRECT.** You could make a perfect copy of a bad speech. It would have all of the mis-quotes of the original but the sound quality would be good.
B. This is probably true, but irrelevant. This answer choice isn't talking about whether it's *possible* to reproduce the scene.
C. This is probably true, but it depends on what is meant by resemble. But this doesn't talk about whether resemblance is possible.
D. This is a bad argument. It's quite possible for people to imitate other people even if they are different. But this doesn't make the error of comparing irrelevant qualities.
E. Winning a prestigious award is not the same thing as being enthralling. It's possible both books are very, very boring. But this doesn't make the error of comparing irrelevant qualities.

Question 22

QUESTION TYPE: Sufficient Assumption

CONCLUSION: A poetry reader can enjoy a poem even if they don't precisely understand the poet's meaning.

REASONING: Poets → Personal expression → ambiguous words

ANALYSIS: The reasoning tells us that all poets use ambiguous expressions. That means that it is impossible to precisely figure out their meaning. But the argument doesn't connect the premises to its conclusion.

The correct answer tells us that readers can still enjoy poems despite that ambiguity.

————————————

A. It doesn't matter whether the readers try to understand words. It only matters if they can enjoy the poem even if they don't understand the precise meaning.
B. We don't care about what writers think. The conclusion is about whether readers can enjoy poetry.
C. **CORRECT.** Everyone who reads ambiguous poets can still enjoy their work even if they don't get the precise meaning.
D. "Most" isn't good enough. The conclusion says "no" poetry reader will fail to enjoy the poems.
E. That's great for those readers. But it doesn't tell us if readers who don't have a precise understanding can still enjoy the poems.

Question 23

QUESTION TYPE: Paradox – Exception

PARADOX: Most lamps in the early Paleolithic occurred when the Magdalenian culture was dominant.

ANALYSIS: The correct answer talks about different kinds of lamps. But having many different types of something doesn't mean you will have more of something overall.

Imagine having 300 types of lamps, but only 1-2 examples of each type. A culture that only had 1-2 types of lamps would have more lamps if they had 5,000 lamps of each type.

The wrong answers help us explain why more lamps from the Magdalenian period were found, or why more Magdalenian lamps were produced.

A. This shows that we are better at identifying the lamps from the later Magdalenian period. There may have been as many lamps in the early period but we haven't figured out that they are lamps.
B. This would explain why we have found so many Magdalenian lamps. We've found more Magdalenian stuff, period.
C. This shows that it was easier for the Magdalenians to make lamps. So they made more.
D. If you had a fire pit, then you didn't need a lamp for light inside your cave: you had a fire, instead. (The Magdalenians came later, not earlier.)
E. **CORRECT.** More *kinds* of lamps does not equal more lamps, total.

Question 24

QUESTION TYPE: Information to Evaluate the Argument

CONCLUSION: Orwell's book *1984* has influenced many of this newspaper's readers.

REASONING: 1,000 people surveyed said that Orwell's book *1984* was the book chosen second most often, after the bible.

ANALYSIS: Being chosen second-most often doesn't necessarily mean much. It could be that 980 readers chose the bible, and only 20 chose *1984*. That doesn't amount to much.

(The people surveyed only picked one book. They didn't choose "bible first, *1984* second". Instead, they each chose one book, and *1984* was selected second most often.)

A. This doesn't matter. It only matters how many of those surveyed were influenced by *1984*
B. **CORRECT.** If only ten people chose *1984* (and 980 chose the bible, and 10 chose other books) then we have no evidence that many readers were influenced by *1984*.
C. The conclusion is only about the readers of the newspaper, so this doesn't matter. The sample of 1,000 was big enough to get a sense of the readership's opinions.
D. This doesn't matter. The conclusion was only about *1984*.
E. It doesn't matter if the books were read. It only matters if the books influenced their lives. We're all influenced by the Iliad, even if we haven't read it.

Question 25

QUESTION TYPE: Weaken

CONCLUSION: People's decision not to exercise costs society a lot of money.

REASONING: Sedentary people cost society $1650 on average.

ANALYSIS: We need to find a reason why reducing sedentary-ness won't reduce costs, or why we can't reduce sedentary-ness.a

The correct answer shows that sedentary-ness is often not a choice. Further, the poor health that causes sedentary-ness could also be the cause of the increased costs associated with being sedentary.

_____

A. This doesn't tell us whether those people are classified as sedentary or not. And it doesn't weaken the argument that being sedentary costs us money.
B. This might explain why some people are sedentary. It doesn't weaken the argument that they cost us money.
C. **CORRECT.** This shows that bad health (which costs a lot) *causes* sedentary-ness. So being sedentary is often an effect, not a cause.
D. Of course. But this doesn't weaken the idea that we cost the system more by choosing to exercise less.
E. This shows that exercise can make us feel good. But it doesn't weaken the idea that laziness costs society money.

Question 26

QUESTION TYPE: Sufficient Assumption

CONCLUSION: Vermeer was not constrained by lack of props. He could have had as many props as he wished.

REASONING: Vermeer used few props, but they were expensive.

ANALYSIS: "Dearth" means lack of. The correct answer tells us that if the lack of props caused the lack of variety then we wouldn't have seen expensive props.

But we *did* see expensive props in the paintings. So there must not have been a lack of props.

_____

A. This could actually weaken the argument by showing the Vermeer lacked props.
B. This doesn't support the idea that Vermeer had access to many other props as well. Maybe he only had a few.
C. This could support the idea that Vermeer *didn't* have access to many props. The ones he used came from family.
D. This could explain why Vermeer used those items. But it doesn't explain why he didn't also use other items, and it doesn't let us prove that Vermeer had easy access to other props.
E. **CORRECT.** We *did* see expensive props, so this answer choice tells us there was no "dearth."

Test 36
Section II - Reading Comprehension
Passage 1 - Computer Communities?
Questions 1-6

Paragraph Summaries

1. Description of traditional communities. Introduction of claim that computer conferences are communities.
2. Evidence for treating computer conferences as communities.
3. Reasons computer conferences aren't really communities

Analysis

The final point is important: real communities are somewhat random compared to a computer conference of people who all share the same interests. This makes real communities diverse, in the broadest sense of the word (education, income, taste, etc.) This comes up again and again.

(Though note that real world communities do also tend to segregate based on education, income and even shared interest in certain topics. That's has no relevance to the questions though)

Question 1

DISCUSSION: The main point is that computer conferences aren't communities, even though some argue otherwise.

––––––––––––––

A. The passage is arguing *against* the idea that conferences are communities. This slightly supports the opposite point.

B. This is absurd. No one said computer *conferences* pose a big threat. It's technology in general that threaten communities. Computer conferences are a tiny part of technology. (lines 4-8)

C. The passage didn't say that conference members couldn't be respectful and polite. But conferences don't have the diversity of real communities; that's the main point. See lines 55-60.

D. CORRECT. Conferences aren't necessarily *bad,* but they can never replace actual communities. It's the main point of the third paragraph, and the first two paragraphs just lead up to this, by introducing the opposing claim.

E. The author never said what would happen if computer conferences became diverse. They were mainly talking about present conferences.

Question 2

DISCUSSION: Communities are random groups of people, and therefore they are diverse (lines 55-59). They are usually located in the same place, and people treat each other well because they depend on each other (lines 1-5).

It also seems important that community members know each other for a while, and they meet each other repeatedly.

_____

A. This sounds like a random group of people who are in the same place. Presumably they treat each other well too; their survival depends on it.
B. We're not told what the political organization is. There are some that are pretty diverse in their views. Since the students are all at the same place, and are diverse, this sounds like a community.
C. **CORRECT.** These doctors are meeting each other only *once*. They're all from the same demographic group: doctors. Doctors tend to be well-off, well-educated and scientifically minded; they're not a very diverse group in that sense. And though these doctors are from different hospitals, hospitals tend to be very similar.
D. These teachers depend on each other, so presumably they treat each other well, as community members should. They come from diverse neighborhoods, and they are all in one location. Sounds like a community.
E. This sounds like a diverse group that depends on each other. They meet repeatedly in the same place.

Question 3

DISCUSSION: The author admits that conferences have some of the qualities of a community. By granting that the other side has a point, their argument is stronger.

_____

A. No! The *author* is the one who claims that computer conferences discriminate. They say this on lines 44-46.
B. That claim was made on lines 36-37. The author isn't introducing a claim that came much earlier in the passage.
C. The author *is* arguing that computer conferences *aren't* communities. They agree with this claim!
D. Huh? The author says that conferences *can* be respectful. How could that possibly be evidence that conferences sometimes *aren't* respectful?
E. **CORRECT.** The author acknowledges the strong point of the other side's argument. Then they go on to argue that conferences are nonetheless not communities. It makes for a stronger argument.

Question 4

DISCUSSION: The author's main argument comes in the fourth paragraph. Conferences aren't diverse. Real communities are (lines 55-60).

———————————————

A. The author admits conferences can be respectful, on lines 42-43.
B. This is the same as A. The author agrees that computer conferences can be respectful.
C. If many people agreed to live same place and talk to each other using only computers, the author still might not think they were a community. A community has to be random.
D. The author thinks the opposite. A community needs educational and economic *diversity*.
E. **CORRECT.** Computer conferences are respectful, but they aren't diverse. Real communities have a tougher challenge: they must be respectful despite being diverse.

Question 5

DISCUSSION: The second paragraph argues that computer conferences are communities. The author is being fair and presenting the opposing argument. This allows the author to make a stronger counterargument in the third paragraph.

———————————————

A. The second paragraph doesn't say anything about the origins of computer conferences. Don't pick nonsense answers.
B. The advocates in the first paragraph said that conferences *are* communities. It's on line 15. Don't pick this type of answer without double-checking what the advocates say.
C. **CORRECT.** The second paragraph gives us the reasons the conference advocates think that conferences are communities. The author then argues against this view in the third paragraph.
D. Nope. If this were true, the argument would have this structure: claim, objection, counterpoint (supporting claim). But the actual structure goes like this: claim, support for claim, counterargument to the claim.
E. Not at all. The third paragraph said conferences *aren't* communities, so the second paragraph did a poor job of anticipating what would be said.

Question 6

DISCUSSION: The author argued that normal communities were diverse, and computer conferences weren't diverse.

———————————————

A. So? Conferences still might not be diverse. We want *actual* diversity, not mere support for diversity.
B. **CORRECT.** This does it. Soon, computer conferences could include people of diverse backgrounds. That would make them more like real communities. The argument's main point was that conferences aren't diverse. (lines 55-60)
C. So? This tells us computer conference members are polite within their own communities. But it doesn't show that computer conferences are communities. The main critique was that conferences weren't diverse.
D. So? There's more to a community than feeling comfortable when dealing with others. A community needs diversity too.
E. So? Real communities might still be good enough at communicating. "More" successful is very vague. Are conferences 50% more successful, or 0.5% more successful?

Passage 2 - Renaissance England
Questions 7-14

Paragraph Summaries

1. Linguists studying the Renaissance ignore technical works written in Latin.
2. But intellectual historians can't understand Latin. So few people study technical works written in Latin.
3. Reasons for the failures: few linguists understand science or other non-literary subjects. Few technical specialists know Latin.

Analysis

This is a neutral, descriptive passage. It tells us about a problem: historians of the Renaissance rarely understand both Latin *and* technical subjects (e.g. law, science, theology). So few people can study the Latin originals of important technical works written during the English Renaissance.

Literary texts written in Latin have been studied. Technical works in English are well understood. But scholars have a big blind spot. Nobody is studying the important technical works that were written in Latin.

This means we misunderstand the Renaissance. England was linked to the European continent. Its intellectuals communicated with intellectuals on the continent who wrote in Latin. We miss all of this if we focus on works written in English.

Question 7

DISCUSSION: The main point is that few people both understand Latin *and* have the technical knowledge to read the texts.

_____

A. No, the main point is that there *hasn't been enough* analysis of those important works.
B. Line 4 says these authors wrote in English. We don't know if they wrote in Latin too.
C. This isn't true. People have studied *literary* Latin from the Renaissance. The passage never claimed that scholars studied only Roman Latin texts. Scholars might have studied medieval Latin texts, for example.
D. Nope. The author of the passage doesn't care *who* analyzes literary works, as long as *someone* does. The problem is that *no one* is studying technical Latin works.
E. **CORRECT.** "Academic specialization" refers to the fact that some people know Latin, and some people have technical knowledge, but few people have technical knowledge *and* know Latin.

Question 8

DISCUSSION: There were two types of scholars. The first group were the literary scholars who knew Latin but only studied literature. The second group were the technical scholars who studied specialized topics. But this group only studied works written in English.

This question is talking about the *first* group: scholars who read Latin works. They read literature.

––––––––––––––––––––

A. The is true of the group that does *not* read Latin works. The question is only talking about the group that *does* read Latin.
B. CORRECT. The neglected Latin texts are those that deal with law, science, etc. The literary scholars haven't been trained to understand science.
C. Not true. The specialists who study Latin do understand Latin. But they don't understand the technical subjects of many important works, and so no one analyzes those works.
D. No! *Few* people have studied books that deal with law and medicine. Only literary works written in Latin have been studied.
E. This is making stuff up. We're never told if those writers wrote in Latin. Line 4 says they wrote in English.

Question 9

DISCUSSION: See lines 37-42. English scholars studied and spoke Latin. They followed what happened in Europe, where authors wrote in Latin.

––––––––––––––––––––

A. The passage says English scholars were fluent in Latin (lines 37-39), so there's no support for this answer.
B. Lines 37-39 imply that the English were just as skilled at Latin as people who lived in continental Europe. The passage never said that Europeans taught the English Latin.
C. This sounds very good, but it says that the writers had *different* concerns. Oops. Lines 45-46 say that writers in England had the *same* concerns as people elsewhere.
D. CORRECT. Line 37 says that scholars ignore the Latin culture of Renaissance England. And they've ignored the links English scholars had with the continent. So it's likely true that the intellectual bonds between England and the continent were stronger than modern scholars tend to realize.
E. The whole point of the article is that modern scholars *underemphasize* the intellectual ties between Renaissance Britain and the rest of the European continent.

Question 10

DISCUSSION: Those writers are famous, and the works they wrote in English are famous. Everyone has heard of Shakespeare. Most people believe Shakespeare to be one of the greatest playwrights of all history.

Lines 4-6 say that these famous authors aren't the only important authors of the English Renaissance. This is a bit *shocking*, given how important we think Shakespeare is.

_____

A. Huh? The passage doesn't mention non-fiction, or "imaginative" works, whatever that means. Reread the relevant section of the passage first, and you'll never be tempted by this type of nonsense answer.

B. The passage never said that Shakespeare *didn't* revolutionize Western thought. They just said that other Renaissance authors were also important.

C. Look all you want through lines 1-6. This simply isn't mentioned there. Don't choose nonsense answers. This phrase was mentioned in line 35: the passage is trying to trick your brain into remembering something it saw in a different place.

D. **CORRECT.** Most people think of Shakespeare as the leading figure of the English Renaissance, and that's why the passage mentioned him. It's surprising to hear that there are English Latin works as important as Shakespeare's plays.

E. The Latin writings of these authors (if they had any) aren't mentioned. Line 4 says they wrote in English.

Question 11

DISCUSSION: The "English-language writings" are the technical works mentioned in the second paragraph. "Intellectual" historians in this passage refers to historians who study works of science, theology and law.

_____

A. Latin language specialists might think that the technical works are valuable. The only reason they don't read them is because they lack technical expertise. (lines 20-21)

B. Hard to say. We know that the Latin works were influential. But that doesn't mean that English works *weren't* influential. Binns' main point is that we need to study all important Renaissance works, no matter which language they are written in.

C. **CORRECT.** "Superficially coherent" means that everything seems to make sense, but that the historians are missing the deeper meaning. Which is true; the historians haven't noticed the Latin works they should be studying, even if the English works all seem to fit together, as suggested by line 35.

D. No one compares English-language writings to those from the European content. This answer just makes stuff up.

E. Binns probably thinks the English works should be studied *together* with Latin works. How else can we understand the intellectual culture of Renaissance England?

Question 12

DISCUSSION: Lines 32-33 say that few historians read the original Latin works.

A. The author never compared science to theology. They were just examples of disciplines with important Latin works.
B. Lines 32-33 say that some translations *were* made. But it is that its usually better to read the original than a translation, and there may be some important works that haven't been translated.
C. **CORRECT.** Scholars who know Latin can't understand the technical subject matter. Scholars who understand science can't read Latin. So few people can read scientific books written in Latin.
D. Huh? This *could* be true, but it's never mentioned. It seems just as likely that English university students studied other subjects apart from science. They probably studied older books.
E. Lines 35-37 say that scholars underestimate how much the English influenced writers in Europe. It sounds like many scientific books were written in Latin, in England, during the Renaissance.

Question 13

DISCUSSION: Milton and Newton are two contrasting examples. It's easy to find scholarship on Milton's Latin poems. It's hard to find anyone who understands Newton's Latin writings. You need to understand science *and* Latin, which is rare.

A. Are Milton's works the easiest to understand of all Renaissance Latin works? Are Newton's the hardest? We don't know. All we know is that Newton's works haven't been studied much, and Milton's have been.
B. Both Milton and Newton wrote in *Latin*.
C. Both Milton and Newton were *English*. There's no comparison made between them and other Europeans.
D. Most people agree that both Milton and Newton are worthy of respect. But while many people have studied Milton's Latin works, few people have read Newton's works in the original Latin.
E. **CORRECT.** This is mentioned in lines 23-27. It's easy to get help if you're reading Milton's Latin, but you won't find much help if you're trying to read Newton.

Question 14

DISCUSSION: The main point of the passage is that Renaissance scholarship has a problem: scholars ignore many important Latin works.

A. Which new approaches? There are problems mentioned, but no solutions are offered.
B. Which views? There is only the author's view: we should study non-literary Renaissance Latin works.
C. Which two views are in dispute? If you can't name the dispute, you shouldn't pick this answer choice. (No one is arguing that Renaissance Latin isn't important)
D. **CORRECT.** The problem is that there are few scholars who can study technical works written in Latin during the Renaissance.
E. Which author? And which misconceptions? These are the questions you have to ask yourself. Binns doesn't criticize anyone in particular.

Passage 3 - Hormones and Behavior
Questions 15-20

Paragraph Summaries

1. **Part 1 of Paragraph 1:** Hormones can affect behavior, not just biological functions.
2. **Part 2 of Paragraph 1:** Description of how hormones balance salt and water in the body.
3. **Part 1 of Paragraph 2:** Salt and water levels can change within certain limits.
4. **Part 2 of Paragraph 2:** Past those limits, biological and behavioral changes occur.

Analysis

This is a dense, scientific passage. But the underlying ideas aren't very hard. The LSAT is counting on you to panic and think you'll never understand the science. You shouldn't let it trick you into not even trying.

There's no sense answering the questions on this type of passage if you don't understand what you've read. So before moving on, read the parts you didn't understand again, until you do understand. Go line by line, figure out what it is saying, and gradually understand the whole thing.

This may seem slow. But that's the point of studying. The more you work at understanding scientific language, the easier it will get. You *need* to train that skill now, so that on test day you'll do better on a science passage if you do get a hard one.

Science majors can ignore everything I wrote above. You may have been wondering why these questions are easy. That's because science passages are usually the easiest passages, *once* you understand what they're saying.

Analysis Continued

Now, for an actual analysis, in plain English. It seems hormones can control stuff within our bodies *and* change our behavior. You may have heard that testosterone makes you more aggressive (which is changed behavior). It's the same principle.

Salt concentration is the example in the passage. Homeostasis means keeping things the same. In this context, it means salt concentration is the same inside and outside of cells. If there's too much salt, we try to get rid of salt, and drink water. If there isn't enough salt, we suddenly have to go to the restroom to get rid of excess water.

Osmolality means how much salt is in the water in our bodies. Osmoregulation is how the body makes sure the salt balance is right. Solutes means salt in our body fluids, more or less. Plasma means blood. So plasma osmolality means how much salt is in our blood.

So if you eat a lot of salt, you'll get thirsty, and the body will try to conserve water. Thirst only comes as a last resort (lines 55-58). If you drink a lot of water or don't eat salt, you won't be thirsty, and you'll have to pee.

Since the hormones cause you to be thirsty/not thirsty or use the bathroom, they influence behavior. That's all the passage is saying.

Question 15

DISCUSSION: The main point is that several types of hormones can influence behavior. We used to think that only reproductive hormones did this. But now we know that peptide and steroid hormones affect whether we are thirsty/crave salt. This is clear from lines 1-13.

These changes in behavior occur along with changes inside the body that force us to preserve/get rid of water and salt, depending on our needs.

———————————

A. This is just a fact about how the body regulates salt. It isn't the main point.
B. This is only part of the example. It ignores how the body gets rid of extra water, and it misses the main point, which is that hormones can influence behavior.
C. Not quite. We already know reproductive hormones could influence behavior. See lines 1-6.
D. CORRECT. Close enough. This covers the explanation of salt regulation given in the second paragraph and the second half of the first paragraph. And it covers the main point of the first part of the first paragraph: hormones can influence behavior.
E. We're not told that hormones are the *only* thing that regulates thirst and taste for saltiness. And we're not told whether the *way* hormones affect behavior is the same in both cases.

Question 16

DISCUSSION: This is from lines 1-6. The point was that we once thought these were the only hormones that influenced behavior. We now realize steroid and peptide hormones also influence behavior.

———————————

A. There's no mention of the history of that research. There are no dates, scientists or important discoveries mentioned.
B. Not at all! The passage makes clear that hormones influence behavior in more ways than we realized.
C. CORRECT. Most earlier research focussed on reproductive hormones. This gives context; it shows that the new research is broader.
D. The passage doesn't say the old ideas about reproductive hormones were wrong. It's just we now know there are *other types* of hormones that also influence behavior.
E. Which procedures are described? And which 'recent' research is mentioned? None of this happens. (No one said the research on reproductive hormones was recent.)

Question 17

DISCUSSION: Vasopressin is mentioned on line 41, but you should read 36-43 for context. It's confusing, but don't look at the answers until you understand it. Once you understand it, the answer is very clear.

In plain English: if you drink lots of water, salt concentration in the blood gets low. So the body tries to get you to pee out water. Your body stops producing vasopressin. Vasopressin holds water in the kidneys. So when it goes away, you go to the restroom.

So if you have to get rid of water, you stop producing vasopressin. But if you need to keep water, your body will probably produce more vasopressin.

_____

A. Steroid hormones aren't mentioned in lines 36-43. This is just here to mislead you. As far as we know, they have nothing to do with vasopressin.
B. **CORRECT.** If you need to keep water, your body will probably increase vasopressin production. The passage already told us we stop producing it if we need to lose water. (Increased osmolality just means we have higher salt concentrations.)
C. Same as A. Steroid hormones are never mentioned in lines 36-43. And more plasma is a fancy way of saying more blood. The passage doesn't say vasopressin does *that*.
D. None of this is mentioned in lines 36-43. They're just using scientific words to confuse you. Vasopressin affects *water*, not salt. And steroid hormones aren't mentioned in this section; vasopressin is a peptide.
E. We're only told that vasopressin is blocked when an animal drinks too much. When an animal is thirsty, some other hormone might take charge.

Question 18

DISCUSSION: The point of the passage is to describe new research: steroid and peptide hormones can affect behavior.

_____

A. **CORRECT.** The new information is that other types of hormones can affect behavior.
B. This is tempting. But lines 1-6 don't say that everyone assumed only reproductive hormones can affect behavior. Previous research focussed on that area, but who knows why? Maybe it was not technically possible to research other hormones back then.
C. There's been no reinterpretation of the old research on reproductive hormones. All we know is that there is *new* research on steroid and peptide hormones. We don't know if this changes the old research or simply adds new information.
D. The theory that hormones can affect behavior is hardly new. Now we just know that more types of hormones can affect behavior.
E. What's the new approach? The passage is mainly focussed on discussing research *results*. There's no mention of method or process.

Question 19

DISCUSSION: In plain English, this is asking which processes are used to manage salt concentrations.

There are four main things that can affect salt concentration: eating salt, losing salt, conserving/drinking water (or thirst) or losing water. Hunger has nothing to do with it, as far as we know.

_____

A. CORRECT. Hunger is never mentioned.
B. See lines 49-51.
C. See lines 40-41.
D. See lines 39-40.
E. See line 46 and lines 12-13. (eating salty foods).

Question 20

DISCUSSION: A second question on the same topic. They're trying to take it easy on us. Vasopressin keeps water in the kidneys (lines 41-42). So holding back vasopressin gets rid of water. This means that other body fluids such as blood are less diluted.

The correct answer is tricky, because it's worded indirectly. C is also tricky. It describes what happens when we *do* have vasopressin.

_____

A. Nope. There's only one thing said about vasopressin: it keeps water in the kidneys.
B. CORRECT. Dilution is a reduction in concentration levels. If a body fluid (like blood) has been diluted, that means it has more water. Blocking vasopressin gets rid of water, and this means body fluids are less diluted by water. See lines 41-42.
C. This is what happens when we *have* vasopressin. This is the *opposite* of what happens when we withhold vasopressin.
D. This is never mentioned.
E. Steroid hormones are never mentioned along with vasopressin. Vasopressin is a peptide hormone.

Passage 4 - Law in South Africa
Questions 21-16

Paragraph Summaries

1. South Africa now has a legal system that protects individual rights. This requires some adjustment.
2. It's hard to create a rights-based legal system from scratch. So judges look to foreign rulings, but must take care not to misuse them.
3. The government has to convince the people that the law is on their side now.

Analysis

This passage is much easier, after the hard science passage. I'm not generally a fan of skipping, but passages like this provide a good argument for it. If you didn't have time to do this passage, you missed some easier points.

Question 21

DISCUSSION: The main point is to describe some of the benefits and challenges of South Africa's switch to a rights-based legal system.

_____

A. Citizens opposed the law. But surely *judges* didn't oppose the law, even under apartheid. Their job is to uphold the law.
B. This is sort of true, but it's hardly the main point. Even if individuals challenge parliament, there are many other problems with the legal system. This answer choice doesn't mention the lack of precedents and other problems.
C. This is *true,* but the passage had another point: the transition will be difficult.
D. **CORRECT.** The transition is happening, even though there are difficulties. The passage gives us an overview of this process.
E. This ignores the first and third paragraphs. Precedent was only mentioned in the second paragraph.

Question 22

DISCUSSION: Lines 10-19 describe the shift in South Africa's legal system. Parliament used to be supreme. Now courts can overturn laws on constitutional grounds.

The passage argues there are difficulties to this system, but that doesn't mean the author thinks we should go back to the old system.

_____

A. Lines 10-19 also mentioned the role parliament had under the *old* constitution.
B. The passage did say the new system would be difficult, but it never argued we should go back to the old system. Certainly not in lines 10-19.
C. **CORRECT.** In the old days, you had to obey parliament's law. Now parliament can't make a law if it violates the constitution. If it does do that, citizens can ask the constitutional court to strike down the law. This is a completely different system.
D. Same as B. The passage *did* say there would be difficulties, but it never said that making the court was a bad idea. Lines 10-19 definitely don't criticize the switch.
E. We're not told why there is a bill of rights. Presumably it was because the old constitution was repressive, but the passage doesn't say, and certainly not in lines 10-19.

Question 23

DISCUSSION: The author seems somewhat hopeful; they never say the new system is a bad idea. But they are aware that there are many difficulties involved in switching legal systems.

A. If this were true, then the passage likely would have said that the new system should be abandoned.
B. Same as A.
C. Doubtful. Why would someone write a whole article about something they didn't care about? The article seems well researched and written with care.
D. CORRECT. The author seems to like the new system, but they emphasize that there will be some difficulty.
E. The *entire* passage says how hard everything will be. That hardly shows complete confidence in the new system.

Question 24

DISCUSSION: This is mentioned in lines 12-14. Under Apartheid, parliament could pass new laws to overturn judgments they disagreed with.

A. There was no constitutional court before; it's new. (See lines 14-16)
B. This is also something in the *new* system. Citizens weren't very powerful under apartheid. (See lines 20-23)
C. CORRECT. Lines 12-14 say this directly.
D. The bill of rights is *new*. It didn't exist in the old system.
E. This might have been true, but it's not mentioned. We only know that parliament could get rid of decisions it didn't like. (lines 12-14).

Question 25

DISCUSSION: The last paragraph mentions another problem: citizens think the law is their enemy. The reasons for this are discussed: the law once was used to oppress citizens.

Examples are given of how people act now: people avoid taxes and cheat the government.

Then the solution is given: convince the citizens the law has changed.

With these structure questions, focus on one sentence at a time, and eliminate answers when part of them is wrong.

―――――――――――――

A. The solution comes at the end of the paragraph, not the start.
B. There were no previous methods mentioned.
C. There are no other solutions mentioned. And this ignores the reasons why citizens mistrust the law, and the examples of how they cheat the law.
D. The first two parts are backwards, and the last part is wrong: citizens do still think the law is their enemy.
E. CORRECT. The problem is that citizens mistrust the law. The examples are: disobeying the law or avoiding taxes. The solution is to educate citizens that the law is now their friend.

Question 26

DISCUSSION: The scholars are mentioned in lines 34-39. They warn that relying on foreign decisions is dangerous. Judges might not understand *why* a foreign judge made their decision. It might be based on local factors that don't apply to South Africa.

―――――――――――――

A. CORRECT. Lines 38-39 say this directly.
B. Mistrust of the law isn't even mentioned until the third paragraph. It's not what the scholars are talking about.
C. The scholars didn't say a correct interpretation was impossible. They just warned against applying foreign law out of context.
D. The scholars didn't say looking to foreign law was *automatically* wrong. They just warned it could be dangerous.
E. The scholars' main concern was applying the decisions out of context, as said in lines 38-39.

Test 36
Section III - Logical Reasoning

Question 1

QUESTION TYPE: Paradox

PARADOX: Laws that order the removal of lead will lead to children ingesting more lead.

ANALYSIS: Three of the wrong answers don't even talk about lead. And C can't account for the increase.

The right answer explains that disturbing the lead will make it easier to ingest.

A. This shows why we should be cautious with lead-free paints. But it doesn't explain why removing lead causes more lead.
B. This doesn't tell us anything about *lead*.
C. This still doesn't explain why removing lead paint will *increase* the amount of lead children ingest.
D. **CORRECT.** If we disturb the lead then it is easier for children to ingest it, even if there is less lead in total.
E. Same as B. This tells us nothing about *lead*.

Question 2

QUESTION TYPE: Weaken

CONCLUSION: Newspaper sales will decline once these electronic news services arrive.

REASONING: These services will lead people get their news faster and more efficiently.

ANALYSIS: This shows that this LSAT is a bit dated. This already happened in real life, and electronic news services (e.g. RSS readers, blogs) plus Craigslist *did* cause a huge decline in newspaper sales and revenue.

But, we have to weaken the argument anyway. The right answer points out that sometimes people *don't* want super-specific news. It's nice to idly browse.

A. **CORRECT.** This is one reason newspaper sales still survive today despite the challenge from the internet. It can be nice to leaf through a paper.
B. This is to be expected: newspaper prices vary too. But this doesn't explain why electronic news services won't beat newspapers.
C. If 30% of people have never used newspapers then those people are irrelevant. The stimulus is talking about whether newspaper will lose already existing readers.
D. This strengthens the argument by showing that the electronic services won't cost more.
E. This strengthens the argument: it will be easy to switch to electronic news services.

Question 3

QUESTION TYPE: Main Conclusion

CONCLUSION: Athlete champions need to have mastery of technique.

REASONING: They all have about the same muscular strength.

ANALYSIS: This argument is ok, but it could be better. At the top level, a tiny difference in strength might make the difference between winning and losing.

The main conclusion is that technique is a requirement (necessary, but not sufficient.)

A. No. All champion athletes have mastery but other people might have mastery as well.
B. The argument implies this is true, but it isn't the conclusion.
C. **CORRECT.** The last sentence is the conclusion. Strength alone is not enough.
D. This is true, but the main point is that technique is required to use muscular strength most efficiently.
E. This is true, but the main point is that you *need* good technique if you are to be a champion.

Question 4

QUESTION TYPE: Point At Issue

ARGUMENTS: Mary argues that computers will let us learn about things without needing to talk to experts.

Joyce argues that computers will lead to more and more specialized knowledge. We'll need experts to interpret that knowledge.

ANALYSIS: Their point of disagreement is whether we will have more of a need for experts (Joyce) or less of a need (Mary)

A. Mary doesn't say whether or not she even thinks more knowledge will disseminate. She might think computers contribute quite a bit, but we'll still need expert interpretation.
B. **CORRECT.** Joyce says people will need to turn to experts and Mary thinks computers will reduce the need for experts.
C. They agree on this point. It's just that Joyce doesn't think ordinary people will understand the information that computers make available.
D. Neither of them talked about a dependency on *computers*.
E. Joyce didn't say that only *computer* experts could explain information to people.

Question 5

QUESTION TYPE: Weaken

CONCLUSION: It's unlikely that Loux would have objected to Zembaty selling the farm rather than giving it to Loux's grandson.

REASONING: Loux never said what should be done with the farm and she didn't seem interested in it.

ANALYSIS: We need a reason why Loux might have objected to the sale, even though she didn't care about the farm.

The correct answer shows that Loux's grandson might have liked the farm even if Loux didn't care for it. Loux might therefore have objected to the sale on her grandson's behalf. She liked her grandson.

A. This strengthens the argument for selling the farm. It was required.
B. This sounds good, but it doesn't mean that the grandson had to have the *farm*. Loux could have just left him a lot of money instead.
C. This strengthens the argument that Loux would not have objected to a sale.
D. This has nothing to do with whether or not the farm ought to have been sold. It's irrelevant, and can't weaken the argument. The cause of a debt doesn't have to be the solution.
E. **CORRECT.** This supports the idea that Loux would have wanted other properties sold instead so that Loux's grandson could have the farm.

Question 6

QUESTION TYPE: Role in Argument

CONCLUSION: It's hard to get rid of our country's chronic food shortages.

REASONING: Direct food aid would drive our producers out of business, worsening the problem. Long term capital investment could cause inflation that would make food hard to buy.

ANALYSIS: This might be a good argument, but we need more information. The argument hasn't excluded all other possibilities. It just shows that two possible methods won't work. The two methods (direct aid and foreign capital) have nothing to do with each other. A lot of the wrong answer choices suggest they do.

The claim about foreign capital shows that one alternative won't work well.

A. The official didn't say if self-sufficiency definitely should be a goal. They just said that direct aid would hurt the possibility of self-sufficiency. But it could be that self-sufficiency is too hard to set as a goal.
B. **CORRECT.** It is one of two pieces of evidence supporting the claim.
C. Not at all: there's no link between those two things.
D. No. The two claims are independent of each, and they support the conclusion that it won't be easy to solve the food crisis.
E. No. The last two sentences are completely separate from each other.

Question 7

QUESTION TYPE: Strengthen

CONCLUSION: We should change work days to be more flexible.

REASONING: Sleep deprivation causes a lot of problems.

ANALYSIS: Most of the wrong answer choices talk about the *amount* of hours worked. But the doctor didn't mention that. They proposed working the same number of hours, but *flexibly*.

A. Overwork is the *amount* of work. The doctor didn't recommend changing the amount. He recommended changing *when* we work. But we could still work long hours, flexibly.
B. **CORRECT.** This shows a connection between flexible hours and sleeping more. The argument didn't make that connection.
C. So? This doesn't help us prove that people would sleep more with flexible hours.
D. The doctor wasn't talking about the number of hours in the workweek. They were talking about when we work those hours. E.g. 9-5 vs. working 10-2 along with 4-8. Both options total 8 hours.
E. Show me where the doctor mentioned the *length* of the workday.

Question 8

QUESTION TYPE: Method of Reasoning

CONCLUSION: The criticisms of the claim are unfounded.

REASONING: "True Belief formed by a reliable process → Knowledge" is the claim.

Some people argue that even if clairvoyance produced a true belief by a reliable process, we still wouldn't believe it.

The Essayist agrees that we wouldn't believe the claims, but argues that it is only because we don't trust clairvoyance is a reliable process.

But *if* we believed in clairvoyance then we would also accept that it produced knowledge.

ANALYSIS: This argument makes a good point. The example of clairvoyance just shows that we don't believe in the reliability of clairvoyance. It can't disprove anything about a general theory of how knowledge is produced *when we believe* in a process. That's because we don't believe in the process of clairvoyance.

Our disbelief in clairvoyance's claims might not be because we have a different theory of knowledge.

A. **CORRECT.** Our beliefs about the predictions of clairvoyance are the reason we don't trust the claims. It isn't because we have a different theory of knowledge.
B. The essayist *agrees* that we reject the claims of clairvoyance. So it hasn't allowed us to form knowledge (true beliefs.)
C. Same as B. The essayist *agrees* that we reject the claims of clairvoyance. And the argument didn't say such claims are wrong.
D. The essayist argues for a single definition of knowledge: A true belief formed by a reliable process results in knowledge.
E. The argument says that clairvoyance *could* be a case of knowledge if we believed it, so it can fit the definition.

Question 9

QUESTION TYPE: Main Conclusion

CONCLUSION: We shouldn't fully condemn Hogan's actions.

REASONING: Hogan thought that Winters was the robber.

ANALYSIS: Basically, Hogan really, really hurt Winters. But he did so because he thought Winters was the robber. So the argument asks us to partially excuse Hogan due to his honest motives.

A. This goes too far. Hogan *is* responsible, but we should show some leniency because Hogan had good motives.
B. No. Hogan is responsible. But the fact that Hogan thought Winters was the robber means that Hogan's violent attack wasn't merely psychopathic.
C. **CORRECT.** We can give Hogan some credit because he thought he was wounding a criminal, rather than an innocent man.
D. This is true, but its just information that supports the conclusion that we shouldn't fully condemn Hogan's violent actions.
E. The argument only said the actions were reprehensible *other things equal*. But other things aren't equal: Hogan should be partially excused because he thought Winters was the robber.

Question 10

QUESTION TYPE: Relationship between arguments

ARGUMENTS: Peter argues that farmers should give plants just enough water and no more. Otherwise insects will feed on their leaves.

Jennifer adds that a plant with little water will also produce pesticidal toxins and further reduce the amount of insects that want to eat it.

ANALYSIS: Jennifer supports Peter by adding completely new information. Her information doesn't have anything to do with Peter's reasoning. It adds new information that supports the conclusion by another method.

A. Not quite. Jennifer's information doesn't have anything to do with the idea that plant leaves will become tougher in texture.
B. Nope. Peter's argument is fine on its own. Jennifer's argument does support Peter, but by providing a completely new reason.
C. Jennifer introduces a *new* premise that has nothing to do with Peter's.
D. Jennifer's info supports Peter's *conclusion*, but has no effect on the premises.
E. **CORRECT.** If plants produce pesticides when they don't have too much water than we shouldn't give them too much water. This has nothing to do with leaf texture - it's independent from Peter's reasoning.

Question 11

QUESTION TYPE: Strengthen

CONCLUSION: Peter's conclusion is that we shouldn't water plants too much.

REASONING: Plants will develop tougher leaves if they have *too little* water. Insects prefer these leaves to leaves that have lots and lots of water.

ANALYSIS: Peter is arguing for giving plants only a small amount of water. This could be harmful. His only evidence is that *drought-stressed* plants get eaten less. Drought-stressed sounds bad.

The correct answer tells us that being drought stressed isn't as bad as being eaten.

_____

A. This doesn't matter. Obviously different crops will react differently. The question is: how will an individual species react to changes in water levels?
B. This doesn't tell us if abundant watering is a good or a bad idea.
C. **CORRECT.** Otherwise, we might be hurting the plants through lack of water even as we helped them avoid getting eaten by insects.
D. This doesn't affect what farmers should try to do when they *can* control water levels.
E. This comparison is between two different types of bugs. It's irrelevant. We want to know whether the same insect species is more or less likely to feed when water is scarce.

Question 12

QUESTION TYPE: Sufficient Assumption

CONCLUSION: People cannot feel secure under vague laws.

REASONING: Vague laws restrict freedom: people can't be sure if their actions are legal.

ANALYSIS: The argument goes from restricting freedom to feeling insecure. We need some kind of connection.

As always on a sufficient assumption question, the right answer must connect the premises to the necessary condition of the conclusion.

The correct answer tells us: Don't know if actions are legal → you cannot feel secure.

_____

A. **CORRECT.** Since people *don't* know if their actions are legal when laws are vague then people also can't feel secure.
B. "Might not feel secure"? That's not a very powerful answer choice. Our conclusion is that people *cannot* feel secure.
C. We're trying to conclude that people *don't* feel secure. This only tells us how to conclude that people *do* feel secure.
D. This doesn't tell us that people will necessarily feel insecure if the laws governing them are vague.
E. This gets it backwards. We get: know your actions are legal → feel secure. That doesn't help us conclude that people *don't* feel secure.

Question 13

QUESTION TYPE: Flawed Reasoning

CONCLUSION: Psychoses (unlike neuroses) have nothing to do with the environment.

REASONING: Psychoses are more easily treated with medicine than with environmental therapy.

ANALYSIS: This is a bad argument. Just because it's easier to treat something with medicine doesn't mean that no environmental factors played a role in causing the psychosis.

Just like the cause of a bacterial infection is environmental but the best treatment is often medicinal (an antibiotic.)

————————————

A. CORRECT. The argument is ignoring the possibility that environmental factors can make psychoses worse, even if medicine is the best treatment.
B. Actually, the argument's whole point is that organic conditions are best treated by medicines.
C. The argument didn't say that those conditions couldn't be treated environmentally. But the *best* treatment method is medicinal.
D. The argument did consider this. What it *failed* to consider is that you can't always infer the nature of the cause from the treatment.
E. The argument doesn't claim neuroses have no organic cause. But the conclusion is about *psychoses.*

Question 14

QUESTION TYPE: Necessary Assumption

CONCLUSION: Technological expertise wouldn't benefit students' job prospects any more than learning to read, write and study math.

REASONING: Most of the technology we use is designed to be used by non-experts.

ANALYSIS: This argument confuses *today's* technology with the technology that will be required for jobs in the future. It also ignores the possibility that technical knowledge may help you get a job even if most technology doesn't require technical knowledge.

It could be that some very important workplace technology *does* require technical knowledge (even if most *consumer* technology doesn't.)

————————————

A. This doesn't matter. What matters is how *effective* that education is.
B. This is weaker than it sounds, when you negate it. It could mean that skill in operating those machines is enhanced only 5% of the time (more than almost never.) And skill could be enhanced very, very slightly. This doesn't really affect the argument that regular education is about as good.
C. CORRECT. If most jobs *do* demand skill in operating machines intended for experts then students would benefit from technical training to operate those machines.
D. The argument isn't hurt if it would be possible for students to learn both.
E. This would be helpful, but the argument wouldn't be hurt if it was *occasionally* more useful to be technically skilled.

Question 15

QUESTION TYPE: Principle – Parallel Reasoning

PRINCIPLE: Environmentalists shouldn't be the little boy who cried wolf. If they make a mistake then people might not believe them when the situation actually becomes serious.

ANALYSIS: The principle is like the fable of the little boy who cried wolf. He lied and lied and then nobody believed him when the wolf actually came.

The principle is warning us to make sure our arguments are good now: otherwise people won't listen to us in the future.

None of the wrong answers mention future decisions.

―――――――――

A. **CORRECT.** This warns us that if we don't present our facts straight *now* then people won't listen to us in the *future*. The stimulus argued the same thing.
B. This doesn't warn about poor decisions in the future.
C. This is a good argument, but it just tells us how to persuade. It doesn't warn about future consequences.
D. This is like C. It doesn't warn us about future consequences.
E. This does warn about the future. But it doesn't warn about a future *decision*. Instead, it just argues that the future will be bad if we don't take the right action now.

Question 16

QUESTION TYPE: Necessary Assumption

CONCLUSION: Reptiles can't do complex reasoning.

REASONING: Reptiles can't always make major alterations in their behavior.

ANALYSIS: This is full of science-y words, but the reasoning isn't complex. The only piece of evidence is that reptiles can't make major changes. The argument is assuming that reptiles *could* make major changes *if* they could do complex reasoning.

The assumption is: can do complex reasoning → can make major changes.

―――――――――

A. The negation is: animals can make major changes even if they aren't capable of complex reasoning. This doesn't hurt the argument: reptiles *can't* make major changes.
B. This would be helpful, but it isn't necessary. There could be a middle ground between simple response behaviors and complex reasoning.
C. This would strengthen the argument, but it isn't necessary. There are other explanations for the reptiles' behavior apart from complex reasoning.
D. **CORRECT.** If reptiles *couldn't* make changes to their behavior *even if* they were capable of complex reasoning then this argument proves nothing. The only evidence presented is that reptiles can't make changes.
E. Even if complex reasoning and responses to stimuli could both contribute to complex behavior, it isn't clear why that should mean that reptiles can do complex reasoning.

Question 17

QUESTION TYPE: Most Strongly Supported

FACTS:

1. A general theory of art is supposed to explain any aesthetic feature of art.
2. Pre-modern theories mainly concerned themselves with painting and sculpture.
3. All pre-modern theories of art fail to explain some aesthetic features of music.

ANALYSIS: We can conclude that no pre-modern theories succeeded in fulfilling the purpose of general theories of art. (Assuming music is art)

A. This is only true of general theories that fulfill their purpose.
B. It isn't enough to explain music. All of the arts must be explained.
C. This is only true of *pre-modern* theories. Modern theories might be able to explain everything.
D. **CORRECT.** Right. No pre-modern theory could explain music, so they all fail their purpose, unless music isn't art.
E. Pre-modern theories might have been able to explain *some* aspects of music. It's just that they couldn't explain *all* aesthetic aspects.

Question 18

QUESTION TYPE: Necessary Assumption

CONCLUSION: If everyone accepts themselves as they are (and isn't dissatisfied with him or herself) then society is unlikely to be happy.

REASONING: No one can truly be happy unless they are pursuing excellence and personal change.

ANALYSIS: The argument is assuming that we can't pursue excellence unless we are dissatisfied with ourselves. That could be true, but it's something the argument ought to prove.

A. It isn't necessary. It's only necessary that no one can be happy if they aren't willing to change.
B. **CORRECT.** If people who are satisfied with themselves are just as likely to pursue excellence then they could still be happy. There wouldn't be any need to avoid accepting yourself.
C. This would weaken the argument. It's arguing that dissatisfaction *increases* the odds of finding excellence.
D. The argument seems to be saying that we should never be content with our abilities if we want to be happy. This weakens it.
E. The stimulus doesn't even mention something being painful to obtain. This is irrelevant. This answer choice plays on outside assumptions that being dissatisfied is painful.

Question 19

QUESTION TYPE: Flawed Parallel Reasoning

CONCLUSION: It is not true that whoever likes potatoes likes turnips.

REASONING: My father likes turnips but not potatoes.

ANALYSIS: The argument gets this backwards. It makes a conclusion about people who like potatoes. But the father like *turnips* and dislikes potatoes.

To prove the conclusion we would need evidence of someone who likes potatoes but dislikes turnips.

A. This is just a terrible argument. It concludes something about paperbacks based on a book that *isn't* a paperback.
   But the conclusion is that *no* paperbacks are expensive. The stimulus only said that *not all* people who ate potatoes like turnips. Two different concepts.
B. **CORRECT.** This makes the same error: It takes information about something that is not a novel and uses it to make a conclusion about novels. Ugh. And like the stimulus, it concludes "not all."
C. This is a good argument.
D. This is a good argument. It's not true that everyone who likes physics also likes pure math: Erika is at least one exception
E. This is a bad argument. The premise is: OC → CF. The conclusion reverses this and gets CF → OC. But it isn't the same error as the stimulus.

Question 20

QUESTION TYPE: Principle – Strengthen

CONCLUSION: It isn't inconsistent to support freedom of speech yet also support limiting TV violence.

REASONING: TV violence will cause more harm than the harm caused by limiting free speech in this case.

ANALYSIS: The principle must not only support the idea that we should restrict TV violence but it should also support the idea that we generally don't limit free speech. The critic is only arguing for a very small restriction on free speech.

A. This shows we should consider the consequences, but it doesn't allow us to support limiting a basic right.
B. **CORRECT.** We can support free speech while recognizing that it sometimes must be limited.
C. We have no idea if banning TV violence will make people happy. Maybe most people like TV violence.
D. This is too extreme. The critic is arguing for a very limited restriction on free speech. He does not say that free speech should always be limited anytime it causes the slightest harm.
E. This doesn't tell us if we should tolerate restrictions in *these* circumstances.

Question 21

QUESTION TYPE: Flawed Reasoning

DESCRIPTION OF THE GAME: Five numbers are drawn. If you pick the five numbers, you'll win the pot. There is not a winner every week: someone only wins if their numbers are picked.

ARGUMENTS: Sandy says it's best to play after there has been no winner for a bit. There's more money to be won.

Alex thinks that it will be harder to win because there are more players.

ANALYSIS: Alex is wrong. How likely you are to pick the winning five numbers is not affected by the number of players.

Alex said you're less likely to *win* with more players. That's incorrect. You have a 1-in-100,000 chance of winning each week, no matter how many people play (you don't need to calculate these odds of to answer the question, of course.) Multiple people can pick the winning number. That doesn't reduce your odds.

Even if you were the only one playing you would still lose for 99,999 weeks for every week you won.

If you had to pick a number between one and ten and you win 2$ if you guess right, your odds of winning aren't affected by how many people play.

_____

A. Sandy didn't say that. Sandy just said it's smart to wait for a bigger pot.
B. **CORRECT.** Alex is mistaken: the odds of picking five numbers correctly never change.
C. Sandy didn't say anything about the odds of winning. He just talked about how big the pot would be if you did win.
D. If Alex had said this, he would have been correct. The odds of winning in any given week *are* unaffected by whether anyone won the previous week.
E. Show me where Sandy talked about the odds of winning. He only talked about how big the prize would be.

Question 22

QUESTION TYPE: Necessary Assumption

CONCLUSION: Decaf can't possibly cost more because it's more expensive to produce.

REASONING: The decaffeination process is not very expensive.

ANALYSIS: The argument sounds very good. If decaf coffee doesn't cost more to process, then how could it possibly cost more to produce?

Well, there could be other costs apart from processing. The negation of the correct answer tells us that the beans could cost more to buy. That would explain the higher price.

_____

A. Actually, the argument admits that decaf costs more to process. It just doesn't cost much more.
B. It doesn't matter what causes differences in product prices as long as the cause isn't production costs in the particular case of decaf coffee.
C. Even if there was a lot of competition, the argument's point that processing doesn't cost much is still true.
D. If retail sellers *did* expect that consumers would pay more for decaf then that could explain why the price is higher. The assumption in this answer choice definitely isn't necessary.
E. **CORRECT.** If decaf beans cost a lot more then that could account for the price difference, even though the processing cost is the same.

Question 23

QUESTION TYPE: Complete the Argument

CONCLUSION: The likely conclusion is that the decline of strikes is not evidence of union weakness.

REASONING: A strong union doesn't need to call strikes. Strikes are evidence of a weak bargaining position.

ANALYSIS: The whole point of the argument is to disagree with the newspaper article's assertion that unions are weak. So the logical conclusion is that unions are not weak.

———————————

A. This is true according to the argument, but it isn't the main conclusion.
B. This has nothing to do with strikes or union strength. It just tells us that unions might form alliances.
C. **CORRECT.** The newspaper article's conclusion is unfounded. The whole argument is directed at proving the newspaper wrong.
D. The stimulus criticizes the idea that unions exist to call strikes. It's in the second sentence.
E. This doesn't tell us whether or not we have strong unions. The whole point of the argument was to answer that question.

Question 24

QUESTION TYPE: Method of Reasoning

CONCLUSION: The likely conclusion is that the decline of strikes is not evidence of union weakness.

REASONING: A strong union doesn't need to call strikes. Strikes are evidence of a weak bargaining position.

ANALYSIS: The argument agrees with the newspaper's evidence. But it adds new context that supports a different conclusion.

———————————

A. The author agrees that strikes are declining. But they think that is a sign of union strength.
B. The analysis isn't outdated. It's simply wrong. Strikes were never the main point of unions.
C. **CORRECT.** The argument re-interpreted the evidence about the lack of strikes. It argued that lack of strikes means unions are strong instead.
D. The argument didn't talk about the newspaper's motives. It just disagreed with the paper.
E. The argument didn't have anything to say about the interests of management. It only talked about the common goals of unions and other members of society. That doesn't necessarily include management.

Question 25

QUESTION TYPE: Flawed Reasoning

CONCLUSION: Diatonic music is popular *only* because of how the human brain is wired.

REASONING: Diatonic scales have dominated world music. If the popularity of a scale were based on social conditioning then we would expect diversity.

ANALYSIS: The conclusion is *very* strong. It says that social conditioning plays *no* role in our preference for diatonic scales.

That goes way too far. The argument provides some evidence that innate dispositions affect our liking of diatonic scales, but it didn't prove that we are unaffected by social conditioning.

A. "Some" people could mean 3 people out of 6 billion. It's a very vague and often useless term.
B. The argument doesn't have to explain this, because it's arguing that innate dispositions explain the popularity of *diatonic* music.
C. The argument doesn't have to explain why scales exist. It just has to explain why we all seem to prefer diatonic scales.
D. **CORRECT.** The conclusion stated that social conditioning played *no* part. That's a pretty strong conclusion. The argument only has good evidence that innate dispositions played some role.
E. Animals are not obviously relevant to why humans appreciate diatonic music. If animals showed a strong preference then we might want to investigate, but the argument isn't obliged to consider animals.

Question 26

QUESTION TYPE: Strengthen

CONCLUSION: There is a fifth universal force: mutual repulsion between particles of matter.

REASONING: This would explain why we have measured smaller amounts of gravity than theory would predict.

ANALYSIS: If you strip aside the science-talk, this question isn't hard. The correct answer simply tells us that the idea of a fifth force doesn't contradict any other established findings.

That helps by showing that the finding is plausible.

A. It doesn't matter when the equipment became available. The researchers had it and were able to use it for their experiments.
B. **CORRECT.** This would support the idea that a fifth force exists: it isn't contradicted by any other scientific findings.
C. This would weaken the idea that it is a separate universal force. We're arguing the opposite.
D. This provides an alternate explanation for the mis-measured gravity and it weakens the argument.
E. This just tells us about the context of the time when the discovery was made. It doesn't affect the argument.

Test 36
Section IV - Logic Games
Game 1 – Fruit Stand
Questions 1-6

Setup

This is a grouping game. There are only two options for the fruit. They can be in the cart, or not in the cart.

As with many in/out grouping games, you can combine all of the rules into two diagrams that cover every variable. This can seem difficult, but it isn't so hard if you take it step by step. Just keep adding little pieces until you've built a big diagram.

It's important to be able to take the contrapositives. Sometimes we can't add a rule onto a diagram the way it's given, but we can add the contrapositive. Taking the contrapositive is easy:

1. Reverse the terms.
2. Put a line through them, or remove the line if they already had one.
3. Change any "and" to "or", and vice versa.

So: A --> B becomes "not B" --> "not A".

Or, a plain English example: If you have a pet, then you have a cat or a dog (pretend it's true)

P --> C or D

Not C and not D --> no pet

The first step for most people on an in-out game should be to diagram all of their rules and contrapositives.

Note For Advanced Students: I personally just add each rule to a single large diagram, but that's an advanced tactic. If you want to try that yourself, just skip the step where I draw each of the rules individually. Instead, attach each new rule on to your existing diagram.

The advanced method is a lot faster and more efficient, but it can lead to error if you're not 100% confident with sufficient-necessary statements

Here are the four rules drawn with their contrapositives:

① K ⟶ P̸
   P ⟶ K̸

---

② T̸ ⟶ K
   K̸ ⟶ T

---

③ O ⟶ P and W   W̸ or P̸ ⟶ Ø

---

④ T or W ⟶ F   F̸ and T̸ ⟶ W̸

Now I'll show you how to combine these into a single large diagram. Start with one rule and draw it in the middle of your page. The first rule is as good as any.

Now look for another rule that you can match up to it. You need a rule that has "K" as the necessary condition, or that has "not P" as the sufficient condition. If that sounds complicated, think of it like playing dominoes: you need to make both sides match to join something together.

We can add in the second rule: "Not T leads to K"

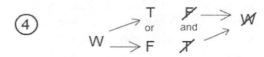

The next rule tells us that oranges have two necessary conditions. Pears are one. So without pears, we can't have oranges.

Therefore, not P leads to not O.

The next rule mentions W. W requires figs or tangerines. The contrapositive is "no F" and "no T" --> no W.

(the "not both" in the rule is useless. "Or" already implies that we could have both.")

We already have no T on this diagram. We can add no F in above.

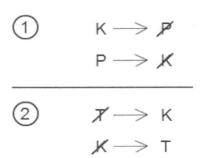

I've also connected no W to no O. It may seem superfluous, since no T also leads to no O.

But, it's possible to have T but still not have W. In that case, it's important to know that O is still out.

This diagram is done, so now you can flip it around and do the contrapositive. Remember to cross out (or remove the line from) everything you flip. Lastly, change "and" to "or" and "or" to "and."

It's also a very good idea to be looking over the rules again when you're drawing the contrapositive. It's easy to make a mistake, and a mistake is often disastrous.

The new diagram starts from O. O leads to P and W (rule 3).

P leads to not K (contrapositive of rule 1). Not K leads to T (contrapositive of rule 2). And we can simply draw in rule 4 to show that W leads to T or F.

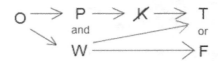

(It may seem superfluous to draw W's rule. If O is in, then we already have T, which satisfies the rule. But...O doesn't *have* to be in. Neither does P. So we should know what happens if W is in but not O or P.)

A quick note about these two rules:

(1) $K \longrightarrow \cancel{P}$

    $P \longrightarrow \cancel{K}$

_____

(2) $\cancel{T} \longrightarrow K$

    $\cancel{K} \longrightarrow T$

They look very similar, but they mean different things.

 If K is in, P is out. And vice versa. So one of K and P is *always* out. And they could also both be out. This type of rule means we can't have both of the variables in together.

The next rule says that if T is out, K is in, and vice versa. One of T and K is always *in*. And they could *both* be in.

The reason both T and K could be in (and P and K could both be out) is that you can only follow the arrows left to right. So K being in doesn't tell us anything about T.

To sum up: an important deduction here is that one of K and T is always in, and one of P and K is always out. We have at least 1 fruit always in and at most 5 in.

Main Diagram

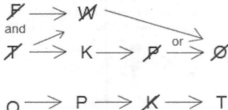

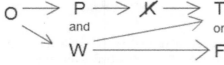

Deductions

1. One of either T or K is always in.
2. One of either P or K is always out.

Question 1

A is wrong because O leads to P *and* also W *and* also T or F.

B is CORRECT. O, W and F could all be out. Their being out isn't a sufficient condition for anything else being in.

C is wrong because O also leads to T or F, through W.

D is wrong because we can't have O without P.

E is wrong because we K leads to no O.

Question 2

On this question, you should look for a type of rule where one variable being out causes another to be in.

For example, T being out causes K to be in. So any answer without T and also without K is wrong. We always need one of K or T to be in.

There are no other rules of that type.

One of T or K always has to be in - you can't make a scenario without them. So they're the only possible right answers. **D is CORRECT.** It says T could be the only fruit for sale.

Question 3

(I'm reproducing the diagrams from the setup)

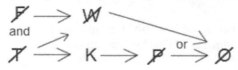

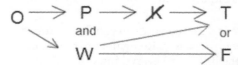

We're told that four of the scenarios work, and only 1 doesn't work. We should start with the longest string of variables: it's the one most likely to violate a rule. **E is CORRECT.** If P is in, you can't have K.

Many people think **A** can't be true. But there's no reason we can't have T and K together. K being *out* means that T is in. So they can't both be out. But they can both be *in*. K being in is *not* a sufficient condition for T being out.

None of the other answer choices have any rule violations. It's also important to see if some variables being out cause other variables to be in. There's only one pair of variables like that in this game: T and K. We always need one of them in. But **B, C** and **D** all do have either K or T.

So since those answer choices don't violate any rules, and they all have T or K, they all work.

Question 4

W being out tells us that O is also out (rule 3).

Answers **D** and **E** are tempting because they include O, but they also include other variables that could be in, so they don't work. The answer choices say that *both* variables must be missing.

A is wrong. We don't need kiwis, ever. We only need kiwis *or* tangerines.

B is wrong because we could have just one kind of fruit: T or K. Question 2 disproves this answer choice.

C is **CORRECT.** We're always missing one of either K or P. Since O and W are also out, that means we have three variables out of six automatically missing. So we can't have more than 3 variables.

D is wrong because while we don't have oranges, we could have pears as long as we don't have K.

E is wrong because it's possible to carry Kiwis.

Setup Diagrams

Question 5

This is a very funny question. I've never seen another like it...the local rule has nothing to do with the right answer.

If the stand has watermelons, then it must have T or F. But it turns out that doesn't tell us much.

Instead, we have to consider the answer choices in light of the general rules.

A could be true. The stand doesn't have to carry figs as long as it has tangerines.

B could be true. The stand doesn't need T as long as it has F.

C could be true. There's no reason the stand has to carry pears. No rule says pears must be in, ever. And there's no relation between pears and watermelons.

D could be true. Oranges require pears, but pears don't require oranges.

E cannot be true, so it is **CORRECT.** If the stand has P, then it doesn't have K. And without K, the stand needs T. So if the stand has P it must have T as well.

The funny thing is, **E** is always true, whether or not W is in. I've never seen a local rule question where the local rule is irrelevant.

Question 6

People seem to find it really hard when the LSAT asks us to change a rule. I'm not sure why. It's easy!

Get ready for this mind-blowing technique I'm about to show you.

We normally have an arrow connecting "not T" to K. Now this question is telling us to get rid of that rule.

So, just erase the arrow...

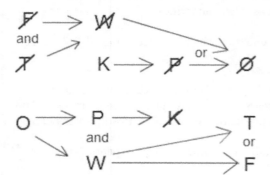

All you need is an eraser, and you're set. All the other rules apply, I just removed the connection between K and T in both diagrams.

Previously, one of K or T always had to be in. Now we've removed that rule. So nothing *has* to be in.

Pears could be the only fruit, since they no longer force T to be in. So **A** is wrong.

B is wrong because neither F nor P are sufficient conditions for any other fruit to be in.

C is **CORRECT.** If W is in, then either T or F have to be in. But they aren't, so this answer choice is wrong.

D is wrong because P and F don't force any other fruit to be in the stand. W needs F or T, but we have F in this answer choice.

E is wrong for the same reasons as **D. E** also includes O, but O just needs P and W, and they're already in.

Game 2 – Talk Show
Questions 7-13

Setup

This is a linear/grouping game. We need to figure out which order the telephone calls go in, where they're from, and whether they are live or taped.

Yikes. Fortunately, the rules let us tie down most of these variables.

First off, notice that the setup tells us how many calls come from each city. Two are from Vancouver, two from Seattle and 1 from Kelowna.

Now for the rules. I'm going to draw the first two rules together. We know that M and Isaac come before everything else. The third call is from Kelowna, and it is taped.

So M and Isaac's calls must be before the call from Kelowna.

(I'm referring to "I" as "Isaac", because "I" is confusing, sounds like I'm referring to myself)

The third call is the only call from Kelowna

The two Seattle calls are live. It doesn't matter how you draw that, as long as you remember it. Here's how I drew it:

If G and F are after H, then we know exactly where H goes: third. It can't be any other way.

There are only five spots. Isaac and M are before H; they fill the first two spots. Since G and F come after H, H must be in the middle.

We know that H calls from Kelowna. Two of the remaining calls are from Vancouver, and two are from Seattle.

The last rule says that M and F are not from Seattle. They must be from Vancouver.

That means that Isaac and G *must* be from Seattle.

Main Diagram

Remember that the Seattle calls are live.

Question 7

Another list question. Eliminate the answers by choosing a single rule and seeing which answer choices violate it. Then repeat for the next rule.

A is wrong because Isaac and M have to be the first two calls.

B is wrong because F and G must come after H.

C is wrong because Isaac and M have to be the first two calls.

D is wrong because H has to come before F and G.

E is **CORRECT.**

Question 8

A is **CORRECT.** All we know about F is that she calls from Vancouver and she is after H. There's no reason she couldn't go in 5.

B is wrong because Isaac or M have to be first.

C is wrong because Isaac or M have to be first.

D is wrong because Isaac has to be first or second.

E is wrong because M has to be first or second.

Question 9

If the first call is from Seattle, then Isaac must go first, because M calls from Vancouver. M comes second and H comes third (as always).

$$\frac{I}{S_L} \quad \frac{M}{V} \quad \frac{H}{K_T} \quad \underline{\quad} \quad \underline{\quad}$$

A can't be true, because M comes after Isaac.

B can't be true, because rule 4 says F comes *after* H.

C *must* be true, and is **CORRECT.** Isaac goes first, M goes after and Henry goes third.

D can't be true. Isaac goes first, since the first call is from Seattle.

E can't be true, because Isaac has to go before M in this scenario.

Question 10

If a taped call airs first then M must go first. Isaac calls from Seattle, and Seattle is always live.

So the first call is a Vancouver call, from M, and is taped. The second call is from Seattle and is live.

$$\frac{M}{V_T} \quad \frac{I}{S_L} \quad \frac{H}{K_T} \quad \underline{\quad} \quad \underline{\quad}$$

A could be true. We have no rules for which order F and G have to appear in.

B could be true, for the same reason as **A.**

C can't be true. Isaac has to go second. Isaac calls from Seattle, and Seattle is a live call. **C** is **CORRECT.**

D *has* to be true. Henry always makes a taped call from Kelowna, third.

E could be true. We have no rules for what order F and G appear in.

Question 11

A is **CORRECT.** We know that Gwen is in Seattle, because F and M *can't* be in Seattle. And all Seattle calls are live.

Henry's call has to be *taped*, because H is third and the third call is taped. **B** is wrong.

Mel is from Vancouver, so we don't know if Mel's call if live or taped. **C** is wrong.

D doesn't have to be true, because F is from Vancouver. We don't know whether Vancouver calls are live or taped.

Isaac *can't* be taped. Isaac is from Seattle, which means Isaac makes a live call. **E** is wrong.

Question 12

Henry makes a taped call from Kelowna in spot 3. If no taped calls are consecutive that means that calls 2 and 4 must be live. And *that* means that calls 1 and 3 must be taped.

T-L-T-L-T. The Seattle calls can only be live, so they must go in 2 and 4. The Vancouver calls go in 1 and five.

There's only one order possible. Remember that M and F call from Vancouver, and Isaac and G call from Seattle.

A is **CORRECT.**

$$\frac{M}{V_T} \quad \frac{I}{S_L} \quad \frac{H}{K_T} \quad \frac{G}{S_L} \quad \frac{F}{V_T}$$

Question 13

If a taped call airs second, then that means M from Vancouver called second. Isaac from Seattle (who is always live) called first.

$$\frac{I}{S_L} \quad \frac{M}{V_T} \quad \frac{H}{K_T} \quad \underline{\quad} \quad \underline{\quad}$$

A *must* be true. So **A** is wrong.

B is **CORRECT.** The Vancouver call must air *second*.

C, D and **E** are all possible. We have no idea whether F or G comes first. We only have rules for what happens before H.

Game 3 – Bus Ride
Questions 14-18

Setup

This is a grouping game. We have three rows of two bus seats, and have to figure out where everybody sits.

This game is quite hard. You have to know all of the rules. Really, you have to know them: memorize them. *Don't* try to understand this game if you don't know the rules.

I've made a list of them below. There are only 5, so commit them to memory or write out the list yourself while trying this game. If one of my explanations says something must be true and you're not sure why, it's almost certainly because of one of the rules.

I find it easiest to draw this vertically. But if you drew a horizontal diagram, that can work too.

Here's how I drew it:

```
      W     A
1    ___   ___
2    ___   ___
3    ___   ___
```

The first rule is the most restrictive rule. G and H both sit in the aisles. G comes right before H.

There are only three aisle seats. So G and H can either go in 1 and 2, or 2 and 3.

Whenever a restrictive situation can only be drawn two ways, I always draw those two scenarios. I find it is very useful to help me think through the diagram.

```
      W     A           W     A
1    ___   ___      1   ___   ___
2    ___    G       2   ___    G
3    ___    H       3   ___   ___
```

These will also serve as guides when we have to make sketches for later questions.

We *could* make exhaustive scenarios for the next four rules, but there are too many to be useful.

Instead, I recommend making a numbered list of the last four rules, memorizing them, and/or referring back to the list quickly as needed. This game centers on the rules.

The next rule is that if M is in an aisle seat then L is in the same row as H.

$$M_A \longrightarrow \boxed{LH}$$

We know that G is always above H. So we can expand on this rule by including that.

$$M_A \longrightarrow \boxed{\begin{array}{c} G \\ LH \end{array}}$$

The third rule is that if G and K are in the same row then M is behind I.

I placed H under G, because G is always over H. This rule actually lets us figure out quite a lot, but I've put that in a separate section later.

The fourth rule is that if K is in a window then M is in row 3.

$$K_W \longrightarrow M_3$$

If M is in the aisles, then K must be in a window seat (because only three variables can fit in the aisles.)

So if M is in an aisle seat then K will force M to be in seat 3.

The final rule tells us that if K is in 3 then Imamura is in 1.

$$K_3 \longrightarrow I_1$$

Scenarios

This isn't essential. I'm adding this section to show you how you *could* build scenarios to help you on this game.

I didn't use these on the questions, but drawing them helped me get a better intuition for the game.

When you have a conditional rule, it's good to think through all of its implications. Consider the third rule. If G and K are in the same row, M, is behind I:

That's pretty restrictive. It covers five variables. We can only fit three variables in the window or aislse columns.

There's no room for I to be over M in the aisle seats, because G and H are already there. There are four variables but only three spots.

So they have to go in the window seats. K has to go above them. It's the only way to fit all three and still have space for H.

	W	A
1	K	G
2	I	H
3	M	

The only other way to place K and IM would be to put K in 3 and IM in 1-2. But then G would be in 3 and there would be no space to put H below.

By default, L will go in the bottom of the aisle seats:

```
      W     A
 1    I     G
      ___   ___
 2    L     H
      ___   ___
 3    K     M
      ___   ___
```

So if K and G are in the same row, there's only one way to place the variables.

Therefore we can make a further deduction is that K and G can't go together unless they are in the first row. We can add this to the main diagram:

```
         W     A
    1    ___   ___

 K  2          G
    ___   ___
    3          H
    ___   ___
```

There is one more scenario worth drawing. We should figure out what happens if M is in an aisle seat, since there are many restrictions when that happens.

If M is in an aisle seat, then K, L and I are in window seats. If K is in a window seat, M goes in seat 3:

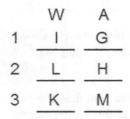

$K_W \longrightarrow M_3$

```
      W     A
 1    ___   G
 2    ___   H
 3    ___   M
```

If M is in the aisles, H and L are on the same row. This fills row 2:

$M_A \longrightarrow \boxed{LH}$

```
      W     A
 1    ___   G
 2    L     H
      ___   ___
 3    ___   M
```

That leaves K and Imamura to be placed in rows 1 and 3. It turns out we can't place K in row 1. Why? Then K would be beside G. We saw that scenario earlier: if K is beside G, M has to be directly below Imamura.

So K must go in 3 and Imamura in 1:

```
      W     A
 1    I     G
      ___   ___
 2    L     H
      ___   ___
 3    K     M
      ___   ___
```

This scenario involved almost every rule. So if you weren't sure how to do it, go back and review the rules, or try drawing it yourself. It's a useful exercise to be sure you're applying the rules correctly.

As I said, you don't need these scenarios to get this game correct. But drawing them correctly will help your diagramming skills.

Solving A Rules Based Game

Some of my diagrams for the individual questions may seem mysterious, so I want to explain what I'm doing.

Questions 15-18 are all "local rule" questions. The game gives you a new rule, and you can combine this rule with the existing rules to make new deductions.

Take question 15 for example. The question says that L and K are in window seats.

If you properly memorized the rules, you'll notice a rule is triggered by this new condition. If you didn't memorize the rules, look at the list to the right.

If K is in a window seat, M is in row 3.

This simple deduction lets us solve everything. There are only two places to put M in row 3: window or aisle.

From there, you can continue to make deductions until everything is solved. See question 15 for the full walkthrough.

In general, the process should be:

1. Identify local rule
2. See which regular rules it affects.
3. Make a deduction
4. Continue combining those deductions with the regular rules, until you're done.
5. Check if you found the answer.

I encourage you to try this process for each question before looking at my explanations.

Master Diagram

	W	A			W	A
1	___	___		1	___	G
~~K~~ 2	___	G		2	___	H
3	___	H		3	___	___

(The "not K" rule is from one of the optional scenarios)

$$M_A \longrightarrow \boxed{\begin{matrix} G \\ LH \end{matrix}}$$

$$\boxed{\begin{matrix} KG \\ H \end{matrix}} \longrightarrow \boxed{\begin{matrix} I \\ M \end{matrix}}$$

$$K_W \longrightarrow M_3$$

$$K_3 \longrightarrow I_1$$

Scenario when K is beside G:

	W	A
1	K	G
2	I	H
3	M	L

Scenario when M is in an aisle seat

	W	A
1	I	G
2	L	H
3	K	M

Question 14

The fact that this is not a list question should set off alarm bells. The game's author expected you to make deductions, and they think you should be very comfortable with the rules and how they interact.

If you're still unfamiliar with them, reread the rules and look over the list in the main diagram section. Otherwise this game won't make sense.

A is wrong because if K is in 3 then Imamura must always be in 1. It's the fourth rule from our list.

B is wrong because if G is in the same row as K then M has to be behind Imamura. This question says we have to put M in the aisle seats. G, H, M and Imamura would make four variables in the aisles seats.

C is wrong because G can never be in a window seat. It's the first rule.

D can't be true. If M is in an aisle seat, then L is in the same row as *H*, not M.

E can be true. If K is in 3 then Imamura is in 1. There's nothing wrong with that. L would be in 2, beside H, so it doesn't matter whether K or M is in the aisle.

```
      W     A
1     I     G
     ___   ___

2     L     H
     ___   ___

3     ___   ___     K M
```

E is **CORRECT.**

Question 15

If L and K are in window seats, then M must be in seat 3 (K window --> M seat 3.)

There are two possibilities. M could be in row 3 in the window, or M could be in the aisle.

If M is in the aisle then L must be in the same row as H. I covered this scenario in the setup.

K can't be in the same row as G, because then M would have to be directly beneath Imamura. So K goes in 3 and Imamura goes in 1.

```
      W     A
1     I     G
     ___   ___

2     L     H
     ___   ___

3     K     M
     ___   ___
```

If M is in the window, then we still have to place K and L in their window seats. We can't place K with G, because then M would have to go underneath Imamura. So K goes in row 2, and L goes in row 1.

Imamura will go in the third aisle seat.

```
      W     A
1     L     G
     ___   ___

2     K     H
     ___   ___

3     M     I
     ___   ___
```

(*Question 15 continued on next page*)

(continued from previous page)

A is **CORRECT.** Moore is in the aisle in the first scenario I drew for this question.

B is wrong. If Imamura is in the third window seat, then L, K and imamura fill the window column. M would have to sit in the aisle.

But if M is in the aisle, K is in the third window seat. It's covered in the first scenario above. Otherwise, K would be with G.

C is wrong. If G and K are in the same row then Imamura is above M. But they can't fit in the aisles or the windows. In the aisles, G and H are there and only one space is free. In the windows, K and L already take up two spaces.

D is wrong. M is in row 3 because K is in a window seat. G is always in row 1 or 2 because G is above H.

E is wrong. This question places L in a window seat. To go beside L, M would have to go in the aisles.

But the second rule says that if M is in the aisle, L to go beside H, not M.

Question 16

If M is in row 1, then M must be in a window seat. If M were in an aisle seat, then K would be in a window seat, and that would force M go to in row *3*.

In fact, K must be in an aisle seat, so that M doesn't go in row 3.

Finally, K must be in row 1. Why? The only spare aisle spaces are 1 or 3. If K were in 3, then Imamura would be in 1. But that wouldn't work, because *M must go in 1.*

We can therefore also deduce that G and H must be in 2 and 3.

This was a complicated sequence of rules. Work through it on your own if you're not clear how it works.

So the drawing looks like this:

```
        W     A
  1     M     K
        ___   ___
  2           G
        ___   ___
  3           H
        ___   ___
```

It doesn't matter whether Imamura or L are in rows 2 or 3. Those aren't sufficient conditions for anything.

A is wrong because H must sit in row 3.

B *could* be true, but it doesn't have to be. There are no rules for L and Imamura.

C *could* be true, but it doesn't have to be. There are no rules for putting L and Imamura in spots 2 and 3.

D is **CORRECT.** If K were in a window seat, that would force M to be in 1, not 3.

So K sits in the aisles. If she sat in row 3, then Imamura would be in row 1 of the windows, and there would be no space for M to go there.

E could be true, but doesn't have to be. There are no rules to tell us where to put L and Imamura.

Question 17

If K is in the aisle seat of row 3, then Imamura is in row 1. (fourth rule):

```
      W     A
  1   I     G
      ___   ___
  2         H
      ___   ___
  3         K
      ___   ___
```

A has to be true. Both G and Imamura are in row 1.

B could be true, but it doesn't have to be. We have no rules telling us where to put L and M if K is in the aisle. **B is CORRECT.**

C has to be true. G, H and K are all in the aisle in this question, leaving no room for L.

D has to be true. There's only space left in the window seats. G, H and K fill up the aisle seats on this question.

E has to be true. If K is in the third aisle seat then G and H will have to be in 1 and 2.

Question 18

If Imamura isn't in row 1 then K must not be in row 3 (contrapositive of the final rule.)

And if G isn't in 1 then G must be in 2 and H is in 3.

K also can't go in row 2, beside G. Why?

That would force Imamura to be above M...but there's no space for the two of them in either the window or the aisle. K would be in row 2 in the window seats, and G is in 2 in the aisle seats.

So K is in row 1, in either the window or the aisle.

```
      W     A
  1   ___   ___   K
  2         G
      ___   ___
  3         H
      ___   ___
```

A is wrong because if G is in row 2 then H must be in row 3.

B is wrong because if K were in row 2 then Imamura would have to be right above M. But there's no room for that if K and G fill row 2.

C is **CORRECT.** Moore could be in 2 in a window seat and Imamura could be in row 3 on a window seat. K would go in row 1 of the aisle, and L would be in row 1 of the window. It looks like this:

```
      W     A
  1   L     K
      ___   ___
  2   M     G
      ___   ___
  3   I     H
      ___   ___
```

D is wrong because that would force K into a window seat. And if K is in a window seat then M also has to go in an aisle seat. Imamura, M, G and H can't all fit in aisle seats.

E is wrong because the only free aisle seat is in row 1. But if M were in an aisle then K would be in the window. And when K is in the window, M goes in row 3, not row 1.

Game 4 – Pilots and Copilots
Questions 19-23

Setup

This game isn't so bad, compared to most games. It combines linear and grouping, but everything can be grouped into two simple scenarios. It's good practice for the harder games that also require scenario creation.

The first task of any game (and often the hardest) is figuring out your layout. I prefer a vertical layout for this game. You can draw a column for pilots and copilots, and four rows.

I've drawn it below, and added in the rule that K goes second. It's a good idea to read over all the rules first and draw the simple ones directly on the diagram.

```
    P      CP
1  ____   ____

2   K     ____

3  ____   ____

4  ____   ____
```

Next, F takes off before G, and someone comes in between them.

F and G are both pilots. We can't put F-G in 3-4 because no one would come between them. So F must go in 1, and G can go in either 3 or 4.

We also know that L (a pilot) has U as his copilot. We can combine all of these rules into two scenarios: one with G is in 3 and one with G is in 4.

Scenario with G in 3:

```
    P      CP
1   F     ____

2   K     ____

3   G     ____

4   L      U
```

If G is in 3, then L must go in 4. It's the only space left for a pilot.

If G is in 4 then L must be in 3:

```
    P      CP
1   F     ____

2   K     ____

3   L      U

4   G     ____
```

To recap:

1. K is in 2 because a rule places him there.
2. F is in 1, because F has to be kept separate from G.
3. G can go in 3 or 4.
4. L goes in the place G doesn't go.
5. U goes with L.
6. There are no rules for R, S and T, the remaining copilots. They are random variables.

Main Diagram

Scenario 1

	P	CP
1	F	___
2	K	___
3	G	___
4	L	U

Scenario 2

	P	CP
1	F	___
2	K	___
3	L	U
4	G	___

Question 19

Clearly, the first question expects us to have made a few deductions: it isn't a list question.

We know that F is always in spot 1. That's the only way to keep F at least one space apart from G.

Only answers **A** and **B** have F. **B** is wrong because it includes Umlas: U has to go with L.

A is **CORRECT.** There are no rules telling us where to put R, so R can go in 1.

Question 20

We've got a local rule on this question: R comes after U. So we have to ask which scenario we're in.

U can only be in 3 or 4. U must be in 3 for this question, so that R can go after.

	P	CP
1	F	___
2	K	___
3	L	U
4	G	R

A could be true. F could come before S if S went in spot 2.

B *has* to be true. K comes in 2 and R comes in 4.

C can't be true, because T can go in spot 2 at the latest. U and R fill up 3 and 4. **C** is **CORRECT.**

D *has* to be true. S can only go in 1 or 2. Meanwhile, R must go in 4. So R is always after S.

E could be true if T went in 1. Then T would be earlier than K.

Question 21

If L is earlier than G then we must be in scenario 2:

	P	CP
1	F	
2	K	
3	L	U
4	G	

We're looking for something that could be false. All the wrong answers *have* to be true.

A has to be true. F is always in 1 and U is in 3 in this scenario. (of course, U can never be earlier than 3 in *any* scenario.)

B must be true. It's the only way to put L ahead of G.

C also must be true. *One* of Reich or Taylor can go in slot 4, after Umlas's flight. But they can't both go there at the same time, so one will always be before U.

D doesn't have to be true. We have no rules telling us where to put S. So while Simon *could* fly earlier than Umlas, he doesn't have to. **D is CORRECT.**

E has to be true. L has to go in 3 in order to fly before G. And since U always flies with L, U has to be in G too.

Question 22

We have to figure out how many different teams could go fourth. First, L and U could be assigned to slot four:

	P	CP
1	F	
2	K	
3	G	
4	L	U

That's one possibility.

Second, G could go in slot 4 with R, with S, or with T. There's no rule preventing any of those copilots from going with G.

	P	CP
1	F	
2	K	
3	L	U
4	G	

LU, GS, GR, GT. Four possibilities means that answer **C** is **CORRECT.**

Question 23

	P	CP
1	F	___
2	K	___
3	L	U
4	G	S

If S comes after L, then LU must be in 3 and S must go in 4 with G.

R and T will fill in 1 and 2, in either order.

G therefore must come after R. So **A** is wrong.

B is just like **A**. G must come after both R and T.

C is wrong too. L comes after R and T, just like G.

D is **CORRECT.** We have no rules to tell us whether to put R in 1 or T in 1.

E can't be false. U is always in 3 with L, and R has to go in either 1 or 2.

Test 37
Section I - Reading Comprehension
Passage 1 - Jury Trials
Questions 1-7

Paragraph Summaries

1. Some people say that forcing juries to agree unanimously can lead to unnecessary retrials.
2. Statistical evidence: most juries aren't hung. Second point: A hung jury means that a jury deliberated seriously, which is what we want.
3. Unanimity helps protect the innocent from false convictions. And it ensures that every juror is listened to (which leads to true deliberation).

Analysis

This passage is an argument. It presents the case for the opposing side, then argues against it.

It's not a bulletproof argument. For instance, there's no evidence that hung juries always indicate true deliberation. It could just be some jerk refusing to admit he's wrong. That possibility was mentioned in the first paragraph, and the author didn't address it.

Their main point is that unanimous verdicts make trials fairer, and they don't cause many problems.

Question 1

DISCUSSION: The main point is that we should keep the unanimity requirement.

It doesn't lead to many downsides (paragraph 2) and it has benefits (paragraph 3).

_____

A. Not quite. The requirement *is* being reexamined. This passage argues against a proposal to scrap the requirement.
B. This is not the author's point at all. Lines 31-33 show that the author thinks a hung jury is a sign that the jury did its job.
C. The author never mentions evidence. And they *don't* think hung juries are a sign of a flaw in the justice system. See lines 31-33.
D. The author's point is that the unanimity requirement *forces* jurors to be conscientious. They can't leave the room unless *everybody* agrees, so they have to talk about it.
E. **CORRECT.** Fairness is mentioned in paragraph 3, and it seems to be the author's main concern. In paragraph 2 the author argues costs are minimal, if any. So we should keep hung juries.

Question 2

DISCUSSION: The author is a strong defender of unanimity. The entire passage argues that we should keep the requirement, and not change it one bit.

———————————

A. Cursory means: not paying much attention to something. The author spends the *whole* passage praising the unanimity requirement.
B. The author clearly praises the requirement. See lines 39-40, for example.
C. There's no caution. The author completely disagrees with the idea that we should get rid of the requirement, and doesn't think we should change the it, at all.
D. CORRECT. The author has nothing but good things to say about the unanimity requirement.
E. The passage may have some logical flaws, but the author uses arguments (reason) to make their point.

Question 3

DISCUSSION: The third paragraph says unanimity helps promote fair trials. It also guarantees that every juror has their opinion heard, because everyone had to agree.

———————————

A. CORRECT. The unanimity requirement is a strong measure. The author thinks we need to ensure fairness, even if juries sometimes are hung.
B. Maybe? The entire passage is about juries, the author never says what judges should do.
C. Lines 40-41 say that we sometimes convict the innocent, even with the unanimity requirement. It's possible for 12 people to be wrong, and it's unlikely unanimity will completely get rid of false convictions.
D. The author never says *who* should be on a jury. They seem to think anyone can serve. The system forces people to act responsibly, because everyone must agree.
E. Why would the author believe this? They spend the whole passage praising the jury system. This is the flip side of answer choice C. We don't know whether the author thinks false convictions will or will not be eliminated. The author never mentions that possibility.

Question 4

DISCUSSION: The last paragraph said that unanimity makes trials more fair. Lack of unanimity means we couldn't be sure whether juries were reaching correct verdicts.

The author thinks unanimity is very important. The correct answer provides a strong closing.

————————————

A. Huh? By this point, the author is done discussing the argument against unanimity. And traditions of argument were never mentioned.
B. The author never said anything should be debated in public. They think everything is fine as it is.
C. **CORRECT.** This is a bit over the top, but it matches the author's opinion. You don't have a real democracy if some people are denied the vote. Likewise, you don't have a real jury trial unless everyone's opinion is considered.
D. Not really. The author implies that the public still trusts juries (lines 53-54). How many citizens would have even *heard* about a debate over hung juries? There's no way the legal system has been undermined by this.
E. The author never mentioned the methods of lawyers. This *might* be true, but the author might also argue that unanimity is even more important than scientific legal methods.

Question 5

DISCUSSION: You may not know what recalcitrant means, but in context the meaning is clear.

The passage is describing a stubborn juror who holds up the trial and won't agree with the majority.

————————————

A. **CORRECT.** Obstinate means someone who won't change their mind.
B. You can be stubborn without being suspicious.
C. You can also be stubborn *and* careless. You come to a snap judgment, then never change your mind even though your opinion is stupid.
D. Conscientiousness and stubbornness have nothing to do with each other. Conscientious means "thoughtful".
E. Naive means someone who doesn't know what's going on. But stubborn people can know what's going on. You might refuse to change your mind because you know you're right.

Question 6

DISCUSSION: The author talks about not listening to everyone's opinion in lines 45-54. We'd lose something important, and society would begin to doubt jury verdicts.

Explicit means something the author *actually said*. You must be able to find the answer in the passage.

_____

A. The author said *hung juries* tend to only occur in close cases. But unanimity is important in many cases. Unanimity can affect a trial even if a jury ends up not being hung; it could force people to change their minds.
B. Search all you want, you'll never find this. We're looking for something the author said. (People might dismiss a dissenting juror's opinions while being respectful.)
C. CORRECT. Lines 53-54 say this directly. This type of questions tests whether you can find the relevant section of the passage, and then read *all of it*.
D. This is probably true, but the author doesn't say anything about it.
E. The author thinks the opposite: they think unanimity is very useful.

Question 7

DISCUSSION: Not much to say, except that you need to be able to find a specific line that supports your answer.

_____

A. Not necessarily. It's possible that the other eleven jurors could be wrong. The author never says whether the minority or majority tends to be right.
B. Yikes, that's a broad statement. The author might think there are many flaws with the justice system, even if they think unanimous juries are fine.
C. Not necessarily. Lines 4-5 mention that juries are often used in serious criminal cases.
D. CORRECT. Lines 29-33 strongly suggest this. You can't have a unanimity requirement without occasionally having hung juries.
E. Lines 45-50 imply that every juror does get a fair hearing when there is a unanimity requirement. The other jurors are forced to listen to the dissenter.

Passage 2 - Marie Curie
Questions 8-13

Paragraph Summaries

1. A description of how Marie Curie discovered radium and polonium. Other results of Curie's research.
2. How radiation works. Why Curie could not have known (the evidence wasn't there).
3. In Curie's time, chemists and physicists debated what the atom was like.
4. Curie was a physicist; their theory about atoms was incorrect. That explains why Curie didn't discover how radiation worked. But her work helped later researchers.

Analysis

The passage is favorable towards Curie. It praises her discoveries, and explains away her failure to discover the cause of radiation. Physicists and chemists are mentioned in paragraph 3 to give context: Curie was a physicist, and believed that the atom was not divisible. That explains why she couldn't have figured out how radiation worked. Quantum mechanics (the correct theory) came later.

Most of the questions deal with Curie's failure to explain radiation, and how she isn't really to blame. Reread paragraphs 2-4 if you have some doubts on this point.

Question 8

DISCUSSION: The main idea is that Marie Curie was a pioneering researcher. She is not to blame for not figuring out the mechanism of radiation.

———————————

A. Who knows? We're not told who discovered quantum mechanics, or why. All we know is that quantum mechanics explained radiation. But radiation might not have been necessary for quantum mechanics.
B. **CORRECT.** Marie Curie took us forward, even if she made some mistakes. Paragraphs 2-4 are devoted to rationalizing Curie's failure to correctly explain radiation.
C. Lines 56-60 contradict this. We should forgive Marie Curie's failure to identify the real cause of radiation.
D. Not so. Marie Curie couldn't explain radiation, but she made other important discoveries, such as radium and polonium (lines 9-10).
E. We're not told whether Curie had any influence on chemists. And this is way off base: the passage was about *Curie*, the chemists were only mentioned in passing.

Question 9

DISCUSSION: The passage's point in paragraphs 2-4 is that current critics forget that it wasn't always obvious how the atom worked. They also forget how important Curie's discoveries were.

A. The passage doesn't mention any obstacles.
B. The passage said quantum mechanics explained radiation. But that doesn't mean knowledge of radiation was necessary for the discovery of quantum mechanics.
C. The critics might know what physicists believed. But they don't realize that the physicists' opinions were reasonable at the time, even though they were wrong in the end. It's important to know the facts, but context can be even more important.
D. CORRECT. Curie and many other intelligent physicists had a flawed conception of the atom. This doesn't make them idiots; there was good reason to believe in an indivisible atom until quantum mechanics came along. Further, the critics ignore the importance of Curie's discoveries, such as radium.
E. The critics might understand the reasoning, but think that Curie's discoveries were nonetheless unimportant.

Question 10

DISCUSSION: The answer is in the first paragraph. Lines 5-10 are the most important. Line 10 says that radium and polonium were "previously unknown".

A. CORRECT. Line 10 says no one knew about radium and polonium, the other radioactive elements in pitchblende.
B. Doubtful. Scientists knew pitchblende had uranium, and they knew uranium was radioactive. They probably thought pitchblende's radioactivity came from uranium.
C. Careful. We know physicists and chemists disagreed about *atoms*. This prevented Curie from forming a correct theory of radiation. But maybe physicists and chemists didn't care much about radiation. They may not have tried to develop theories to explain it.
D. Lines 44-46 say it wasn't clear if atoms existed. So presumably there was some research being done to settle the question. In any case, the passage never claims there *wasn't* research.
E. We don't know. Physicists are only mentioned in paragraph 3, for their theories on the atom. We don't know what they thought about radioactive elements. Maybe they thought there were many, but they hadn't been discovered yet.

Question 11

DISCUSSION: The author praises Curie's discoveries and defends her failure to discover the true cause of radioactivity.

_____

A. **CORRECT.** The author mentions Curie's accomplishments, and argues that critics ignore the context of Curie's time. She couldn't have figured out radiation, because quantum mechanics hadn't been discovered.
B. The only scientific dispute is the one between physicists and chemists, in the third paragraph. It's a dispute *from the past*, and it has already been resolved.
C. The only currently accepted theory mentioned is quantum mechanics. We're not told why this was accepted. This answer choice also ignores Curie.
D. The final paragraph does explain why radiation occurs. But there's no mention of a debate that led to the discovery of the true cause of radiation.
E. The only theory mentioned is quantum mechanics, and the passage clearly suggests it is correct.

Question 12

DISCUSSION: The first paragraph describes Curie's successes, and introduces her failure to explain the cause of radiation.

_____

A. Not quite. The passage only talks about Curie's research. There's no mention of other radiation researchers.
B. The fight between physicists and chemists has long been settled. They were only mentioned to provide context for *Curie's* failure.
C. **CORRECT.** More or less. We know what Marie Curie did and did not accomplish. On the whole it's positive.
D. Nope. The first paragraph is just a collection of facts. It didn't say how the author would complete the argument.
E. No. Curie did have an incorrect explanation of radioactivity (lines 47-48), but that *doesn't* mean her discoveries weren't important or useful. (lines 58-60).

Question 13

DISCUSSION: Postulate means 'describe' or 'theorize'. Mechanism in this case means "method".

In simpler words, Curie couldn't tell us h*ow* radiation occurred.

_____

A. **CORRECT.** Curie could observe radiation (the phenomenon), but she couldn't explain it.
B. There's no mention of any experimental machine.
C. Scientists didn't cause radiation (the phenomenon). It existed without their help.
D. Huh? Isotopes are never mentioned in the first paragraph. This answer choice is playing with your outside knowledge that radiation involves isotopes.
E. No. Theories can be wrong. A mechanism refers to the way that radioactive elements produce radiation, in the real world.

Passage 3 - Invisible Man
Questions 14-21

Paragraph Summaries

1. Ellison merged African-American and European themes in *Invisible Man*. Critics wanted him to support political action, and wanted him to help develop an African-American literary style.
2. Ellison argued these critics were censoring individual authors. They were asking African-American authors to segregate themselves and muffle their creativity.
3. Ellison's novel was like jazz. It borrowed from foreign themes to create a unique style.
4. Ellison's protagonist *was* part of a community.

Analysis

This passage is an argument. The opposing claims come in the first paragraph. The rest of the passage defends Ellison against his critics. The main point is that Ellison wasn't wrong to write an individualistic novel that was influenced by European styles.

Since the book was written in 1952, the "political struggle" refers to the struggle to end segregation and poor treatment for African-Americans. Intellectuals and writers are always an important part of community struggles. That's why the critics were disappointed Ellison was pursuing his own path.

Question 14

DISCUSSION: Support the answer using a specific line from the passage.

Remember that the passage praised *Invisible Man*. So critical answers are likely wrong.

_____

A. **CORRECT.** This is the point of paragraph 3. If jazz can mix cultures, then so can Ellison.
B. The paragraph never said whether *Invisible Man* or jazz were effectively used for political action.
C. We are told that Ellison liked and promoted jazz. But jazz might not have needed Ellison's help, and we're not told whether Ellison's promotion had any effect on jazz's popularity.
D. The passage praises *Invisible Man*. So the book shows the opposite: we *can* combine African-American and European concepts.
E. The passage never mentioned whether *Invisible Man* was popular. Also note that this is a criticism, while the passage praised the novel. That's enough to rule out this answer choice.

Question 15

DISCUSSION: Ellison's critics thought Ellison should have helped the communal political struggle, and they didn't like that he used foreign influences.

_____

A. CORRECT. The goal of the political movement was to improve conditions for African-Americans. Ellison's critics might have liked his novel better if it had improved social conditions for African-Americans.

B. The critics wanted Ellison to help with *present* struggles: winning political battles and creating an African-American literary style.

C. Same as B. The critics cared about contemporary struggles. They wanted Ellison to help with the present, not the past.

D. Careful. The critics wanted *African*-American literature to be separate. It's doubtful they cared whether American literature in general was distinct from European literature.

E. The critics didn't like the book. They probably would have been *unhappy* if it had many readers.

Question 16

DISCUSSION: In context, we can see that Ellison was accusing his critics of wanting to keep the African-American art and European art separate, the very thing they were fighting against in society (African-Americans fought against segregation in the 1950s, when Ellison's novel was published).

_____

A. What general tendency? Ellison had a specific point: his critics wanted African Americans to self-segregate their art from the broader culture.

B. Ellison argued that authors from different communities didn't necessary disagree on style and esthetics. Ellison found much to like in European novels.

C. Huh? No one suggested Ellison himself felt isolated from his culture.

D. No one mentioned the audience of the book. The whole passage is about the book itself.

E. CORRECT. African-American critics expected Ellison to use only the styles of the African-American community. He argued that this was censorship and segregation.

Question 17

DISCUSSION: The third paragraph shows that Ellison isn't alone: jazz also borrows from European culture.

_____

A. Within the discipline? Jazz is music, a different discipline from writing.

B. This is gobbledegook. Jazz is used as an example to strengthen the argument in favor of Ellison. The point of the paragraph wasn't to tell us how important jazz is.

C. Jazz wasn't the *source* for Ellison's novel. It's mentioned because it also borrows from foreign themes.

D. It's true that Ellison liked jazz. But we're not told why, or what his perspective on it was.

E. CORRECT. The critics make it seem like Ellison had done something heretical, something that no African-American had ever done before. But *jazz,* one of the great African-American musical traditions, had done the same thing. We realize that Ellison wasn't alone within the African-American community; other arts had borrowed from foreign influences.

Question 18

DISCUSSION: What a fun question. All you have to do is read the paragraph on jazz and make sure your answer is in there.

_____

A. This isn't said, and it contradicts our everyday experience. Many people like jazz.

B. There's no comparison made between jazz and other types of modern music.

C. CORRECT. Lines 34-37 say this. It was the *whole point of mentioning jazz.* If you got this wrong, take it as a sign that you're going through the passages too quickly. You'll do better if you reread sections you didn't understand.

D. We don't know, the themes of jazz aren't mentioned.

E. We know Ellison liked jazz, but that's all. We have no idea if jazz influenced literature in general.

Question 19

DISCUSSION: When you think you've found the right answer, look for it in the passage. You can *always* find it for detail questions, and then you'll be 100% certain you're correct.

Audiences are mentioned only once, in lines 26-29. Ellison argues his critics don't think very much of audiences. The critics believe that audiences have narrow perspectives. Ellison thought differently, and those lines imply he thought audiences could understand his work.

_____

A. Who knows? Ellison simply may not have wanted to write a political novel. But he might have believed political novels were more successful.

B. We aren't told if Ellison's work was popular and whether the criticism affected its popularity.

C. CORRECT. Ellison's work was unique and expressive (lines 24-26). He probably thought audiences could understand such a work. It's hard to write a book you're sure no one will want to read. Lines 26-29 show he thought audience had broad perspectives.

D. This is never mentioned. The audience was only mentioned in lines 26-29.

E. Lines 26-29 contradict this. Ellison thinks audiences don't have narrow perspectives.

Question 20

DISCUSSION: The main point of the passage is to defend Ellison against his critics.

A. The passage never said whether Ellison was better or worse than other novelists.

B. Jazz wasn't necessary to the argument. The author could have used any African-American art form that drew on foreign influences.

C. The author didn't say whether Ellison's work was relevant to the political struggles of African-Americans in 1952. The last paragraph says that Ellison's novel is linked to the African-American community, but political and social issues aren't mentioned.

D. CORRECT. The criticism comes in the first paragraph. The rest of the passage argues against the critics.

E. Huh? The passage never said if Ellison's novel was "art for art's sake". And it never said whether political novels were good or bad.

Question 21

DISCUSSION: You should be able to eliminate the wrong answers by finding them in the passage. If you can't do this fast enough, then practice doing it. It's a trainable skill, and you can get faster at it.

A. Line 31. You should know the third paragraph is about jazz, and look there to find the line.

B. CORRECT. This isn't mentioned.

C. His response is in lines 20-23.

D. Lines 47-50 show that Ellison was influenced by Europeans and African-Americans. Lines 13-15 also mention European influence.

E. Lines 33-36 mention that some jazz musicians used American theatre music that was influenced by Europe.

Passage 4 - Decision Making
Questions 22-26

Paragraph Summaries

1. Researchers have found that people fear loss more than they value gains. This explains some irrational political decisions.
2. People act to avoid loss more than to seek gains. But, if there is a certainty of loss, people will risk an even bigger loss if it gives them a tiny chance of no loss.
3. If a country thinks it has lost something, it will risk an even larger loss to get it back. The Falklands war is an example.

Analysis

This is an interesting decision on the rationality (or lack thereof) of decision making. Research shows that we'll do stupid things to avoid a loss. That's the main theme of the passage. The paragraphs are devoted to explaining specific parts of this phenomenon, and giving examples.

Let's look at some examples to explain the research. First, the old findings: people fear loss more than they value gains.

Let's make a bet. You give me $100, and I'll flip a coin. Heads, I keep the money. Tails, you get $300.

It's a very good bet, for you. If you could take this bet as many time as you wanted, you'd become the richest person on earth.

Analysis Continued

So, want to take the bet? If you're like most humans, you hesitated. Sure, you could triple your money. But think of how much work it took to get $100. *Your* $100. You're not going to gamble it away, are you?

You pay $100 to play and win $150 on average. But because humans fear loss, we don't like that bet.

Now, the new research. It says that if we're faced with a near-certain loss, we'll risk a *big* loss to avoid it. Let's look at an example.

You're walking home with a crisp new $100 bill in your wallet. A mug with a gun comes up and tells you to hand it over. He doesn't want the wallet, he just wants the money. You'll never see this guy again.

Objectively, your situation isn't that bad. Your maximum loss is $100. That's nothing, in the grand scheme of things. You should feel lucky he hasn't hurt you.

But some people act irrationally in this situation. They try to resist, or run, or fight. They'll risk their life to save $100. Rich or poor, the instinct is the same. Humans don't like certain losses.

Note the difference between subjective and objective. $100 is a small objective (actual) amount, but it seems like a larger subjective (perceived) amount because we really don't like certain losses.

Question 22

DISCUSSION: It sounds like the attacking country is acting rationally. If the country succeeds, then they've gained new land and great wealth. If the country fails, they just face a small loss.

The *other* country will probably act irrationally when trying to get the territory back.

The old theory was that a person would only take a risk if there would be a big payoff. It looks like the benefits for the attacking country far outweigh the risk. So their actions fit with the old risk model.

A. **CORRECT.** The earlier research found that countries will take risks only if the benefits greatly outweigh the possible harm (lines 17-22). That seems to be the case here: the gains are large and the risk is small.
B. Since the victim has experienced a *loss*, they'll probably act irrationally when they try to get the territory back. We fear loss more than we like gains. Only one country has lost something here; so the two countries will view the situation differently.
C. The new research doesn't change what the risks of any move are. It changes how we *see* risk. We see a loss as being unusually bad. The 'objective value' of a risk is not how we *see* a risk. It's instead how big a risk really is.
D. Hard to say. The risks seem objectively good: the country has gained great wealth and it only risks a small loss.
E. Maybe? The leaders might just want to steal mineral wealth.

Question 23

DISCUSSION: The question makes us think about how people weigh risk. And it introduces the research results that follow: people need a very big payoff to take a risk.

If you have a 50% chance to lose $100, and a 50% chance to gain $201, you *should* take that bet. But most people hesitate. They need things to be very lopsided in their favor before taking risks.

A. Lines 32-35 suggest that people tend to react the *same* way to risk.
B. It's not a rhetorical question: the author has an answer for us. Rhetorical questions tend to be unanswerable.
C. **CORRECT.** The previous view was that people need a big payoff before they'll take a risk. Lines 33-35 answer the question from lines 24-27 and suggest that people often do behave as the old theory predicted.
D. In plain English, this means that how we see things (subjective) is the same as how they actually are (objective). But the experimental results in lines 33-35 show the opposite. People turn down good bets because they fear risk.
E. This sentence is confusing, because it describes something that never happens. The easiest way to eliminate it is to focus on one small part you can disprove. Was there ever any 'previously unaccepted research' mentioned? No? Then this answer can't be right.

Question 24

DISCUSSION: Inference questions test whether you can check your answer against the passage. 100% of the time you should be able to support the correct answer with a line from the passage.

———————————

A. Not so. States might have correct information about the risks. But their *perception* of what risks they should take will probably be off base.

B. CORRECT. This is implied; evidence about normal people is used to describe how countries act. Countries are run by people, and they likely see risk the same way as ordinary people.

C. Unfortunately, we don't know if this is true. Just because we can describe how countries act doesn't mean we know how to stop conflicts.

D. The author would agree with the first part. But the second part isn't supported. Rational decision making generally shouldn't lead to severe consequences (on average at least).

E. This isn't true at all. The new research only described people who faced a certain loss. In all other cases, people want the benefits to greatly exceed risks. Just matching risks isn't enough.

Question 25

DISCUSSION: The passage discusses new and old research. It applies the research to decision making in international politics.

———————————

A. We know people fear risk, but we don't know why, psychologically speaking.

B. The psychological results are more than hypotheses. They've been tested and confirmed using experiments.

C. There is no talk of research by political scientists. Only psychological research is mentioned.

D. CORRECT. The new consideration is that people will take large risks to avoid a certain loss. The other field of inquiry is international politics. Specifically, the Falklands war is discussed.

E. What are the two theories? I only see one: the theory of decision making. The new results don't really contradict the old results, they complement them. The old research never investigated situations with a certain loss.

Question 26

DISCUSSION: As with question 24, you should be able to support the right answer from the passage. If you don't, you're just guessing.

———————————

A. The author never criticizes researchers. The old research is still true; the new research just expands on it.

B. The author thinks there *is* enough research support for these ideas. That's why they talk about the Falklands war as confirmation of the theories...they think the theories are correct.

C. CORRECT. The Falklands war was an example of stupid risk taking to avoid a loss. Britain felt it had lost the Falklands, so it likely would have been willing to risk *huge* danger to get them back.

D. The whole passage argues *against* this. Governments will avoid risk, unless they fear a loss. In that case, they'll take really dumb risks. It's scary, but not hard to understand.

E. This is never mentioned. As far as we know, the earlier research is consistent with the new research.

Test 37
Section II - Logical Reasoning

Question 1

QUESTION TYPE: Strengthen

CONCLUSION: It wouldn't be such a good idea to start mediation late in the process of a grievance.

REASONING: There isn't a reason given. The president does mention that grievances are expensive overall.

ANALYSIS: The president likes mediation. He just doesn't think it will work in later stages. The wrong answers all weaken the idea that mediation is useful at any stage: they contradict the president.

To strengthen the president's argument, we need to show that mediation is not useful at a late stage.

A. This weakens the president's argument that a mediator would be a good idea if used early.
B. That's nice. But for disputes that aren't solved, the president is arguing that mediators may cut costs.
C. **CORRECT.** If the mediator arrives late in the process they won't be able to help the two parties agree. The positions will often have hardened.
D. This would be true at the start or the end of the mediation process. But the president thinks mediators are a good idea at the start.
E. This weakens the president's argument that we should use mediation in the early stages.

Question 2

QUESTION TYPE: Must be True

FACTS:

1. The depth of pilings determines how solid a bridge is.
2. Pilings used to be driven in to the point of "refusal", where they wouldn't go any deeper.
3. The Rialto Bridge met the standard for refusal. 24 hammer blows would drive the pilings in by less than 2 inches.

ANALYSIS: We don't know anything about how safe or unsafe the standard of refusal was.

We *can* conclude that the pilings could have gone deeper. The 24 hammer blows were still driving in the pilings, just not by much.

A. Presumably the standard of the time was fairly safe. We have no evidence it wasn't, and the Rialto Bridge met the standard.
B. This is exactly the same as A. We have no evidence the standard was unsafe. People probably would have stopped using the standard if it was unsafe.
C. If Da Ponte met the contemporary standard then that means he met the standard of his time.
D. Huh? The stimulus clearly state that all bridges built before 1700 had pilings driven to refusal. Presumably some bridges were built during 1588-1700.
E. **CORRECT.** 24 hammer blows drove the pilings in by less than two inches. That isn't much, but they were still being driven in.
   The standard of refusal determined that they were "deep enough", but the pilings could have gone deeper.

Question 3

QUESTION TYPE: Flawed Reasoning

CONCLUSION: Joan will have to do the class presentation to pass.

REASONING: If she had gotten an A on her paper, she could have passed even without the presentation. But Joan didn't get an A on the paper.

ANALYSIS: This is an incorrect negation. We had: Get an A → Doesn't need presentation.

The argument incorrectly switches this to: A → Does need presentation.

But it's possible Joan wouldn't need to do the presentation even though she didn't get an A on her paper. Joan might otherwise have had excellent grades, and a B+ on the paper.

———————————

A. Actually, the argument did consider this possibility: but it's a mistake! It doesn't have to be the case that Joan needed one or the other.
B. **CORRECT.** We have nothing to tell us that not getting an A is a sufficient condition for having to do the class presentation.
C. The argument wasn't concerned with the overall grade. It only considered whether or not Joan could pass.
D. This is the same thing as A. The argument didn't ignore this possibility: it assumes that this is true, but it has no evidence for the claim.
E. Other students are irrelevant. This is only about Joan.

Question 4

QUESTION TYPE: Weaken

CONCLUSION: People who lived 100 years ago probably read more.

REASONING: They had fewer distractions back then.

ANALYSIS: The correct answer points out that people didn't have much free time to read or waste time 100 years ago.

The wrong answers try to show that it would have been hard to read. But you don't need to buy a book to read a book. And you might still read a bad book if you had nothing else to do.

———————————

A. That doesn't mean people wouldn't read books. Take what you can get.
B. **CORRECT.** People had fewer distractions but also less time to be distracted.
C. So? There are a lot more people today, too. That could explain the large number of books. Back then people could have read from libraries or borrowed books.
D. This doesn't tell us much. And you don't have to buy a book to read a book. You can borrow it from a friend, for example.
E. This doesn't change the fact that there were fewer diversions a century ago.

Question 5

QUESTION TYPE: Sufficient Assumption

CONCLUSION: No strictly physical theory can explain consciousness.

REASONING: Consciousness appears to come from physical processes. But physical theories can only explain physical structures and functions.

ANALYSIS: It's odd that consciousness can't be explained by physical theories: it seems to come from physical processes.

The answer tells us that consciousness requires a broader explanation than physical theories provide.

————————————————

A. This doesn't tell us that consciousness isn't a physical phenomenon.
B. **CORRECT.** This means physical theories are inadequate because they can only explain physical structures and functions.
C. That doesn't mean that a physical theory couldn't explain the functions and structures of consciousness, someday.
D. This weakens our conclusion that physical theories can't explain consciousness.
E. This doesn't tell us anything about consciousness.

Question 6

QUESTION TYPE: Strengthen

CONCLUSION: You'll get a fair price at Gem World.

REASONING: Gem World certifies its diamonds in writing. At most jewelry stores the diamond's assessor is also the seller.

ANALYSIS: We shouldn't care too much about a written assessment. Gem World could be both the assessor and seller, and write their own assessments!

The correct answer shows that Gem World's written assessments come from an outside source.

————————————————

A. This would weaken the argument that Gem World is special.
B. This sounds good, but it could mean that the assessors at Gem World have years of experience of setting too high a price for their gems. This doesn't tell us they're honest.
C. Higher quality could mean even higher price.
D. This weakens the argument that a written assessment is useful.
E. **CORRECT.** The main problem at other stores is that the assessor and the seller are the same person. This shows Gem World is different.

Question 7

QUESTION TYPE: Must be True

FACTS:

1. Newton's physics was highly successful.
2. But it was surpassed by Einstein's physics.
3. This happened despite the fact that Newton's physics was highly successful and substantiated.

ANALYSIS: We can conclude that highly successful, substantiated scientific theories can be replaced.

The wrong answers talk in general terms. We only have evidence about one situation: Newton's theory.

A. We only know this happened once, in the case of Newton and Einstein.
B. **CORRECT.** Newton's theory had long standing success and was substantiated. But then it was replaced.
C. We only know this happened to Newton. It might not happen to other theories.
D. We have evidence this isn't true. Newton's theory was only dominant for a couple of centuries.
E. Not necessarily true. We only know this is true in the case of Newton and Einstein.

Question 8

QUESTION TYPE: Paradox - Exception

PARADOX: Companies want conscientious employees yet conscientious workers who are laid off take a long time to find work.

ANALYSIS: The correct answer shows the importance of rates/percentages vs. amounts.

We have no idea what amount (number) of people from both groups are unemployed.

We only know that lazy people get hired within 5 months at a higher *rate* (percentage.)

A. **CORRECT.** The stimulus talked about the *rate* at which people from both groups were hired. It doesn't matter how many of them there are. It only matters what percentage get hired.
B. This shows that conscientious people are picky and won't take just any job. So it takes them longer.
C. This would make employers thinks those conscientious people were bad candidates.
D. This gives lazy people an unfair advantage over conscientious people.
E. If something is less urgent then it can take longer without causing a problem.

Question 9

QUESTION TYPE: Complete the Argument

ARGUMENT: The environment and natural ability are both important for language learning.

ANALYSIS: The logical conclusion is to ask how much natural ability and the environment each contribute to language learning.

_____

A. Not quite. There's nothing in the stimulus to indicate that there's some obstacle to a full explanation.
B. We already know that innate mechanisms play a role. This is redundant.
C. We already know this isn't true: the environment plays a role.
D. The stimulus doesn't even mention parents and peers. Presumably they are part of the environment, but this is a non-sequitur.
E. **CORRECT.** We know both are factors. It will be important to figure out which is more important.

Question 10

QUESTION TYPE: Method of Reasoning

CONCLUSION: Carla argues that historians should use general and objective views of history.

REASONING: It is impossible to know whose perspective to take, if we try to take a subjective view.

ANALYSIS: Carla believes that Mark's idea would make history inaccurate.

_____

A. Carla doesn't say that. She just thinks Mark's ideas are wrongheaded.
B. Carla might think we can understand an individual's feelings. But in history, *which* individual should we try to understand? The British or the French? The general or the foot soldier? That's the problem.
C. **CORRECT.** If we followed Mark's advice then history would no longer be objective.
D. Mark didn't deplore any historical writing. Read carefully.
E. Neither Carla nor Mark even mentions what profession Mark has. He might not be a historian. This is totally unsupported.

Question 11

QUESTION TYPE: Point At Issue

ARGUMENTS: Mark argues that we need to see history as it was experienced by individuals.

Carla argues that we will lose all objectivity if we try to view history from an individual standpoint.

ANALYSIS: They disagree on whether we ought to view history from an individual perspective (Mark) or whether we should take a broad view (Carla.)

_____

A. They both talk about understanding past events. But they disagree on what method we should use for understanding.
B. Participants might have an objective view of the *ramifications* (consequences) of the events. (i.e. "if we lose/win this battle, the country will be conquered.") That's different from having an objective view of the events themselves. Carla and Mark disagree on the latter point only.
C. Carla agrees we could do this but thinks that the picture would be distorted.
D. **CORRECT.** Carla says no, we should make broad, objective statements. Mark says yes.
E. Neither of them says whether we should make stuff up.

Question 12

QUESTION TYPE: Must be True

Facts/Chain of REASONING:

Good meal → Good food → Good soil → good farming → culture of maintenance of natural resources.

ANALYSIS: This is definitely a question to diagram. It's one long chain of conditional statements. You *need* to get it all straight in your head before trying to answer the question.

_____

A. **CORRECT.** The final statement is having a *culture* of maintenance of *natural* resources.
B. It's the other way around. Farming needs natural resources.
C. This is backwards. Soil needs farming, but farming might not need good soil.
D. This is backwards. Cuisine needs culture, but culture might not be sufficient for cuisine.
E. There could be many reasons why food is bad. All we know is that soil and farming are *necessary* for good food. But they aren't sufficient.

Question 13

QUESTION TYPE: Method of Reasoning

CONCLUSION: Aiesha argues that reflecting posts could cause more accidents.

REASONING: Drivers go faster and closer to the edge when roads are lit by reflecting posts. That causes more accidents.

ANALYSIS: Aiesha doesn't disagree with any of Adam's facts. But she adds context that shows that people will respond by driving recklessly. Even though they *could* theoretically drive safer.

A. Aiesha agrees with this, but thinks that other factors increase danger.
B. Aiesha doesn't say how to reduce road accidents. She just claims that Adam's idea won't work.
C. **CORRECT.** Seeing the edge of the road would make safe driving easier. But most drivers respond by driving recklessly.
D. Aiesha didn't say this was irrelevant. But she pointed out that drivers tend to respond with risky behavior.
E. Aiesha doesn't think people will drive more safely with road-side lighting.

Question 14

QUESTION TYPE: Weaken

CONCLUSION: VDTs cause headaches.

REASONING: People who use VDTs often have more headaches than other office workers.

ANALYSIS: On survey questions, try to think whether an answer shows that the data is flawed somehow.

Answer D does this. People with headaches misreport how often they use VDTs.

A. This doesn't tell us that one group was affected more than another.
B. The conclusion was only about how often headaches occur. The severity doesn't matter.
C. This supports the conclusion, assuming eyestrain can lead to headaches.
D. **CORRECT.** This shows the data is flawed, and biased towards showing that people with headaches use VDTs more often.
E. This shows the samples are equal and strengthens the argument.

Question 15

QUESTION TYPE: Necessary Assumption

CONCLUSION: Interpretations of a literary work tell us more about the critic than the author.

REASONING: There is no single valid interpretation of any work. Interpretation involves imposing meaning rather than discovering meaning in the work.

ANALYSIS: The wrong answers are particularly weak on this question, but they disguise themselves in language that sounds plausible. Remember the conclusion: a review tells us about the critic. Only B addresses this point.

The argument assumes that we can learn about critics from their reviews. If we can't interpret authors' writing, then why can we interpret critics' writing?

———————

A. The argument implies that there is a way to distinguish the validity of an interpretation. It says "there are a number of equally valid" interpretations. That implies that some interpretations are less valid.
B. **CORRECT.** If meaning doesn't reflect anything about the interpreter then it isn't clear how interpretations tell us anything about the critics.
C. This isn't necessary. The argument already says that intentions aren't necessary to an interpretation
D. Similar to C: this doesn't matter. The argument said that it isn't necessary to consider an author's intentions.
E. This doesn't tell us whether critical reviews tend to tell us more about critics or authors.

Question 16

QUESTION TYPE: Flawed Reasoning

CONCLUSION: Electronic media will get rid of the traditional school.

REASONING: Printed books helped bring about the traditional school. Electronic media is fulfilling the role of printed books.

ANALYSIS: The argument hasn't shown that books are necessary to schools. They just helped schools arise, centuries ago.

———————

A. This isn't circular reasoning. The evidence for the conclusion is that books are being replaced by electronic media. It's bad evidence, but the argument isn't circular.
B. There isn't a single expert mentioned.
C. The argument hasn't even managed to prove that schools *could* go away.
D. **CORRECT.** Books helped schools to arise. But the argument hasn't proven that they are necessary for schools.
E. This is densely worded but meaningless. The argument didn't mention how valuable schools are or how they operate (in what medium.)

Question 17

QUESTION TYPE: Paradox - Exception

PARADOX: Seat belt laws lower the *rate* of traffic accidents. A certain city passed seat belt laws two years ago but has the same *number* of traffic accidents.

ANALYSIS: All of the wrong answers show how some other factor either increased the number of deaths or caused the statistics to be bumped upwards.

The right answer just tells us a fact about the people who died. We don't know why they weren't wearing seatbelts. And it could be only a small minority of people who don't wear seatbelts, and die.

Note that the stimulus first talks about the *rate* of deaths, and then switches to the *number* of deaths. Those aren't the same thing, though only answer choice C addresses this.

A. Higher speed limits generally lead to more deaths.
B. This would increase the number of deaths reported even if the actual number of deaths decreased.
C. More traffic means more potential accidents.
D. A law that nobody pays attention to won't have much of an impact.
E. CORRECT. This doesn't tell us anything. We don't know why these people disobeyed the law, and why fatalities didn't decline in the city.

Question 18

QUESTION TYPE: Principle - Must be True

FACTS:

1. Some people say space exploration is too expensive.
2. It's also very risky.
3. And cutting budgets increased the risk of space exploration.

ANALYSIS: About the only information we can get from the passage is that there are a couple of problems with space exploration and that if we cut costs we'll make the safety problem worse.

A. CORRECT. By trying to solve the cost problem we increased the safety problem.
B. Unfortunately, it's not clear that we made any scientific progress. We just cut costs a bit.
C. Safety was sacrificed for cost, not speed.
D. We have no clue if the mistakes were bureaucratic or instead were causes by defects in the manufacturing process. We only know that cost-cutting was the ultimate cause.
E. This isn't clear. We haven't been told of the benefits of space exploration. They might be large enough to justify the risk.

Question 19

QUESTION TYPE: Necessary Assumption

CONCLUSION: Hatha yoga helps us quit smoking.

REASONING: Hatha yoga + counseling were as effective as self-help groups + counseling.

ANALYSIS: This is a really bad argument. First, we're not told how much each group reduced its smoking. It's possible it was a very tiny change.

Second, it's possible that individual counseling was the major reason for each group's success. That would mean that Hatha yoga and self-help groups are equally useless.

We can ignore individual counseling since it was an equal factor for both groups. That means that Hatha yoga must be exactly as effective as self-help groups.

———————

A. This still doesn't tell us how large a reduction each group experienced. It would be hard to say that Hatha yoga was a powerful tool if it only reduced cravings by 5%.
B. It doesn't matter how many smokers can practice Hatha yoga. It only matters how effective Hatha yoga is for those smokers who can practice it.
C. **CORRECT.** If this is true, then Hatha yoga must also be a powerful tool. Individual counseling was the same for each group. So Hatha yoga must be exactly as powerful as self-help groups.
D. This would be nice, but the main question is whether Hatha yoga helps quit smoking. It doesn't matter if it's harmful in some other way.
E. Other forms of yoga are quite irrelevant.

Question 20

QUESTION TYPE: Strengthen - Exception

CONCLUSION: Some researchers say that Antarctic seals store oxygen in their spleens.

REASONING: No specific reason is given, apart from the fact that seals must store oxygen on long dives.

ANALYSIS: A lot of the wrong answers provide pretty weak support. But any support at all is enough to strengthen an argument.

B is the weakest answer because it doesn't specify that *Antarctic* seals can store oxygen in muscles. Further, there's no evidence that storing oxygen in muscles lets seals store oxygen in the spleen.

———————

A. This shows that it possible for an animal to store oxygen in their spleen.
B. **CORRECT.** First, this doesn't tell us that *Antarctic* seals can do the same. Second, muscle tissue isn't the spleen, and it increased muscle tissue storage doesn't indicate that the spleen can store oxygen.
C. This shows that Antarctic seals must store oxygen *somewhere*. Perhaps in the spleen.
D. This shows that the spleen may have a special function in Antarctic seals. And it seems related to dives.
E. Blood vessels allow oxygen to be used. So extra blood vessels in the spleen could show that oxygen was being stored there.

Question 21

QUESTION TYPE: Flawed Parallel Reasoning

CONCLUSION: There is no increased health risk from eating fruits and vegetables that had pesticides.

REASONING: Some studies show that eating fruits and vegetables decreases the risk of *cancer*. The studies did not separate organic fruit and vegetables and those that had pesticides.

ANALYSIS: The conclusion is about *health* risks while the evidence is about *cancer* risk. The argument confuses two types of risk.

There's another error. The study mixed up the organic and non-organic fruits and vegetables. Overall, fruits and vegetables reduce cancer risks.

But if we separate non-organic from organic, it's possible that non-organic fruits and vegetables would increase health risks, while organic varieties decrease them.

———————————

A. **CORRECT.** Modern power plants decrease the incidence of *certain* diseases. But the conclusion says that nuclear power plants do not present an overall risk to *health*. Health includes *all* diseases.
This also repeats the error of lumping together both groups into one study, then assuming that what is true of the whole group is true of each part.

B. This is a bad argument. It has proven that either exercise or diet could work. But it hasn't proven which strategy is more useful. Yet the argument doesn't make the error in the stimulus of confusing two terms.

C. This is a bad argument. Motorcyclists receive one year of instruction while car drivers just pass a test. One would hope a year of training would make motorcyclists safe. But this argument doesn't make the error of confusing two types of risk.

D. This is a bad argument. We don't necessarily care whether a cutting board has fewer microbes. We care whether it has fewer microbes *that are harmful*. There are microbes everywhere, and most don't hurt us. But this argument doesn't confuse two types of risk.

E. This is a good argument. Lack of a health benefit to doing something means there is no health risk to not doing it.

Question 22

QUESTION TYPE: Principle – Strengthen

CONCLUSION: Judges shouldn't be merciful based on motives.

REASONING: Motives are hard to be sure about. And even bad motives can be presented as good.

ANALYSIS: The wrong answer choices all miss the point: the argument is talking about how we should treat someone who claims to have had good motives.

The argument claims we should have no mercy, because its too hard to tell what motives are real and truly good.

The wrong answers all focus on what laws should exist. That's completely different from how a judge should decide a case.

————————————

A. This talks about which laws should exist. But the stimulus talks about what judges should do.
B. CORRECT. That is what judges will be doing if they ignore motives. They will punish everyone who does something wrong, even those who really had motives that ought to have excused them. The author is fine with that.
C. The argument isn't talking about what should be allowed. It's talking about how we should punish those acts that already aren't allowed.
D. We *can* enforce laws. If you're punishing someone, you're enforcing the law. The argument is just arguing we should ignore motives when we punish people.
E. This has nothing to do with the argument, which is about whether we should consider motives.

Question 23

QUESTION TYPE: Point at Issue

ARGUMENTS: Roxanne argues that buying old ivory won't increase the demand for new ivory.

Salvador argues that buying old ivory *will* increase the demand for new ivory. There isn't enough old ivory, so some people buy new ivory instead.

ANALYSIS: They disagree on whether we should buy antique ivory.

————————————

A. Neither of them talks about any other substances.
B. CORRECT. Roxanne says yes. Salvador says that demand for new ivory would increase.
C. Both of them agree we should try and protect elephants. They disagree how we should do so.
D. Salvador might think that refusing to buy new ivory would help. But he thinks refusing to buy old ivory would help even more.
E. Both of them agree about this. Roxanne thinks we should only buy ivory older than 75 years.

Question 24

QUESTION TYPE: Principle – Strengthen

CONCLUSION: Salvador concludes that buying old ivory will increase the demand for new ivory.

REASONING: There isn't enough old ivory to meet demand. Some people buy new ivory instead. (Presumably if there were even more demand for old ivory then more people would have to switch to new ivory)

ANALYSIS: Some people buy new ivory only because they can't get old ivory. These people don't care about elephants. Let's call them "ivory fans"

If fewer people buy old ivory, then there will be more old ivory for "ivory fans" to buy, and they won't buy so much new ivory.

Salvador doesn't care about the motives of "ivory fans". If he can free up old ivory for them to buy then elephants will be saved.

So anyone who *does* care about elephants should stop buying old ivory. This will indirectly reduce ivory fans' demand for new ivory.

_____

A. Salvador doesn't talk about spreading knowledge. He just says not to buy any ivory.
B. We don't know if acceptable substitutes are available.
C. Salvador is arguing that we shouldn't purchase old ivory either (an object in existence at the time the species became endangered.)
D. We have no evidence that workers will engage in restraint.
E. **CORRECT.** Salvador's plan is aimed at reducing the damage other do to elephants. He wants fewer people to buy new ivory, even if they don't care about elephants.
   If people who do care about elephants stop buying old ivory, then people who don't care about elephants will buy the old ivory instead. This will spare elephants.

Question 25

QUESTION TYPE: Weaken

CONCLUSION: You aren't any safer in a car with air bags.

REASONING: Air bags lower the risk of serious injury. But cars without air bags have more accidents.

ANALYSIS: Try to think of a situation that is consistent with the stimulus, but that shows airbags are effective.

For example, cars with air bags could only be 1% more likely to be involved in an accident. And those accidents could be minor. Meanwhile, air bags could lower the risk of serious injury by 80%.

When I put it that way, would you rather be in a car with air bags or without them?

_____

A. The argument doesn't say this. It just points out that cars with air bags are more likely to be in an accident, on average.
B. The argument didn't say whether cars without air bags have other safety features.
C. The argument implies this occurs. It's talking about probabilities: cars with air bags are more likely to have accidents. But of course both groups can have accidents.
D. **CORRECT.** I'd rather be in more accidents but avoid serious injury. The reverse sounds painful.
E. The argument doesn't say this. Some very minor accidents might not require air bags.

Question 26

QUESTION TYPE: Parallel Reasoning

CONCLUSION: Ashley is unlikely to collect a stone that didn't originate in Tanzania.

REASONING: All known deposits of Tanzanite are from Tanzania.

ANALYSIS: This is a good argument. It's possible we'll discover Tanzanite outside Tanzania. But the argument is appropriately cautious: it's only "unlikely" that Ashley will get a rock from outside Tanzania.

All of the answer choices use the same terms: frogs, owls, lagoon, and island. So pay very close attention to the relationship between those terms, and choose the one that is as uncertain as the stimulus.

A. This is a bad argument. The lagoon has many frogs, but there might also be many frogs outside the lagoon but still on the island.
B. This is a bad argument. The frogs are only *eaten* by the owls. But this doesn't say that the owls only *eat* frogs from the island. The owls could eat frogs from other islands.
C. Frogs are the only animals to live in the lagoon but that doesn't mean that all frogs live in the lagoon. The owls could therefore eat frogs that live outside the lagoon.
D. **CORRECT.** All frogs live in the lagoon, as far as we know. If owls eat only frogs then they'll only eat animals from the lagoon unless we discover frogs that live outside the lagoon.
E. This is a good argument, but it's more strongly worded than the stimulus. The stimulus said all *known deposits* of Tanzanite are on the island. Answer choice D said that all *known frogs* live in the lagoon. This answer is too certain: it says that every frog (known *and* unknown) *does* live in the lagoon.

Test 37
Section III - Logic Games
Game 1 – Boarding School
Questions 1-5

Setup

This is a grouping game. We have to figure out how to arrange females and males between eight dormitories. There are five females and three males. Here's how to set it up:

F	F	___	___
R	T	V	W

North is on the top and South is on the bottom. I've added in the rule that says that R and T north are filled with females.

Rules 2 and 4 are important to remember. There are only three males (rule 2). If a male is in a dormitory, then the other wing is female (rule 4).

There's no single best way to diagram that. The main thing is to commit them to memory somehow. Here's what I drew:

$M = 3$

$M \longrightarrow F$

We can combine these rules to figure out that three of the four dormitories will have one male and one female, and one dormitory will be all female. This means that one of either R south or T south will be male.

Why? Well, look what happens if they're both female:

F	F	___	___
F	F	___	___
R	T	V	W

We have no space to spread the men out across 3 dormitories. So we can draw our diagram like this to remind ourselves that at least one of them must be male.

F	F	___	___
M/F	M/F	___	___
R	T	V	W

The final rule lets us split our setup into two scenarios. It says that if males is in V south, then males are also in W north.

So we can see what happens if V south is male, and we can see what happens when it's female.

F	F	F	M
M/F	M/F	M	F
R	T	V	W

Here I've made Veblen South Male. That means V north and W south are female, according to rule 4.

The other scenario is more boring. But should draw it to remind yourself that you can't put males in V south unless your diagram follows rule 5 and looks like the diagram up above.

Drawing a way to keep yourself from forgetting the M in Vs --> M in W north rule.

F	F		
M/F	M/F	F	
R	T	V	W

You might think we need to put F in W north as well. But we're not drawing the contrapositive. We're just trying two options: males in V south (rule 5 triggered), or no males in V south (rule 5 not triggered).

Main Diagram

Scenario 1 (where M is in V south)

F	F	F	M
F/M	M/F	M	F
R	T	V	W

Scenario 2 (where F is in V south.
         i.e. all other situations)

F	F		
M/F	M/F	F	
R	T	V	W

Rules:

1. If M is in a dormitory, then F is in the other wing.
2. Five F, three M.
3. If M is in V south, then M is in W north.

Question 1

The first thing to do is to try diagramming the new information.

F	F	F	___
M/F	M/F	F	
R	T	V	W

We've used four of our five available females. We only have one left. But the questions asks for *two* places where females can be assigned.

So the right answer must include one of the two females already placed in R and T north.

It's also important to check where males *have* to go. We have to put one male in each of R, T and W. So the full diagram actually looks like this:

F	F	F	___
M	M	F	
R	T	V	W

A is wrong because it says females go in Tuscarora South.

B is wrong because R south has to be male.

C is wrong because R south has to be male.

D is **CORRECT.** We know there are definitely females in T north. Females could also go into W south...it doesn't really matter as long as Males are in one spot in W.

E is wrong because T south has to be male.

Question 2

I'm looking at the main diagram in order to think about this question.

F	F	___	___
M/F	M/F		
R	T	V	W

Where couldn't we put two females? Well, the only obvious place is in R and T south. Then there would be no place to split up the three males in across three dormitories.

That's why **B** is **CORRECT.**

F	F	___	___
F	F		
R	T	V	W

That's a much faster method than the alternative, which is to draw out each scenario and see what works.

A and **C** both have females in R south and one other place. That's fine. There are no rules associated with females being in any of the places mentioned, and all setups leave room for three males in three separate dorms.

D and **E** both involve females being in Wisteria South and one other place. Again, there are no rules telling us what to do if females are in those places. Both setups leave space for three males to go in three separate dorms.

Question 3

The first step with a local rule question is to draw the local rule in our diagram.

F	F		F
M/F	M/F		
R	T	V	W

The second step is to ask if we can make any new deductions by combining the rule with our existing rules. The last rule mentions Wisteria North. If men are in V south then M also has to be in V north.

Hmm. We *don't* have M in Wisteria North. So we *can't* put M in Veblen South. We must put females there. Therefore **D** is **CORRECT.**

Question 4

Like the last question, the first step here is to draw the local diagram.

F	F	F	M
F/M	M/F	M	F
R	T	V	W

We saw this in our setup; it's scenario 1. Males go in W north because of the last rule. Females go in V north and W south because men can't fill both spots in a dormitory.

Males could go in either R or T south (in fact, they *have* to go in one). So the places men can't go are the places marked F on our diagram.

D is **CORRECT,** because it lists all of those places.

Question 5

F	F		
	F		
R	T	V	W

I've drawn the local diagram above. You can see that the major constraint is that males have to be assigned across all three of the open dormitories. We need an M in R, V and W. That means we must put M in R south, so really the diagram looks like this:

F	F		
M	F		
R	T	V	W

So we need one male in V and W.

A and **B** are wrong because they put an M in R south.

C is tricky to eliminate. But if you put F in Veblen North and Wisteria North, then M goes in Veblen South and Wisteria South.

This answer choice vioates the last rule. M in Veblen South means M in Wisteria North. This answer choice puts F in Veblen North.

D is **CORRECT.** There's no rule against putting Females in Veblen and Wisteria South. We can put males in the North, so we'll have males spread across three dormitories.

E is wrong because Veblen is completely filled up. Now only Wisteria is left for the two males, and we can't put two males in the same dormitory.

Game 2 – Red and Green Trucks
Questions 6-11

Setup

This is a linear game with a twist. Not only do we have to figure out the order of the trucks, we also have to figure out which colors they are. Fortunately, the rules about color let us figure out almost everything about this game.

The first rule tells us we can't have two reds in a row. That means we always need a green between two reds (green is the only other color.) Here's how I drew that:

```
___   ___   ___
 r     g     r
```

The variables go on top of the slots, and the colors go on the bottom.

The next rule is straightforward sequencing. Y comes in front of T and W. We'll put it directly on our diagram later, but for now here's how to draw it.

```
        T
     /
  Y
     \
        W
```

The next two rules are interesting. If exactly two trucks before Y are red (rule 3), then Y must come at fourth at the earliest. There are two red trucks and a green truck in front of Y. Y could go fifth if there is more than one green truck in front of Y.

But...we also know S is sixth (rule 4). Y can't go last (because T and W come after Y), so S must come after Y.

T, W and S all come after Y. That means Y has to go fourth at the latest.

If Y has to go fourth at the latest and fourth at the earliest...then Y just has to go fourth!

S, T and W fill up spots 5, 6 and 7. Here's to draw all that:

			Y	T/W	S	W/T
1	2	3	4	5	6	7
r	g	r	g			

The three trucks in front of Y are r, g and r because that's the only way to fit in two red trucks. So Y must be green, since we can't have two reds together.

S is in sixth. T and W come after Y in 5 and 7, in either order. We don't know anything about the colors of trucks 5, 6 and 7: they could even all be green.

Lastly, Z comes before U (rule 5). X wasn't mentioned in any rule, so it could go anywhere in spots 1-3. I've drawn these directly onto the diagram:

Z — U, X

			Y	T/W	S	W/T
1	2	3	4	5	6	7
r	g	r	g			

Z --U and X are drawn overhead and separated by a comma to indicate that they all must go before Y. The comma indicates that we don't know if X comes before Z and U, after them, or even in between.

As far as I know, I invented this style of drawing. It's an easy way to keep track of all remaining variables. This frees up mental space and lets you focus on the question.

Question 6

As with all list questions, take one rule and go through the answer choices in turn to see what can be eliminated.

A is **CORRECT,** by process of elimination.

B is wrong because Y needs to be fourth.

C is wrong because Y needs to be fourth.

D is wrong because T needs to be *after* Y.

E is wrong because Z needs to come *before* U.

Question 7

Two trucks can't both be red if they come beside each other. From our diagram, the only trucks that are definitely beside each other are T/W and S.

B is **CORRECT.** T and S are always beside each other (even though T could be in 5 or 7.) Therefore at least one of them has to be green.

A is wrong because X could go in 1 or 3 and therefore be red. And there's no rule stopping S from being red.

C is wrong because U could go in 3 and therefore be red.

D is wrong because T and W could both be red if S is green.

E is wrong because Z could go in 1 and X could go in 3. Then they would both be red.

Question 8

If X is in 3, then Z and U must be in 1 and 2 respectively. The truck in 2 is always green, so U must be green.

Therefore answer **C** is **CORRECT.**

Z	U	X	Y	T/W	S	W/T
1	2	3	4	5	6	7
r	g	r	g			

Question 9

If three trucks are green then there's only one way to set things up. The last three trucks have to be red, green, and red.

We can't do something like green, red, red because then two reds would be together. (We already have the first two greens in 2 and 4). Here's how it looks:

Z — U, X

			Y	T/W	S	W/T
1	2	3	4	5	6	7
r	g	r	g			

Clearly, S must be green. **A** is **CORRECT.**

Question 10

For ten, just look at your main diagram and see how many trucks are in fixed positions. Y is in 4 and S is in 6.

They're they only ones we can be sure about. T and W can switch places with each other. Z, U and X don't have a fixed order.

B is **CORRECT.**

```
Z — U, X
                         Y    T/W    S    W/T
  ___   ___   ___   ___   ___   ___   ___
   1     2     3     4     5     6     7
   r     g     r     g
```

Question 11

A is wrong because U comes after Z. U could go third and be beside Y, if X went before U.

B is wrong because X could go third, after Z and U. There are no rules for X.

C and **D** are wrong because both W and T can go in 5 or 7. If either goes in 5, then it's beside Y.

E is **CORRECT,** because Z has to go before U. U will always be between Z and Y, since Z and U come before Y.

Game 3 – Bookshelves
Questions 12-18

Setup

This is a grouping game. It's also one of my favorite games, because it lets you figure out almost everything before you start. I love those games.

But it isn't always obvious how to do that, so I'll show you how to approach this sort of game.

First, the basic diagram looks like this:

1 ____

2 ____ ____

3 ____ ____ ____

If you're unsure how to set up a game, take a look at the first question. Notice they've set it up the same way I have.

Next, you should draw the variables. This is important whenever variables are split into groups.

Once you've finished your setup, you should look back at this diagram and remember which variable is a novel, a monograph, etc. On logic games, it's very important to load that type of information into your short term memory.

g : F,H

m : P,S

n : V,W

Now, I said something about splitting the game into three scenarios. You can do that with the second and third rules (I'm going to ignore the first rule for a moment.)

The monographs, P and S, can't go with each other (rule 2). And they can't go with V, either! (rule 3)

V, P and S must all be kept separate. So there is one for each group.

For instance, one of P/S could go in 1, the second could go in 2, and V could go in 3. It looks like this:

1 __V__

2 __P/S__ ____

3 __S/P__ ____ ____

You may find it tough to see this type of deduction during a game. The trick is to look for rules that mention the same variable. Rules 2 and 3 both mention monographs.

There are only two other ways of arranging that, shown below.

1 __P/S__   1 __P/S__

2 __V__ ____   2 __S/P__ ____

3 __S/P__ ____ ____ 3 __V__ ____ ____

I'll call them scenarios 1, 2 and 3, in order. (I'm numbering the scenarios based on where Vonnegut appears)

V, S and P must always be keep separate. *Always.* This is the cardinal rule of this game. If you remember it, the game is easy. If you forget it, the game is hard.

Now we can look at the first rule. You must always put at least one of the novels (V or W) on the same shelf as F. So F needs two spots: one for F and one for the novel.

Remember these two things:

1. V, P and S are separate
2. F always goes with V or W

Did you memorize the two things from the previous page? Seriously, that's all you need to follow along and do this game. Go memorize them if you didn't let them sink in.

In the first scenario, V is already in group 1. So W has to be the novel that accompanies F. Only group two has the two spaces to fit them in. That leaves H to go in group 2.

1   <u>V</u>

2   <u>P/S</u>   <u>H</u>

3   <u>S/P</u>   <u>F</u>   <u>W</u>

In the second scenario (when V is in 2) we have more options. F could go in 2 with V, or F could go in group 3 with W. The only thing we can't do is put W in 2. Then both V and W would be together and there would be no novel left to go with F.

So W has to go in 3, and then F and H are split between the other two groups.

1   <u>P/S</u>

2   <u>V</u>   <u>   </u>

3   <u>S/P</u>   <u>W</u>

In the third scenario (when V is in 3), there's only space for F to go in group 3. V is already in group 3, so the novel requirement is satisfied. That leaves H and W go fill the other spots in groups 3 and 2.

F can't go in group 2 because there would be no novel there.

1   <u>P/S</u>

2   <u>S/P</u>   <u>H/W</u>

3   <u>V</u>   <u>F</u>   <u>H/W</u>

Main Diagram

Scenario 1

1   <u>V</u>

2   <u>P/S</u>   <u>H</u>

3   <u>S/P</u>   <u>F</u>   <u>W</u>

Scenario 2

1   <u>P/S</u>

2   <u>V</u>   <u>   </u>

3   <u>S/P</u>   <u>W</u>   <u>   </u>

Scenario 3

1   <u>P/S</u>

2   <u>S/P</u>   <u>H/W</u>

3   <u>V</u>   <u>F</u>   <u>H/W</u>

Notice that I've kept P, S and V in the first column on each scenario. They divide the scenarios. Little details like this make your diagrams clearer.

Question 12

For the first question, pick a rule and use it to eliminate answer choices. Repeat for each rule.

A is wrong because the semantics monograph and the Vonnegut novel are together on the second shelf.

B is **CORRECT.**

C is wrong because F doesn't have V or W on the same shelf.

D is wrong because P can't go with S.

E is wrong because P can't go with S.

Question 13

We can use the three scenarios to figure out this question. The *main* deduction is that P, S and V all have to be on separate shelves.

A is **CORRECT.** If a grammar were on the first shelf then we can't keep P, S and V separate.

B could be true in the first scenario.

C could be true in the first scenario.

D could be true in the third scenario.

E could be true in the first scenario.

1	V		
2	P/S	H	
3	S/P	F	W

(First scenario)

1	P/S		
2	S/P	H/W	
3	V	F	H/W

(Third scenario)

Question 14

This is just a general must be true question. Think about the three scenarios.

A doesn't have to be true in the second scenario: V is on the second shelf and the monographs are elsewhere.

B doesn't have to be true. In two of our scenarios the second shelf has a monograph.

C doesn't have to be true: in the third scenario Vonnegut (and no monographs) are on the third shelf.

D is **CORRECT.** Why? Lack of space elsewhere. After we place P, S and V, we only have three open spaces to place F, H (two grammars) and W (a novel).

One possibility is that F goes with V in scenario 2, in which case the only space left for F and H is the third shelf.

The other major possibility is that F goes with either W or V on the third shelf.

In both cases at least one novel and grammar are on the third shelf.

E is wrong because in scenario 3 there is no linguistics monograph on the third shelf.

Question 15

We must be in scenario 3 if both grammars are on the same shelf. It's the only way to fit F + H + a novel (in this case, Vonnegut.) Remember, F always has to go with a novel.

Here's scenario 3 again, with H on the third shelf:

1 P/S

2 S/P   W

3 V   F   H

We can see **A** is wrong because no monographs can be on the third shelf.

B is wrong because the first shelf has to have a monograph on it.

C is wrong because V has to be on the third shelf.

D is wrong because F has to be on the third shelf. If we put F on the second, there would be no room to fit H as well as a novel.

E is **CORRECT.** Either S or P can be on the first shelf.

Question 16

Another must be true question. When a game has many of these, it's a sure sign you need to have made many deductions.

A doesn't have to be true. In scenario 1, V is on the first shelf.

Scenario 3 proves **B** doesn't have to be true. We could fit V, W and F on the third shelf.

C doesn't have to be true, the scenario from question 15 proves both grammars can be on the same shelf.

D doesn't have to be true. The scenario from question 15 proves we can put W on the second shelf with either monograph (S or P.)

E is **CORRECT.** If we put W on shelf one then we can't put P, S and V on separate shelves.

Question 17

If the Farsi grammar isn't on the third shelf then it must be on the second. That means V must go on the second shelf so that F goes with a novel. We're in a version of the second scenario.

```
1   P/S
2   V     F
3   S/P   W     H
```

We can't put a monograph on the second shelf. So **A** is wrong.

We can't put H on the second shelf, so **B** is wrong.

S could go on the third shelf. **C** is **CORRECT.**

V has to go on the second shelf, not the third. F has to go with a novel. But if we put W on the shelf instead of V, we couldn't keep P, S and V separate. **D** is wrong.

E is wrong. W can't go on the second shelf. Then P, S or V would have to go together.

Question 18

If P and H are together, then they must be on the second or third shelves (we can't both fit on the first).

F must be on the other shelf, because F needs an open space to go with a novel.

```
1   S              1   V/S
2   V     F        2   P     H
3   P     H    W   3   V/S   F     W
```

In the first case, V has to go in second, because F needs to go with a novel.

In the second case, V and S are interchangeable. F already has W, so the novel requirement is satisfied (W can't fit anywhere else.)

A is wrong because P could go in 2.

B is wrong because in the 2nd case, V goes in 3.

C is wrong because S can go in 1 or 3 in the second scenario.

D is wrong because S could go in 3 in the second scenario.

E is **CORRECT.** In both scenarios there is no space for W to go anywhere else.

Game 4 – Swimmers
Questions 19-24

Setup

This is a linear game. It's slightly different from a standard linear game. We have ten spots, but really it's just two lines of five spots that each repeat once.

Since the swimmers all repeat, we can just draw two horizontal rows over top of each other:

1	2	3	4	5
6	7	8	9	10

Any swimmer that goes in 1 goes in 6. If they're in 2 they're also in 7, and so on.

K isn't before directly before L (rule 1). We can draw it like this:

It's important to remember that spot 5 is directly before 6. So K can't be in 5 if L is in 1 and 6.

Next, we're told that J can't go in 9 (rule 2). Since swimmers repeat laps, this means that J also can't go in 4.

1	2	3	4	5
			J̶	

6	7	8	9	10
			J̶	

Next, Ortiz is somewhere after Miller (rule 3). This is a normal sequencing rule:

M — O

The rule gets more interesting because we can combine it with the final rule. O has to come directly before J, once. So we get this:

M — [OJ]

Note that the rule said that J only has to come after at least one of O. That means that O could be in 5 and J could be in 1 and 6. It's not worth drawing these exceptions separately - just keep this in mind.

We can add this rule onto our main diagram by showing that O can't go in 3 and 8 (because J can't go in 4 and 9). We can also say that O can't go first and M can't go last (because M has to go before O.)

Lastly, J can't go second (because O can't go first, and J has to go directly after O). This comes in handy on question 23.

1	2	3	4	5
Ø	J̶	Ø	J̶	M̶

6	7	8	9	10
Ø	J̶	Ø	J̶	M̶

Question 19

Eliminate the answers one by one using the rules.

A is **CORRECT.**

B is wrong because J can't be in 4. That would cause J to also be in 9.

C is wrong because O has to be in front of J.

D is wrong because M has to go in front of O.

E is wrong because K can't go in front of L.

Question 20

This is a fun question. If J is in 8, we have to place O right before J, in 7. That means M has to go in 6 (and 1) in order to be before O.

```
 M       O       J
___     ___     ___     ___     ___
 1       2       3       4       5
 Ø               Ø       X́       Ḿ

 M       O       J
___     ___     ___     ___     ___
 6       7       8       9       10
 Ø               Ø       X́       Ḿ
```

So we've placed those three variables. We've got K and L left to place in 4 and 5. K can't go before L, so K must go in 5. L goes in 4.

That means we've placed all 10 variables! **A** is **CORRECT.**

Question 21

If O is in 4 then J must be in 5, because J has to come right after O. The only other restriction will be that K can't come before L.

```
                         O       J
___     ___     ___     ___     ___
 1       2       3       4       5
 Ø               Ø       X́       Ḿ

                         O       J
___     ___     ___     ___     ___
 6       7       8       9       10
 Ø               Ø       X́       Ḿ
```

C and **E** are wrong because they don't have J in lap 5 - other people are placed there.

A and **B** are wrong because they don't place J in lap five.

Often, local rule questions can be quickly solved once you make a single deduction: J must be in five.

D is **CORRECT.** I've shown it by process of elimination, but as further proof, this order works: K-M-L in spots 1, 2 and 3, O-J in spots 4 and 5.

Question 22

A is wrong because J can't go in lap 9. Laps 4 and 9 are the same.

B could be true. The following order proves it: MOJLK. **B** is **CORRECT.**

For **C,** L can't be in 5 because there's no place to fit M-O-J without placing K right in front of L. If you put M-O-J in 1, 2, 3, you would get MOJKL.

And OJ can't go in 3 and 4, because J can't go in 4.

D is wrong because M has to go before O.

E is wrong because if O is in 6 then O is also in 1. That doesn't work because M has to go before O.

Question 23

Jacobson can't swim lap 2. If J is in 2, then O is in 1 (because O has to be directly before J). That leaves no room for M to come before O.

Answer **B** is **CORRECT.**

It might seem like **D** is also right. Two problems. First, if J is in 6, then O could be in 5. Then O would come directly after J. Second, **D** and **A** are really the same answer choice: If J is in lap 6 then J is also in lap 1. Two answer choices can't be right.

Question 24

This is another process of elimination question.

A is wrong because J needs to be directly after O.

B is wrong because K can't be before L.

C is **CORRECT.**

D is wrong because J can't go in 9.

E is wrong because M has to be before O.

Test 37
Section IV - Logical Reasoning

Question 1

QUESTION TYPE: Complete the Argument

CONCLUSION: The logical conclusion is that the criminals didn't think they were doing anything wrong.

REASONING: Several examples are given where criminals rationalize their actions.

ANALYSIS: None of the criminals think they have done anything wrong. The logical conclusion is that they don't think they are criminals.

No one likes to think that they are a bad person. Everyone has a reason for the things they do.

_____

A. This goes too far. We don't reward people for borrowing money, even though there's nothing wrong with borrowing money.
B. If someone borrows money, that doesn't make them a victim of a criminal.
C. **CORRECT.** All of the statements indicate that the criminals didn't believe they were doing anything wrong.
D. The criminals haven't even mentioned the justice system.
E. If an embezzler thinks they merely borrowed money then why should they think they deserve any sentence at all?

Question 2

QUESTION TYPE: Weaken

CONCLUSION: VNO works in humans.

REASONING: Human test subjects experience subtle smells when their VNO is stimulated.

ANALYSIS: The wrong answers point out that the human VNO is not very developed. But we already knew that. That doesn't weaken the idea that our VNO cells still can do _something_.

The right answer shows that the scientists may have activated nose cells by mistake.

_____

A. **CORRECT.** If this is true then researchers might have actually stimulated the nose while trying to stimulate VNO cells.
B. This would explain why we can only see it microscopically. But it doesn't weaken the argument that its still functional.
C. The VNO is really tiny in humans and we don't seem to use it. So it makes sense that the chemicals are different. This doesn't weaken the argument that the VNO is still slightly functional.
D. This could explain why those other animals can routinely use their VNO while we cannot. But it doesn't weaken the argument that its possible to stimulate our VNO.
E. This strengthens the argument, since the VNO was linked to smell in humans as well.

Question 3

QUESTION TYPE: Most Strongly Supported

FACTS:

1. Students always preferred the painting that the instructor said had hung in prestigious museums.

ANALYSIS: We can only make a limited statement about these two paintings: the students seemed to be influenced by the professor's description description. That's all.

We can't make any general statements amateur art or paintings that are in prestigious museums.

———————

A. This is an extreme statement. The students might like *some* amateur art. But they might like prestigious art even more.
B. If both paintings were made by amateurs then the instructor was only lying half of the time.
C. This is also pretty extreme. Some people don't like abstract or religious art, for example. But plenty of that hangs in prestigious museums.
D. **CORRECT.** Otherwise, both groups probably would have preferred the same painting.
E. We have no idea. Maybe the effect of the lie was so powerful that it badly distorted the results. It could be that almost everyone would have preferred one painting over the other if they were presented neutrally.

Question 4

QUESTION TYPE: Flawed Parallel Reasoning

CONCLUSION: Greta Harris must be a rich CEO.

REASONING: Most rich CEOs went to prestigious business schools. Greta went to a prestigious business school.

ANALYSIS: Most Xs are Ys does not mean that all Ys are Xs.

Or if I say that most pets are fish (true, people have lots of fish), that does *not* mean that all fish are pets.

The number of rich CEOs is very small and the number of people who get MBAs from fancy schools is fairly large.

The argument reversed a "most statement", and also took it as an absolute statement.

———————

A. This is a bad argument because people don't always get the problems "associated" with their profession. But it doesn't make an error about reversing a most statement.
B. This doesn't have to be true. Otto could make a great career as "the opera singer who never practices." This doesn't make the error of reversing a most statement though.
C. Not quite. This is a bad argument. It could be that Italians are good singers but hate listening to opera. But it doesn't reverse a most statement.
D. This is a bad argument because it doesn't establish that bent nails actually cause good luck. But this argument doesn't reverse a most statement.
E. **CORRECT.** Lots of opera singers know languages. But there aren't very many opera singers and many more people know languages. So it doesn't have to be true that anyone who knows languages is an opera singer.

Question 5

QUESTION TYPE: Paradox

CONCLUSION: Farmers once managed to increase productivity with fertilizer. Now they want to increase productivity again, but fertilizer use is dropping.

ANALYSIS: Sometimes a certain tactic will be effective up to a point but then stop working. The right answer tells us this happened with fertilizer.

———————————

A. This just tells us there will be lots of mouths to feed. It doesn't say anything about fertilizer.
B. If this is the case then we would expect fertilizer to be used for soybeans as well.
C. This doesn't explain why farmers don't try again with fertilizer now.
D. CORRECT. Fertilizer use has reached its limit. It made impressive gains in the past but now it can't do much to improve productivity.
E. This describes something temporary. The decline in fertilizer use only began in 1985, five years after these events.

Question 6

QUESTION TYPE: Most Strongly Supported

FACTS:
1. Monkeys chose suede over wire, when both suede and wire had milk.
2. And milk over suede, when the suede had no milk.

ANALYSIS: The experiments offer two clear comparisons. Suede and wire are compared, and suede wins. But when wire has milk and suede doesn't, milk wins.

We have *no* idea how effective suede and milk are as substitutes for the monkeys' mothers.

We can only make a conclusion about the two situations that were directly compared.

———————————

A. Actually, the monkeys chose food over suede.
B. We have no evidence for this. The researchers didn't test fur.
C. This wasn't tested. The comparison was only between suede/wire and then wire + food vs. suede + no food.
D. The study did *not* test how convincing the substitutes were compared to the infants' mothers.
E. CORRECT. Assuming suede is warm and comfortable, the monkeys preferred food. The two tests establish that they prefer suede over wire, unless only the wire has food.

Question 7

QUESTION TYPE: Point at Issue

ARGUMENTS: Hazel argues that the company should switch to automatic bill processing so that the process will be more efficient.

Max argues that automatic processing is perceived as being less human. Fewer people will buy and the company will lose money.

ANALYSIS: Their main point of disagreement is whether or not the company should switch to electronic order processing. Along with that, they disagree whether electronic processing would increase or decrease profits.

A. Max might agree that electronic processing is more accurate. That doesn't do much good if customers are scared away.
B. I almost picked this. But Max would probably agree that faster order processing is good as long as it isn't electronic.
C. **CORRECT.** Hazel says yes, as processes would run smoothly. Max says no, as customers would stop buying.
D. Neither of them talks about this. There might be some things the business shouldn't do even if profits would increase.
E. Hazel might agree with this, but disagree that customers would stop buying as a result.

Question 8

QUESTION TYPE: Complete the Argument

CONCLUSION: The logical conclusion is that stability will decrease if a nation has advanced technology.

REASONING: People in countries with advanced technology will be able to see how other people live. They will question their customs and change them.

ANALYSIS: If we have prosperity, then we have technology. And technology undermines customs. So prosperity will undermine customs.

A. Not quite: the issue of justice isn't addressed.
B. **CORRECT.** If they have prosperity then they'll have all the latest technology (1st sentence.) That undermines customs and tradition, which will reduce stability.
C. Laws can't do much if technology is undermining your customs.
D. Actually, *acquiring* technical skills seems likely to undermine culture. It is the latest technology that changes customs.
E. Hard to say. Perhaps even gradual assimilation will undermine customs.

Question 9

QUESTION TYPE: Sufficient Assumption

CONCLUSION: If we think we're just objects controlled by natural laws then morality will decline.

REASONING: Not believe responsible → not ashamed at immorality → moral decline

ANALYSIS: The missing link is between thinking we're subject to natural forces outside our control and not thinking we're responsible for our actions. The chain should be:

Thinking we're subject to forces → Not believe responsible → not ashamed at immorality → moral decline

---

A. This doesn't let us connect anything to people not believing they were responsible.
B. **CORRECT.** If that happens, then they won't become ashamed at immorality and morals will decline.
C. This doesn't let us connect natural laws to believing you're not responsible.
D. So? We don't even know if those theories are correct.
E. We're trying to conclude "decline in morality." This doesn't help.

Note:

It's very useful to diagram sufficient assumption questions. They're almost always in this format:

Example: The conclusion is: A → D

The premises are one of the following. There is a gap between letters. :

A   B → C → D
A → B → C   D
A → B   C → D

In each case the right answer will provide the missing link.

Question 10

QUESTION TYPE: Method of Reasoning

CONCLUSION: Lydia concludes that squirrels are likely after sugar.

REASONING: Lydia examines what she thinks is the only alternative, and dismisses it.

ANALYSIS: Lydia makes a decent argument. She just says that squirrels are "probably" after sugar. She's open to the possibility of another reason.

A. This means: ignoring information that could prove her wrong. Lydia didn't consciously do that.
B. This would be: all squirrels go after sugar. So this squirrel must go after sugar. Lydia didn't make that kind of argument.
C. This would be like B. "I can see this squirrel is making a hole in the bark. He must be after sugar."
D. Tell me, what "well-understood phenomenon" does Lydia make an analogy to?
E. **CORRECT.** Lydia squirrels aren't after water and therefore they must be after sugar.

Question 11

QUESTION TYPE: Weaken

CONCLUSION: Galina concludes that the squirrels aren't after sugar.

REASONING: The concentration of sugar in maple sap is very low and squirrels would have to drink a lot to get much sugar.

ANALYSIS: Galina doesn't make a very good argument. If the squirrels aren't after sugar, why are they going for the sap? It's only sugar and water.

A. This is irrelevant, since maple sap doesn't have a high concentration of sugar.
B. This just tells us that other squirrels are copycats. It doesn't explain why they want the maple sap.
C. This sort of supports Lydia. But it's pretty weak. Less frequently could mean 49% of the time rather than 50% of the time.
D. **CORRECT.** This ruins Galina's argument. The squirrels raise the concentration of sugar by letting the water evaporate. Smart squirrels.
E. This just shows it would be pointless to go after sap. Galina and Lydia are presumably only talking about those seasons where squirrels can get sap.

Question 12

QUESTION TYPE: Necessary Assumption/Flawed Reasoning

CONCLUSION: When people complain about representatives, we can know that the politicians are just doing what they were elected to do.

REASONING: People make the specific complaint that politicians are ineffectual. Politicians only seem that way because they must make compromises to secure government funds.

ANALYSIS: This is a very subtle question. The conclusion talks about complaints in general. But the evidence only comes from complaints about ineffectuality.

We have no idea what people are like when they make general political complaints.

A. **CORRECT.** The stimulus' evidence is about what is true when people complain that their politicians are ineffectual. But then the conclusion talks about what is true when people complain about their politicians in general.
B. The argument didn't talk about increasing government resources. It talked about securing (existing) government funds.
C. The argument was simply clarifying why politicians behaved the way they do. It doesn't matter whether the public would be satisfied with such an explanation.
D. This isn't necessary. If compromise only disappointed the public 95% of the time, would the argument be weakened?
E. This is silly. The argument isn't claiming that nobody else displeases the public.

Question 13

QUESTION TYPE: Strengthen - Exception

CONCLUSION: The dermatologist thinks that the rash was caused by telephones.

REASONING: The rashes were on the side of the face where the patients held their telephones.

ANALYSIS: It seems odd that telephones could cause rashes, since most people use telephones and don't have rashes. The wrong answers all help show how some people could get rashes from phones.

The right answer just tells us that most people use telephones. We already knew that.

_____

A. Allergenic plastic could explain the rashes.
B. This helps rule out the possibility that some other device caused the rashes.
C. This shows that telephones were used for long enough to cause a rash.
D. **CORRECT.** So? Most people don't have rashes from telephones. This information doesn't help us blame telephones for the patients' rashes.
E. This shows that the proposed cause (telephones) came before the proposed effect (rashes.)

Question 14

QUESTION TYPE: Parallel Reasoning

CONCLUSION: Reducing government spending wasn't the only reason the scholarship program was cut.

REASONING: The government could have cut even more spending if they had cut military spending.

ANALYSIS: The point is that cutting spending wasn't the *only* reason the scholarships were cut. This is a good argument.

It doesn't claim that the government *should* have cut military spending. But there must be some additional reason scholarships were cut. (e.g. "scholarships are useless, but national defense is important.")

Another important part of the argument is that achieving the goal would have been *even easier* if they had cut military spending. Clearly, cutting spending wasn't their only goal.

Most of the wrong answers don't even involve a goal.

_____

A. This is a good argument, but it doesn't show a goal or that Phyllis had an easier way to reach her goal.
B. This is a good argument. But it doesn't show that there was an even better way to achieve a certain goal.
C. This just tells us how Sally and Jim could have avoided their problems. It doesn't say their real reason for doing something was different from their stated reason.
D. This is a good argument. Roger was just being kind. But Roger didn't say what his goal was for adopting the cats.
E. **CORRECT.** Thelma's actions support her goal, but she could have done even better by doing something else. So there must be an additional reason.

Question 15

QUESTION TYPE: Necessary Assumption

CONCLUSION: Punishing crime more harshly might cause an increase in our tendency to ignore others' welfare.

REASONING: Harsh punishment → less guilt → more transgressions

ANALYSIS: The argument has shown that threat of harsh punishment leads to more transgressions. But that might not be the same as the same as ignoring the welfare of others.

A. If legal penalties *do* determine the morality of an action, this argument is still good. That has nothing to do with ignoring the welfare of others.
B. **CORRECT.** The argument has proven that harsh punishments lead to transgressions. But if transgressions can't make us ignore the welfare of others then the conclusion is unsupported.
C. The argument didn't talk about being concerned for your own well being.
D. The argument is claiming that harsh punishment will actually lead to *more* transgressions. The argument would be stronger if harsh punishment never deterred anything.
E. The argument wouldn't be hurt if a handful of people are complete psychopaths and never feel shame.

Question 16

QUESTION TYPE: Flawed Reasoning

CONCLUSION: We shouldn't believe connoisseurs' assessments of whether a painting is real.

REASONING: Connoisseurs claim they can know about a painting based on the emotional impact it has *on them*. But the same painting will have different emotional impacts on different people

ANALYSIS: The argument makes a claim about connoisseurs based on evidence about the general population. That's a bad idea. It's quite possible that connoisseurs are different from the public and they all have similar emotional reactions, since they know the subject matter [paintings] very well.

Experts tend to have similar opinions. So if a painting makes an expert feel "exaltation", it's likely other connoisseurs feel exaltation too.

This common reaction could let the connoisseurs judge the authenticity of a painting.

A. This doesn't matter. The conclusion was that we should ignore connoisseurs.
B. Rembrandt was only given as an example. But emotional reactions to all paintings will be different.
C. **CORRECT.** Experts will often agree on something even when non-experts have differing opinions.
D. The argument doesn't say that emotional impact is irrelevant. It just says that the emotional impact will be very different for different people. So it could be hard to use as an objective criterion.
E. Rembrandt was just used as an example. Most paintings can provide emotional impact. It is that impact that connoisseurs use. The argument is about connoisseurs rather than painters.

Question 17

QUESTION TYPE: Necessary Assumption

CONCLUSION: We can reduce traffic fatalities by lowering speed limits.

REASONING: Last year the government lowered speed limits and traffic deaths declined.

ANALYSIS: This argument makes a causation-correlation error. It presents no evidence that the speed limit change *caused* the decrease in traffic deaths. That could have been a coincidence.

_____

A. If highway traffic increased then the argument would be even stronger. We would expect more accidents if there are more drivers.
B. The argument would still be ok if 49% of drivers (not a majority) obeyed the speed limit.

Most people do in fact disobey highway speed limits. But they'll drive slower if the limit is lowered, even if they still go above the limit.
C. This is very tempting. But it says "number of automobile accidents". The conclusion talks about *fatalities*. You can be in an accident but not die.
D. The argument would be ok if the new speed limit was only enforced at the same level of strictness as the old speed limit.
E. **CORRECT.** If this were true then we shouldn't be surprised that fatalities fell. They probably would have fallen even without the reduction in the speed limit.

Question 18

QUESTION TYPE: Weaken

CONCLUSION: A large comet could have killed the dinosaurs.

REASONING: The comet would have sent a cloud of dust into the atmosphere and cooled the planet.

ANALYSIS: The correct answer says that species very much like the dinosaurs survived. That's strange. If *all* of the dinosaurs died then we would expect similar species to have died too.

_____

A. So? The argument just says that the comet explanation is plausible. It's to be expected that some paleontologists will disagree. But they haven't proven the comet theory is implausible.
B. **CORRECT.** We would have expected these species to die if they had the same vulnerabilities that dinosaurs had. Otherwise, why didn't some dinosaurs survive as well?
C. There might be some other way of figuring out if the theory were true. This doesn't matter.
D. Of course. Some animals might have been adapted to survive in a cooler climate. But the dinosaurs could still have died if they weren't well adapted to cool weather.
E. "Fully understood" is a very high standard. We might be able to conclude that a comet would have killed the dinosaurs even if we can't figure out all of the consequences.

Question 19

QUESTION TYPE: Necessary Assumption

CONCLUSION: Government by referendum is worse for society.

REASONING: Big government projects usually benefit special interest groups the most, at first. Big projects are less likely to receive funding if power is equally distributed.

ANALYSIS: The argument is assuming that infrastructure projects are good, even if they benefit small groups at first.

A. **CORRECT.** If large projects never improve society then its not clear why there would be a disadvantage to government by referendum.
B. The argument hasn't shown that large scale projects will occur at all if the government doesn't do them.
C. The argument doesn't make any claims about the democratic process.
D. It doesn't matter what the purpose of equal distribution of power is. It only matters that enhanced welfare will be not be an *effect*.
E. It doesn't matter if there are other ways. The argument just claims that this particular way will reduce welfare.

Question 20

QUESTION TYPE: Sufficient Assumption

CONCLUSION: You don't deserve praise if the desire for praise motivates you to help others.

REASONING: We deserve praise only if we're trying to help others.

ANALYSIS: The argument hasn't shown that people who want praise also lack a desire to help others. We can have multiple motives for any action. We may like to help others as well as ourselves.

A. **CORRECT.** If we can't have both motives then this is a good argument. Desire for praise means no desire to help others.
B. This sounds good, but the argument hasn't proven that those actions are motivated *solely* by a desire for praise. People can have multiple motives.
C. The argument hasn't said that people motivated by praise are indifferent to the welfare of others.
D. People might well advance the interest of others if they take action to help them. So they could deserve praise.
E. This shows that we're correct to focus on motives. But this doesn't let us say that people who desire praise also lack a desire to help others.

Question 21

QUESTION TYPE: Principle - Strengthen

CONCLUSION: Laws should have an immunity period before they can be repealed.

REASONING: The long term benefits of laws often aren't obvious, while the short term pain of a law is usually clear.

ANALYSIS: The theorist says we should wait. The consequences of a law are only clear in the long run. He thinks the long run is most important.

———————————

A. Not quite. The theorist argues repeal should be independent of what voters think the *short-term* consequences will be. But if voters correctly think the long term consequences are bad then maybe we should repeal a law.
B. **CORRECT.** If the long term consequences are most important then it makes sense to wait until the long term consequences become clear.
C. The theorist doesn't compare the difficulty of repeal to how much work it took to pass a law. Their main point is just that we should wait a bit, no matter if the law was hard or easy to pass.
D. The theorist doesn't think short term consequences are that important. They're interested in the long term.
E. This doesn't make sense. If a law provided tons of benefit in the short run and only some benefit in the long run, we should still pass it. It's beneficial all around.

Question 22

QUESTION TYPE: Flawed Reasoning

CONCLUSION: This druid stone discovered in Scotland must be recent.

REASONING: The druid stones discovered in Ireland are old.

ANALYSIS: This is a silly argument. The fact that Irish druid stones are old doesn't mean that *only* Irish druid stones are old.

———————————

A. Old always means the same thing: made a long time ago.
B. The argument doesn't even use a word that means "most."
C. This isn't circular reasoning. There is (bad) evidence presented: the stone is Scottish, not Irish.
D. The argument is making a claim about the *present*, not the future. It's talking about how old the stone is, right now.
E. **CORRECT.** The argument assumes that *only* Irish stones are old because all Irish stones are old. But Scottish druid stones could be old too.

Question 23

QUESTION TYPE: Necessary Assumption

CONCLUSION: Sheila thinks it is not a good idea to install speed bumps and warning signs.

REASONING: She thinks that people who hit speed bumps could have accidents if they are driving too fast.

ANALYSIS: Most people slow down when they see speed bumps and signs that say "slow down!" They don't want to hurt their cars.

Sheila is assuming that at least some people won't slow down and will still drive fast enough to hurt themselves on the speed bumps.

————————————

A. It doesn't matter how bad the problems are in other cities. The proposal is limited to Crownsbury.
B. Sheila is clear that Robert is actually trying to address accidents. This answer choice is way off base.
C. **CORRECT.** If every driver slowed down then no driver could drive too fast and have an accident on a speed bump.
D. It's not necessary that *any* people affected by the problem be harmed. It's only necessary that some of the people *causing* the problem (the speeders) would be harmed by speed bumps.
E. The proposal is limited to residential streets. Non-residential streets are irrelevant.

Question 24

QUESTION TYPE: Relationship Between Arguments

ARGUMENTS: Robert argues we should slow traffic with speed bumps to prevent accidents.

Sheila argues that Robert's plan could cause accidents.

ANALYSIS: Sheila doesn't disagree with anything Robert says. She just points out a disadvantage to his plan that he may not have considered.

————————————

A. Sheila doesn't deny that the problem is serious. But she thinks that Robert's solution will cause harm.
B. **CORRECT.** Robert might slow some traffic but his plan will also cause some accidents when people hit the speed bumps too fast.
C. Sheila didn't propose an alternative plan.
D. Sheila didn't question Robert's motives. She just warned his plan had hidden dangers.
E. Sheila thinks it's worse than that: Robert's plan could cause harm.

Question 25

QUESTION TYPE: Strengthen

CONCLUSION: The historians say that the decline in wheat production was due to too much irrigation, not enough drainage and buildup of salt in the soil.

ANALYSIS: There is no reasoning given for the hypothesis. So we just have to find some that shows that salt was the main problem.

_____

A. The problem was too much salt, not lack of water. The land was actually over-irrigated.
B. **CORRECT.** If salt was the problem, then this explains why barley did better than wheat.
C. This tells us a fact about barley production but it doesn't explain why barley overtook wheat.
D. This weakens the theory that salt was the cause.
E. This confirms the idea that barley took over but it doesn't help us conclude that salt was the problem.

Test 38
Section I - Logical Reasoning

Question 1

QUESTION TYPE: Sufficient Assumption

CONCLUSION: The new health program will cause increased health risks for employees.

REASONING: A rapidly increased amount of exercise increases anyone's risk of a heart attack.

ANALYSIS: The stimulus doesn't tell us how hard people will exercise in the new program. It's only sudden, increased exercise that causes an increased risk of heart disease.

A. **CORRECT.** This tells us that the exercise program is intense enough to cause an increase in heart disease risk.

B. This doesn't necessarily mean much. It could be that both exercise programs are quite tame and involve less exercise than employees get outside of work.

C. This doesn't tell us if there will be a sudden increase in exercise for those employees. It's only a sudden increase that it harmful.

D. A sudden change in policy is not the same thing as a sudden increase in exercise.

E. This doesn't tell us if the new program is strenuous or not.

Question 2

QUESTION TYPE: Main Point

CONCLUSION: It is not a coincidence that the two desks were designed independently.

REASONING: No product like this had ever been released previously. The two products were incredibly similar in how they looked and how they worked.

ANALYSIS: The entire argument is aimed at showing that it is very suspicious that the two products look the same and work in the same way. The main point is that it can't be a coincidence.

A. This is true, but it's only part of it. Soccer balls have many characteristics in common. This product was *new* and that's why the similarity was significant.

B. This isn't certain. It could be that OCF copied Ergotech and managed to release the product first.

C. **CORRECT.** There must have been some leaking of information from one company to another. At least, that's the argument.

D. That would explain why the two desks worked the same way. But it wouldn't explain why the two products looked incredibly similar as well. Mere coincidence isn't enough to explain this.

E. This goes against what the argument is saying. The argument was claiming that the identical appearance was odd because the first product truly was unique until the second arrived.

Question 3

QUESTION TYPE: Principle - Strengthen

CONCLUSION: The chemist claimed the anthropologist had committed fraud.

REASONING: The anthropologist did not report her negative test results. The anthropologist claimed that the test had been performed incorrectly.

ANALYSIS: The stimulus doesn't tell us what counts as fraud. The correct answer (E) gives a very strict definition: you pretty much have to report everything that could even be incorrectly seen as a disconfirmation of your idea.

_____

A. The anthropologist did not report *anything*. That's the problem.
B. This tells us that someone can commit fraud despite doing some honest things. The anthropologist only did something *dishonest*. And this answer choice doesn't actually help us define fraud.
C. This supports the *anthropologist*.
D. The anthropologist *didn't* report any results.
E. CORRECT. The experiment certainly could be *interpreted* as disproving the anthropologist; even if the experiment was actually flawed and couldn't disprove anything.

Question 4

QUESTION TYPE: Strengthen

CONCLUSION: The anthropologist claims she did not commit fraud.

REASONING: The anthropologist claims that her experiment was tainted with acid and therefore wasn't accurate.

ANALYSIS: The anthropologist hasn't explained why acid should be a problem. The correct answer tells us that acid hides toxin T. So it is impossible to test for toxin T if acid is there. There's no need to report results if a test is guaranteed to be ineffective.

_____

A. This doesn't add anything to the claim that the anthropologist shouldn't have reported her results. It doesn't explain why the experiment wouldn't work with acid.
B. So? The anthropologist didn't claim storage time was to blame. Acid was the excuse.
C. CORRECT. This would explain why acid would invalidate the results. The presence of acid ruins the test by making it impossible to detect toxin T.
D. This *weakens* the argument. The anthropologist could have simply tried another test.
E. This doesn't explain what acid has to do with it.

Question 5

QUESTION TYPE: Point at Issue

ARGUMENTS: Naima argues that we should adopt the new system as fast as we can. It will operate more smoothly once we switch.

Nakai argues that the cost of switching now would outweigh the benefits.

ANALYSIS: Nakai doesn't disagree that the new system has benefits. But he also thinks that the costs of switching are too high.

———————————

A. Nakai thinks that the benefits would occur. But he also thinks that the switching costs would outweigh the benefits.
B. Neither of them claims that the proposed new system is the best system possible.
C. Nakai agrees the conversion is possible but he thinks it would cost too much to be worth it.
D. Naima might think the current system works well enough. But she thinks the new system will work even better.
E. **CORRECT.** Naima thinks we should convert as soon as we can. Nakai thinks that we should keep the current system (and delay conversion) as long as we can.

Question 6

QUESTION TYPE: Flawed Reasoning

CONCLUSION: For health-related guidance, experts are useless.

REASONING: Some articles on health claim that specific foods have benefits while other articles claim those same foods have disadvantages.

ANALYSIS: The argument's evidence doesn't say that the studies contradicted each other. Instead, one study claim a benefit (e.g. more alertness) while another study claimed a downside (e.g. higher cancer risk.)

The "conflicting" studies did not claim whether coffee was good or bad *overall*. They just mentioned a specific benefit and a specific drawback.

———————————

A. Coffee is just used as an example to show how expert advice can seem contradictory.
B. The argument is just making a statement about whether expert advice is reliable. It doesn't matter whether we want it or not: that won't change how reliable expert advice is.
C. The conclusion is restricted to experts' *health* claims.
D. The argument claims that expert opinion is *untrustworthy*.
E. **CORRECT.** Perhaps coffee lowers our risk of cancer but increases our risk of heart disease. It's possible for something to be both good and bad.

Question 7

QUESTION TYPE: Principle - Parallel Reasoning

PRINCIPLE: You should have someone else check your work: they'll be better at catching errors. It's easier to spot someone else's errors than to see your own.

ANALYSIS: Most of the wrong answers ignore the two elements from the stimulus:

1. We want to catch errors.
2. Someone else should do it, because they aren't you. You can't see your own mistakes.

Answer D is a straightforward application of the principle. Sometimes (but not often) the correct answer has a situation similar to the stimulus.

————————————

A. This has nothing to do with having someone check your work. It's just a statement about teachers' math abilities.
B. This does talk about how it's easier to understand our own views. But that's the opposite of the stimulus: it was easier to spot *someone else's* errors. And this has nothing to do with checking work.
C. This does talk about catching errors. But the stimulus talked about having someone else check your work, simply because they weren't *you*. This is a different situation.
D. CORRECT. This is exactly the same principle: someone else is more likely than you to catch your errors.
E. This doesn't talk about catching errors.

Question 8

QUESTION TYPE: Necessary Assumption/Flawed Reasoning

CONCLUSION: We don't need to listen to the officials who claim we should fly more.

REASONING: The officials drove to an out of town meeting.

ANALYSIS: There are two criticisms that work. First, the officials' advice might be good, even if the officials aren't following it. The pundit is making an ad hominem attack: claiming their argument is bad because they were hypocrites.

Second, it could be that the officials had good reason to drive. Maybe the out of town meeting was 10 minutes out of town. It wouldn't make sense to fly.

————————————

A. This is an assumption made in the *officials'* argument. The pundit is not arguing we should try to keep the airline.
B. The pundit didn't seem too concerned with what options the airline had. The main question was: should we listen to the officials?
C. It doesn't matter who paid for the trip. The pundit's main point was that they didn't fly.
D. It doesn't matter which option was more expensive. The officials argued that more people should fly, and the officials didn't fly. That's the critic's main point.
E. CORRECT. The critic is assuming that his ad hominem attack is sufficient to disprove the officials' argument. Ad hominem almost never makes a good argument.

Question 9

QUESTION TYPE: Paradox

PARADOX: An asteroid strike could have killed the dinosaurs. It would have raised enough debris to block the sun and kill plants. But most of the debris would have settled within six months, too soon to kill plants.

ANALYSIS: On many paradox questions, there's no way to think of a right answer ahead of time. Here, you just have to keep an open mind for other ways an asteroid strike could kill *all* the dinosaurs.

The right answer provides an alternate way the asteroid could have killed the dinosaurs: the dust caused disease. The disease could have occurred even if most of the dust settled.

A. Poor carnivores. But we haven't established that the herbivores would have lost their food: the dust settled very quickly.
B. This doesn't matter, since the asteroid strike would hurl dust into the entire atmosphere.
C. That's interesting. But the debris cloud settled down very fast, so the cool temperatures wouldn't have lasted for long.
D. Ok, so "many" dinosaurs would have been killed. But this doesn't tell us that the asteroid strike was enough to kill *all* of the dinosaurs.
E. **CORRECT.** This could kill all of the dinosaurs. The atmospheric debris went everywhere. And if enough of it stayed airborne even after most of it then settled then respiratory infections could have killed all of the dinosaurs.

Question 10

QUESTION TYPE: Weaken

CONCLUSION: Bernard says that Cora is wrong when she says the original keyboard was designed to slow us down.

REASONING: The technological limitations Cora mentions have disappeared, yet we are still using the same keyboard.

ANALYSIS: We need to strengthen the idea that the original keyboard was designed to slow people down. So we must explain why nobody has switched to a more efficient keyboard.

The right answer tells us that people want to keep buying the keyboards on which they were trained.

A. **CORRECT.** If people learn on the original keyboard then they'll want new machines with the same layout. It doesn't matter if another keyboard is theoretically faster: it's hard to switch.
B. This doesn't explain *why* word-processors have the same keyboard.
C. This might lead us to believe that it's worthwhile to keep the standard keyboard. But some other keyboard might be even faster, so this doesn't help Cora.
D. This means that people would have to stop typing while they learned the new layout. But it doesn't tell us if that is particularly hard to do or how long it takes. So this doesn't explain why we still have the old keyboard.
E. Then why haven't we switched? This explains nothing.

Question 11

QUESTION TYPE: Flawed Reasoning

CONCLUSION: Grades aren't necessary for teaching purposes.

REASONING: The best students won't be motivated by grades and neither will the worst students.

ANALYSIS: The argument didn't mention those students in the middle: the ones who have some motivation but who might need the incentive of grades to do their best.

_____

A. The argument didn't even mention a fixed body of material. Read carefully.
B. The argument mentioned that bad students aren't interested in grades or study materials.
C. This doesn't matter: the conclusion was only about an *academic* purpose.
D. This doesn't tell us if the worst students would respond to grades. Once they were "quite interested" in the material they might become like the best students.
E. **CORRECT.** There is usually a middle ground of students who have some self-motivation but who aren't completely self motivated.

Question 12

QUESTION TYPE: Necessary Assumption

CONCLUSION: Large government job training programs aren't a good idea anymore.

REASONING: Periodic retraining can be efficient only if it meets companies' short term needs.

ANALYSIS: The argument is assuming that large government programs cannot meet the short term needs of individual companies.

The wrong answer choices don't even say anything about large government programs.

_____

A. This talks about the past. The stimulus talks about what is appropriate in the present.
B. This talks about what happens if the pace of change slows. But the stimulus is talking about what is true at the *current* pace of change.
C. There could be a single type of retraining program that is most efficient as long as it isn't the government program.
D. **CORRECT.** If large government programs do meet companies' needs then they could be efficient.
E. This doesn't affect how well government programs work.

Question 13

QUESTION TYPE: Most Strongly Supported

FACTS:

1. Eating fruits and vegetables is correlated with lower stroke risk for the middle aged.
2. Fruits and vegetables are rich in folic acid.
3. Low levels of folic acid are correlated with lots of homocysteine, which can block arteries.

ANALYSIS: There isn't much evidence here to say that lack of fruit *causes* strokes. But it is associated with fewer strokes.

This is a crucial difference - we don't know very much. We're not even told if homocysteine *causes* blocked arteries. It's just associated with blocked arteries. Some other agent could be the one responsible.

Further, we don't know what the relationship is between blocked arteries and stroke. (Really - the stimulus doesn't say)

We *can* say there is a correlation between lower risk of stroke and more folic acid. This is because fruit is correlated with a lower risk of stroke and more folic acid.

This correlation is only true in the case of fruit, but we have at least some support for that statement.

A. The other way around. *More* homocysteine is correlated with more strokes.
B. **CORRECT.** More fruit leads to both more folic acid and less risk of stroke. Since folic acid and low stroke risk occur together, they are correlated.
C. Same as A, this gets things backwards. *More* homocysteine is correlated with more strokes.
D. This is also backwards. More folic acids is correlated with fewer blocked arteries.
E. We have no idea if folic acid can prevent strokes. We only know that folic acid is *associated* with a lower risk. It could be a total coincidence.

Question 14

QUESTION TYPE: Necessary Assumption

CONCLUSION: British people have more money to spend on vacations now.

REASONING: Foreign vacation costs about as much as it used to (i.e. it is expensive.) Yet a much higher percentage of Britons now travel abroad.

ANALYSIS: This argument is ignoring the possibility that Britons are simply spending money they don't have (i.e. going into debt.)

It's also ignoring the possibility that Britons have decided they like foreign travel more now than they did 30 years ago. Perhaps they could have taken foreign vacations back then but they just didn't want to.

The conclusion is unusual in that it says "vacations" instead of "foreign vacations." Normally such a switch is important, and you may have noticed it here. But, it doesn't make any difference this time. Always watch out for such subtle changes but don't assume they're always important or intentional.

A. This wouldn't affect anything. The argument's claim is about the total amount of money that Britons have to spend on foreign travel. If travel were less expensive then they could take more trips but have the same amount of money to spend.
B. The argument is talking about what Britons do. Foreigners are irrelevant.
C. It doesn't matter what Britons spent the money on. The main point is that they weren't spending it on foreign travel.
D. **CORRECT.** It's possible that preferences have changed. It could be that people simply prefer to travel abroad now when they didn't have such a preference 30 years ago.
E. The opposite of this is that people could be wealthier even without having more money to spend on travel. This doesn't destroy the argument because it leaves open the possibility that people aren't wealthier but have found more money to spend on travel.

Question 15

QUESTION TYPE: Most Strongly Supported

FACTS:

1. Mystery stories tend to have a smart detective and a dumb companion.
2. They use the same clues, but only the detective can figure things out.
3. Including the dumb companion lets readers try to solve the mystery.

ANALYSIS: We don't know how many mystery stories are like this, we only know that it happens "often." We also don't know if readers usually *do* solve these mysteries. They might fail most of the time.

But since readers had a "chance" to solve the mystery then there must have been enough clues for the readers to solve the mystery.

_____

A. We only know that mystery stories "often" feature a brilliant detective. That isn't necessarily most of the time.
B. We know that mystery readers are given "a chance" to solve the mystery. That doesn't mean they will "often" solve the mystery.
C. **CORRECT.** Those mystery stories that feature a dull companion will often have enough clues. If readers have a "chance" to figure out the story then there were enough clues to do so.
D. We have no idea. The brilliant detective is likely interesting and may divert us now and again. The point was that the dull companion diverts us from the solution to the mystery. No one cares about the dull companion's actions apart from that.
E. We're not told who uncovers the clues.

Question 16

QUESTION TYPE: Flawed Parallel Reasoning

CONCLUSION: The city should not increase the size of the police force to deal with rising crime rates.

REASONING: More police officers will only address the symptoms of increased crime. They won't eliminate the cause.

ANALYSIS: This is a bad argument: increasing the size of the police force might be a good short term measure. In the long run, it's better to address root causes. But lack of crime may be an urgent issue and it could make sense to deal with it by hiring more police.

So hiring police could make sense as a short term strategy even if it isn't the best long term strategy. Also, there's no evidence police make things worse in the long run.

_____

A. This is a good argument. Overly demanding rules make things worse in both the short run and long run.
B. Dams prevent floods in the short run but make floods worse in the long run because they dry up swamps. So dams may not make sense even as a short term strategy. This is a decent argument.
C. This is a good argument. On balance, security alarm systems save the most money, because security guards are expensive.
D. **CORRECT.** The drug presents a short term benefit and no long term harm. Therefore it may be a good idea to take it. The argument is wrong and makes the same mistake as the stimulus.
E. This isn't really a good argument. We might be able to reduce criminal activity even if we never fully understand the causes. But this doesn't make the error of confusing lack of long term advantage with lack of *any* advantage.

Question 17

QUESTION TYPE: Weaken

CONCLUSION: Automobile insurance should cost more if you drive more.

REASONING: A person's chance of being involved in an accident increases with the number of times that they drive.

ANALYSIS: We need something that shows that high-frequency drivers are also more likely to be safe drivers. Answer choice B does that.

———————————

A. This doesn't tell us anything about people who drive *frequently*.
B. **CORRECT.** This shows that infrequent drivers may actually be riskier than frequent drivers. We should charge *them* more.
C. This shows that infrequent drivers are *safer*.
D. If long distance trips are riskier then this strengthens the argument.
E. This *strengthens* the argument by showing that high-frequency drivers are also higher risk.

Question 18

QUESTION TYPE: Role in Argument

CONCLUSION: Automobile insurance should cost more if you drive more.

REASONING: A person's chance of being involved in an accident increases with the number of times that they drive.

ANALYSIS: The claim is the argument's conclusion. The argument gives examples to show that behavior that increases risk also increases premiums. Therefore, the fact that frequent driving increases risk means that people should pay more for that behavior as well.

The conclusion doesn't have to be the final sentence. The "after all" in the last sentence indicates that it is supporting another phrase.

———————————

A. It's the conclusion. Every other statement supports it.
B. **CORRECT.** It is supported by every other statement.
C. Which premise is supported by this claim? You won't be able to find it, because it doesn't support any. Always identify the premise that is supported before choosing this type of answer choice.
D. The argument doesn't mention any potential objections.
E. Which term is clarified? As with C, make sure you can answer that question before picking this type of answer.

Question 19

QUESTION TYPE: Complete the Argument

ARGUMENT: We can't view happiness people deserve all on its own. We also have to consider the happiness that someone brings to others.

ANALYSIS: The final sentence of the argument tells us that we should measure the happiness people deserve based on how much happiness they bring to others.

This leads to C: happiness is judged in terms of happiness.

_____

A. The essayist seems to agree that bad people are less deserving of happiness.
B. The essayist implies that happiness is valued: we judge the happiness people deserve *based on the happiness they bring to others*. That shows we value the happiness people bring.
C. **CORRECT.** Happiness is to be determined in terms of how happy we make others.
D. There might be other ways for a person to become happy. The argument doesn't address this point, so it can't be the conclusion.
E. A bad person might be happy. We just wouldn't think they deserve it.

Question 20

QUESTION TYPE: Most Strongly Supported

FACTS:

1. Big shifts in climate cause migration.
2. Migration mixes ideas, which is necessary for quick advances in civilization.

ANALYSIS: There isn't really much we can do with these two statements. Shifts in climate don't necessarily lead to advances in civilization. And intermingling of ideas could happen without shifts in climate.

The correct answer simply rephrases point one. If shifts in climate cause migrations then people will only stay settled (and not migrate) where the climate doesn't shift too much.

_____

A. We only know climate can be a cause. There could be other more important causes of migration.
B. We only know some climactic shifts can lead to more civilization. But some other shifts might simply be disastrous.
C. **CORRECT.** If there were drastic shifts in climate then the populations would move and wouldn't stay settled.
D. We have no idea if populations settle everywhere they *could* settle.
E. Intermingling ideas is only a *necessary* condition for advanced civilization, not a sufficient condition.

Question 21

QUESTION TYPE: Most Strongly Supported

CONCLUSION: It is best to study only the basics, but to cover them in depth.

REASONING: Deep knowledge of a few subjects will provide the basis for future study. But memorization of many facts without context will not prepare one for understanding anything.

ANALYSIS: There are two opposing education viewpoints. One is that we should study broadly, without depth. The other is that we should have a narrow focus, but learn well each subject that we study.

The stimulus argues that the second method will make us much better at learning on our own once we finish school.

————————

A. Learning how plants and animals are useful is not the same as understanding them in depth.
B. This has nothing to do with the different types of study mentioned in the stimulus. (Detailed vs. Broad.)
C. This doesn't tell us much. The stimulus was arguing both for learning from a teacher and learning on your own, later.
D. **CORRECT.** Detailed study of a small part of a subject gives us the tools to understand the rest of the subject later.
E. The stimulus didn't say which method was more effective. And it advocated learning only a *few basic* subjects, but learning them well.

Question 22

QUESTION TYPE: Parallel Reasoning

CONCLUSION: Building a dam wouldn't help agricultural productivity in the region.

REASONING: A dam would help the upstream lands but hurt the downstream lands even more.

ANALYSIS: This is a good argument. It shows that benefits in one area are *outweighed* by benefits in another area. The overall effect (on agriculture) is negative. The conclusion is mild: it only says the overall effect is not positive.

————————

A. This compares across areas (health vs. taste) whereas the stimulus compared agricultural benefits to agricultural drawbacks. Also, this doesn't tell us that the benefits of less disease definitely outweigh the worse taste.
B. This argument might be correct, but we would have to know whether businesses would also reduce their transatlantic phone calls.
C. **CORRECT.** This compares time saved to time lost, and finds that time lost in city delays offsets time saved by the new highway. The conclusion matches the stimulus: it merely says the highway will not reduce transit time (actually, the highway would increase transit time.)
D. This is a bad argument. If an illness *can't* be cured by rest alone then you ought to see a doctor. It only says diseases can *often* be cured at home.
E. This is a bad argument. It could be that the only plants damaged by the chemical are weeds. In that case, many gardens could benefit.

Question 23

QUESTION TYPE: Flawed Reasoning

CONCLUSION: Irradiated food isn't safe.

REASONING: The studies that found that it was safe were flawed.

ANALYSIS: Because the studies were flawed, we no longer have evidence irradiated food is safe. But we also don't have any evidence it is unsafe. We know nothing about irradiated food.

We have no clue about how safe or unsafe it is, so we can't make any conclusions.

The correct answer uses abstract language. Proof of denial of a claim is another way of saying: "you're wrong! And I have proof."

A. **CORRECT.** Failure to prove a claim is: no longer being able to prove it is safe. Proof of a denial of a claim is: It must be unsafe.
B. The argument didn't say anything about future studies.
C. The argument didn't claim any study supported its conclusion.
D. This would be an argument against the studies that concluded that irradiated food was safe.
E. It doesn't matter if the independent scientists know more. It only matters if they're able to detect flaws in the method of the study. You can detect flaws in the method of a study without knowing much about the subject matter.

Question 24

QUESTION TYPE: Necessary Assumption

CONCLUSION: A young child's food preferences can be changed based on what you feed them.

REASONING: If you feed a one year old child salty food for a year then they will develop a taste for salty food.

ANALYSIS: A whole year is a long time in the life of an infant. We might expect their tastes to change naturally. The argument is assuming that a child's tastes do not switch from sweet to salty naturally over the course of the year.

A. **CORRECT.** If you feed a one year old for a year, they become two years old. The argument is assuming that two year old children do not naturally prefer salty food.
B. The argument assumes this *doesn't* happen, unless you feed them salty food.
C. The argument would actually be much stronger if two years olds *do* naturally dislike salty food (unless you've been feeding it to them for a year.)
D. The argument would be stronger if children fed salty food developed a taste for salty food even if it tasted unpleasant.
E. The argument doesn't say what type of food is better for a child. This is irrelevant.

Test 38
Section II - Logic Games
Game 1 – Clown Car
Questions 1-7

Setup

This is a sequencing game. They aren't too common, but they are very standard. If you know one you can easily solve any of them. The trick is to turn all the rules into one large diagram that tells you how everything is ordered.

(on recent LSATs, the LSAC has thrown in conditional rules, because people were getting too good at pure sequencing games)

The diagram I'm going to show you is simple. The ordering goes from left to right *for those things that are connected by lines.* If a letter has a line to the right of it that connects it with another letter than the 2nd letter is later. If 2 variables have no lines between them then we have no idea which one goes 1st.

This will be easier with pictures so let's diagram the first rule:

You can see that V goes before both Y and Q, because there is a line between V and both of those letters.

There is no relationship between Y and Q because no line directly connects those 2 letters.

Here's rule 2:

As you can see, we just add new rules on to the diagram.

It's important to learn how to read these diagrams. There is no relation between Z and Y because there is no line between them. We can only read from left to right.

Here's rule 3. R is before T and that T is before V:

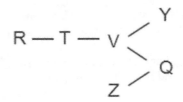

Some people understand this type of diagram instantly. But for others it's not so easy.

If you're still not sure how this works, put your finger on the R. You can see how R is connected to all the other letters by tracing a line from left to right with your finger.

If you can trace a continuous line from R to another letter *without going backwards* then R is before that letter.

If you have to go backwards or if there is no line between 2 letters then there is no relationship between the letters.

So R is before T, V, Y, and Q. You have to go backwards to connect R to Z, so there is no relationship between them.

Both R or Z could be 1st. Likewise both Y and Q could be last.

If you're still not sure how to read the diagram, then go back and read over each individual rule and think about how they fit together.

Apply those rules to this diagram and see how to match everything up. Now let's add rules 4 and 5. W is after R, and S is after V.

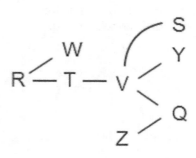

And we're done. There's no contrapositive because these rules aren't conditional statements.

This is just an ordering diagram; it tells us who can go 1st, who can go last and how all variables are related to each other.

Since there is just one diagram it is very important that you understand. Look over the diagram and see who can go 1st and who can go last. R and Z are the only variables that can go 1st because no variables come before them. S, Y, W and Q are the only variables that can come last because no variables come after them.

Master Diagram

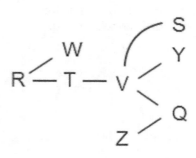

Question 1

For list questions it's better to use your rules than your master diagram. Pick one rule and go through the answer choices to see which ones you can eliminate using that rule.

A is wrong because T is before R.

B is wrong because Q is before V.

C is wrong because Q is before Z.

D is wrong because W is before R.

E is **CORRECT,** because it violates no rules.

Question 2

For a could be true question, you can eliminate answer choices by asking: does this have to be false?

A can't be true because R, T and V must come before Y.

B can't be true because only Z can go before R.

C can't be true because R, T, V and Z must go before Q.

D could be true. S could be fifth if Z, Y and Q went after S. **D** is **CORRECT.**

E can't be true because S, Y and Q all have to come after V.

Question 3

If Z is the seventh clown then Q must be the 8th clown. R must be first, because only Z could have gone before R.

R __ __ __ __ __ Z Q

A is wrong because only Z can normally go in front of R, but now Z is seventh.

B is wrong because now only R and W can go before T.

C is **CORRECT.** The only limit on W is that it cannot go before R. W can go anywhere from 2nd to 6th in this scenario.

D is wrong because now S, Y Z and W must go after V.

E is wrong because if Z goes seventh then Q goes eighth.

Question 4

If T goes fourth then both Z and W must go before T. We don't know where Z has to go apart from that.

V must go fifth because V goes after T and because S, Y and Q all go after V.

The diagram below indicates that Z, R -- T and W comes before T. The commas show that they could be in any order (as long as R is before T).

Z,R — T,W
__ __ __ T V __ __ __

A *could* be true but it doesn't have to be. R could go first and Z could go second or third.

B *could* be true but it doesn't have to be. Z could go first, or third.

C *could* be true, but it doesn't have to be. W could go second instead, and Z could go third.

D must be true. T goes, V goes after T and before S, Y and Q. There's only room to place V in fifth. **D** is **CORRECT.**

E could be true, but doesn't have to be. Y could also go sixth, if both S and Q went after Y.

Question 5

If Q is fifth then W, S and Y must all go after Q. It's the only way to fill the three spots after Q.

$$\underline{\quad} \ \underline{\quad} \ \underline{\quad} \ \underline{\quad} \ \underset{Q}{\underline{\quad}} \ \overset{Y\,,\,S\,,\,W}{\underline{\quad} \ \underline{\quad} \ \underline{\quad}}$$

A is wrong because Z could go anywhere in front of Q, including first.

B is wrong because T could go second if R went first and Z went after T.

C is wrong because V could go third if R and T went first and second and Z went after V.

D is **CORRECT.** W has to go after Q in order for us to place Q fifth.

E is wrong because it doesn't matter where Y goes as long as it is after Q and V.

Question 6

If R is second then that means Z gets out before R. There's no other variable that could go first.

$$\underset{Z}{\underline{\quad}} \ \underset{R}{\underline{\quad}} \ \underline{\quad} \ \underline{\quad} \ \underline{\quad} \ \underline{\quad} \ \underline{\quad} \ \underline{\quad}$$

All of the wrong answers talk about variables that have no rules linking the two of them.

A is wrong because there is no rule telling us whether S goes before or after T.

B is wrong because there is no rule telling us whether to put T before or after W.

C is wrong because there is no rule telling us where to put W, as long as it is after R.

D is wrong because there is no rule telling us where to put Y and Q in relation to each other.

E is **CORRECT.** Z has to go first if R goes second. Every other variable has to come after R.

Question 7

Some people find this question difficult, because we have to modify our diagram. But the process isn't any different from when we did our initial setup. V goes before Z? So draw a line from V that shows it's before Z. Then add in your other rule that says that Q goes after Z.

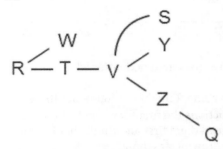

See, that wasn't so hard. If you feel stuck on a question that asks you to change the rules, just change one thing at a time. You'll eventually reach the goal that way.

A is wrong. R has to go first since Z now has to go after V.

B is wrong for the same reason. T now has to go second or third: only R and W can go before T.

C is wrong because R, T, V and Z all have to go before Q.

D is wrong because only R, W and T can go before V.

E is possible, and therefore **CORRECT.** R, T, V, W, and one of S or Y could all go before Z.

Game 2 – Farm Exhibition
Questions 8-13

Setup

This game is a mix of linear and grouping. We have to figure out which tasks the volunteers demonstrate, and the order they demonstrate the tasks

The first rule is incredibly important. Frank goes first, then Gladys, then Frank and Gladys in either order. It looks like this:

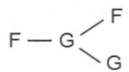

On it's own, that doesn't tell us much. But the second rule says that Frank can't go in 1 or 6. So Frank can only go in second or third (for his first task.) If Frank goes in fourth, there's no room for the two Gladys' plus the other Frank.

We'll get to the other rules after, but watch what happens if we put Frank in third.

		F	G	F	G
1	2	3	4	5	6

There's no other way to put it since Frank can't go in 6. And that takes care of all the Franks and Gladys'. So only Leslie is left to go in spots one and two.

L	L	F	G	F	G
1	2	3	4	5	6

We'll call this scenario 1, and come back to it later.

Scenario 2 isn't as interesting. Putting Frank in 2 doesn't let us figure much out. Though we do know Leslie goes first, because Gladys can't go before Frank.

L	F				
1	2	3	4	5	6

So Leslie always goes first, no matter what.

When doing a game, I might not figure out these ordering deductions the first time I look at the rules. That's why I read them first and think about them briefly before drawing anything.

Look for rules that mention the same variable. These can be combined to make deductions.

Now that we have ordering figured out, let's look at the other rules. They're all about tasks.

Rules 3 and 4 tell us which tasks Gladys and Leslie *can't* perform.

G ⟶ H̶ and M̶

L ⟶ T̶ and H̶

Both rules mention H. Since Gladys and Leslie can't demonstrate H, only Frank is left. Frank must demonstrate H.

The next rule says that T must go right before M.

This TM rule produces interesting results in the first scenario. Leslie can't demonstrate T, so only Frank or Gladys can demonstrate T.

Except, M comes after T. And Gladys can't demonstrate M. So Frank can't demonstrate T, because then M would be with Gladys.

So it must be Gladys that demonstrates T, and Frank demonstrates M. GF demonstrates TM.

The second Frank must demonstrate M, because it's the only Frank with a Gladys in front.

L	L	F	G	F	G
		H	T	M	
1	2	3	4	5	6

The first Frank therefore has to demonstrate harvesting (since no one else can demonstrate harvesting.)

That's about all we can figure out. We know most things when Frank is in 3, but we don't know very much when Frank is in 2. This game depends on knowing all the rules quite well.

It's also important to note that W, S and P all have no rules.

Master Diagram

Scenario 1

L	L	F	G	F	G
		H	T	M	
1	2	3	4	5	6

Scenario 2

L	F				
1	2	3	4	5	6

Rules

1. Gladys doesn't demonstrate H or M.
2. Leslie doesn't demonstrate H or T.
3. Frank therefore demonstrates H.
4. Frank doesn't go first or sixth.
5. T is demonstrated directly before M.
6. Leslie goes first (a deduction from the setup)

Question 8

For list questions, pick one rule and test each answer choice with that rule, eliminating them one by one.

A is wrong because Frank can't be in 1.

B is wrong because *two* Franks are in front of the first Gladys.

C is **CORRECT.**

D is wrong because Gladys can't demonstrate M.

E is wrong because T has to be directly in front of M. Here it is in front of S.

Question 9

When you see a general question, it's a strong sign the LSAC expected you to make deductions using the rules.

Here, **A** is **CORRECT.** Rules 3 and 4 tell us that Gladys and Leslie both can't demonstrate harvesting. So Frank *must* demonstrate harvesting.

The correct answer to question 8 shows that Leslie can demonstrate milling (rather than Frank) so **B** is wrong.

The correct answer to question 8 shows that Gladys can demonstrate threshing (rather than Frank.) So **C** is wrong.

Weaving, Plowing and Spinning all have no rules and could be demonstrated by anybody. That shows that **D** and **E** are wrong.

Question 10

If L is 4th, then we are in scenario two.

There are four spaces after the first Frank, and we need to fit in 2 Gladys and one Frank.

The question just assigned Leslie to one of those four spaces.

(The other Leslie has to go in 1, because one Leslie always goes there.)

L	F	__	L	__	__
1	2	3	4	5	6

Since we can't put Frank in 6th, Gladys must go there. And Gladys must also go third because we need a Gladys in between the two Franks.

L	F	G	L	F	G
1	2	3	4	5	6

Harvesting can only be demonstrated second or fifth (since Frank has to demonstrate harvesting.)

B is **CORRECT,** since it says second and no answer choice says fifth.

Question 11

On this question, Gladys demonstrates P right before Frank demonstrates T.

M comes right after T. So we have the order PTM. M is demonstrated by Leslie since Gladys can't demonstrate M.

It must be the second Frank that demonstrates T, because Gladys has to come after the first Frank.

There are two possible scenarios.

L	F	G	G	F	L
	H		P	T	M
1	2	3	4	5	6

L	F	G	F	L	G
	H	P	T	M	
1	2	3	4	5	6

This must be true. Frank always demonstrates H. The second Frank demonstrates T, so the first Frank (in spot 2) demonstrates H. **A is CORRECT.**

B is wrong. There are no rules attached to spinning, so either Gladys or Leslie could demonstrate it.

C is wrong. There are no rules attached to weaving, so either Gladys or Leslie could demonstrate it.

D is wrong. Gladys *can* perform the fourth demonstration, but she doesn't have to. In the lower scenario, Frank performs the fourth demonstration.

E is wrong, for the same reason as **D**. In the lower scenario, Gladys is in six instead f L.

Question 12

This is a general, "must be true" question. We can use our rules and previous scenarios to show which answers could be false.

We know from the first scenario of our setup that Frank can go third. So **A** is wrong.

The two scenarios from Question 11 disprove **B** and **C**. Gladys doesn't have to go in either 4 or 6.

Leslie *always* performs the first demonstration. F can't go first, and Gladys goes after F. So **D** is **CORRECT.**

The scenarios from question 11 prove **E** is wrong. Frank can go second.

Question 13

For a could be true question all of the wrong answers will definitely be false.

A can't be right because Frank is never first and only F can demonstrate H

B M can't go second because T has to go before M. Only Leslie can go first, and Leslie can't demonstrate T.

C is wrong because Leslie goes first and Leslie can't demonstrate T. It's the same error as **B.**

D is wrong because M has to go after T. That can't happen if T is last.

E is CORRECT. There are no rules attached to W. It can go anywhere that is open. L always goes in spot 1, and we have no rules to tell us what L must demonstrate. So L could demonstrate W in spot 1.

Game 3 – Job Applicants
Questions 14-19

Setup

This is a grouping game. Seven candidates are divided between three departments.

It might not be obvious how to draw the basic setup diagram. If you're ever stuck on how to represent a game, you can glance down at the first question. The layout of the answers usually shows the most efficient way to draw everything.

We should put the departments vertically. I've placed F in P because the last rule says F goes there.

(It's important to read the rules first, in part because you can spot some obvious rules that go directly on the diagram)

M ___

P _F_ ___ ___

S ___ ___ ___

The first two rules tell us that H and Y must go together and that F and G can't go together.

$$H \longleftrightarrow Y$$

$$F \longleftrightarrow\!\!\!| G$$

It's important to realize that H and Y form a pretty restrictive bloc. They can only go in P or S, and they'll take two of the three spaces.

The rule that F and G can't go together tells us that G goes in M or S, since F is in P. You can add "not G" beside P in all future diagrams.

The next rule says that if X is in S, then W is in S. We can draw this using sub-scripts.

$$X_S \longrightarrow W_P$$

You might think this game looks pretty open ended. But it would be a big mistake to stop here. None of the rules can be directly combined, but we can still draw deductions.

Look for the most restrictive variable. There are only two options for placing H and Y. We can put them in P, or we can put them in S.

When there are only two options, you should always try both. Often it leads to deductions.

If we put H and Y in P, then everything is settled. X has to go in M.

Why? Well, if X went in S, then W would have to go in P (rule 3). But P is full. So X goes in M, not S.

M _X_

P̸ P _F_ _H_ _Y_

S _W_ ___ ___

G and I take up the other two spaces in S because every other spot is full.

M _X_

P̸ P _F_ _H_ _Y_

S _W_ _G_ _I_

We'll call that scenario 1.

There are a couple of possibilities if H and Y go in S instead of P.

```
  M  ____
ø P   F   ____ ____
  S   H    Y   ____
```

If X also goes in S then W goes in P (rule 3).

```
  M  ____
ø P   F    W   ____
  S   H    Y    X
```

G then has to go in M, because G can't go with F in P. That leaves I to go in P.

```
  M   G
ø P   F    W    I
  S   H    Y    X
```

We'll call that scenario 2.

The third alternative is simply where X doesn't go in S. It could go in P or M. G can go in M or S, but not P since F and G can't go together.

```
  M  ____
ø P   F   ____ ____
✗ S   H    Y   ____
```

We got these scenarios first by seeing where we could put HY. Then we added in the third rule, Xs --> Wp

Scenarios aren't essential, but I find they help us think through the rules.

Main Diagram

Scenario 1

```
  M   X
ø P   F    H    Y
  S   W    G    I
```

Scenario 2

```
  M   G
ø P   F    W    I
  S   H    Y    X
```

Scenario 3

```
  M  ____
ø P   F   ____ ____
✗ S   H    Y   ____
```

Rules:

1. If X is in S, then W is in P.
2. Always put H and Y together.
3. Don't put F and G together.
4. Put F in P.
5. There are no rules for I.

Question 14

As with all list questions, pick a rule and test each answer choice to see if it violates the rule.

A is wrong because when X is in S, W has to be in P. That's the third rule.

B is wrong because F isn't in P. That's the fourth rule.

C is wrong because F can't be with G. That's the second rule.

D is wrong because H and Y aren't together. That's the first rule.

E is **CORRECT.**

Question 15

We know F is always in P. And G *cannot* be in the same group as F. So the right answer has to include G.

That leaves only answer choices **B** and **D.** Either it's only G that can't go in P, or it's G, H and Y.

We know from scenario 1 that H and Y *can* go in P.

```
   M    X
 ⌀P    F    H    Y
   S    W    G    I
```

So **D** is **CORRECT.** Only G can't go in P.

Question 16

We're trying to lock down all the variables. Ilias is the variable with no rules: the hardest variable to lock down. It makes sense to start with the answer choices that mention Ilias.

C is **CORRECT.** If we put W and Ilias in S, then we need to put H and Y in P, because it's the only place they'll fit. That fills up P.

We still have to place G and X. We can't put X in S. Why? Because if X is in S, then W must go in P (3rd rule).

But this answer choice tells us W is in S, not P. So X must go in M.

We therefore place G in the open space in S.

In other words, **C** describes our first scenario:

```
   M    X
 ⌀P    F    H    Y
   S    W    G    I
```

D is wrong because it doesn't let us decide where to put X, W and I. Any of them can go in M or P.

E is wrong because it doesn't let us decide whether to put W/G in M or S.

A is wrong because we already knew F was in P. This only tells us where W goes. I and G are interchangeable in this scenario.

B is wrong because we don't know how to place X, W and I. They could go in M or P.

Question 17

Since we're placing variables in sales, we should figure out which rules apply to sales.

$$X_S \longrightarrow W_P$$

That's the only rule specific to sales. Start with answer choices that involve X being in sales.

B is CORRECT. This isn't possible. If X and G are in sales then H and Y are forced to go in P along with F. That fills up P. But X being in S means that W *also* has to go in P. There's no room!

E involves X, but the scenario works and so the answer isn't right. H, Y and X are all in S. W has to go in P along with F. G must go in M to avoid F. That leaves I able to go in P, which works.

A is fine. H and Y go in P. W goes in S and X goes in M (X has to go in M so that he doesn't force W into P.)

C is fine because it means H, Y and G are all in S. That allows us to put X, W and I in either P and M. No rules apply to them when they're in P or M.

D is fine because it means H, Y and W are in S. That leaves G to go in M (so it avoids F). X and I can go in P, as there are no rules that apply to them when they are in P.

Question 18

We know F is in P. This new rule tells us X must be in P too.

That forces H and Y to go in S, as that's the only place that has room for them. The only other restriction is that G can't go in P.

M _____

~~G~~ P   F   X   _____

S   H   Y   _____

A is wrong because G's only restriction is that he can't go in P.

B is CORRECT. H and Y must go together. There is no longer room for them in P, so H can't go in P.

C is wrong because Ilias can go anywhere. There are no rules that cover Ilias, and this scenario doesn't force Ilias to be in any particular spot.

D is wrong because there are no rules attached to W apart from the rule that W is in P if X is in S. But X *isn't* in S, so W can go anywhere.

E is wrong for the same reason as **D.**

Question 19

If X isn't hired for P, then there must be a split of G and X between S and M. G can't go in P either.

```
    M   G/X
 ⌀ P    F    ___   ___
    S   X/G   ___   ___
```

A is wrong because F can *never* be hired in sales. Rule 4 says F goes in P.

B is wrong because Y always goes with H. This answer choice therefore wants us to put H, Y and W in S. But we only have two spaces.

C could be true and is therefore **CORRECT.** F is already in P, so we just have to add H and Y. Then W and Ilias could go in S. X goes in M to avoid forcing W into P.

D is wrong because Garcia can *never* be hired for production. The second rule says that F and G never go together, and F is always in the production department.

E is wrong because H and Y always go together. So this answer choice wants us to put H, Y and W all in P along with F. That's four people for three spaces.

Game 4 – Musical Instruments
Questions 20-24

Setup

This game looks superficially linear, but it's really more of a grouping game. The most important element is mastery of the rules; we're not able to deduce much during the setup.

Each piece is performed by two instruments. It's important to write this down somewhere you'll be able to see it clearly and refer back to it.

N : F,L

O : H,M

S : G,H

T : F,G

V : L,M

We only have two rules:

- N or T goes second
- Each piece must share an instrument with the piece before or after it.

The second rule does not mean that a piece has to share instruments with *both* of the pieces beside it: one is enough.

That's a common mistake on this game, so I'll say it again: A piece only has to be linked with either the piece before it *or* the piece behind it.

A piece *does not* have to be linked to both the pieces before and behind it.

I found it useful to write down the pieces that could go beside each piece. For instance: N plays F or L. T has F and V has L, so N needs one of either T or V beside it.

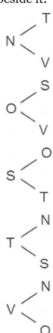

Keep the above chart somewhere you can refer to it easily. The game depends on quick access to this information.

Finally, here's how we can layout the five pieces.

$$\underset{12345}{\underline{}\;\overset{N/T}{\underline{}}\;\underline{}\;\underline{}\;\underline{}}$$

The lines underneath show where we *must* have links. The piece is spot 1 can only be linked to the piece in spot 2. There doesn't have to be a link between 2 and 3, because the piece in spot 3 could be linked to the piece in spot 4 (while spot 2 is linked to spot 1.)

Therefore, when N is in 2, either T or V must be in 1. They're the only ones who could allow a link between 1 and 2. When T is in 2, one of N or S must be in 1.

Main Diagram

N
　　T
　　V

O
　　S
　　V

S
　　O
　　T

T
　　N
　　S

V
　　N
　　O

N : F,L

O : H,M

S : G,H

T : F,G

V : L,M

T/V　　N
1　　2　　3　　4　　5

N/S　　T
1　　2　　3　　4　　5

Question 20

As with all list questions, go through the rules one at a time and eliminate answer choices one by one. In this case, choose one piece, and check whether it shares an instrument with at least one piece beside it in each answer choice.

A is wrong because S is in 2. Only N or T can go in 2.

B is wrong because O needs to be beside S or V. Instead, O is between N and T.

C is wrong because S needs to be beside O or T. Instead S is beside V.

D is **CORRECT.**

E is wrong because T needs to be beside N or S. Instead, T is beside O.

Question 21

There a fast, easy way and a hard, tedious way to answer this question. The long and the hard way involves drawing out each scenario. I prefer the fast and easy way.

Ask yourself what the most restricted variables are. Only N and T have special rules. And they share an instrument: the fiddle. They're the only ones who play the fiddle.

So if the fiddle is in spots 3 and 4 then N and T have to be in spots 3 and 4. Check if it works.

It doesn't work, because one of N and T has to be in spot 2. So **A** is **CORRECT.**

None of the other instruments have any restrictions. S and T could play the guitar in 3 and 4, N and S could play the harp in 3 and 4, V and N could play the lute in 3 and 4, and V and O could play the mandolin in 3 and 4.

All of those scenarios still allow one of N or T to be in the second spot.

270

Question 22

This question changes our rules. Now we need links between every spot.

$$\underset{1}{\underline{\quad}} \underset{2}{\overset{N/T}{\underline{\quad}}} \underset{3}{\underline{\quad}} \underset{4}{\underline{\quad}} \underset{5}{\underline{\quad}}$$

My instinct is that the right answer will involve one of the variables that can be linked with N and T: S or V. They're the obvious choice to test first, because only N/T have rules.

And that turns out to be true. **A** is **CORRECT.** V can go in 1.

$$\underset{1}{\overset{V}{\underline{\quad}}} \underset{2}{\overset{N}{\underline{\quad}}} \underset{3}{\overset{T}{\underline{\quad}}} \underset{4}{\overset{S}{\underline{\quad}}} \underset{5}{\overset{O}{\underline{\quad}}}$$

When you put V in 1, N has to go in 2. Then T has to go in 3, because it's the only other piece linked with N. Then S is the second instrument linked with T. Then O is the second instrument linked with S.

B is wrong because N or T always has to come second.

C is wrong because O shares no links with N or T. So there would be a gap between 2 and 3.

D and **E** are wrong because N and T both play F. So N and T have to be beside each other. Otherwise there's no way to link the piece in spot 2 with *both* spot 1 and spot 3. We have to do that, thanks to the new rule in this question.

Question 23

We need a link between the first piece and the second piece.

N, S, T and V all share links with N and T (the pieces that can go second.) So any one of them could go in 1.

Onyx doesn't share an instrument. Onyx can only go beside S or V. So **B** is **CORRECT.** If Onyx goes in 1 then we won't have a link between 1 and 2.

Question 24

If S goes fifth, then O or T has to go fourth. They're the only two pieces that can go beside O, and we *need* a link between 4 and 5.

Watch what happens if we put T in 4:

$$\underset{1}{\underline{\text{V}}} \quad \underset{2}{\underline{\text{N}}} \quad \overset{\text{O}}{\underset{3}{\underline{}}} \quad \underset{4}{\underline{\text{T}}} \quad \underset{5}{\underline{\text{S}}}$$

We have to put N in 2, and then we can link it with V in 1. But then O is left to go in 3. And O has no links with N or T. So this scenario doesn't work.

So O has to go in 4. It's pretty easy to place the rest. N and V share links, and T and N share links. Every combination works as long as we don't put V in 1 and T in 2.

$$\underset{1}{\underline{}} \quad \underset{2}{\underline{\text{N/T}}} \quad \underset{3}{\underline{}} \quad \underset{4}{\underline{\text{O}}} \quad \underset{5}{\underline{\text{S}}}$$

We can't put N third. T would be in second, and V would be in first. But T and V don't share a link. So **A** is wrong.

B is wrong because O *has* to be fourth. We saw that putting T fourth doesn't work.

C is wrong for the same reason as **B.**

D is possible. N could go second, so V and N would link the first two spots. T could then go third, where it would be linked with N.

We don't need a link between 3 and 4, because O and S are linked in 4 and 5. So every variable has a link with at least one of the pieces beside it, and **D** is **CORRECT.** It's drawn below.

$$\underset{1}{\underline{\text{V}}} \quad \underset{2}{\underline{\text{N}}} \quad \underset{3}{\underline{\text{T}}} \quad \underset{4}{\underline{\text{O}}} \quad \underset{5}{\underline{\text{S}}}$$

E is wrong because only N or T can go second.

Test 38
Section III - Reading Comprehension
Passage 1 - Forests in the Americas
Questions 1-8

Paragraph Summaries

1. Natives had changed many forests in the Western Hemisphere before Columbus arrived. They usually did this using fire. Nonetheless, some researchers think climate change could have changed forests, or that natives only rarely burned forests.
2. But there's much evidence of burning.
3. Native fires helped some species. For example, berries and pines. Unusual plant patterns provide evidence that natives burnt forests.

Analysis

There are many details here. You don't need to know them; you never need to. Instead, you need to know three things:

1. What's the point of the passage? (arguing against the researchers)
2. You need to understand it, in broad terms. Reread anything you don't understand.
3. You need to know where to find details. That's the point of the paragraph summaries. I usually do mine in my head, and they're shorter. But they let me find information quickly when I need to. So if you have to know about evidence of burning, you look in paragraph 2. If the question is about plant species, the answer is probably in paragraph 3.

Question 1

DISCUSSION: The main idea is that the researchers in the first paragraph are wrong. Native Americans did frequently change forests before Columbus arrived.

_____

A. This gets the emphasis backwards. It should be 'despite the claims of some scholars, forests were burnt'.
B. Scholars don't all agree! The very first paragraph gives us two scholars who disagree.
C. **CORRECT.** The scholars are in the first paragraph, and the evidence is given in paragraphs 2 and 3.
D. Actually, the scholars in the first paragraph *still* disagree. The passage doesn't prove it's point by citing "general agreement". It presents *evidence* to argue with the scholars.
E. This ignores the fact that scholars in the first paragraph don't think there was much burning (lines 9-10). *That* was the disagreement.

Question 2

DISCUSSION: Burned forests had more pines and berries (Lines 36 and 44). The forests also tended to have only one kind of tree (lines 37-38). The forests sometimes turned to grassy meadows (lines 27-28).

These are just a few changes, others are mentioned. You should check wrong answers against the passage before eliminating them. Four of the answers are eliminated using the passage, I've given line references below.

If you can't do this quickly, then *practice*. It's a trainable skill, and it will help you greatly.

———————————

A. CORRECT. Lines 37-39 contradict this. Burning tends to turn mixed forests into forests with only one kind of tree.
B. See lines 31-34. Burning lead to undergrowth.
C. See lines 35-37.
D. See lines 29-31.
E. See lines 27-28.

Question 3

DISCUSSION: Lines 44-50 tell us that Nicaraguan pines grew at low elevations after fires. Nicaraguan forests are contrasted with Mexican forests, which only grow at high elevations. Lines 50-52 say there has been some recent forest burning.

———————————

A. Lines 39-40 mention these, but we're not told if these forests are recent.
B. Same as A.
C. These are mentioned on lines 46-50. Pines at high elevations are *natural*. They aren't the result of burning.
D. Same as C.
E. CORRECT. It takes a bit of searching, but this is supported by lines 44-50. Lines 50-52 tell us that Nicaraguan forests were burned recently.

Question 4

DISCUSSION: This looks tricky, but the elevations give us a clue. They're only mentioned in lines 44-50. Nicaraguan forests were burnt, at low elevations. The result was forests full of nothing but pines.

Lines 37-38 tell us that burnt forests are homogeneous. And the Nicaraguan forests are homogenous pine, so B is the answer.

———————————

A. This isn't right because the high altitude pine forests were *natural*. See lines 49-50.
B. CORRECT. See the explanation above.
C. Heterogenous forests are natural forests that haven't been burned. See lines 37-38.
D. Same as C.
E. Lines 18-20 mention charcoal, but we're not told about elevations.

Question 5

DISCUSSION: Support the right answer using the passage. There's not much else to say.

———————————

A. This is unlikely. Lines 53-57 say that pine forests in Nicaragua went away when humans lefts. Human fires are non-random, while natural fires are random.
B. Lines 32-34 say that mature forests do have herbaceous undergrowth.
C. The passage argues that natives had a big impact. That doesn't mean settlers didn't also have a big impact.
D. CORRECT. Lines 35-37 support this. Berries were more common because of fires, for example.
E. Hard to say. The passage implies that controlled burning is different from natural fires, which are random. Lines 53-57 say that the pine forests disappeared when humans weren't around.

Question 6

DISCUSSION: The wrong answers can all be eliminated, and should be eliminated, using lines from the passage. There's nothing to explain here, apart from providing line references.

A. **CORRECT.** This is never mentioned. Indeed, there's no need for fires to be the same in all areas. Different regions might have different purposes for the fires.
B. See lines 29-31.
C. See lines 31-34.
D. See lines 18-21.
E. See lines 27-28.

Question 7

DISCUSSION: You have to read the earlier lines to understand what 'succession' means. It refers to human-sculpted pine forests that changed back to their natural state when humans went away.

A. No. In this case, the succession is forests returning to their natural state when humans stopped burning them.
B. The opposite: the Nicaraguan pine forests turned back to tropical forests.
C. Close, but it's implied that *natives* settled the land then abandoned it.
D. **CORRECT.** Pine forests turned into natural, mixed forests.
E. Nope. Lines 55-56 talk about settlements being *abandoned.*

Question 8

DISCUSSION: The main point of the passage is to argue against the researchers mentioned in the first paragraph. The author argues that natives did affect forests by burning them.

A. **CORRECT.** Specifically, the skeptics mentioned at the end of the first paragraph.
B. The common belief is that the Americas were virgin nature when Europeans arrived. This is mentioned in lines 1-4.
C. What evidence is being countered? The skeptical researchers in lines 8-15 don't show any evidence to support their views.
D. Which two viewpoints? There are only two presented. There is the opposing viewpoint, and the author's own viewpoint: natives did sculpt the forests using fire.
E. It isn't the geographical record that needs correcting. The record is clear that natives burnt forests. It's the common myth (lines 1-4) and the opinions of certain researchers (lines 8-15) that need correcting.

Passage 2 - Authority
Questions 9-14

Paragraph Summaries

1. Definitions of intellectual and institutional authority. Example of legal systems, which mix both types of authority.
2. Critics' claim: courts only have institutional authority; intellectual authority doesn't exist. Author's rebuttal of critics.
3. Critic's rebuttal: intellectual authority is often institutional authority in disguise. Musicology example.
4. Author's final argument: sure, legal precedent *is* institutional authority, but it is sometimes overruled by arguments from intellectual authority.

Analysis

This argument has an unusual amount of give and take. The critics are allowed to make several good points, which the argument rebuts. Be sure you know who is speaking at each point.

The overall conclusion is that intellectual authority exists and that courts do use it. But note that the author doesn't completely disagree with critics. The critics make decent points, but they ignore the real role of intellectual authority within the law.

Question 9

DISCUSSION: The main idea is to argue that intellectual authority exists and that courts do use it.

The wrong answers are ridiculous. They say courts only have intellectual authority. That's silly. Everyone knows that courts can make the police enforce their decisions. A judge can send you to jail! That's pure institutional authority.

This is a long question. But if you stop think about what they mean, you can *easily* eliminate the four wrong answers.

_____

A. Who argues that *courts of law* only have *intellectual* authority? It's nonsense. It would mean a criminal would only go to jail if the judge had convinced him he deserved to.
   Words have meaning. Make sure you know what an answer means before you pick it.
B. Courts have *no* power? That's absurd. A judge can order the police to enforce his decisions. That's real power!
C. Nobody argues courts have only intellectual authority. This is as absurd as answers A and B.
D. **CORRECT.** The critics say courts are purely institutional. But in lines 46-51, the author points out that courts will reconsider past decisions for intellectual reasons.
E. *Nobody* says courts only have intellectual authority. The police and government enforce courts' decisions, even if their decisions are bad. Everyone knows that.

Question 10

DISCUSSION: Some good arguments aren't accepted by institutions. ("Imprimatur" means acceptance.)

If you don't know what imprimatur means, you can read lines 20-23 to get the sentence in full. "Not...imprimatur." It's talking about arguments that fail.

The passage continues the same theme in lines 23-26. They mention that some good arguments don't get accepted by institutions.

The LSAT often gives you several ways to understand a single line if you don't know a word.

––––––––––––––

A. CORRECT. Lines 23-26 explain lines 22-23. Most people don't know that "imprimatur" means acceptance. But the passage continues with the same idea, in simpler language. It pays to read beyond the lines specifically mentioned. The full sentence "Not...imprimatur." also shows that the passage is talking about arguments that fail. (lines 20-23)

B. The arguments probably *do* challenge institutional beliefs. That's why institutions don't accept them.

C. Who knows? If institutional beliefs changed, then a decision might not be accepted even if it was like past decisions.

D. The arguments *were* convincing, but the institutions didn't accept them. Think of Galileo and the church. His argument were rejected based on institutional authority.

E. Lines 22-26 never mention forcing an institution to believe your idea. This answer is just making stuff up.

Question 11

DISCUSSION: The author's main argument about intellectual authority in the court system is in the final paragraph. The right answer adds new context to that paragraph.

––––––––––––––

A. The author never said judges were perfect. It's okay for them to make bad decisions as long as intellectual authority eventually corrects them.

B. So? This is to be expected. It would be deeply weird if every legal system in the world had *exactly* the same percentage of flawed reasoning.

C. "Many" could be as few as 15-20% of cases; this is vague. We need something that tells us judges rarely use intellectual authority.

D. So? This could just mean that all legal systems use intellectual authority, but some use it *even more* than the others.

E. CORRECT. This means judges aren't using intellectual authority very often. The author thought that intellectual authority was mainly used to reconsider decisions. (lines 51-54)

Question 12

DISCUSSION: This is a hard question to pin down using the passage. The author doesn't give an opinion about several of the answer choices.

You're allowed to use common sense (as long as you don't contradict the passage), and it comes in handy here. It's unlikely that institutions *never* accept good arguments. The world wouldn't work very well that way. Since the author seems sensible, he probably disagrees with that as well.

A. Lines 1-3 say that intellectual authority never forces its opinion on anyone.
B. **CORRECT.** This is no good. Intellectual authority *always* accepts well-reasoned arguments. And institutions might accept well-reasoned arguments if the conclusions helped the institution. The author is unlikely to agree with this *very* extreme statement.
C. Lines 1-3 say that intellectual authority never depends on convention.
D. The argument never says whether institutional authority can attack institutional beliefs. It might: we've all heard of the head of some corporation challenging the corporation's values. Since the author doesn't give his opinion, this doesn't contradict him.
E. Institutional authority could conflict with precedent if institutional beliefs change (the institutional attacks wouldn't have to be well-reasoned). The author gives no opinion on this point, but this is reasonable based on what we know of institutions.

Question 13

DISCUSSION: In the third paragraph, the critics claim that intellectual authority often depends on institutions (line 28-30).

The rest of the paragraph is an extended example supporting that claim. Line 30 says "for example".

A. The *first* paragraph defined the two types of authority.
B. Not at all. The musicologists' argument *was* accepted by their institution.
C. Which "genius" was later found out to be not a genius? This is not at all what happens.
D. **CORRECT.** The example supports the general claim made at the start of the paragraph. The musicologists' authority was institutional, in disguise.
E. The musicologists are just an example. The critics don't really care about musicologists; they could easily have used another example to prove their point.

Question 14

DISCUSSION: The author says precedent is an institutional tool. It can sometimes be overturned based on persuasive reasoning (intellectual authority).

A. Nope. Precedent is doing something just because others did it earlier. That may be sensible sometimes, but it's not intellectual.
B. Not always. Sometimes an earlier decision is also the best decision. Then intellectual and institutional authority will agree.
C. **CORRECT.** It's nice not to have to rethink decisions from scratch every time you hear a case. But you need to make sure your precedents are good. Some will get old and need changing (lines 46-50).
D. Lines 46-50 make clear that judges *can* reconsider earlier decisions.
E. The author seems to like the current system. The fact that judges can overrule decisions is a useful safeguard on institutional authority.

Passage 3 - Historical Sociology
Questions 15-20

Paragraph Summaries

1. Abrams argues that individuals influence society and society influences individuals.
2. We shape history, but our actions are also limited by our historical circumstances. (Julius Caesar changed the history of Rome. But he couldn't fly to New York, for example, despite his power.
3. Abrams' advice to sociologists for how to understand history.

Analysis

Abrams makes a good point. We influence society, and society influences us. You can't separate the two (though some sociologists do separate them). Abrams calls this dual influence "structuring".

Contingency isn't a word people use often, but it's important. A contingency is something random that meaningfully affects your life.

Your parents. Your hometown. Your name. Your native language. All of these are contingencies. They've determined the course of your life, but you didn't choose them. You were given them at birth.

Other things can be contingencies. You have an important job interview, and it's sunny outside. Studies show that companies hire more people they interview on sunny days.

It was your choice to interview for that job, but some factors beyond your control (contingencies) can affect whether you get it.

The last paragraph is hard, and demands analysis. Abrams is saying that we should look at certain important historical events. We need to know what the event was, what broad forces made it possible, the historical figure who helped direct the event and the results of the event.

For example. Napoleon losing at Waterloo, (the final battle of the Napoleonic wars):

We'd need a description of the battle. We'd need discussion of the history of the Napoleonic wars up to that point and Napoleon's return. We should mention that Europe was tired of war, and other social factors. We should know about the technologies that made the battle what it was. The weather, if it was important, etc.

Then we should discuss Napoleon himself. Who was he? How was his life shaped by his historical circumstances? How did he shape the history of the world around him?

Finally, we'll need to know the results of the battle, both for Napoleon and society.

Question 15

DISCUSSION: The main idea is that sociologists have to consider how individuals influence society *and* how society influences individuals.

———————

A. This sounds like nonsense, and probably is. Best not to spend too much time on this type of answer until you look at the rest.
But you can conclusively disprove it. No one said structuring can't be applied. Abrams' main criticism was that sociologists didn't seem to be aware of structuring. That's clear from the first paragraph. They can't argue against structuring if they aren't aware of it.
B. This is only half of Abrams' argument. He also said that individuals influence society.
C. Sounds good, but this is way off. Abrams argued social structures and individuals influenced each other. This says social structures and *history*.
D. **CORRECT.** Lines 4-8 say that sociologists focus on each of these, but rarely together. Abrams argues we must study both processes at once.
E. Abrams criticizes sociologists. See lines 8-12. He thinks they need to study how people affect society *and* how society affects people.

Question 16

DISCUSSION: The paragraph ends by describing how academic sociologists should study history.

It makes sense to sum things up by saying what benefits Abrams' structure will bring.

———————

A. This is dumb. Everyone knows that individuals have *some* influence on history. We don't need a special method to figure this out.
B. Not quite. Abrams says that sociologists do talk about the influence between individuals and society. But they only focus on one part at a time (lines 6-8). Abrams argues that individuals and society both influence each other.
C. Abrams *is* a historical sociologist. He's criticizing *sociologists*, and he claims they should use his *historical* sociological methods.
D. The formation of societies? Abrams is talking about all of history, even after societies are formed.
E. **CORRECT.** It's hard to judge how individuals and society affect each other, but Abrams' approach may help.

Question 17

DISCUSSION: Lines 21-30 describe contingencies. They are events that influence us, even though we may have little control over them.

This question is testing two things: 1. Can you locate the relevant part of the passage? 2. Can you read it?

It should be very easy. Each wrong answer can be eliminated using a line from the passage. The area you have to search isn't large. You should never get this sort of question wrong. If you do, practice finding the wrong answers in the passage.

———————

A. Line 21 says that *all* contingencies are social phenomena.
B. **CORRECT.** Historical structuring is the name of Abrams' method. It isn't a historical event.
C. Line 26.
D. Lines 21-22.
E. Lines 29-30.

Question 18

DISCUSSION: Abrams' method is described in lines 49-54. You should read those lines once or twice before looking at the answers. Then eliminate wrong answers by checking to see if they contradict any of the criteria.

Broadly speaking, the right answer should consider both social forces and an important individual. The answer should mention the consequences the event will have for each.

———————

A. **CORRECT.** This report talks about social forces *and* an individual. Then it does step 4, which is to think about the consequences of the bill for society and for individuals.
B. This doesn't mention social forces.
C. This doesn't describe social forces.
D. This doesn't describe social forces.
E. This doesn't mention an important person. And it should have discussed the consequences of the event itself, not some hypothetical situation where the event didn't happen.

Question 19

DISCUSSION: The first paragraph tells us Abrams critique of sociologists, and introduces his ideal method: structuring.

———————

A. Abrams' method isn't evaluated in the first paragraph.
B. We aren't given much detail. We're just told in general terms that individuals and society influence each other.
C. This simply doesn't happen. Which challenge is anticipated? There would have to be something like: "Now, some might object to this theory because..."
D. Which terms are examined? This isn't there. An example would be: "By society we mean _____, and this is the role it plays in influencing individuals..."
E. **CORRECT.** We're told that individuals and society both influence each other. That's the essence of Abrams' entire theory.

Question 20

DISCUSSION: Contingencies are random historical events that affect our lives. They didn't occur because of the choice of an individual, at least not initially.

Answer C *could* be a contingency, but it doesn't have to be. As far as we know, that person lives in the city because of their own choice and not because of a random contingency.

Examples of contingencies: birth year, gender, height, eye color, native language.

Example of non-contingency: College major, husband/wife, workplace, etc. Basically anything you can choose.

A. If something happens to you randomly and it affects your future behavior, then it's a contingency.
B. The person didn't choose to be born in a farming area, but it affected their actions. It's a contingency.
C. **CORRECT.** You generally choose where you live. If you choose something, it isn't a contingency. And the decision isn't very important ("visiting friends").
D. Definitely a contingency. If your parents are catholic, and you're catholic, their religion probably has something to do with your beliefs. It's your own choice, but it's not completely your own choice.
E. You don't choose to be born poor. If that affects your future decisions, then it's a contingency.

Passage 4 - Medical Empathy
Questions 21-27

Paragraph Summaries

1. Medical students must learn to care about their patients. Ethical training that uses stories might help.
2. Most ethics training is very abstract. It would be better to train students using stories that show realistic situations.
3. Reading stories makes you use your imagination and imagine perspectives different from your own.
4. Doctors don't have to give up their own moral ideas. But stories can help them understand how to deal with other humans.

Analysis

This passage masks simple ideas with fancy words. Narrative just means story, for example. If you don't understand a section, reread it slowly. You'll likely find you can understand it after all. The more you practice understanding a passage, the easier it will become for all future passages.

There's not really much to analyze here. The only difficulty on this passage is being sure about what it means.

With one exception: to do well, you *have* to notice lines 17-19. The author praises the conceptual clarity of the traditional curriculum. So even though the author criticizes the curriculum, they don't think it's all bad.

This is extremely important. Always watch for nuances in an author's opinion. This nuance comes up again and again and again. I had to cite those lines seven times.

Also note that narrative doesn't necessarily mean "fiction". It's possible to use real-life ethical stories to train doctors.

Question 21

DISCUSSION: The main point is that medical students could develop more empathy if they read ethical stories.

_____

A. **CORRECT.** This is a mouthful, but it's a fancy way of saying what I said in the box above.
B. This goes too far. Lines 17-19 say that traditional ethics courses can be useful. The author's objection is that narrative training would be *even more* useful. You could use both traditional classes and ethical narratives.
C. Not at all. The passage is talking in general terms. Some medical students may already have enough empathy and ethics to treat patients even if they don't get any extra training. And the author's main focus is on narrative training. They don't think the other types are as important.
D. The passage never says that narrative ethical training is becoming popular. And the ethical situations aren't necessarily complex. But medical students are so busy that even simple ethical situations might cause trouble for them.
E. Lines 60-62 make clear that doctors will still use moral principles. The author just wants them to be more flexible and empathetic.

Question 22

DISCUSSION: You should start back at line 34. The author is talking about imagining the lives of people apart from ourselves. We need to imagine how it feels to be someone else with different beliefs.

It's even useful to read down as far as line 46. Don't just stick to the line mentioned in the question.

─────────────

A. It's more than this. We need to be able to put ourselves into another's shoes.
B. No! We don't need to identify with one side over another. The important thing is to imagine how different people feel about a situation.
C. This has nothing to do with imagining someone else's perspective. And the author doesn't mention solving problems.
D. CORRECT. If you're reading a book, you're not directly involved in the situation. To keep interested, you must use your moral imagination.
E. You can imagine something without acting upon it.

Question 23

DISCUSSION: You'll want to match the correct answer to a statement from the passage. Anything less is guessing.

─────────────

A. Line 5 says medical students are so busy that they might not learn empathy. But they might still have time for ethics courses. The problem is that those courses don't do enough (lines 20-21).
B. Narrative literature doesn't necessary mean fiction. You can tell a real story and use it for ethical training. It may be even more effective to use a real situation to teach ethics. The most important thing is that the lesson is in the form of a story.
C. The passage was recommending *narrative literature*. Practical experience might help too, but it's never addressed.
D. Lines 17-19 show that abstract ethics courses have some value. The author never says we should use *only* narrative ethics. They just think we need more narrative.
E. CORRECT. Doctors get lots of scientific training, and they already get abstract ethical training (line 9 and lines 15-17). But lines 4-5 show that empathy is still a challenge; so doctors need another kind of preparation.

Question 24

DISCUSSION: The author's goal is probably to persuade medical schools to use narrative literature to train medical students.

_____

A. Close, but first the author would have to convince medical schools that they *should* use narratives.
B. Lines 17-19 say that current ethics classes are useful. So they aren't counterproductive.
C. The author wasn't talking about all narrative literature. That's incredibly broad (it includes all novels, for instance). The article is recommending we use ethical stories written to train medical students. That's a tiny subset of all narrative literature. Also, lines 55-57 say that narrative literature doesn't have to lead to situational ethics.
D. CORRECT. The first paragraph says that doctors risk ignoring their patients instead of empathizing with them. The author thinks that narrative literature will keep doctors in tune with their fellow humans.
E. The author hasn't said what the value will be. They haven't said what harm will come from doctors who aren't empathetic, and they don't say what the benefits of empathetic doctors are.

Question 25

DISCUSSION: You should find the four wrong answers in the passage. There's never much else to say on "exception" questions.

_____

A. This is mentioned on lines 47-52.
B. Lines 30-31.
C. Lines 60-62. If you're more flexible with your moral principles then you have a new way of dealing with people.
D. Lines 45-46.
E. CORRECT. This is never said. Doctors are more *prepared* to face ethical dilemmas, but they're probably not *insulated* (kept apart) from ethical dilemmas.

Question 26

DISCUSSION: You should find the four wrong answers in the passage. If you don't, you're guessing.

_____

A. Lines 22-23. "Multifarious" is a hard word, but you probably know the word 'multi' from words like multiple.
B. Lines 9-10.
C. CORRECT. New technology is never mentioned.
D. Lines 19-21.
E. This is the *whole point* of the passage.

Question 27

DISCUSSION: The author doesn't think the normal method is good enough. However, lines 17-19 show that the author thinks traditional ethics courses have some value.

The passage is critical of ethics training. So it's weird to see that the most positive answer is correct. But the wrong answers are too negative: the author doesn't hate traditional training.

_____

A. Lines 17-19 show that the author thinks that traditional courses have some value.
B. Same as A. One effect of traditional training is that medical students get conceptual ethical clarity.
C. 'Indifference' towards the effects? The author clearly cares; they want medical students to learn empathy and ethics.
D. The author approves of some of the effects, lines 17-19 provide an example.
E. CORRECT. Lines 17-19 show partial approval of effects: students get conceptual clarity. But the author clearly disapproves of the method (abstract courses). They think that courses using narrative literature are required as well.

Test 38
Section IV - Logical Reasoning

Question 1

QUESTION TYPE: Must be True

ARGUMENTS: Mrs. Smith doesn't think it's fair that her son had to miss recess when he had not thrown raisins.

The principle argues that it's like a traffic jam caused by an accident: even the innocent must suffer.

ANALYSIS: The principal's analogy expresses resignation. Even innocent travelers are caught in traffic. He is implying that Mrs. Smith's son was innocent yet nonetheless had to miss recess.

_____

A. The principal doesn't say how many people he thinks were responsible.
B. **CORRECT.** The principal implies that he is aware her son threw no raisins. But her son must suffer regardless, just like those caught in a traffic jam.
C. The accident is just an analogy. The principal doesn't say what causes the jam.
D. The principal doesn't say anything directly about the accident. His analogy implies Mrs. Smith's son is innocent, but he doesn't say anything more than that.
E. The principal doesn't say if the strategy worked or even if it was his idea.

Question 2

QUESTION TYPE: Flawed Reasoning

ARGUMENTS: Mrs. Smith doesn't think it's fair that her son had to miss recess when he had not thrown raisins.

The principal argues that it's like a traffic jam caused by an accident: even the innocent must suffer.

ANALYSIS: The principal ignores the school's responsibility. _They_ decided that all students had to suffer. The situation wasn't inevitable.

_____

A. The generalization is that all students in the class had to suffer. That's true: all students missed recess.
B. No it doesn't. The situation is just an analogy to get across the idea that people can suffer even when they do no wrong.
C. **CORRECT.** The school didn't have to punish _all_ of the children.
D. The principal implies he knows that her son it _not_ guilty.
E. The principal didn't introduce any facts. He just made an analogy to a traffic jam.

Question 3

QUESTION TYPE: Main Conclusion

CONCLUSION: Animals and plants are interdependent.

REASONING: Animals would die without plants and plants would die without animals.

ANALYSIS: For a main conclusion question, think about the argument as a whole. It isn't enough that an answer choice is true: it has to be the main point of the argument.

Here, the argument uses examples to show that animals need plants and plants need animals.

―――――――――

A. Animal life isn't necessary for photosynthesis. Photosynthesis depends on the sun. Animal life is responsible for *replenishing carbon dioxide*.
B. This is true, but the main point is much broader.
C. This is true, but the main point was that plants and animals depend on each other.
D. This is true: humans breathe and emit CO2 like other animals. But the main point is about interdependence.
E. **CORRECT.** Plants and animals need each sother.

Question 4

QUESTION TYPE: Principle - Strengthen

CONCLUSION: The government gas company is within its rights to sell gas appliances.

REASONING: A private company could do the same thing.

ANALYSIS: It's possible that different rules apply to a government company than to a private company.

The right answer tells us not to worry about this.

―――――――――

A. **CORRECT.** Simple enough: if a private company can do it than so can the government.
B. This would support the idea that the government company *shouldn't* sell appliances.
C. This goes way too far. We're not trying to say that private companies should bow down before the government company.
D. Owners of private companies *did* complain.
E. So? Here a *government* company competes with a private company.

Question 5

QUESTION TYPE: Strengthen - Exception

CONCLUSION: There will soon be more headaches, fatigue, etc.

REASONING: Oil refinery workers exposed to MBTE have a lot of headaches and fatigue, etc. MBTE will soon be used as an additive in gasoline.

ANALYSIS: This isn't a very good argument. It could be that oil refineries themselves cause headaches, and MBTE isn't to blame. Or it could be that MBTE in gasoline is not present in high amounts and it won't hurt anyone.

The wrong answers take care of these objections and also show that the sample of oil workers was representative.

––––––––––––––

A. This shows that it's likely MBTE causing the headaches, rather than something else in the oil refinery.
B. CORRECT. This just tells us something about headaches. It doesn't strengthen the idea that MBTE causes them.
C. This shows that the prediction is true in the areas that did start using MBTE.
D. This shows that MBTE seems to be causing problems in those regions where it is used.
E. This shows that the sample was representative and strengthens the findings.

Question 6

QUESTION TYPE: Necessary Assumptions

CONCLUSION: Computers can not be experts because human experts do not store their past experience as rules and facts.

REASONING: Human experts can draw on past experience to form an intuitive reaction to a new situation.

ANALYSIS: The argument implies that computers store information as rules and facts. Human experts don't store their knowledge this way.

The argument is assuming there is no way to translate expert knowledge into something that computers could understand.

––––––––––––––

A. This doesn't matter. We don't even know how much originality designers built into computers.
B. CORRECT. If there is a way to translate expert knowledge into something a computer can understand then computers might be able to mimic experts.
C. This doesn't matter. If humans don't rely on such information then the argument is stronger because computers rely on rules and facts.
D. Even if computers can sort through more information they still might not be able to understand the *type* of knowledge that experts have.
E. It doesn't matter if experts rely on intuition while building their model. It only matters if they can successfully use intuition once they have finished building a model.

Question 7

QUESTION TYPE: Principle
Parallel Reasoning - Exception

(*author's note:* ugh, what a long question type)

CONCLUSION: Drivers get worse when they are sleepy but often don't realize it.

ANALYSIS: The two elements of the principle are:

1. An altered state.
2. Lack of awareness of the altered state.

A. We have an altered physical state and poor awareness of it.
B. **CORRECT.** Disliking arithmetic is not an altered physical state. And the teachers are presumably aware that they aren't good at arithmetic.
C. Noxious fumes can change our abilities even if we aren't aware of it.
D. It's hard to tell how faint you are, even if everyone else can see your face is pale.
E. This is another example where we may not be aware of our own state of mind.

Question 8

QUESTION TYPE: Flawed Reasoning

CONCLUSION: The politician argues his opponent is wrong.

REASONING: The opponent doesn't practice what he preaches.

ANALYSIS: This is an ad hominem attack. That never makes for a good argument.

A. There wasn't really any characterization of his opponent's lifestyle: he just said he lived in the country. He didn't say "beautiful countryside" or anything like that.
B. Huh? The argument didn't hinge on where apartment buildings could be built.
C. This is irrelevant, just as the opponent's living situation is irrelevant. We should only care about the quality of the argument.
D. **CORRECT.** The argument is good or bad because of its reasoning. It doesn't matter how the opponent lives.
E. This is irrelevant, just as it is irrelevant that he now lives in a house. We need to assess an argument's reasons instead.

Question 9

QUESTION TYPE: Paradox - Exception

PARADOX: People are very concerned about recycling plastic yet much more glass is recycled than plastic.

ANALYSIS: The right answer tells us where the materials come from. That doesn't matter.

The wrong answers explain difficulties in recycling plastic or easiness in recycling glass.

_____

A. This shows that it may not be possible to recycle as much plastic as glass.
B. This shows that it is much easier to recycle glass.
C. **CORRECT.** This tells us why we ought to be concerned about recycling each material. But it doesn't explain the low plastic recycling rate.
D. This shows that it's hard to effectively recycle plastic.
E. This shows that some plastic cannot be recycled.

Question 10

QUESTION TYPE: Complete the Argument

CONCLUSION: Technological progress tends to make workers less satisfied in their work.

REASONING: Technological progress makes workers' skills less valuable. Workers' satisfaction depends on believing that their skills are needed.

ANALYSIS: Technology reduces the need for workers' skills. And they can only feel satisfied if their skills are needed. So technology will make workers less satisfied.

_____

A. Unhappy workers could still make good quality products, thanks to technology.
B. Hard to say. Workers might be glad about prosperity and progress overall even if they feel a bit less satisfied in their work.
C. This is too strong. Workers might welcome the increased wealth that comes from technology even if they feel less satisfied about their work.
D. **CORRECT.** Technology reduces the need for workers' skills and so they will feel less satisfied.
E. We don't know this is true. There could be many new jobs, but the jobs might not require much skill from workers.

Question 11

QUESTION TYPE: Main Conclusion

CONCLUSION: We can restore land to biodiversity without reducing meat production.

REASONING: The prairie supported as many bison as cattle, and bison provide as much meat as cattle.

ANALYSIS: The stimulus is not saying what we *should* do. It's saying what we *could* do. This is a major distinction on the LSAT, and it explains why answer choice D is wrong.

A. The bison were not "an earlier north American agricultural technique." They were part of a natural ecosystem.
B. This is only true of bison. It might not be true of all animals, such as chickens.
C. The argument is arguing that we *could* restore the prairie and that there won't be consequences.
D. The argument didn't actually say we *should* restore the ecosystem. Maybe it would cost quite a bit in the short term. The argument just said we *could* restore it without major consequences for meat production.
E. **CORRECT.** We could restore the prairies and still eat bison meat.

Question 12

Question twelve was removed. Very, very occasionally an LSAT question will have an error and be taken out.

Question 13

QUESTION TYPE: Weaken

CONCLUSION: TV doesn't really affect which breakfast cereals children like.

REASONING: One group of children watched TV and the other didn't. Both groups liked sugary cereals.

ANALYSIS: The correct answer shows that peer pressure could explain why the non-TV group had the same preferences as the TV group.

A. **CORRECT.** This shows that TV influences all children, since children are influenced by their peers who watched TV.
B. There could be other environmental factors apart from TV that cause children to prefer sweet cereals. Maybe they see billboards, or hear radio ads, etc.
C. This is likely, if you think about it. TV ads repeat frequently. The main point is that there was no difference between the group that was exposed to the ads and the group that wasn't.
D. This would strengthen the argument. Both groups reacted the same to low sugar cereal even though one group watched TV and the other didn't.
E. This doesn't matter: the conclusion was about children. Their minds may work differently.

Question 14

QUESTION TYPE: Flawed Reasoning

CONCLUSION: Reducing speed limits doesn't save lives or help the environment.

REASONING: Cars will spend more time on the road, where they can pollute and could get into an accident.

ANALYSIS: According to this argument, we'd all be safest if we drove at 150 mph, and got to our destinations really, really fast. See the flaw?

Cars aren't as dangerous if they're going slowly. And cars may pollute more at high speeds even if they are the road for less time.

A. If motorists ignore speed limits then the argument is stronger. Speed limits certainly won't make a difference if they are ignored.
B. The conclusion was only about pollution and safety.
C. This fact would strengthen the argument. The argument claims more cars are dangerous.
D. **CORRECT.** Emissions might increase quite a bit with speed. Time is not the only factor.
E. The argument doesn't assume that road time is the *only* factor. The author of the argument might agree that drunk driving increases the risk of accidents, for example.

Question 15

QUESTION TYPE: Weaken

CONCLUSION: Loggerheads live and breed in distinct groups. Some live in the pacific and some live in the Atlantic.

REASONING: Loggerheads in the Pacific have similar DNA.

ANALYSIS: The argument hasn't shown that loggerheads in the Atlantic have *different* DNA from those in the Pacific. Maybe all loggerheads just form one big group that's fairly similar.

A. This would just show the pacific group is widespread. It strengthens the argument.
B. This tells us Atlantic turtles behave differently than Pacific turtles. It somewhat strengthens the argument.
C. This just tells us a fact about loggerhead population. It doesn't show that the two populations aren't different.
D. **CORRECT.** This shows that Atlantic loggerheads have DNA similar to that of pacific loggerheads. This weakens the argument that the populations are distinct.
E. The argument didn't say that the loggerheads *couldn't* interbreed. It just said that they generally didn't breed.

Question 16

QUESTION TYPE: Sufficient Assumption

CONCLUSION: People who trust others tend to view a hard task as a challenge rather than a threat.

REASONING: People who are confident view hard tasks as challenges. People who do not believe that others distrust them are confident.

ANALYSIS: The argument switches between not thinking you are distrusted by others and trusting others yourself. Those are different things. The right answer shows that if you trust others then you don't think people distrust you (and therefore you are confident.)

We have nothing connecting "tends to trust others" to anything else. The right answer *has* to make this connection and answer choice C does.

———————————

A. This is backwards. It should say: "People who *don't* believe that others distrust them."
B. This would only get us: don't think others distrust → confident → challenge, not a threat AND trust others. Trust is a necessary condition when we need it to be a sufficient condition as in answer choice C.
C. **CORRECT.** We get: trust others → don't think others distrust → confident → challenge, not a threat.
D. This doesn't allow us to connect anything to people who trust others.
E. How exactly would this let us prove that people who trust others view tasks as a challenge? It's totally unrelated.

Question 17

QUESTION TYPE: Flawed Parallel Reasoning

CONCLUSION: We shouldn't consider Mullen's proposal to tax the rich.

REASONING: Mullen is rich.

ANALYSIS: This is an ad hominem attack, and it's worse than usual. First, it doesn't matter who makes an argument. Attack the argument, not the person making it.

Second: Mullen might actually be in favor of paying more tax. Several US billionaires such as Warren Buffet have called for higher taxes on the rich.

The structure is: don't listen to this person saying the proposal is good, because this person will be *hurt* by the proposal.

———————————

A. Here the person will be *helped* by the proposal.
B. **CORRECT.** Here Dr. Han will be hurt by his own proposal.
C. This is just plain ad hominem. The witness has no personal stake in it.
D. Here Timm would benefit from his own proposal.
E. Here Dr. Wasow has nothing obvious to gain or lose from his proposal.

Question 18

QUESTION TYPE: Role in Argument

CONCLUSION: Yang concludes that researchers should focus on the function of the brain rather than the structure.

REASONING: Yang claims that focusing on the structure will lead to failure. Flying machines modeled after birds all failed.

ANALYSIS: Subsidiary conclusions are fairly rare, and not well understood. It means a conclusion that is supported by evidence and supports the main conclusion. For example:

$$A \rightarrow B \rightarrow C$$

A is the evidence. It lets us conclude B, a subsidiary conclusion. B leads to C, the main conclusion.

———————————

A. The main conclusion is that researchers should focus on the function of the brain, *because* focusing on the structure will lead to failure.
B. **CORRECT.** It is supported by the analogy about early flight machines and it supports the idea that we shouldn't focus on the structure.
C. It is not a principle of research. We don't know how many people agree with Yang.
D. This is true of the example about birds. But the statement about the brain structure is not a general claim.
E. Yang hasn't given us any context about the brain.

Question 19

QUESTION TYPE: Most Helpful to Know

CONCLUSION: Yang concludes that researchers should focus on the function of the brain rather than the structure.

REASONING: Yang claims that focusing on the structure will lead to failure. Flying machines modeled after birds all failed.

ANALYSIS: Yang's analogy about flying machines is important. It would be very helpful to know if the first non-bird flying machines were made possible by studying the structure of birds.

———————————

A. **CORRECT.** If this were true then Yang's analogy isn't much good. Studying the structure of the brain might give us ideas for building an intelligent computer, even if we eventually used a very different structure.
B. This would be more helpful in evaluating Anders' argument. It would show us if the brain's type of thinking matched the proposed thought process for "thinking machines."
C. This doesn't matter. The brain is more complex than an aircraft; it might take much longer to build a thinking machine. Or it might not. But it doesn't affect Yang's argument.
D. This doesn't matter. It would only affect how feasible the research proposed by Anders' would be. This doesn't affect Yang's argument that we shouldn't focus on structure.
E. It's to be expected that some flying machines not modeled on birds failed. What's important for Yang is that some *worked*, unlike flying machines modeled on birds.

Question 20

QUESTION TYPE: Necessary Assumption

CONCLUSION: An all-consuming hobby is not a successful strategy to get over loneliness as a teenager.

REASONING: Sometimes shy adolescents can make friends through a hobby. But if they lost interest in the hobby then they might get even lonelier.

ANALYSIS: This argument isn't quite good. We don't know what happens once a teenager drops a hobby and gets lonelier. Maybe they go and make new friends in a bit. Having a hobby might have taught them how to meet people.

A. Even if adolescents don't want more friends they may still lose the friends they have if they abandon the hobby.
B. **CORRECT.** If a successful strategy for getting past loneliness *can* intensity that loneliness then perhaps a hobby can be a successful strategy even though it could make you lonelier.
C. It doesn't matter what adolescents do if they *don't* make any friends from a hobby. The strategy has failed in that case.
D. This doesn't have to be true. Perhaps no strategy is successful.
E. It doesn't matter why teenagers start hobbies. The question is: will the hobbies help them make friends?

Question 21

QUESTION TYPE: Flawed Reasoning

CONCLUSION: Democracy doesn't promote freedom.

REASONING: Some democracies haven't been free and some oligarchies have been free.

ANALYSIS: If something promotes freedom then that means it increases freedom *on average*. It could be the case that democracy promotes freedom even if there are occasional failures.

And just because democracy promotes freedom doesn't mean that all other societies will be unfree.

A. No. Democracy isn't a necessary or a sufficient condition for freedom. It just tends to make more of it, on average.
B. This gets it backwards. We're trying to show that democracy leads to freedom, usually. This says freedom leads to democracy.
C. The historical examples are quite relevant. If all past democratic societies were unfree then the claim starts to look a bit shaky.
D. **CORRECT.** Not everything is a necessary or sufficient condition. For example, exercise promotes health even though it isn't necessary or sufficient.
E. What personal point of view? The political scientist doesn't say anything about him or herself.

Question 22

QUESTION TYPE: Necessary Assumption

CONCLUSION: Sugar plays a role in mood elevation.

REASONING: Sugar → insulin → removal of all amino acids except tryptophan → tryptophan enters brain → serotonin

ANALYSIS: This argument plays on the common knowledge that serotonin has something to do with being in a good mood. It's easy to forget that this argument doesn't actually tell us anything about what serotonin does.

The argument assumes that serotonin helps elevate the mood.

A. This isn't necessary. It's only necessary that serotonin elevates mood.
B. This is like A, and it isn't necessary. The argument would be ok if not consuming sugar was simply neutral for mood.
C. It doesn't matter if there are other ways to produce serotonin. It's only necessary that tryptophan is *one* way to produce serotonin.
D. **CORRECT.** If this isn't true then it's not clear why sugar would elevate mood.
E. We don't have a clue about this. There could be something else about protein that elevates mood, even if the amino acids in it block out tryptophan.

Question 23

QUESTION TYPE: Principle - Parallel Reasoning

PRINCIPLE:

Civil disobedience AND Self Interest AND no interest for others → Not justified

Civil disobedience AND required by conscience → Justified

ANALYSIS: There could be infinite ways of showing that something is an act of justified civil disobedience. But we only have one. If the conclusion says "justified" then we must have "required by conscience."

If the conclusion says "not justified" we must have "Self interest" and "no interest for others."

A. We could only conclude it was justified if Keisha acted because her conscience required her to. This doesn't say she did.
B. Acting out of conscience is a sufficient condition for justified civil disobedience but it isn't a necessary condition. There could be other ways of committing justified civil disobedience even though her conscience didn't require her to.
C. Close, but this doesn't tell us that Georgette's conscience *required* her to act.
D. **CORRECT.** Here we go: Georgia acted partly on behalf of others, so we can't conclude "not justified." And since her conscience *required* her to act then we can conclude "justified."
E. Similar to B: conscience is a sufficient condition, but it isn't a necessary condition. It's possible there is a way to commit justified civil disobedience by another method.

Question 24

QUESTION TYPE: Most Strongly Supported

CONCLUSION: We land dwellers have rotating limbs ending in digits (e.g. arms with fingers, legs with toes.)

New evidence shows that an aquatic ancestor of land mammals might have been the first to evolve this trait.

ANALYSIS: We don't have very much information in this stimulus. The wrong answers all talk about things of which we know nothing.

A. Who knows? Maybe the *Acanthostega* was very successful. Its skeleton was only too feeble for *land* movement, but the animal may have done just fine in water.
B. There's no evidence for this extreme statement. For example, most fish have spines but so do land animals. Does that mean a spine is a disadvantage for land animals?
C. No. The fact that the *Acanthostega* couldn't move on land is evidence *against* this idea.
D. We have no clue. We only have information on *one* aquatic species and we don't know if the *Acanthostega* found its limbs to be an advantage or not.
E. **CORRECT.** The anatomical characteristics are the rotating limbs with digits. Some aquatic animals refers to the *Acanthostega,* which had such limbs.

Those limbs likely present a survival advantage on land because they are useful for land movement and most land animals kept this feature.

Question 25

QUESTION TYPE: Must be False

FACTS:

1. European music is popular because the music could be successful outside of its original context.

ANALYSIS: This question depends entirely on nuances of phrasing. Check the stimulus carefully before choosing an answer choice on this type of question. All of the wrong answer choices can be justified by a specific phrase or word in the stimulus.

A. This could be true. The stimulus only said that European music has had a *strong* influence. It isn't necessarily the most influential music worldwide.
B. This could be true. The stimulus is just giving *one* reason why European music has been influential.
C. This is true of European music and it could be true of Chinese music as well. The stimulus didn't say European music was unique in this respect.
D. **CORRECT.** The stimulus says that European music is a sophisticated achievement because it is still intelligible even when it is independent of its original function. This answer choice contradicts that idea by saying that music is even more sophisticated when it isn't intelligible.
E. This could be true. It's one of the reasons European music stands out: it doesn't lose its appeal.

Question 26

QUESTION TYPE: Point At Issue

ARGUMENTS: Tony says that only novels can accurately show human lives, because they exist over time.

Raoul believes that short stories show life best. Life does not unfold linearly, but it's instead a series of unconnected events. Short stories can portray these events.

ANALYSIS: They disagree on how we should understand humans. Do we need a long view (Tony)? Or can we understand someone with a brief glimpse during an important event (Raoul)?

A. **CORRECT.** This restates Raoul's opinion. Tony completely disagrees: he thinks we can only display someone's character by showing their gradual evolution through life experience.
B. Both of them *agree* that novels and short stories have different ways to show character.
C. Raoul doesn't disagree with this. He just thinks that the method used by short stories is better.
D. They might both agree that novelists have other methods for creating sketches.
E. Tony wouldn't necessarily disagree. He just thinks novels show a more important part of character: gradual evolution with time.

Appendix: LR Questions By Type

Strengthen

Test 34

Section II, #14
Section III, #21
Section III, #24

Test 35

Section I, #4
Section I, #15
Section IV, #10

Test 36

Section III, #7
Section III, #11
Section III, #26

Test 37

Section II, #1
Section II, #6
Section II, #20
Section IV, #13
Section IV, #25

Test 38

Section I, #4
Section IV, #5

Flawed Reasoning

Test 34

Section II, #1
Section II, #3
Section II, #9
Section III, #4
Section III, #10

Test 35

Section I, #6
Section I, #17
Section IV, #7
Section IV, #8
Section IV, #13
Section IV, #18
Section IV, #24

Test 36

Section I, #19
Section III, #13
Section III, #21
Section III, #25

Test 37

Section II, #3
Section II, #16
Section IV, #16
Section IV, #22

Test 38

Section I, #6
Section I, #11
Section I, #23
Section IV, #2
Section IV, #8
Section IV, #14
Section IV, #21

Weaken

Test 34

Section II, #11
Section II, #12
Section II, #17
Section II, #25
Section III, #6
Section III, #18
Section III, #20

Test 35

Section I, #8
Section I, #13
Section I, #23
Section IV, #5
Section IV, #17
Section IV, #20

Test 36

Section I, #2
Section I, #8
Section I, #10
Section I, #12
Section I, #25
Section III, #2
Section III, #5

Test 37

Section II, #4
Section II, #14
Section II, #25
Section IV, #2
Section IV, #11
Section IV, #18

Test 38

Section I, #10
Section I, #17
Section IV, #13
Section IV, #15

Sufficient Assumption

Test 34

Section II, #2
Section II, #10

Test 35

Section I, #20
Section I, #22
Section IV, #14
Section IV, #19

Test 36

Section I, #18
Section I, #22
Section I, #26
Section III, #12

Test 37

Section II, #5
Section IV, #9
Section IV, #20

Test 38

Section I, #1
Section IV, #16

Most Strongly Supported

Test 34

Section II, #4
Section II, #19
Section III, #19

Test 35

Section I, #12
Section I, #19
Section IV, #1
Section IV, #3
Section IV, #21
Section IV, #26

Test 36

Section I, #4
Section I, #16
Section III, #17

Test 37

Section IV, #3
Section IV, #6

Test 38

Section I, #13
Section I, #15
Section I, #20
Section I, #21
Section I, #24

Paradox

Test 34

Section II, #5
Section II, #7
Section III, #2

Test 35

Section I, #10
Section I, #21
Section I, #25
Section IV, #4
Section IV, #12

Test 36

Section I, #9
Section I, #13
Section I, #23
Section III, #1

Test 37

Section II, #8
Section II, #17
Section IV, #5

Test 38

Section I, #9
Section IV, #9

Parallel Reasoning

Test 34

Section II, #6
Section III, #25

Test 35

Section IV, #23

Test 37

Section II, #26
Section IV, #14

Test 38

Section I, #22

Complete The Argument

Test 34

Section III, #12

Test 36

Section III, #23

Test 37

Section II, #9
Section IV, #1
Section IV, #8

Test 38

Section I, #19
Section IV, #10

Flawed Parallel Reasoning

Test 34

Section II, #24
Section III, #23

Test 35

Section I, #24
Section IV, #6

Test 36

Section I, #21
Section III, #19

Test 37

Section II, #21
Section IV, #4

Test 38

Section I, #16
Section IV, #17

Principle

Test 34

Section II, #20
Section III, #1
Section III, #16

Test 35

Section I, #2
Section I, #7
Section IV, #11

Test 36

Section I, #15
Section I, #17
Section III, #15
Section III, #20

Test 37

Section II, #18#
Section II, #22
Section II, #24
Section IV, #21

Test 38

Section I, #3
Section I, #7
Section IV, #4
Section IV, #7
Section IV, #23

Role in Argument

Test 34

Section II, #22
Section III, #14
Section III, #26

Test 35

Section I, #9
Section IV, #2
Section IV, #15

Test 36

Section III, #6

Test 38

Section I, #18
Section IV, #18

Must Be True

Section II, #23
Section III, #13

Test 36

Section I, #11
Section I, #14

Test 37

Section II, #23
Section II, #7
Section II, #12

Test 38

Section IV, #1

Necessary Assumption

Test 34

Section II, #13
Section II, #16
Section II, #21
Section III, #3
Section III, #5
Section III, #9
Section III, #11
Section III, #17

Test 35

Section I, #14
Section I, #18
Section IV, #16

Test 36

Section I, #3
Section I, #20
Section III, #14
Section III, #16
Section III, #18
Section III, #22

Test 37

Section II, #15
Section II, #19
Section IV, #12
Section IV, #15
Section IV, #17
Section IV, #19
Section IV, #23

Test 38

Section I, #8
Section I, #12
Section I, #14
Section I, #24
Section IV, #6
Section IV, #20
Section IV, #22

Thank You

First of all, thank you for buying this book. Writing these explanations has been the most satisfying work I have ever done. I sincerely hope they have been helpful to you, and I wish you success on the LSAT and as a lawyer.

If you left an Amazon review, you get an extra special thank you! I truly appreciate it.

Next, I'd like to thank Steve Schwartz of LSAT Blog. These explanations wouldn't exist if not for him. He originally commissioned them for sale on his blog, and was supportive in offering guidance to make them better.

Thanks also to Anu Panil, who drew the diagrams for the logic games. Anu, thank you for making sense of the scribbles and scans I sent you. You are surely ready to master logic games after all the work you did.

Thanks to Alison Rayner, who helped me with the layout and designed the cover. If this book looks nice, she deserves credit. Alison caught many mistakes I would never have found by myself (any that remain are my own, of course).

Thanks to Ludovic Glorieux, who put up with me constantly asking him if a design change looked good or bad.

Thanks to Paul Germanotta, who diligently proofread the logical reasoning sections of this book. Any typos that remain are my own, of course.

Finally, thanks to my parents, who remained broadly supportive despite me being crazy enough to leave law school to teach the LSAT. I love you guys.

About The Author

I'm an LSAT instructor in Montreal, Canada. I've taught courses for Testmasters and Ivy Global, and offer private lessons.

I took the LSAT way back in 2007, and scored a 177. I still remember how intense it was to study for this test, and what it felt like to see my scores go up and down on practice tests.

I attended law school at the University of Toronto and McGill University, but left after deciding I wouldn't enjoy being a lawyer.

I love teaching the LSAT, and I feel privileged to be able to earn a living doing something I enjoy.

I first wrote these explanations to sell as pdfs on LSAT Blog, and later decided that a print book would be a good idea too.

You can find me at www.lsathacks.com and www.reddit.com/r/LSAT, where I am the moderator.

Feel free to get in touch by email, my address is graeme@lsathacks.com. Or you can call 514-612-1526, I'd love to hear from you.

Dedication

To Rachel Chatham, who is both a fair- and foul-weather friend,
partner, and associate; she is a woman who, no matter what kind of straits we are in,
always tells me that everything is going to work out fine.

Author Tom Ralston

With Thanks To

I sincerely thank all my employees, who have stuck by my company throughout the rains of recession. Our ship took in lots of water. Since a large part of our reputation is built on doing very creative concrete, I believe that our work has been viewed by many as a luxury item, and, because of that perception, we were bypassed by many potential clients. The fact is that we would construct any type of concrete project, from foundations to retaining walls to removing and replacing concrete sidewalk squares. Moreover, owning a concrete company that continually tries new and unproven methods of decorative concrete construction can be costly as well as risky. We are constantly testing new ideas that involve pouring mock ups, brain storming sessions, and general trial and error.

I am also clear that the company's struggles translate to employee struggles. This makes me all the more appreciative of their tenacity and great can-do attitude. However, weathered and waterlogged from our financial trials and tribulations, our key employees continued to fight the good fight; they continue to inspire me with their attitudes and their hard and creative work … they never give up.

Once again, a special thanks go out to my astute and dedicated office manager, Rachel Chatham, who has to put up with quite a lot just to work with me. Also, to my fellow artisan, estimator, and project manager, who also helps to keep me grounded, Bill Goff; to twenty-one-year veteran estimator and project manager, Tracy Whitesell; and to my very talented and dedicated concrete craftsmen and artisans: foremen Lupe Rodriguez, Victor Gomez, Sergio Diaz, Antonio Fuentes, and Enrique Chavez and Matt Sanchez; and to my finishers, Luis Medina and Sammy Ramirez, Alphonso and Jose Fabian; to my perennial employee of the month Cipriano "Cippy" Hernandez; to detail specialists Chris Cravey and Jesus Delattore, as well as to my secretaries, Carolyn Bradley and Holly Christianson.

Contents

86
Hillside Gallery

42
Constructing the Hillside Project

Foreword

Two years ago, I saw a photo of a backyard with an amazing pool, spa, and landscape. It was a night shot, so the pool and landscape were glowing from the lighting that had been installed in the walls surrounding the pool.

What I was struck by was not the pool, the large oak trees, or the great lighting. I wanted to know more about the walls. "How did he do those walls?" was my first thought. My second was: "What an amazing use of this property." The hillside looked like a piece of pottery. The walls meandered, curved, and flowed in and out of the hillside, holding back the earth in just the right places. There was also a set of steps, leading up to a new patio that overlooked the property, flanked by more of these curving walls.

I had a chance several months after seeing this photograph to hear Tom Ralston speak at a conference about this very project. He was teaching a seminar for concrete contractors on how to build concrete walls. In the seminar, as he does in this book, Tom gave specifics not only on the physical part of the project, but also on how he runs his business—how he estimates and bids, how he designs a project, how he works with homeowners and subcontractors, how he manages his crews, and much more.

Working at Concrete Network, I've seen a million images of projects that some of the best contractors in the world have been willing to send our way. But the projects Tom does are different. He's different. Rarely do you find an artist or contractor with his skill willing to share the intimate details of his work—from how to properly do tie wires on concrete retaining walls to his unique way of coloring walls with color hardener.

I met Tom roughly ten years ago at a World of Concrete event. I've always been drawn to Tom, as many people are. I think the main reason is because he's so enthusiastic about his craft and about helping other contractors succeed. He loves doing both, and it shows. Tom pushes the concrete industry forward, he makes us better. He's just crazy enough to try things no one else will try.

I remember another project where he created walls, floors, and steps (in a high-end residential home, no less) that replicate an ocean-washed cliff, complete with multiple stain colors, bug holes, sand and crushed glass embeds, and a purposefully worn finish. Few contractors would or could pull off a project like this that would have to withstand the homeowner seeing it up close every day. Tom does this repeatedly. The homeowners love the results. After each project, he shares exactly how he did it, so other can learn.

Artists see things that others don't see. It has been said that Michelangelo could look at a piece of marble and see the finished sculpture before he began. Tom sees concrete projects the same way. He can look at a hillside, a property, a home and see something amazing.

Don't just read this book—digest it. Live with it. Keep it within arm's reach as a reference for your projects. Learn how to see a property with his eyes.

—Thad Orr
Concrete Network

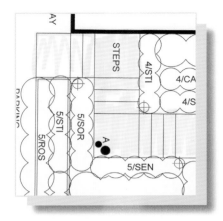

Introduction

This book was written, in part, to help in both the designing and building of residential hillside concrete projects and to examine various pitfalls that contractors face when considering a hillside project. Also, it is my hope that homeowners and designers alike will get some creative ideas and a bit more confidence before they carve into the hillside. This book also addresses the many challenges that builders or contractors will likely face when asked to construct a hillside hardscape project—especially without the aid of adequate plans, details, and specifications. It will also help contractors navigate through negotiations and designs with homeowners or project managers.

Most of the people who ask me to bid on residential hillside projects do not have an engineer's specifications or recommendations in hand before they start. During the recent economic recession, the housing and construction industries were among the worst hit, and even less money was spent on projects that were not absolutely necessary. People tended to cut back on expenses in every area.

Choosing to have all of the necessary engineering and design done by professionals adds thousands of dollars to the cost of a hillside project. Conceivably, it would mean employing an architect, a civil engineer (who may address hydraulics, drainage, and property line matters), a soils engineer, and a structural engineer. I do not wish to discredit, devalue or negate any of those particular professionals or the work that they do, but my experience is that people just do not have the additional money to spend on their services.

Even when residential projects have a plan, they tend to be minimal like the one above. They are lacking the necessary working details. Most residential plans that we get do not have any recommendations for footing thicknesses or rebar schedules, exact elevations for wall heights (or any at all), let alone a design that includes actual colors or textures pre-determined for the various components of the project.

A minimally detailed plan for a hillside that actually required far more than what is shown on the sketch.

The actual project was much more involved than the plan indicated.

It is my preference to work from plans that are fully loaded with engineering and design. It is so much easier to have elevations, engineering, and designs laid out so you can work from predetermined, specific parameters. Also, I do not recommend that a contractor or builder engage in any project with which they do not feel comfortable; if there is any uncertainty, it is important to hire engineers for consultation prior to construction. The recommendations in the book reflect where I have found success on a structural level, and illustrate what my aesthetic sensibilities have been. Issues specific to hillside construction are addressed and various ways these issues can be handled are illustrated, even though other professionals may take issue with what I prescribe. Our company's expereinces and the various formulas that we have found successful will, we hope, help you be successful, too.

Additionally, we give contractors, homeowners, and landscape architects ideas and inspiration to work with barren hillsides and create works that have lasting beauty and utility.

Being from Santa Cruz, California, an area with mountains and hillsides, I have been involved with countless hillside expanses in my twenty-five years of experience. The transformation that can take place on a hillside, going from nothing to something, is truly amazing. The end results never fail to impress or surprise the homeowner. In fact, everyone involved with the project, including those who build it, is able see the transformation and is touched by the enthusiasm. I have had customers so pleased that they write notes to me about how excited they are with their new landscape.

Just a few months after one particular project was completed, I received a letter from a customer, who wrote:

Dear Tom,

This hillside project that your team produced evolved throughout a process to something that turned out spectacularly. Every time I walk outside, I am truly amazed at the quality of work and how well each different area blends together with the next. I look forward to starting a project with your team on the rest of my property in the near future … having you win the WOW Award at the 2012 Decorative Concrete Awards Competition, was simply icing on the cake.

Designing and constructing a hillside expanse can be tricky. Over the years I learned that the generous amount of time spent hatching the idea and creating plans is merely a starting point for the evolution of the final product. This book shows the process step-by-step, to help the contractor, designer, and homeowner navigate this lengthy, creative process. The pictures and photographs of projects featured in this book show just how dramatic the changes can be.

The West Coast is rich with individuals who love to do things that are different and unique. This trait has afforded me the opportunity to design and work on unique projects.

My clients clamor to create the *avant-garde* and progressive designs that flourish on the West Coast and are embraced by pockets of creative people across the country.

Certainly, decorative and architectural concrete construction has been positively influenced by people of this mindset. The concrete countertop movement was spawned on the West Coast by concrete gurus Buddy Rhodes of San Francisco, Fu-Tung Cheng of Berkeley, and David Hertz of Los Angeles. These people have been innovators of concrete countertops (as well as concrete design), which now have become commonplace in most states and around the world. I have been fortunate to be able to co-present with all three at World of Concrete seminars on concrete countertops and have learned a great deal from them.

Tom Ralston (right) receives the WOW Award at the 2012 Decorative Concrete Awards Competition from The American Society of Concrete Contractors at the World of Concrete event. The WOW Award is the highest ranked award in the overall competition. Clay Fischer of the ASCC congratulates Tom with the award. The winning project, featured in the 2012 April issue of *Concrete Décor* magazine, turned an area that wasn't being used into an expanse with beautifully sculptured walls, stairs, and an oval upper patio.

Another revolution in decorative concrete was started in large part by West Coast innovator Brad Bowman, whom I have always held in high regard. Brad was from Carmel, California, and studied sculpture before delving into concrete construction and producing the first cast-in-place stamps for concrete. Brad was the innovator of stamped concrete and other techniques that led to the creation of the well-known franchise Bomanite. The Bomanite Company has used Brad's innovative practices as a springboard to develop other unique systems over the years.

In the early 1970s, Robert Freis, of Southern California, began manufacturing concrete imprinting tools known as "cookie cutter" stamps. These were initially made of aluminum and later from high-impact plastic. Robert is responsible for developing many innovative stamps and systems for decorative concrete.

This kind of creative concrete work has benefitted from great publicity. Magazines like *Sunset, Architectural Digest, Interior Digest, Concrete Décor, Concrete Construction Magazine*, and various architectural and home design magazines and newspapers have featured unique, *avant-garde* projects, spreading these ideas across the United States.

Hillsides: A Great Canvas for Skill and Imagination

A naked hillside canvas prior to the beginning of the project.

*E*very hillside concrete project provides an opportunity to create something unique, and something that will last (the Roman Coliseum is still hanging around!) and serve as a tribute to your own humble legacy as a concrete designer and craftsman. Many of us who embark on decorative concrete work come to realize that we have a particular artistic flair that we never knew we had.

My own experience is that I could never draw to save my life, and I never excelled in art classes. I do remember writing poetry in the second grade for a contest and I got my poem printed in the single page flyer at school; I thought that was pretty cool. I started playing piano and guitar when I was younger but never became completely serious in either discipline. Whatever creative endeavors I did undertake, they were anything but visual. So, I never thought I was an artist. Working with decorative concrete, however, has allowed me to tap into an artistic bent that has been very rewarding. I experienced an inexplicably strong desire to create unique decorative concrete, and, quite frankly, I have become somewhat obsessive about it.

As I continue to engage in decorative concrete work, I have come to realize that I *am* an artist. I am innately driven to pursue decorative concrete as some are driven to write poetry, play piano (not very well), sing, or write songs. Now I understand why.

Because I love decorative concrete, I look for it and see it everywhere. I am constantly in awe of architecture, especially when there is concrete involved. I get inspired by others' works in stone and concrete, both ancient and modern, and glean ideas from sources as diverse as clouds and seaweed, random rocks that I see along the road, or even certain trees. My camera is an invaluable aid in my creative process. I keep it close, and use it to capture the fleeting images my muse presents. I am constantly searching for unique, fascinating, and interesting ideas that I can incorporate into a new hardscape.

Design ideas can come from all kinds of sources. Landscape design and architecture magazines are one great source. It never ceases to amaze me how many books and publications are out there that can serve as guides. *Concrete Décor* and Concrete Network.com have plenty of examples of people's creative concrete ideas. There is a lot of material hidden in landscape books. I have one called *Dream Gardens*. It is focused on softscapes, but there are innumerable ideas you can draw upon. Spend time in the bookstore and library, or build your own library that you can reference whenever you want.

It is really helpful to study concrete design. It is like pretty much anything else on the planet that you want to do well. A strong desire and spirit can overcome a lot of inadequacies or shortcomings, but you still need a foundation of knowledge to become familiar with all the various avenues that need to be pursued in order to become a good decorative concrete contractor.

When I first travelled in Italy, I took numerous pictures of staircases. I have dozens of pictures of steps taken at the Coliseum and at little villas here and there. I constantly gaze at, and sometimes allow myself to meditate on, concrete construction of all kinds. If the concrete catches my attention and is unique, I try to figure out why. I ask myself how someone came up with the idea and how they actually constructed the piece.

I am sure that my "original" designs are influenced by these studies and observations of other's works. All artists consciously and unconsciously adopt and adapt what they see around them.

In the music world, we know that The Beatles admittedly copied from Chuck Berry, Little Richard, and The Everly Brothers. So much of their foundation was developed through other people's material. That's what we do in concrete design—we become students of other artists' concrete aesthetics and techniques. The techniques are important. Whatever the source of inspiration, designs for concrete pieces that are used as floors, walls, countertops, or pool decks are rendered inferior or perhaps even useless if the form does not function properly.

New York's High Line project turned a former stretch of elevated railway into a park. Here, concrete design, shape, and texture create a "boardwalk-like" effect.

Tom with TRC office manager and friend, Rachel Chatham, as well as past client Jorgen Hendrickson at the High Line in New York City.

An old axiom says that "when the student is ready, the teacher will appear." The key is being a "student," striving to continually be present and looking for ways to become better at your craft.

Become a student of design. Follow your enthusiasm and passion. The projects and the talents will follow accordingly.

Experience will help develop your creativity, too. What you learn on one project may inspire you on another. Soon, you will develop a vast set of experiences, you'll gain exposure and a good reputation, and your career will move forward.

A.

D.

F.

E.

G.

B.

C.

A. The Coliseum in Rome is inspirational for a decorative concrete contractor.

B. The Spanish Steps in Rome are elegant and functional. While others leisurely congregated, I was awed by the staircase and its design.

C. A door into the Diocletian Bath House in Rome.

D. A travertine concrete floor in Venice, constructed in the 1500s with marvelously warm concrete pigments.

E. This photo was taken from a small plane en route from Panama City to the outer island of Boca Del Toro.

F. A Boca Del Toro floor inspired by the pattern of the sea floor as seen from the air.

G. Jungle floors inspired by nature; it took many beta tests to create this particular look.

Develop Yourself

Develop your charisma and enthusiasm, and continue to be a student. If you can, go to concrete seminars and join associations. You meet people who do nothing but what you do. That's what you talk about. Hanging out with like-minded individuals enables you to live, eat, and breathe your concrete passion.

Get involved with the American Society of Concrete Contractors (ASCC) to help you develop your craft and art. I was speaking with a man the other day who said, "I'm an artist, I paint on concrete. I am not a concrete contractor. I don't think the association is for me." I said, "Well, a lot of the guys who pour the concrete you paint on are in the ASCC; it still starts out as their concrete, even if you end up painting on it. You should develop a relationship with these people. This will allow you to further your career in a positive way." The ASCC also has a Decorative Concrete Council (DCC) that is an association specifically involved with all decorative concrete. If you join these associations, you can talk to all types of individuals about problems and solutions. Then you are going to have a whole head full of information that you can use in discussions with homeowners. You will be better prepared to converse with your client.

Another thing you can do is continue your education. Go out and see what other people in the industry are doing. I have learned so much from other people and continue to do so. One man from France just showed up at my office fifteen years ago. He showed me the coolest trick, pouring one color concrete atop another color and making craggy fissures. Since then, I've developed that technique in a different way and used it countless times. Someone just showing up at your doorstep is not going to happen very often, unless you become a part of the community. Keep learning. Attend seminars on sealing, structural information, concrete mix, and design. Stay sharp, and keep up with innovations in the decorative concrete industry.

As a result of getting involved with organizations like the ASCC and the DCC, and continuing to push myself, I have met people and mentors whom I can call on to help me. I also have many people calling me to ask for advice about certain ideas they are trying to incorporate. This interaction keeps my brain churning with decorative concrete ideas.

It is also absolutely important to take business classes. For example, I recently went to an estimating class, and it reminded me how important it is to establish certain production rates so that your project estimates are accurate. Taking seminars for technical details is really a good idea. I once traded concrete work for business classes and found them to be helpful and eye opening. I had done a job for an architect who developed a 175-store franchise in the United States, and he had created a manual for developing and managing a business. I exchanged the work I did for him for his course in professional management. It was a crash course in business with one four-hour session per week for approximately eight weeks. I learned a tremendous amount from him. Most concrete workers have not taken business classes, and this can help set you apart

A great publicity shot, showing off flooring and hardscape samples: Some samples will have the same color with different textures, while some will have the same texture with different colors. By seeing samples on site, a client is better able to visualize the final product in the expanse where it will be used. By getting approval in advance, we help build immunity against later complaints.

Samples created for clients' approval fill a "boneyard" in our home lot. These are just a few of the many samples Tom Ralston Concrete casts for clients to see, touch, and experience before they make their decision.

This display helps entice clients to our home office. Sample racks show what can be done with textures and colors, and thereby help with sales.

from your competitors. Your knowledge and enthusiasm will impress clients.

You should also develop a stong knowledge of concrete color. By working with it, in it, and around it for so many years, I've developed a pretty good sense of what's possible in concrete color. I have listened to designers and engaged them in conversations regarding tastes for colors, designs, etc. You are going to need to be able to present clients with various options for color. Ask them if they are going to keep the current exterior color of their home, and offer them options that work well with that color. Let them know you're going to provide them with samples. It is a good idea for clients to be able to come to your office or yard to view various samples, so they have some idea of what they would like. It is a good way to start the discussion of colors and textures and gives a client the chance to touch and experience the sample they may choose for the project. More often than not, a client will ask for a particular color or texture that might not be in our sample racks. In these cases, we provide them with up to three dust-on color samples. We do not offer integral samples without a charge, because we have to go to one of our concrete ready-mix vendors and ask them to make a full yard of concrete, which usually costs more than $150.

I encourage clients to provide visual examples of what they like and ask them to show us images from magazines and books that show various styles, textures, and ideas. Maybe they will stumble upon things we have not seen or done before. Seeing what they have in mind, and discussing ideas with them, is part of the evolution of design. With regard to color, I ask them to bring in a color swatch—a stone, a piece of tile, or basically anything that is representative of the kind of color they would like to use.

Share your knowledge. We educate clients about colors, textures, and various options and combinations as best we can. Choosing colors and textures for a client's concrete work is a big deal. It is concrete, after all, and it has a lot of mass. It is heavy, and it is permanent. We want them to feel comfortable with their decisions, so they will have a lifetime of satisfaction.

If you have a client who focuses only on price, there may be a good chance that you will not be able to accommodate him or her, but you can still counter with ideas that are creative and offer decorative solutions for their hardscape. Charge in with enthusiasm. Let them know that "If we get your job, we are going to put every ounce of our creativity and technical expertise into it." My goal is to leave my clients happy.

Remember, It's a Team Effort

I do consider myself a creative person. But part of being creative is listening to the ideas of other. You will find inspiration from people who have no design experience and think, "Wow, I never thought of that."

Clients often have no idea how concrete works and so can offer a fresh and unique perspective, pushing us as designers to try new things. We design by evolution. Many factors and many different minds play a part in a final design. For example, our foreman may make a little change in the swoop of a wall because he either thinks it looks better or because he can't do it the way I asked him to. After a bit of field trial and error, *voilà*, the result looks great. Design changes can also come from the homeowner, from me, or from the estimator/project manager—it's a collaboration of minds that ultimately makes these projects turn out well. It is helpful to have creative brainstorming sessions before the project begins, to get a firm direction.

When the job is complicated, you are likely to need a team of subcontractors. Build a network of competent and personable professionals. Make sure you have good relationships with your engineer, electrician, landscaper, plumber, arborist, carpenter, and general contractor in case you need to bring them on board.

Remember, the work of each subcontractor reflects back on you. Build a portfolio of quality, competent professionals who you can bring on the site to make the project look great. You want everyone to rave about it.

Choose subcontractors who are friendly and communicative. It is really important that everyone working with you be communicative—especially your subs.

I have a lighting specialist who will come out to a project even before I have a signed contract. He'll even do a mock light-up before we have the job up and running because we have a good relationship and he trusts that the jobs I ask him out on will be worth his while. He'll show clients different styles and educate them about their options. He works with homeowners to evaluate their preferences and ensure their ultimate satisfaction. He went out with me recently to visit a site where the work was in progress. We had to drive forty miles to get to this site at night, and we started putting in lights to ensure that the job would come out as well as we could possibly make it. Who was going to pay for that? We were. But if you don't make efforts like this, how are you going to have a job that is extraordinary?

Connecting with your clients is important—let them know that you and your team will work exceptionally hard to make sure they are completely happy with the finished product.

Tom gets into his samples. A photographer from *Concrete Construction* magazine asked Tom to pose for an article.

Build Your Job Photo Library
(and Buy a Good Camera)

A portfolio of your work—inspiring pictures to share—isn't something you can provide early in your career. I didn't become a successful concrete contractor overnight. But if you really love this work, your enthusiasm will allow you to evolve into a seasoned decorative concrete professional. Along the way, you can develop your portfolio.

You need to get a good digital camera so that people can see examples of your work and seek out your services. Spend at least $500 to $800. I highly recommend the Canon Rebel. Whatever you get, spend time learning how how your camera works. Buy it from a store with an educated sales staff who can help teach you. Learn how your camera works with your computer and other technology. With my iPad, I can instantly download photos into a selected file. Look for ways like this to save time.

Cameras can be adjusted to take big pictures that use up a lot of memory or little pictures that might look okay on your computer but will wash out and look grainy when printed. Invest in memory cards, and set your camera to take pictures at the highest resolution possible. This is really important if you want to submit a photo to a journal, magazine, or newspaper. Generally, print media want images that are a minimum of 300 dpi (dots per inch). For websites, you only need 72 dpi. Also make sure to document your work in the highest resolution. You can take away those dots, but you can't add them.

The size of your image matters, too. Standard print sizes are 4" x 5," 5" x 7," and 8" x 10". For a full-page, 8.5" x 11" image, you need a resolution of 300 dpi *at this size*. Again, the salesperson and the camera manual are key to making sure you are prepared for a big centerfold spread in a magazine!

This backyard paradise is shown with its built-in lights blazing and its fountains flowing. A shot like this can inspire clients to upgrade their plans.

You want images worthy of submission for print so you can send pictures to publications that will help promote your business: local newspapers and magazines, trade websites like Concrete Network, and national trade journals like *Concrete Décor* magazine. Be proud of your work and be smart about marketing it. It starts with the digital camera.

Remember, though, you can't put that fancy camera to work without the property owner's permission. You cannot legally publish pictures of someone's private property, or put them on your website, if you don't have the owner's signed permission. So, add a permission clause to your standard contract to take pictures and use these for marketing purposes for your company. Make sure you discuss this with the homeowner, so they understand that these images will only be used for promotion of your business. And make sure you have it in writing if they prefer to remain anonymous or how they wish to be credited when you either publish the images or simply show them to future clients.

Once you have their signed permission, you have to get pictures that produce the "wow" effect. A talented photographer, a little staging, and the right natural lighting make the difference between an image that *shows* your work and an image that *shows off* your work.

A camera can only do so much; you need to learn to take good pictures. First, you'll want to make sure the project is looking its best. You may want to come back a month or two after the project's completion to give seeded grass a chance to grow and plants a chance to bloom. Don't let orange buckets or the odd broom detract from the glamour of your work. Make sure all tools have been removed from the site and all surfaces are clean. If there is a hose, coil it out of sight. You would be surprised at how many pictures are not up to par or rejected by a publisher because of an errant "thing" hanging out in the photo.

Some professional photographers may bring an expert to help with the staging. This is the art of making a patio—or any other project—look like a paradise. A stager may bring colorful cushions for the furnishings, matching tableware and napkins, as well as a floral centerpiece and potted plants. Professionals know that a wet patio reflects color more richly. Wet everything down before photographing it, if you can. The next time you watch a movie, notice if the street looks wet. Trust me, this doesn't happen by accident in most film locations! This being said, the judges for a recent Decorative Concrete Contest asked that the hardscape not be wet down prior to shooting the picture, as sometimes the surface water promotes glare and creates an unnatural look. As an option, you can simply seal your concrete work first to enhance the color.

Timing is everything. It is important to shoot photographs in the early morning or late afternoon when the lighting is soft and doesn't bleach out your images. The midday sun tends to wash out nature, make colors pale, and create too much contrast between shadow and light. In fact, sunlight can be so harsh you probably won't be able to look at the images on your digital camera very clearly, unless you step out of the sun.

An overcast day is ideal. Overcast skies don't cast shadows, allowing you to shoot a landscape with evenly diffused lighting. Taking lots of pictures helps, too. You never know what kind of angle will work out the best, or in what light, so keep looking for the best angles and keep snapping photos.

Finally, be sure to shoot from angles that flatter your work and make it the focus of the picture. Your work should be central. That maple tree may look lovely, but it is no testament to your concrete skills. Still, I like to play with colors of plants and floral life as a backdrop

Look how rich the east to west photo of our hillside concrete work is in the morning. The light from the morning sun helps capture the rich color finish we worked so hard to create on the stairs and walls. This is a great shot to use to sell a fancy finish.
Photo by Bud Ralston.

This midday shot is washed out, and the richness of the concrete colors on this Saratoga hillside is lost.

The same shot taken at night adds an aura of romance. This could be a money shot for couples on the fence about whether or not to sign a contract and turn their backyard into a honeymoon-like resort.

Our Lumi Lumi product is rather quiet in the daylight.

By contrast, this photograph shows that our Lumi Lumi product is quite dramatic at night.

or highlight in my hardscape photos. I believe that hardscape can be very much enhanced by surrounding plants. In fact, I am constantly badgering the landscape contractor I work with the most to get his plants in the ground so we can get some really good photos.

Once you have good photographs, put them to work. For starters, have your own website, and make sure your website shows that you do amazing work. You can find web designers, photographers, and business majors at local colleges to help you with this, all for a very reasonable price. It is an important investment. You may want to place an ad at a local college or university to see if any photography students would like a part-time job helping you with project photos. I have had very good luck with this. With a photographer in hand, you can do your own staging, making sure the project is clutter free. It might help to power-wash the project the day before, as well.

Also, upload your images onto your iPad or electronic tablet so they are ready to show to clients. And get prints made and put together an old-fashioned photo album (and another as backup). Take your portfolio everywhere with you. It doesn't hurt to have it on hand if the guy sitting next to you at the diner takes an interest in your work. Show him pictures that impress him, and leave him with a business card when you go. The latest rendition of our TRC business card has one of our best projects on the back of the cards as well, with a little wreath that says "2012 Best Decorative Concrete Project." This has been a big hit that drives our potential client to our website, so he can see more.

Women tend to drive home-improvement projects in most households, and couples and individuals come to decisions more easily when you facilitate the communication process with pictures and examples. Your images are going to give them ideas they never imagined, too, and may spur upgrades and additions.

A lot of times clients will come to your shop. Be ready to show them all your photographs. I turn my big monitor around for their viewing, and I'm able to show them everything from interior stairs 2-inches thick that wrap over plywood to fireplaces and patios. I organize my pictures by the jobs, but also by the subject—such as hillside walls and steps; pool decks; interior floors—so I can quickly and easily show them examples of what I am talking about. I am also in the process of installing a flat screen in my office that will have a beautiful running slideshow of some of our nicest projects.

It is a great idea to show before and after pictures, too, because they are so dramatic. Potential clients will see how transformative your work can be and how good you are. I learned this from the senior editor of *Sunset Magazine* years ago, who said, "There are few things in construction that are as dramatic as a good before and after picture."

We use our business cards to show off one of our award-winning projects.

Logos stamped in concrete are another way to brand and market your company's work.

Our company logo may remain in our projects for centuries. I think we can get some "Return On Investment" in that amount of time. These bronze logos can cost as much as $100 each, so be sure the project has good exposure.

Marketing Yourself

A picture can be worth a thousand "wows." An image my photographer shot helped us win the Decorative Concrete Council's coveted WOW Award.

In addition to creating a website rich with photos and having your portfolio of images on hand at all times, there are other ways to market your busiess. We always remember to place company barricades on projects that are ongoing. We also stamp almost all of our jobs with our company logo. Note: Whenever you want to place a logo on a client's work, make sure you ask first! It doesn't hurt that my family has been in this business for so long. Our company has been in the local newspaper at least ten times in the last ten years.

If you are starting out, your local chamber of commerce and Rotary club can provide important connections in your community or in nearby wealthy communities where you want to focus your business. We have our business on Facebook, too. Somebody in your company should be versed in marketing, as it will help immensely with sales.

How It All Begins

The Lead

We are now talking about basics. Likely, the lead is a phone call or Internet inquiry to your company for your service. That inquiry needs to be returned quickly! Always get back to a client within the first few days to let them know you are interested—or not interested—in the project. This goes a long way toward keeping your company's reputation intact; your chances of landing a project are always better if you can return contact before your competitors.

Reputation is the best source of new business. If someone contacts you because you were recommended, you have an instant foot in the door. You should approach every job as though it will help produce such leads in the future. Moreover, you should strive to get the kinds of jobs that will be noticed by your client's friends and family and will further build your reputation. Your efforts should be geared toward leads that will fit well with your company's talents and your ability to develop the particular projects. We were asked to bid a project for a client whose contractor recommended that they use Tom Ralston Concrete for all of their hardscape work. When the contractor asked if the clients wanted to meet with me, and they said, "No, that's fine, we know the kind of work Tom Ralston's company does." This was the result of many years of developing and executing good decorative concrete work that turns the ordinary into the extraordinary. Remember, whether it is in the details of operations or marketing, leave no stone unturned. Keep pushing forth.

Hopefully, your clients will know something about your work and your specialty. I am wary of potential clients who simply pull our name out of a phone book and may only be shopping for the most economical option.

Hillside concrete work is usually expensive to build. If you are trying to produce a hillside project with lots of merit, you don't necessarily want to be the low bidder. Being the low bidder often doesn't do anything for your bottom line except to eat into it. You wouldn't believe how often this happens to me. I look at a bottom line and realize I just used my company's money to subsidize a project … *again*! You may have produced a project where everyone is happy, but you have just used the company's money to complete it.

Not all leads are good leads. Keep your feelers up for bad leads, and hone your instincts for detecting them. Try to evaluate the potential customer's intent. If you realize the client is only out to get different bids, you may want to pass and move on. Building a hillside project can be so complicated and time-consuming that you may end up wasting your efforts on the would-be client who merely wants to draw out as much information from you as he or she can.

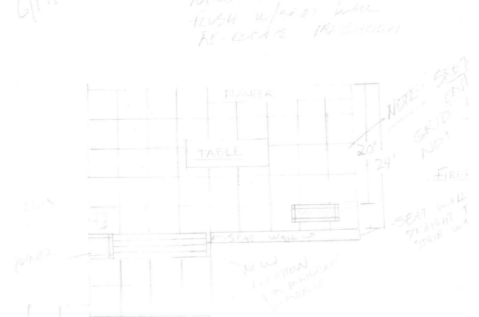

My photographer once observed that the clients who ask a lot of questions are knowledgeable; with them you can have a really good project. And while this is often true, sometimes the opposite is also true: any times, clients who ask countless questions are nervous. They don't have any idea what they want. While this situation can be normal, the client I am talking about usually goes on and on about various possibilities. They might say, "Oh, I can't have that, I won't be happy with that" or "Can we mix the colors for the band and then mix them in a different way for the field?" Many times they are very pleasant and even exceptionally sweet. But they also can be the most difficult clients. It is important to try to identify clients who are going to be problematic.

An indecisive client can cost you lots of money. Charles Vander Koii, who conducts seminars on concrete estimating and project managing, talks about the "ding dong" factor. He (somewhat jokingly) describes "ding dongs" as clients who don't really know what they want and continually change their minds, right to the end of the project, costing you time, money, and loads of stress. I have been on jobs where clients cost my company thousands of dollars out of pocket because the clients weren't sure sure what they wanted.

Some people need to see something before they know if they like it. This is what you want to avoid in the concrete business: "Wow, I didn't know it was going to look like this … can you change this, please?"

The instinct for detecting a bad client is something I continue to develop, even after decades in the trade. The bad client is not always easily discernible. Here are some warning signs: Folks who ask lots of questions but, at the same time, are very impatient. They talk over you and ask "how much" for everything. They might ask how much less it would cost if they had weekend warriors do some of the phases to prepare the work for you. Or, they tell you that they are getting three to four bids. Sometimes, they will want to brainstorm with you to see what they could creatively do in tandem with your company to save money.

More often than not, these clients want you to bid the job in different ways and have many options in terms of costs and aesthetics. In just about every case, where I have completed multiple proposals followed by multiple contracts, I end up losing money.

It is nice to develop a good relationship with a client and to build up their trust and confidence in you. I have spent up to a year and a half with certain potential clients. I think they hire me because I have demonstrated an immense amount of passion for their project. I have shown that I want, as much as they want, to see their project come out spectacularly (sometimes it seems I want it even more, especially when I go beyond our budget).

This "before" picture shows a hillside home with a wooden deck. The deck was demolished, and the area was completely reconstructed with decorative concrete.

This project was challenging. It involved lots of thought and planning to construct these aesthically pleasing curved walls that support a new patio area, complete with an outdoor kitchen, fountain, seat walls, and a fire pit. Arbor by David Hooks Construction.

The First Visit

With most new projects I bid, I find that my enthusiasm for this type of work is contagious. I'm able to engage potential clients even before we start discussing their designs. The ideas start flowing pretty quickly after that. Soon after that initial contact, I set up a meeting on site, with my camera in hand.

If the opportunity presents itself early in the conversation, I try to be realistic about costs for the project. If I am able to, I give a rough range of what the total cost will be. "This looks like it could be anywhere from $150,000 to $200,000," I will say. It is important to watch the clients' faces to see if they are serious about the investment in their property. Don't be afraid to overshoot in your estimate. That's the nature of a hillside project. These projects are usually expensive to build because there are so many unknowns when you begin. Something is always going to run over budget. *Always.*

It is hard to estimate how elevations are going to affect the amount of concrete used without having serious civil engineering work done in advance. It is also hard to know, without soil tests, what you are going to encounter in the subgrade, e.g. shale rock or sand. Many times I have found that clients are not willing to invest the money to hire soil engineers, surveyors, and civil engineers who could produce a plan that includes the exact height of retaining walls and the exact location of stairs, for example. So, the client needs to understand that time and work estimates may change. Even when you do have soil reports, surprises may still be in store.

This barren hillside is calling out to be "sculpted" and reconfigured for both function and form.

The "after" photo shows the same hillside after a major reconfiguration and pool deck additions.
Photo by Bud Ralston.

This is why stating a high price right up front is necessary. Usually there will be additional costs. I don't care how good a plan is, with hillside construction it seems that there is always something that arises that was not considered. I have had contracts with more than 65 line items, and the owners have tried to drive down costs on just about every one of the line items, time and again. If I start aggressively negotiating at a lower cost for the majority of line items, I am usually going to drive my project into the red.

I talk to my clients about the challenges of hillsides, while also trying to fill their heads with ideas—elevated patios, firepits and fireplaces, built-in lighting and sound systems, meandering staircases, curving walls with beautiful colored or stained finishes, and built-in seating. I show them pictures to gauge their likes and whet their appetite. Keep in mind, at this point, you run the risk of having a potential client take your ideas and run away with them.

Also, take a look at the neighborhood the home is in. Can this project be seen as a marketing project, that is, one that has the potential to attract other potential clients in the area? There have been many times where I have begun working in a neighborhood and, as time has gone on, I have been asked to do other projects close by—sometimes, very good projects.

On-Site Evolution

The entire time I am on site, I'm taking photos so I can sketch out ideas and plans to help my clients visualize the project. I also like to document the stages of development.

On the first visit, take pictures of the proposed project area. I take ten to twenty pictures from various angles and start pondering how to make the space useful but also aesthetically pleasing. Function and form will start to develop. The photos can also be good references for estimating difficult line items and phases, too.

Print out the pictures on stock paper, and then draw on them to start designing your project. For most of the projects shown in this book, we didn't have a landscape architect. We, the contractor, and the owner became the designers and architects, volleying ideas to arrive at a shared vision for the project. These initial photos help me with perspective and remind me of the expanse of the hillside, as well as other pertinent factors to consider.

Take "before" photos of the site from several different angles, and try to remember where your vantage point is so you can take the "after" shots from the same spot. These photos will be important for your marketing efforts later.

Photos are also important for documenting the work being done. Get excavation shots. If you are doing a project that doesn't have an engineer or inspector on site, take all the pictures so you can to document how big and deep footings are and how much reinforcing you have in the concrete. I take lots of pictures with tape measures to show how deep and wide the footings and piers are. If anything ever comes into question, you have photographs to document what you've done.

It's important to organize your photo files digitally. I take photos, and so do my project managers and estimators. All the photos go into the project folder on the computer. I have a separate computer drive where all of these pictures are located. I also have them backed up every night off site. (In 2001, I had my office broken into and four of my computer towers were stolen; I lost more than 3,000 pictures of jobs.).

Visually document the progress on each job. For example, you may need to confront your foreman with "look at the mess you left," or "you don't have enough reinforcement here." Or, you may want to show off the work to the rest of your foreman and say something like, "Look what a great job Victor is doing with his crew." These photos are essential for good communication. This can be especially helpful if you have workers whose first language is not English.

During the bidding process, I might bring along a member of my team—a plumber, carpenter, landscaper, electrician—to meet with the prospective client. I have great subcontractors and want the client to see that. My landscaper can create conceptual drawings better than I can, so many times I will ask him to do just that for one of these initial meetings.

Before we invest a lot of time, I tell customers "we'll draw a working plan for you," and it will be a basic, conceptual plan that we can bid from and work with. Developing a basic plan with parameters can be worth anywhere from $750 to $2,000, or perhaps even more, but I will let a potential client know that if they give us the job, we won't charge them for the plan. In this recession, we have had to give away a lot more than we used to in order to survive.

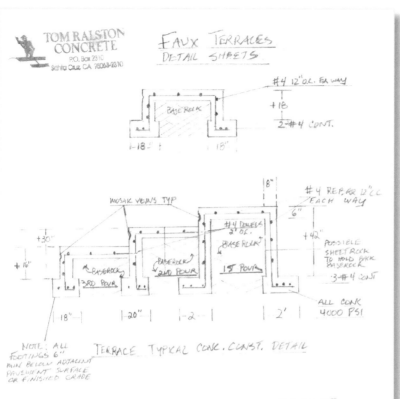

TOM RALSTON CONCRETE
P.O. Box 2310
Santa Cruz, CA 95063-2310

FAUX TERRACES
DETAIL SHEETS

"Faux terrace" details were drawn in-house by TRC to specify structural elements for a tricky monolithic pour that required stripping on all sides so that the vertical surfaces could be finished with craggy veins.

A photo of the faux terraces, almost complete.

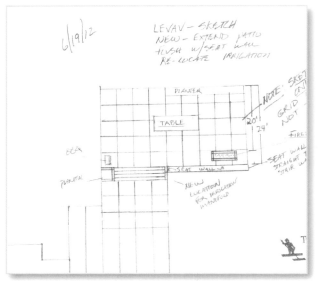

This TRC patio sketch was primarily drawn to show the client how a fire pit would fit in the patio area. The sketch also shows clients how a particular style of staircase would look, as it leads down from an upper yard to a lower pool deck.

TRC used a photo taken of the proposed stair area to sketch a conceptual design for concrete walls and stairs.

The concrete staircase built from TRC conceptual design, as shown in the sketch above.

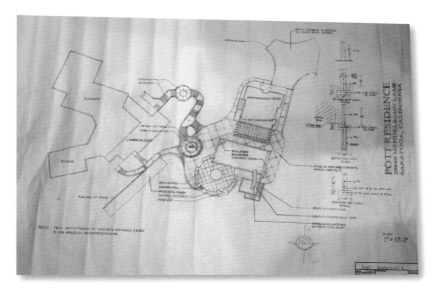

An in-house TRC design for stairs. A horseshoe planter divides the stairs; one side leads to a bocci court and spa area and the other side leads to a guest house and swimming pool.

The completed stairs, horseshoe wall, and walls.

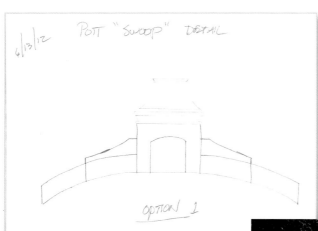

This detail was drawn to show a client what a vertical swooped back would look like. This particular drawing has three curves: a circular curve for the bench around the fireplace, a vertical curve (swoop) for the top of the seat wall, and an actual concave at the seat back.

The poured-in-place bench seat, with vertical, horizontal, and concave curves.

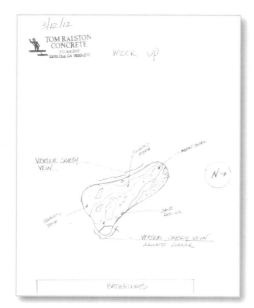

The finished, stained, Geo Strata Rock.

A conceptual sketch for a Geo Strata Rock for Pleasure Point Park in Santa Cruz, California.

Local Regulations

The contractor needs to know what engineering and inspections are required. Building codes usually state that if you construct walls more than 4 feet high, for example, you need a professional engineer. If the project is more involved, you may ask the owner to pay a fee for the engineering consultation.

It Costs Time

Developing a relationship with the homeowners, giving them ideas and ways ways to upgrade their projects, takes an enormous amount of time.

In the construction arena, you will need to be prepared to do lots and lots of free work to make a sale. That's really part and parcel of what we do as contractors. We go out to look at job sites, meet with clients, survey their project, take pictures of their project, make suggestions, discuss design possibilities, perhaps draw sketches or rough plans, and then work up a proposal. Or work up many proposals with various options.

Sometimes, unfortunately, you will get no return on your investment of time. Clients and contractors alike can be very self-serving and deceitful in trying to get the best deal for their project. Some will simply use you for ideas or for pricing, so that the contractor of their choice can match your bid or come in below it.

In the past, I have let a client or contractor know if they have been rude or disrespectful about procuring bids. These are the demanding types that push and push for a bid and then completely ignore your requests for the results of the bid; they do not answer phone calls, email, or any other type of communication. Unfortunately, that is just the way it is sometimes. You are paying your dues; putting in your investment of time.

Hopefully, through, the free work you do to make a sale will pay off. You will keep banging away at your potential client with enthusiasm, and ultimately your energy will help get them excited about their upcoming project.

The WOW Award I won was the result of a lot of hard work behind the scenes, free work, and passion for the project. I think that when you have a passion for a particular project, you will more likely produce something with extraordinary results.

Being recognized for your work helps to fuel that passion. All of my crews share that passion for their work. We discuss various ways to make our concrete work more efficient and easier, and we figure out ways to create unique concrete projects. We look for things that have never been done, concrete work that is different and challenging.

While the process of bidding a job can be very stressful and nerve-wracking, the elation that that comes with the completion of an excellent project keeps driving us to do unique and custom work.

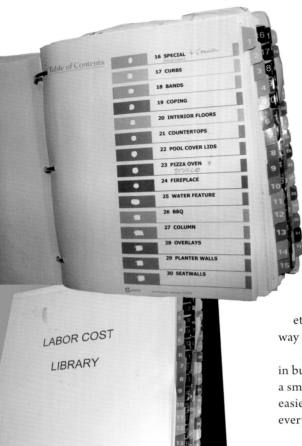

LABOR COST
LIBRARY

My labor cost library's table of contents is my essential reference when putting together a project bid. I have spent years compiling data with regard to hours per task, and it is still a work in progress.

Estimating Your Work

How do you estimate a job? If you ask ten professional estimators, you will get ten different answers. My strategy is to estimate it the way I am going to build the job. It has a logical, sequential order. I am using numbers that I am comfortable with.

For instance, for a hillside project, I first have to grub: remove plants and existing wooden stairs, scrape away the grass, and haul all that debris away. How much rough grading is it going to take? Am I going to have to haul off dirt? Our landfills want clean dirt separately, and they will not take it if it has any debris or organic material in it. How long is separating the soil going to take me? Am I going to have to do dumping or pay trucking fees? What other equipment needs will I have? Then, the estimate moves to the next phase and task, perhaps to layout and footing excavation, and then to labor and materials for reinforcing, etc. The way in which we estimate and build a job on paper follows sequentially the way in which the job is constructed.

Experience and documentation save me hours of work. For the first four years I was in business, I had more than fifteen employees, and I was just breaking even. When I had a smaller crew and worked in the field every day, it was a lot easier to manage and a lot easier to oversee production. When you have a larger company, you simply cannot be on every job on every day.

Estimating is very time consuming. Years ago I noted that for approximately every $10,000 earned on a job, I spent an average of an hour estimating the project.

Everyone has his or her own way to estimate a project. Some people are really good at flying by the seat of their pants, throwing out unit prices based on what they think is competitive. I am not comfortable working that way. I am not even comfortable giving a simple ballpark estimate when we first start to discuss a project. I find that when I do, expectations have already been set and clients will use the ballpark as a baseline.

I like to use documentation of past and current jobs when estimating. I keep extensive records of time and costs on each job. For instance, I can look up past jobs and figure that, if I have 5,000 square feet to grub, in an area inaccessible to a tractor, I am going to need men with picks and shovels. Two men can clear about 700 square feet a day. Four guys would be 1,400 square feet. So you have 3.5 days with four guys, or 15 man-days. That's the beginning of the estimate. If I am able to get a tractor in, I can grub 2,500 square feet of hillside per day.

I see an estimate as the sum total of all the parts of a prospective project (e.g. layout, excavation, tractor work, formwork, reinforcing, etc.) and, more generally, the costs for labor, material, equipment, subcontractors, overhead, and profit. A bid is made by adjusting that estimate up or down to make your price more competitive or to make it more profitable. A very good question to ask is, "How much is this project really worth and what should I sell it for?"

If you are an artist, you will be excited by the blank canvas (the hillside) that calls out to you to develop it. It's important to step back, and pour some cold reality on yourself. This

TRC BUDGET SHEET Date: 4/24/12 Job Name: DOB / RES WALL & GUEST HOUSE

ADDED FTNGS/PIERS 50 LF × 3' WIDE × 2' DEEP — PIERS @ 6' OC, 12"Ø × 6' DEEP

Code	Description	Crew Size	Man Days	Labor Costs	Material Quantity	Material Costs	Equipment	Equipment Costs	Sub Costs	Other
1	LAYOUT	2.5	.5	120	REBAR #4 PIERS 216'	55	BOB CAT-1-DAY	200	DUMP FEES 8.5 YRDS	200
2	EXCAVATION	3	3	720	REBAR #4 STIRRUPS 229#	45	DUMP-1-DAY TRUCK	100		
3	CAGES 9-12	1	1	240	REBAR #4 FTNGS 165 LF	42	PICK UP TRUCK	50	CONC PUMPER	475
4	TEMPLATE & REBAR PLACEMENT	2	2	480	CONC PIERS 2 YRDS	264	REBAR BENDER	50		
5	POUR FTNGS/PIERS	2.5	1	240	CONC FTNGS 6.5 YRDS	858				
6	STRIP & CLEAN	1.25	.25	60	2×4'S 60'	40				
7	SUPERVISION	1.25	.25	25	STAKES 1-BNDL 8'	25				
8					DOBIE BLOCKS 15	12				
9	TOTAL MAN DAYS →		8.0		TIE WIRE	5				
10					REBAR #4 DOWELS 150 LF	40				
11										
12				1885		1286		400		675
13		×1.65 %			×1.05 %		×1.25 %		×1.10	
14				3110		1455		420		743
15										
16		TOTAL		5728		$5,725.				
17										
18					÷ 8.5 YARDS = $674 PER YARD					
19					÷ 50 LF = $115 PER LF					
20										

A spreadsheet shows estimates for time, labor, materials, and equipment based on past experience. This is the final estimating sheet for a hillside.

is a business deal. You must separate your artistic aspirations from what a project like this will really cost.

You should have a pretty good idea how many man-days you need for every single task. The way we break it down is by phases and tasks.

As you will see on the example of the time card that we use (see page 37), we have about 37 construction phases and about 45 tasks. Our phases are ordered and start with 01 Foundation; 02 Slabs; 03 Patios, etc. Our tasks start with 01 Layout; 02 Excavation; 03 Bobcat; 04 Formsetting, etc. An estimating sheet will follow and combine those numbers. For example, 0407 means a man is placing and finishing a pool deck (pool decks are 04; place and finish is 07). Even administrative work—project managing time—is a task, coded at 00. When putting together the estimate, you need to have all of your phases and tasks in order exactly as you would build the job.

Remember, this is only an estimate!

As I noted earlier, hillsides often have surprises. The soil may turn out to be "fluffy," and you have to dig down further to reach something solid you can build on. Perhaps you will have to introduce a pier system to adequately build your walls and footings. Or you may have ultra-hard rock that needs to be excavated.

You bid should include disclaimers and exclusions, noting that it is built on normal conditions. It is important to note exactly what you are going to do in a quantitative way, as well as state exactly what your bid will cover and what it will not. My contracts and proposals always say, "The work we are obligated to do is limited to the scope of and quantity of work stated in your contract's line items."

For example, if I am going to put in footings, and I have specified them to be 18" wide and 18" deep by 100 lineal feet, then I will budget 9.5 yards of concrete. When I draft my contract, this particular line item will indicate that I have 9.5 yards of concrete budgeted for this particular footing. If, upon footing excavation, we find the soil is suspect and it soft and fluffy (completely unsuitable for building solid footings), we will strongly recommend that the soil be removed. The ramification is that we now have considerably more dirt to haul off, dump fees to pay, and then we need to add extra concrete and rebar. If it comes in at fifteen yards, I will charge the same amount per yard that we have budgeted in the contract. Each of my line item prices have the exact yardage on the contract or, when applicable, they will have exact square footage, lineal footage, and tonnage if that is relevant. If I run into issues, I am able to ask for compensation. When I go in and do a retaining wall that is 6 feet instead of 4 feet, priced by the square foot, I can charge for that extra.

The client can see that it is logical and fair. It is an additional expense that one is not able to include in an initial estimate. That doesn't mean it will be easy to get your client to agree to it. Nobody wants to pay more for their project, and you may have to argue for your extras, but having a clearly written bid and contract will certainly help your cause.

All my contracts state they they only cover "the quantities laid forth herein." Sometimes estimates are too high. For example, if we put in 30 lineal feet of concrete instead of the 50 outlined in the contract, the client has the right to ask for a refund or price break. It is good for the client and the contractor. You have to play it fair and have it all clearly documented.

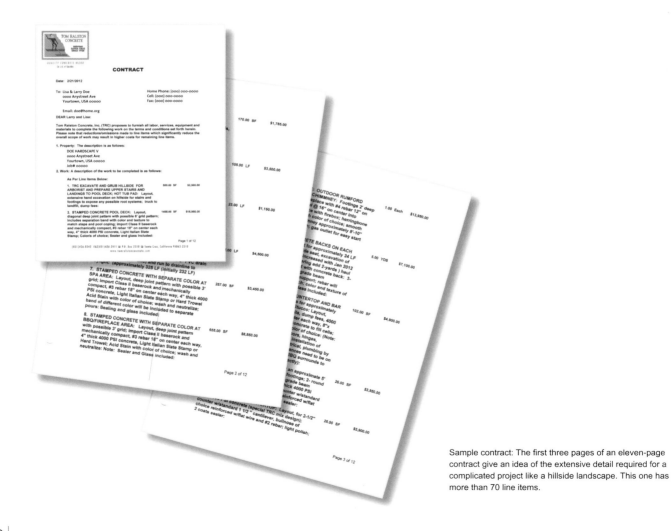

Sample contract: The first three pages of an eleven-page contract give an idea of the extensive detail required for a complicated project like a hillside landscape. This one has more than 70 line items.

Pricing and Managing Your Work

Starting out as a decorative concrete contractor, one of the things you need to know is that there will always be creative risks. I have found that no matter how much thought you put into an estimate, especially for projects that are as complicated as a hillside expanse, it is hard to nail all of the components into profitability. There is necessary creative risk. You just never know exactly what kind of effort you will be expending in order to complete the project. Sometimes you're going to win, sometimes you're not, but along the way you have to be diligent about keeping records so you can make intelligent decisions about future projects.

You are building decorative concrete experience and a really good database. Sometimes this is the only silver lining in a project gone awry.

A client will invariably tell me, "Hey, Tom, your proposal is putting me over my budget." I like to come back to them, when I can, and point out that a contractor has a budget, too. It is important to be diplomatic, of course. Especially during a recession, it seems the client sees his budget as always more important than yours.

At the time of this writing, I was working on a proposal for a $325,000 project with sixty-five line items (and the line items grew weekly as the clients changed their minds). Off and on, I spent almost 11 months courting this client to get the job. This particular project has four different proposals, five different contracts, and will be very risky. But I saw the potential with this remarkable job to transform the ordinary into the extraordinary.

I feel lucky I have past projects that exemplify what we have done and what we can do. I called past clients and asked if I could bring these homeowners to see their projects. We did some work at the home of a professional quarterback, and we were able to show our new potential clients what we did at his place—fireplace, pizza oven, barbecue, bocce ball court, and outdoor stereo system. We also had just finished a job that was very similar to the one I proposed for them, and I was able to show them that, too.

There are lots of issues when it comes to pricing and billing, especially if the work changes in scope. My masonry subcontractor told me that because he had to put long swoops in a chimney rather than building it straight and plumb, he should charge at least another $700. "I am three days over budget," he said to me. I said, "Well, this is the third rendition of the sketch for the fireplace, and you saw that." He pointed out that the client kept changing her mind, and he didn't include that additional work in his original estimate. While I was sympathetic, I had already given a final price to the homeowner. More importantly, he had moved forward with the extra work without saying there would be additional costs. I did talk to the the homeowner, but he said he couldn't afford any more changes and that he should have been apprised of the additional cost before the fireplace was started, and then he would have had an option.

It is hard to go to a homeowner and say, "Hey, I made a mistake on my estimate, will you give me more money please?" This is true especially after the work has been completed and the work was not in included in the original contract. It is like buying a car and having the dealer come back and say, "I didn't include the leather seats, would you please pay more for them?" It's too late. The deal has been done.

Technically, change orders need to be signed on the day they come to light. This frequently happens on commercial projects, but my experience is that residential work is quite a bit more lax in this regard.

I have lots of friends who are concrete contractors who say it is much harder to work in the residential realm than in the commercial realm. Homeowners are inexperienced at construction, and the jobs are very personal to them. One contractor told me he got out of residential construction because it seemed that the jobs never ended; there was always something else that came up on the punch list. He said he just could not charge enough for his work. Now, he said, in order to bid a commercial job, he has to read a spec book that is as big as a Bible, but in the long run it is worth it. Commercial jobs are exponentially bigger, and he usually deals with a developer or contractor who understands the various nuances of construction. When he requests a change order, he goes through the proper channels and gets approval.

It will be up to you to sort through all of the changes in a residential project and help clients make decisions. I know general contractors who wait until their residential jobs end before they send in the invoices for many of their extras. But presenting a big mark-up at the end may shock clients and compromise your leverage. If there are lots of little changes that will affect the cost of the job, it is better to deal with those as they arise.

Sometimes, you need to increase the cost if there are lots of unknowns on the project or it has inherent difficulties. Or maybe you want to increase the cost because this is a niche project that is in your company's realm of expertise and your competitors will not be able to bring what you can offer to the project. When you are absolutely certain of this, I think you need to play the card, hold tight, and wait for them to negotiate. Your negotiations may be affected by how badly you need the work or how badly you want to do the job. I have had projects that are so compelling that I took them on so that I could produce a stellar, one-of-a-kind hardscape.

If you have estimated the job correctly, you will be able to determine how many man-days a given phase or task may have, which then means that your contract's line items have their budgets built into them. Because we build our contract the way we'll build that hillside, we should have a good idea of how long it should take the crews to complete tasks and phases. Once you get that in an estimate, you will have a budget. When you are awarded the job, you can tell your crews at any given time: "Hey, guys, I only have three days to do this particular phase or particular task. At the end of tomorrow, I need the three of you to be done with it." Even if you *don't* have a budget for a particular phase or task, it is a mistake not to give foreman and crews orders for what should be completed at the end of each day. When crews are aware of a production goal, they perform better. More often than not, they will either beat the budget or at least meet your goals. Of course, if the project is grossly underestimated, or the crews run into unforeseen problems—they hit into a rock subgrade, or run into that fussy client who changes his or her mind on a daily basis—you will not be hitting any goals and can easily end up losing money.

The "father of management" is Peter Drucker, who has written many books on this subject. He says, "Shat can be measured can be managed." If you don't have goals in place, it will be harder to make a profit. I will assume that you will get the job completed in some form or fashion, but not with the assurance that it will come in under budget. If you don't have a budget in the first place, how will you ever know if you are on target? Production rates applied or labor budgets brought to your field crews will equate to a project that is logically well managed. And where does management start? It starts right in the estimate.

I once heard someone say, "Without establishing a budget for your crews, it's like asking them to play a football game without goal posts." You could hypothetically say "How did you do?" and they'd say, "I don't know, nobody won the game, we just kicked the ball around."

All people need goals, and it is rewarding when they reach them. As a manager, you have to keep everybody on task and remind them of production goals.

A great way to estimate is to enlist the help of the foreman who will be working on the job by saying, "Hey, I have this job coming up and we will have this and that task to do. Can you tell me how much time I should allot for each of them?" When you pencil in his estimate, you have gotten him vested in the production of the project and the buy-in will be easier. I wish that I had enough time to do this on more of our jobs, but usually we don't have that kind of luxury.

Understanding Overhead

Basically, there are three compartments to every company: sales, operations, and administrative. Secretaries and the office manager go into the G&A (general and administrative) account as well. Every company has some kind of overhead percentage. Some have more, especially if they have buildings, equipment, property, and office staff. Their percentage is going to be a lot higher, unless their sales volume goes up considerably. If they do $4 million a year, their overhead might shrink down to 20 percent of their overall budget. If their sales shrink to $1 million, that overhead percentage could shoot to 50 percent or higher.

Obviously, some companies that we compete with have less overhead than we have, and others have more. Our overhead runs approximately 35 cents on every dollar to break even. If I want to anticipate a 5 percent profit, I have to apply 40 percent over costs. I have overhead: my office, my employees, and my own salary are the cost of administration. Because our company is small, our estimators are hybrids who also act as project managers and salesmen. Some of their salary could go into sales and some into operations, which makes it difficult to separate the allocation of monies. In our company, they simply go into G&A expenses. When projects get bigger, I can usually compete better than on the smaller projects. Also, one of our yearly goals is to look at which jobs came in profitable and see who the estimator/salesman, the project manager, and the foreman were for that job, so that by category we can see who was responsible for the end results of the project.

Building a successful company is challenging but rewarding. I'm not the greatest business person, but I do have a whole headful of knowledge because I have studied what I needed to. I still need to learn more about the various facets of the concrete construction business.

It is really important for a contractor to understand what his overhead is and how to manipulate the profit margin effectively. At the very least, you need to know where your company's break-even point is. How much do you need to bring in on each job to cover the liability, workers comp, fuel, office staff, and so on? You have to find where the break-even point is, and then you can play around with the percentage of profit. That's what I do, anyway. I say, "I am going to get this job, and I'm going to just get a three-percent profit," or "I'm going to get this job and try for a twenty percent profit because it's really a risky job and I need a cushion for contingencies."

Quite frankly, I didn't know what my break-even point was for the first four years I was in business. I asked general contractor for advice. That was a mistake. They said, "Just get your cost and add 10 percent." So I was adding 10 percent for four years to my job estimates, and when I finally had the wisdom to ask an accountant, I found out that my overhead was 26 percent! I was dragging an anchor around that I didn't know I had, but work was plentiful. A company of my size, with thirty employees or so and office space, and truck payments, typically needs around a 30 percent profit.

I would strongly recommend that a decorative concrete contractor understand his business structure. Find a good accountant who is versed in construction—ask other contractors in your area who they use—and interview him or her. You should find an accountant who is well versed in construction because it is different than other businesses.

I am going to assume that the majority of the people attracted to the decorative concrete industry have an artistic bent and may have a more difficult time focusing on or being interested in financial matters. Me too, but I have forced myself to be somewhat proficient. The other key for me is to offset my artistic sensibilities with someone who is more "left brain," better versed in accounting, numbers, and statistics. I found an office manager with these strengths, and she has become absolutely indispensable.

Keep Those Old Time Cards

Time cards from completed projects, as I've noted earlier, are essential to the work of estimating the cost of a job and calculating a bid.

Time cards also help us see if we are on target for current jobs. The process can be complicated. We use programs like Excel, American Contractor by Maxwell, and a program we developed in-house that we call Job Manager by TRC. If we want to drill down into the job and see what kind of production or profitability we have to date, we can do that.

Our time cards also teach us when we should give up on certain tasks. Geoff Eisenberg of the West Marine Company, whom I highly respect for his business acumen, once said to me, "You either make it or you buy it." You either make the house, or you subcontract with someone else to build it. Our time card entries show us, for instance, if we are making money doing flagstone work for a particular phase of a project. We can compare that project to other flagstone work we've done for other projects. If our time cards show us, over and over again, that if we are not making money doing this sort of flagstone work, we should subcontract that sort of work for future projects.

Or time cards also show us patterns in how our crews work. For example, when we do tall, meandering concrete walls with Victor's crew, we may make money, but with Matt's crew, we may lose money. Each foreman usually has his particular forte, and time cards will help you see what those are.

When you analyze time card records, they will reflect what you are good at and what makes money for you. And that's what you should be marketing. We do incredible interior floors, acid staining, hillside projects, driveways, and patios, as well as unique one-of-a-kind projects. These are what our crews really like to do, too.

The key to making time cards work for you, as I mentioned earlier, is to make sure they are accurate. That's a problem in and of itself. Our foremen are busy and can have up to twelve people on their crew. Every single day, ten to twelve time cards (sometimes even more) come into our time card basket. Our project managers have to go through the time cards to check for accuracy. We see at least a few mistakes almost every day.

We also need to stay on top of our foreman about any materials that are picked

Our time cards include codes for phases and tasks. Before the guys go out on the job, we've already set goals for them. The time cards keep them accountable and help us keep our work estimates for future jobs accurate. It can be complicated: I need to know if I am doing a job with a crew that is super fast compared to other crews. For example, Crew #1 is really fast at pool decks, but Crew #4 is really talented at concrete countertops. This is an individual time card sheet used for every job TRC constructs. The time card includes all phases and tasks so we can track production.

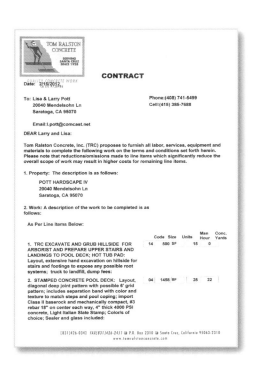

This foreman contract shows budget task man-days.

up for a project during the day. We ask the foreman to attach their concrete tags, pump tags, and any material tags to the time cards. (It should be noted that we would rather have a laborer or truck driver pick up materials as this task wastes a foreman's production time.) Much of the time, when the material tags come in, we have to ask exactly what the materials were bought for because the foremen haven't entered the phase and code. They usually do tell us what job the materials were for, but we need to be more specific: Were the materials for the stairs or the coping? These accurate records will help us figure out how much the job cost us per linear foot or square foot, or whatever.

Your collections of time cards will provide you with enough information to start your own labor cost library. I got this idea from George Headley, who gives seminars about the economics of production. I have a labor cost library that has every single phase and task we have ever done, down to hauling dirt by wheelbarrow from a backyard to a front yard. I work with American Contractor and have set up various computer programs that will allow me, with a click of a mouse, to see how many man-hours a particular task takes per square foot, per lineal foot, per yard, or per ton.

For example, let's say we are bidding a new project and want to find out how much labor we typically spend for placing and finishing a stamped pool deck. We can isolate that task (07) and see what kind of production we usually get per square foot. Or we can choose to isolate the overall phase of 04 Pool Deck to get a broader accounting. In my records, I see that for one particular pool deck it took us .1458 man-hours per square foot to complete the entire pool deck, which included all of the tasks from layout, form set, grading, and finishing to sealing. The pool deck was 2,905 square feet, so when I multiply the .1458 man-hours by 2,905 I see this job took this particular crew 423.5 man-hours, or approximately 53 man-days. Now, if I calculate what we charge per man-day plus overhead and profit, we are looking at around $6.75 per square foot for labor only. Materials, equipment, and subcontractors will be in excess of this, and a conservative cost may be around $12 per square foot without sealing the concrete.

All of these metrics start with a time card, and hopefully the job costs are accurately reflected by the time card entries, even though no two jobs are ever really the same. As I've said before, when you are working on and within Mother Earth, every job is unique. Even the same crews that you put out on a certain type of job can have different production numbers on the next job. But these baseline budget numbers are still essential to help you manage your project's production.

Metrics Log

All my estimators/project managers have cheat sheet shortcuts to our metrics log on their computers. The metrics entries match the numbers we use for our timecard entries: For example, installing pavers is task number 23. A driveway is phase code number 11. If we see 1123, we know that our crew is setting pavers in a driveway.

Our metrics log gives us instant access to lots of information. For example, we can see how long it took to do pavers in a patio in a backyard, as opposed to pavers in a driveway, which is usually right off the street. The equation boils down to how many lineal feet we get done per hour per man and how many square feet we get done per man per day. We try to document all our production rates for each task and ultimately each phase. Again, all this data came from our time cards.

If you don't have this kind of data, you will just be guessing where you make and lose money. A lot of people have a good intuitive understanding of how much a job will cost. As I've said, usually these people are in the field, working side-by-side with their employees. This seems to work for some smaller businesses. But the bigger you get, the less successful you will be if you are trying to manage your growing company just by feel.

 If you bid your projects with "x" amount of money per line item and don't have man-days or man-hours associated with the phase, managing the project will be more difficult. A system like ours also makes it easier to let clients know the schedule with a good deal more accuracy.

To arrive at cost estimates for a project, start with your raw costs: labor, materials, equipment, and perhaps a subcontractor. Then apply profit and overhead.

But finding the time to "stick figure" a job can be difficult. This means sticking a figure to each line item in a budget. I have had jobs that had more than 59 line items, and more than 25 different phases, as well as 30 different tasks. When the estimate was done, there were approximately 750 individual entries (e.g. rebar, form lumber, form building, stripping, and finishing for each item).

Using our metrics log, I can work more efficiently by looking at unit pricing. If I have a job that is very similar to other jobs we've done in the past, I can use the square footage numbers that I've compiled from those previous jobs. If I had 10 pool decks, all somewhat similar, let's say their cost worked out to an average of $10 per square foot. I want 10 percent profit, so that adds another $1 to that square foot, for a total of $11 per square foot. I can use that number and not have to do all that line-item math to get a good general idea of what costs will be.

Note: With hillside work you need to spend the extra time with your estimate. There are too many items that need really good calculations in order to get to an accurate estimate.

Our metrics log is in an Excel spread sheet and compiled from time card entries. It shows us what kinds of production times we have had for various phases and tasks. The log tracks production rates for each step in a project to help the TRC company understand our costs for different varieties of work.

This can take a long time. It took me more than 30 hours to do a detailed, longhand estimate for a $330,000 job, for example. Typically, I use both unit priced numbers that I am comfortable with and some stick figured items. The more difficult job is to determine if there are special conditions that will mean additional costs, like a rocky subgrade or poor access. Or, of course, the indecisive but sweet client who will be an additional cost if he or she keeps calling for changes.

Most decorative contractors that I have run into bid the majority of their work by unit pricing: so much per square foot, per lineal foot, or by the yard. But most of them are also one-man bands: The contractor is also the form setter, estimator, salesman, finisher, bill collector, marketer, and photographer. This contractor wouldn't have time to go through a 975 line item budget and give each line a figure. Especially since he or she could go to all that trouble and still not even get the job.

Making the Sale

Now we've made a sketch or a plan, put together the estimate, and sent our bid to the customer. The client may want to get into some sort of negotiation. This is where it is nice to have a job history. When you are doing something unique and different, you have to work to the best of your ability to build the job on paper and sometimes just draw a line in the sand and say, "I can't go any lower than that."

A word to the wise: Watch out for the clients who want to examine every single line item to see where they can save money. When you start lowering the price for various line items, it can lead to disaster.

More likely than not, you are going to get hurt on a lot of the hillside jobs if you try to bid competitively because these projects are expensive and have many unforeseen complications. Sometimes I bid aggressively on these jobs because I am just trying to keep my best foreman and crews busy. But we should all bear in mind the words of Warren French of Las Animas Concrete, who used to sternly say, "I am not in business to break even."

A pool contractor once gave me some good advice about how to handle a client who wants to get the costs down for an estimate. He says something to the effect of "Well, sure we can reduce the costs, what is it that you would like us to take out?"

Ask the client what he or she is willing to take out or eliminate and give them options: "Let's take out the firepit. That will save you almost $4,000. Let's reduce the height of the walls and that could reduce the size of the footings and we can save money there. Let's change the acid stained concrete to stamped concrete and you will be able to save some money there."

Instead of reducing costs on line items, try to reduce the line items. Ask your client to sacrifice the scope of the project.

When you go out to sell a job, it's easy to worry about other bids and give the cheapest bid because you need the job. But you can't think that way, especially if you are doing difficult projects like hillsides. Instead, stay positive. Show your work, and talk about the things you could do for your potential client. I always let my potential client know that I probably won't be the cheapest bid out there.

If you love what you do, let it show. One of the reasons I am a good salesman is because I eat, sleep, and breathe what I do, and that level of involvement shows through to my clients.

Talk about some of the different creative options you could do for their project. Maybe some will cost the client more money, but maybe they will see it as a good investment. You want to get them excited about your ideas. Have them imagine themselves in their new environment. Make suggestions: "If you put a firepit here, think how fun it would be to have your friends over with a glass of great wine," or "What about a sound system?" You might come up with some appealing options for this homeowner that he or she never thought of. For example, once I suggested radiant heat in a seat wall cap to keep the client warm during the winter months, and the client's response was, "Yes, what a great idea."

Don't let those suggestions and options stop with the sale. Keep coming up with ideas as the project evolves. If you have a great new idea, let your client know right away. My crew does that, too. Most of the time the ideas involve small changes and no additional costs. They might just make the design flow better. For example, we might say, "What if we flared this out, what do you think of that?" My clients are usually enraptured by this kind of engagement. We wow and involve them by continuing to be creative, looking for ways to make their project extraordinary.

Discuss All Changes

As we were working on one hillside project, I told the property owner I was thinking of opening the stairs up more on the pool side than on the hillside, and the husband was ecstatic. But when we got done building the forms, pouring the concrete, and then sealing the concrete, his wife said, "Why did you build them like that? That's not how they were on the plans." She said, "You know, since these weren't built as shown on the plan, I could have you rip them out and redo them at your expense." I said, with as much of a smile on my face as I could muster, "Do you really hate them that much? It is your house and I want you to be happy. But I would not have done this without discussing this with your husband, and he really liked the idea."

Fortunately, after she lived with the stairs for a few days, she ended up not only getting used to them but really liking them.

It is always important, but especially important when you have two people who are the decision-makers, to document significant changes and the times the changes were discussed and subsequently made. Make sure you email and discuss changes with both parties. I always try to gang email all of the parties that need to be kept in the loop. Sometimes it is a general contractor, his client, and his client's spouse, and sometimes there is a designer or architect as well.

If there are two or more decision-makers, do all that you can as a contractor to make sure all of them are aware of decisions being made.

Logo chocolate for TRC to distribute to clients.

Constructing the Hillside Project

Grubbing

Usually when I am drawing up the sketch or plan, I have already walked the site, mentally laying out the patio, stairs, or other hardscape. In these walks, I also note if there are trees or bushes that need to be removed or that can be incorporated in the new plan. We try to incorporate existing trees, but sometimes a tree or two has to be eliminated. Sometimes our team will suggest planting new trees and landscaping. Sometimes we put fences around trees that need to stay to make sure they don't get damaged during construction. If you are working in a permitted situation, most of the time the city arborist will insist that these trees are fenced off.

The first job on a hillside construction site is clearing and grubbing—picking off the vegetation and organic material. Take out all the vegetation—trees, shrubs, and plant matter—that is in the way of the new hardscape or is deemed unsightly.

Step one is removing the vegetation, or grubbing. I have to figure how many square feet a man can grub in a day, factoring in trees, and how far the debris has to be carried or carted by wheelbarrow if there is no access for machinery.

Grubbing by hand is sometimes the most economical, especially when access for heavy equipment is not feasible.

Protective fencing for trees is placed prior to grubbing a hillside with a dozer.

Hillside site prior to grubbing.

Grubbing by dozer is the easiest and most of the time the most economical option.

Experience will help you estimate how much time it will take. Having a record of how many square feet of hillside a man can grub in a day will help you with your estimate. Sometimes, if the grubbing is extensive, I will hire a grading contractor who has lots of great equipment to bring to the site. He may be able to do the job far more efficiently than our company and do it considerably cheaper.

You also need to know if your landfill requires separation of organic material and inert soil, and what the dumping fees are. Are you going to need a larger dump truck or would a smaller dump truck do? How many runs will you need to make to the landfill? Usually it's hard to get a tractor onto the hillside, and you need to allow time to wheelbarrow the dirt from the backyard to the front.

After grubbing, a bench cut is made to prepare for walls and a swimming pool.

Grading and Excavating

After all the organic material has been stripped from the work areas, you need to excavate for walls, stairs, and patios. If you have, for example, an upper patio on your hillside, you have to grade that hillside. Multiple layouts may be required as the stakes can get moved or run over by equipment.

The excavation process always leads to new ideas. You, your crew, your foreman, and the property owner may decide to tweak the layout at this point to improve the design—adding a curve here, a different angle there. Most of these changes won't add anything to the cost, but if they do, it is appropriate to submit a change order for the work at hand.

When you are cutting away for retaining walls, you have to factor in about two feet behind the walls to allow for installation of drainage and waterproofing, such as a geotextiles soil drainage mat or a couple of applications of cementitious waterproofing.

Next you lay out and excavate for footings. This is where we refer back to our structural engineers, especially if the walls will be more than 4 feet in height. If something goes wrong later— for example, if the wall leans out away from the hillside— it will be important to learn if the design was at fault or if the contractor didn't do an adequate job. Remember: It is important to photograph your work on footings or piers. We have our foremen use tape measures to show the depths of the footings and piers before the wall is built as insurance against liability. If the construction is ever called into question, we have this record of our work carefully documented.

I think I have established that concrete contractors, especially decorative concrete contractors, are at high risk for liability claims. We take on the risk of the structural integrity of whatever we are building.

After hand-grubbing and initial excavation, hillside stairs receive an initial layout.

Laying Out Upper Patios

This compacted baserock pad will be a sub-base for a future pool deck.

Because they provide wonderful vistas, upper patios are desired in hillside environments. The upper patio needs to be laid out very similarly to the stairs. Usually on a hillside, the patios are tied in by walls in conjunction with the stairs. Many times we will do the stakes and the walls as a mock-up form, so the clients can see how it will look. That is important.

We like to put seat walls around patios because they help to frame the patio into the hillside. The walls are raised about 18 inches higher than the patio to create seating and a nice definition for the space. On a 20' x 20' patio, you get 50 feet of seats—25 seats easily—without any patio furniture. The upper patio then becomes a gathering place for enjoying that great vista. Upper patios are often enhanced with firepits, lighting, and other such amenities.

A lot of this work has been anticipated in the initial estimate or plan. If you just have a patio that doesn't have walls, there will be a tall edge, depending on how steep your hillside is. The flatter the hillside, the shorter the footing/wall. When a wall is not planned, there will be added concrete where the footing meets the slab. There will be a triangular space around the perimeter of a footing because you can't get dirt to stack at a 90-degree angle; it usually slopes toward the edge. Sometimes, we use an inert material, like sheet rock, to hold back the baserock from falling into the footings, but that is a bit of work. You will need to determine if it is more cost effective to pour the concrete thicker in a triangle or to haul up sheetrock and spend on extra labor.

Setting up mock forms before fastening them securely will allow an owner to see formwork for approval and avoid costly undoing of formwork.

If you can build walls first, to contain the patio, then baserock can be placed right against the wall. We usually wait seven days for the concrete walls to set before we will compact baserock against them.

Walls can also add color to a patio setting. Color variations can create beautiful contrasts in walls, patio, wall caps, and steps.

You can also wire music speakers into patio walls. We've been doing more and more of that. We've also been putting in more electrical outlets in patio walls. Our electrician makes sure that we leave no "electrical stone" unturned.

Hillsides lend themselves to beautiful curvatures. We don't do a lot of straight walls and stairs.

Loosely secured perimeter forms for a hillside wall allow clients to visualize the formwork before form-setters make a deeper commitment.

Perimeter seat walls with upper patios are attractive and have obvious advantages.

Firepits and seat walls are a natural match, and a smooth concrete bench is both easy to sit on and to maintain.

An upper retaining wall and a (mostly) freestanding lower wall make for a nice firepit area.

The built-in seating, retaining walls, and patio surface were created in a variety of finishes, creating the sense of a flowing streambed and natural banks.

Stairs and Stair Layout

There is nothing like a beautiful expanse of steps to define a hillside. We like to arc our stairs as they meander up and down a hillside.

A stairway can be dramatic. The first thing we do when creating a hillside project is to figure out where the stairs will be. Then we consider how the walls will be constructed, i.e. how high, stepped or angled, etc.

The plan for the stairs and walls will evolve as you grade and excavate the site. The original plan is a conceptual layout. Invariably, as we start the construction, we see opportunities to improve the design. When you stand in the space and see how your design relates to the rest of the environment, you may have ideas on how to improve that design. It's important to include homeowners in the evolution of site design, and to make sure you have them on board.

All our stairs typically have rebar reinforcing and usually we use #3 bar on each stair as well as in a grid in the concrete base of the stair runs. Our stairs get 4000 psi concrete with ¾-inch aggregate rock. We don't use pea gravel; we don't pump pea gravel. We only use ¾-inch aggregate, even when the concrete is only 1 ½ inches thick. We have discovered over the years that we get less shrinking and it is a better structural mix. Sometimes, if the concrete is thinner, we'll put in an admixture like Tetra-Guard by Master Builders or Eclipse by W.R. Grace. That greatly helps to reduce shrinkage and cracking.

Laying out hillside stairs with paint for approval.

There's a certain method to forming stairs. Stairs are difficult to place and finish, especially when they have a bullnosed profile, which means there is some kind of protrusion or cantilever. Bullnose protrusions can break off or collapse if stripping is done soon after the stairs are poured. It is a very delicate matter and can be challenging, especially if the concrete sets up sooner than anticipated.

There are different styles of bullnosed profiles to use for stairs. We show clients examples of what we've done, and we can make custom bullnoses if the client has something in mind. We don't want to have too many nooks on the bullnose, however, because it becomes too hard for the finishers to keep the lines that are close together straight.

The bulk of the work is with concrete, but some clients like tile on the risers of the stairs. When tile is placed on risers and treads, an ugly grout joint is sometimes created where two steps meet. One of the things we've done to eliminate this grout joint is to cast a bullnose so that the tile meets with the top and bottom of the bullnose.

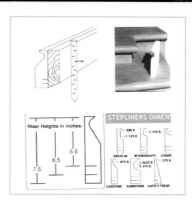

An example of the Stagmire step profile; there are companies that will fabricate custom bullnose profiles, too.

Laying out steps with temporary
wooden risers for client approval.

Laying out a stairway with precut horses or a stair jig is
one way to see how they fit into the hillside.

Another thing we can do is to insert tile into our risers and sometimes into the tread of the step. It's a really beautiful look.

You need people who understand the art of stripping and finishing stairs. It is a thing of beauty to watch our finishers in action. Our metrics formula for stairs shows that one man should be able to handle 35 to 40 linear feet maximum. If we have 240 lineal feet of stairs, we need eight men for that job. In addition, if the stairs get a colored plaster, then we need an additional mixer/dispenser person assigned to the project as well.

You may have to add manpower in certain weather conditions. If it's hot and windy, maybe you are only going to get 25 lineal feet of stairs per man or less—the stairs are going to set up much more quickly. If the weather is too extreme, you may have to cancel the pour. If there's a 50 percent chance of rain, you probably don't want to pour.

Considering metrics for a moment, it is really important to figure in all these man-hours for your bid. In the end, however, it is the finished product that matters. Regardless of your estimate, the job has to look great. If you are on the site and the weather is challenging, or the concrete was late and now is setting up quickly, you might be need to change your plans. Maybe you estimated the need for six men, but now you need eight instead. If you have started the pour, you have only three or four hours of opportunity to get it all right, and you need to do whatever it takes to make the job turn out beautifully.

Most of the concrete pours that are scheduled should have a contingency plan, and you should have workers on stand-by in case you need them.

We will talk about coloring walls (page 62), but coloring stairs is done in the same manner when using a dust-on concrete. We usually start out with approximately a quarter bucket of the color hardener of choice, and then add water to mix a paste with a drill and a paddle. Then we spread it on by hand, using rubber gloves. The texture of the stairs, like any concrete surface, can be varied—you can make a sand-washed finish texture, a stamped finish texture, a Victorian swirl, or a hard trowel texture. Typically, you want to have something on the steps that roughens it up to give you some traction. We also get that result from using a pulverized glass in the sealer. Most of the time, we use a combination of a fern green with an autumn blend of pulverized glass that is lightly broadcast onto the first coat of the sealer and then complete the process with a second coat of sealer. If we want a

Laying out stairs with paint on walls helps to place landings and make sure that wall heights are correct.

Note the buckets of cappuccino-colored hardeners that were used to dust on color on these winding stairs.

An example of tile inserted into concrete bullnose stairs, which eliminates the need for an unsightly grouted edge of tile.

sand-wash finish with muriatic acid and water, we wait till the day after the pour. Then it breaks the skin of the surface and exposes the bits of sand in the color hardener, creating a beautiful worn and weathered look. Another way you can get this texture is by using a sand blaster, but it is more labor intensive. We do it as a sand-wash item, while our competition bids it as a sand-blast item. We get the same look with a lot less labor.

The advantage of using a dust-on color is you can match that color years down the road much easier than if you are using integral color put in at the concrete plant. The dust-on colors also increase the PSI of the concrete, making it a little harder and more scratch-resistant.

Typically, we don't put deep joints in stairs, but if they get really long, we will. We like to leave stairs as one solid piece. However, I suggest using deep joints if your client objects to seeing a small crack develop in the stairs.

Structural Integrity of Walls and Footings

Excavation for walls with a backhoe.

If you have any questions about the integrity of a project, be sure to consult an engineer and get confirmation that it is structurally sound!

If you use an architect or engineer, they will specify how much steel reinforcement or rebar should be used on a project. If you are the designer, you take on the responsibility yourself. Experience is critical. Over the years, I have collected information on reinforcement systems for various wall heights in various soil conditions. If the project is relatively simple, an engineer can use calculations that have been used successfully on other structures.

When a project becomes more complicated, a structural engineer will most likely consult a soils engineer who will look at whether that soil has clay, sand, or shale content, whether it is it near epicenters for earthquakes, and other considerations. Then the structural engineer will make his calculations. Most of our jobs do not have engineered plans because most of our work isn't structural. Most of our walls are 3 or 4 feet high. Anything more than 6 feet is beyond the realm of what we are discussing in this book.

Excavation for walls and drain system by hand.

One of the hillside projects in this book did involve a lot of engineering because the project was over my head on many levels. I interviewed three structural engineers for my client, as well as civil and soils engineers. The project included 10-foot concrete walls and a 2-foot diameter drain line under the pool deck, patio, and lawn area. A swimming pool rested against the 10-foot wall, and there were hundreds of pounds of native soils to export from the site and engineered fill to import. The site was in a backyard on a very steep hillside. I would never bid or construct a project like this without getting proper engineering.

By the time the estimate was drawn up, I had already specified footing widths and depths and determined there would be a pier and grade beam system incorporated in the footings. The grade beam is similar to a beam of steel or wood, except that it's in the earth—a beam of concrete fortified with concrete. These piers attach themselves to the beam of concrete, and the walls are subsequently attached to the grade beams and piers. I use piers extensively in walls; they are immensely important because they provide structure and insurance.

The footings are determined by the engineering. For 3- and 4-foot walls, piers are included for insurance. Usually, I will space them 6 to 8 feet apart. Bigger walls usually mean bigger footings and deeper piers. Also, since it is hillside work, mechanization is a

Hand excavation for piers using a common post hole digger.

Hand excavation for piers using a power auger.

challenge. Usually, if we can't get a tractor up to bore our footings, we use 12-inch diameter hand augers. If you want to go deeper than 4 or 5 feet with a motorized hand auger, you have to detach the shaft and add a second stem/shaft attachment so you can get 8 feet deep. These types of piers are not easy to install. Typically, we put these piers 6 feet on center, sometimes 8 feet on center, in the expanse of the wall.

We insert cages in each footing—four pieces of rebar wrapped in a square so that each corner has a piece of vertical rebar coming up. The wraps are called stirrups and are used to tie the bars in and keep them in place.

Another thing we do with walls when we feel the integrity might be a little tentative or risky is to install a deadman—an additional pier and footing that attaches to the wall system and is placed up higher and attached by a grade beam. A deadman is essentially a square footing and pier connected by a trench on more-or-less a 90-degree angle from the footing, which will serve to anchor the wall system back into the hill. It is another way to get into the solid ground and anchor the footing with more support. Basically you make a trench that goes uphill perpendicular to the wall and at the end of the trench is a 30-inch-square footing with another 12-inch pier in the center. (See photo of deadman, page 52.) Rebar is tied from pier to pier within the grade beam and makes what we refer to as a hairpin. It's a great system that works well in many applications.

Usually for walls 5 feet or less in height, we pour the footings, the piers, and the wall at the same time. For taller walls, we most often pour piers and footings separately from the wall. It is always better if you can pour everything all at once, of course. You only have to use one pump and you get three phases poured.

It is important to document this work in photographs in case there are questions or concerns later in the life of the project.

Wall footing layout for hand excavation.

Piers and grade beam with rebar to help anchor an 8-foot wall that will eventually anchor a patio and barbeque area; remember to take images to document the rebar reinforcement of footings and piers before the pour.

After wall footings have been excavated into the hillside.

Deadman with an anchor pier into a square pad footing and a grade beam connecting to the wall footing system.

Typical pier and grade beam after excavation and ready for rebar.

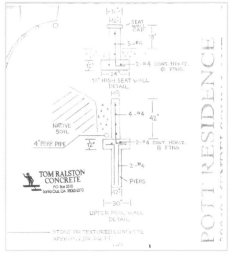

Pier detail drawn in-house for a pier system

Pier grade beam and wall ready for a monolithic pour.

Pier cages fabricated and ready to install.

Forming the Walls

The footings are excavated, allowing at least two feet behind the wall to work and install a drain system, and we've dug our piers. Now we are going to execute our final layout and form and brace the walls. Walls are formed one side at a time. The inner wall (next to the hillside) is built first and then braced, and then the rebar goes in. After that, the inside forms "button up" the walls. Many times our hillside walls are curved. When we make curved walls and need to allow our forms to make various serpentine shapes, we use a masonite ship-lap siding (or as one manufacturer calls it, "Valueform"). It is half an inch wide and comes in 16-foot lengths. This siding requires lots of stakes and bracing. Most of the time we space our stakes at only a foot apart, which insures that our walls will stay perfectly straight. When the bends are even tighter, we usually get the ¼-inch or ⅛-inch 4' x 8' Masonite sheets and then cut to whatever width we need to form the walls at the tighter curved area.

When the walls are straight, you can use form material that is thicker, like 2" x 12" stock made from Douglas Fir. With 2" x 12"s, you can spread your stakes out 2 to 3 feet apart, because the form material is stiffer and more rigid. This has been a really good wall forming system for us.

Ready to form lower retaining wall with oval upper patio wall formed with Valueform that bends nicely for curved walls.

Close up of Valueform's ability to bend for great curvatures as shown at this oval upper patio.

Straight walls meet curved walls and crews have last minute prep work before pouring the remainder of the decorative walls.

Tie Wires and Wedge Ties

What I'm about to describe is a secret we've used for years. It enables us to pour, strip, color, and finish our walls all at the same time and all in one day. The way this is done is by setting up your walls to be able to strip easily. Your forms have to be very secure or you are going to have very unsightly blowouts; to straighten this mess out could be extremely expensive! With a concrete wall that is only 4 feet tall, there are 750 pounds of pressure per square foot at the bottom of the wall. In a 4-foot run, the bottom of the wall is holding back an aggregate weight of 3,000 pounds.

The way we brace them securely is either with wedge ties or tie wire. While most contractors will use the tried and true method of snap ties that are left in place, this method will not work for our particular wall system. The snap ties leave plastic cones in the walls, and the system is not designed to strip and finish in the same day.

When we put the tie wires in, we place them at every stake whether they are 1 foot apart on the wall or 2 feet apart (on center) at the wall. The wires are going to be tied vertically every 12 inches on center, straight up the stake line. They are tied every 12 inches because the material we are using is 12 inches wide and the tie wire or wedge tie will rest on the top of the form. That is, they will be at every 12 inches vertically. If the wall is 4 feet tall, you will have four vertical tie wires or wedge ties. Wedge ties are built for 2" x 4" thick material, so if you are using a Valueform, which is only ⅝-inch thick, you have reduced that thickness between the stakes. The picture at the right give you a good idea what we are describing.

Wedge ties installed with small cleats to take up slack.

A wedge tie is a flat piece of galvanized metal, about half an inch wide and 12 inches long, and about 3/32-inch thick—put two 2" x 12"s together and that's about 3 inches thick—the wedge tie goes underneath, and on the inside it has a little tab that locks around the inside and outside of the 2" x 4." In conventional concrete wall construction, when the forms are stripped on the following day, they are removed by twisting the outside tabs off, which leaves the remainder of the wedge tie in the concrete wall. If you use the wedge ties the way they are designed to work, you won't to be able to finish the wall on the day of the pour. So we have re-engineered the tie system, so to speak, to enable us to strip color and finish concrete walls the same day.

Most retaining walls are 8 inches thick. To make this wall so that it strips easily, we reconfigure the wedge ties. We cannibalize them, as it were, so the little tabs that allow the wedges to slip in and hold the forms in place are flattened with a hammer. This way, you can take a pair of pliers and pull that wedge tie out as soon as the concrete is hard enough that it isn't going to blow out the forms. It's like pulling it out of an 8-inch thick jelly bean. We pull out hundreds of them on any given pour so we

Wedge tie and tie wire combination shown at inside of formwork.

Wedge tie and tie wire combination shown at outside of formwork.

Cutting tie wires to strip forms from walls.

can pull the siding off and start finishing the wall. On pour day, we will assign a laborer or two to the task of pulling these out quickly, so the finishers can focus on coloring and finishing the walls as specified.

If you don't have wedge ties, another way to adequately brace the wall, and still be able to strip, color, and finish, is to double up on tie wire and run it in between the stakes with which you are forming. You have to have opposite stakes on inner and outer sides of the wall, directly aligned so that you can tie wire around either stake. A spacer goes in at the top of the wall, a piece of wood, 1 ½" x 1 ⅝ " at the top of the wall. Even if we use wedge ties to hold our forms together we still will use a tie wire at the top of the wall to allow for ease of edging. Now we can tie the stakes tightly with tie wire because the spacer is creating the proper wall thickness.

Wire ties all have to run parallel to each other, as do the stakes to which they tie. A lot of contractors take a large nail and put it in the middle of the two parallel wires inside the forms so they can twist the wire and pull the forms tight to the spacer. For our application, this is a big mistake! We leave the wires open so we can pull them, unobstructed, straight through and out of the wall. It leaves two little snakebite-size holes, but they are easy to cover up with a wood float.

The wire is designed to pull out easily for stripping forms.

Pulling out wedge ties in the same manner for ease of stripping.

Once the wall is poured, we take those spacers out because the weight of the concrete easily pushes out the forms for space, while the tie wire fastened at each opposing stake holds the wall tight to exactly 8 inches, or whatever spacing you want. Take those spacers out so you can edge the top of the wall nicely. In order to edge it flat and straight, the tie wire has to be above the top of the wall so that your hand-edger tool can be run under the wire and not be obstructed. This is critical. Make sure that the wire is located at least 6 inches above the forms so there is ample room to run the edger tool back and forth on each top side of the formed wall. You need to float and level, then edge, float and level, and edge again. If it is not level and straight, it will look bad and unprofessional

Note: You should not edge the walls too early or the top edge of the wall will have a tendency to ride up and down. The walls have to be edged when the concrete is a little harder and takes its first set, so you don't get undulations and warbling effects.

If the walls are 6 feet tall or higher, don't pour them all at the same time. The weight of that concrete per square foot will be too much; pour in layers. Pour the footing and seal off the bottom of the wall, then go back with a second and third pass. That way, the forms have a chance to do their work and not be overburdened with the weight of all that wet concrete.

Concrete is 4,000 pounds per yard and 144 pounds per square foot—so it is 97 pounds per square foot in an 8-inch wall. Stacking multiple feet of concrete in walls grows the weight exponentially.

Using a Dewalt impact driver to set forms.

Make sure there is enough manpower to strip and finish poured-in-place walls.

Using a Dewalt impact driver to strip forms.

The Pour

Pour day for a concrete contractor is extremely important because he is working with a perishable and fickle product that needs to be tamed. You usually have an average of a four-hour window of opportunity to get the job done. The colors need to be on site and the right stamps need to be in place. Everything needs to be ready: release agents, specialty tools like individual bullnose finishing tools, chisels, small covers for wall tops and bottoms, admixtures, etc. You should have a checklist to make sure all of the men, materials, and equipment are on the job. If you don't have systems in place. you may end up having big problems. You definitely need a foreman, perhaps a project manager, standing back and looking at the infinite details that, if left undone, can reduce a great job to an average one.

Concrete contractor deal with many detailed techniques: detailed formwork, wall pours, coping pours, concrete countertops, stamping, blending colors, preparing for acid staining or acid washing, sand blasting, etc. All of these treatments require different labor metrics or ratios. These are some of the considerations that drive a lot of decorative concrete contractors out of the marketplace. It is complicated, and there is so much to control, especially on pour day. You have to be as diligent and scientific as possible in the decorative concrete business.

Having a really good pumper makes pours much smoother.

Placing and Finishing Walls

Stripping and finishing walls is far more of an art than a science. As soon as you pour, you need to start unscrewing. Use Phillips wood screws in all the forms. That way you don't have to bang around with nails, which increases the difficulty of form setting. Use screw guns. We mostly use 18-volt, cordless, DeWalt impact screw guns. The impact feature works extremely well and allows us to remove screws without stripping as many of the Phillips screw heads.

When screwing forms into place was becoming popular in the late 1980s, it was common to see screw heads constantly strip, which made it extremely difficult to remove forms so that the finishing could begin. I remember one job where the majority of the Phillips screw heads were stripped so badly that the crosses on the screw heads became like hollowed-out cones. We barely got the step treads and risers finished. Make sure you use good screws and a good screw gun with an impact feature. These screw guns are more expensive, but when you are stripping formwork, and concrete is setting up quickly, they are worth far more than what you invested in them.

You might start taking most of the screws out immediately from each stake. If you take screws out too early, your forms will let you know right away as they will bow, and you should put the screws back into place and wait a bit more. As soon as you can only depress the concrete ¼" or ⅜" with your finger, you're more than likely ready to start stripping the forms. Typically, you are ready to strip within three hours of the pour. There is really a level of finesse and an art to knowing when to strip, and every pour is different due to variables such as how long the concrete has been in the truck, how hot or cold it is, etc.

The crew strips the walls very carefully.

Many of the stakes, wires, and wedges have been pulled so that stripping wall forms can take place.

Place and Finish Metrics

A profit and loss sheet examines the direct costs to build a job: labor, material, equipment, and subcontractors. One of the biggest and most difficult costs to manage is labor. In the decorative concrete industry, labor is such a monster to try to harness. I will bring up the adage from Peter Drucker again, "What can be measured can be managed." You are trying to manage your labor and ultimately your costs by employing measurable metrics. I have gone to a great deal of effort to ascribe a certain amount of labor to the various tasks that we use within our company, mostly in our operations and less in sales and administrative. It is obvious that I have a lot more work to do in my company.

As noted earlier, in our company, each phase and task has a particular metric attached to it. For example, our experience and and metrics logs say for each 100 linear feet of coping we should have four men. Our metrics log for stamped concrete says that we should have between 125 and 175 square feet per man for a patio or a driveway. If the pours are more difficult, we have to drive the square footage rate down and, likewise, if the pour is wide open and there are very few deep joints in the surface, then we might be able to get as much as 250 square feet per man or even higher.

We try to be diligent in keeping records of how many people it takes to do a certain job. We record, with our time cards, how many men we used on each phase and task. But I've also noted that many variables and contingencies can throw those metric calculations out of the window. You will need to track your own crews to see what they are capable of.

Through our experience and documented time cards we have arrived at other metrics for various pours. One man can usually handle 125 square feet of flat, stamped work. This metric will be reduced to approximately 90 square feet per man when we are delicately blending in color hardeners to produce subtle variations of color on a patio or pool deck. When it comes to exposed aggregate, one man can handle 80 to 100 square feet of exposed aggregate because it is a lot more labor intensive.

Recently we had a three-part pour with a planter wall, stairs, and patio. We had 160 square feet of planter wall that needed to be stripped, colored, and finished, so I assigned four finishers to that phase. We had 33 lineal feet of stairs, so I assigned one man to that. We had 600 square feet of stamped patio, so I assigned five men for the patio. We had 10 men on that pour, and everything went well.

I want ample man power on pour days, but when the pour is over—many times its over by 1 p.m.—I want the crews moving on to one of the other jobs. Most of the time we are "borrowing" a foreman and his crew for a different job. He and his crew need to return to their own job ASAP.

Your team will include people from outside your company, such as lighting and landscaping people. Another team member important to your company is your concrete pumper. We use concrete pumpers on a weekly basis, and in the summer, sometimes on a daily basis.

We have had really bad pumpers who put our projects in jeopardy. It can be a disaster to have this key team player unprepared. A bad pumper puts a project a risk. A pumper has to keep his pumps in tiptop shape. It is very important that a concrete contractor either have his own pumps or have a top-of-the-line subcontractor who really takes pride in his work.

It's important that every team member that you choose is at the top of his game and is going to make your product that much better and your job that much easier. All of your people on your team, from in-house employees to subcontractors, everybody has to be top notch. On pour day, you're going for the Super Bowl. And you need to be the winner on every pour.

Applying Color to Poured Walls

Thus far, you have read about coloring steps and walls. There are over a thousand dust-on colors that you can make by blending products from the various color hardener manufacturers: Alcantar, Scoffield, Matcrete, Kingdom, Brickform, and Butterworth, just to name a few. Make your own custom blends from a combination of colors from the same or different manufacturers. It is really simple, and you end up with some outstanding custom colors. So if you want to lighten a platinum grey, add some oyster shell, for example. The disadvantage of dust-on color is that it is more labor-intensive than if you just add the color to the concrete. But some of the results you can get with it are extraordinary.

When pouring walls that will be stripped, it is a good idea to have all hands on deck, including the pumper to make sure that there is plenty of labor to ensure a great finished wall.

If the colors vary too much, if there is a snafu with dust-on colors, or if the customer is not happy with the color, you can make a blend of color hardener by adding Acryl glue to the mix. Rub this into the surface until you get the color your client wants and appreciates.

The first step after stripping the walls, when you are using a dust-on-color hardener, is to take a float and strip down any inconsistencies, knocking down any raised or extruded lines created where the form boards met. Also, rub out any small bug holes that are left in the concrete as a result of air pockets at this time. Choose a wooden float for this procedure because it can shape the concrete far more easily than a metal float or hard trowel can; hose tools have a tendency to ride onto the surface rather than cutting and filling it. A wooden float can bring up the cream and cut into the high spots with far more effectiveness.

Now it is ready for the application of color.

It is possible to broadcast dry color onto the walls; however, when you have lots of wall to color, mix it in buckets until it is a yogurt-like consistency and then start stuccoing the wall. Apply the color hardener with wooden floats and work it into the surface to meld these materials together, creating a mechanical bond between the colored material and the grey concrete wall. The newly stripped wall is fresh, green concrete that allows for a great bond with the fresh cementitious stucco mix. Put in the deep joints, which have been previously laid out, as soon as you've done the color stucco.

Mixing color hardener in a bucket with a drill and paddle to prepare for finishers.

Stucco-finishing the walls.

Finishing walls over 6 feet tall requires special attention when stripping; make sure there is plenty of labor on hand to keep finishing under control.

Once you rub that color in with your wooden floats, you are ready to hard trowel. This is an art. Hard trowel it once, and then it is ready for a final hard trowel finish. One of the good things about using this technique is that you can get movement and drifts in the color on your walls that you don't get with integral color. Integral colors are also really susceptible to discoloration if you add water during the finishing procedure—you run a risk of having ugly disparities and blotchiness. Color hardeners eliminate this risk, and another advantage is you get an array of up to 800 colors easily. Color hardeners can have their base cement change from grey to white, creating pastel colors. Sometimes if you want "drifts" of color or movement of color, use small spray bottles to mist-on the color. One thing to watch out for is bubbles . If you trowel the concrete too soon, too hard, and too quickly, the plaster mix will bubble and separate from the concrete wall. If this happens, then wipe out the bubbles with a wood float and wait a while longer to start the troweling procedures.

This wall was 8 feet from the ground on a slight hillside, which made an 18-yard pour very labor-intensive. More than 12 men helped finish the wall on the day of the pour.

Placing Joints

Put deep joints in most of your walls because concrete will most likely crack. A yard of concrete is three feet tall, wide, and thick. In order to make a yard of concrete pumpable, workable, and malleable, you have to add water. The optimum amount of water to add is 25 to 30 gallons of water per cubic yard. As soon as you pour, the water that was used to start the hydration process to give concrete its tensile and PSI strength, starts leaving the concrete immediately. The concrete shrinks. That shrinkage is going to produce cracking and curling. It is going to crack when it shrinks. A flat expanse is like a lake bed. You get the curling phenomenon at the edges because the edges dry faster. In concrete, it is called slab curling. With a wall, you won't get curling so much as shrinkage. You want to chisel in deep joints, ½ to ¾ inches deep, to ensure that this jointed section of the wall has become weakened and will direct the cracking to that line. It is like programming your concrete to seek this weakened line as it shrinks. Once you've established the weakened plane, the concrete should crack there—not always—but it usually will. The twists and turns of hillsides put additional stress on the concrete. You want to get those joints established in a logical place and, if possible, in an aesthetic place. Form and function should complement each other.

Laying out deep joints for a pool deck.

Layout for jointing should happen days before the pour. Many contractors will lay out the joints the day of the pour, or during the pour—but that is wrong. The day of the pour is so hectic, the last thing you want to do is leave this as a final task. You'l also want to get the input of the contractor and/or the homeowner. This is also the time to lay out the lighting . A light fixture can create a weakened point in the wall, so this often dictates a deep joint. You want the joints to make sense and to look incredible, and this will require a thoughtful layout. When patio or deck drains are involved, try to lay out the joint pattern first, whether it is a parallel and perpendicular joint pattern or a diagonal one. You need to lay out the joints first to determine where the drains will be set, since concrete usually wants to crack around the drain grates. Using deep joints to intersect the drains will help alleviate cracking.

Tool in the joints with giant iron chisels. First, scribe a line with a level so that it is plumb. If you have a joint that is off plumb, the eye goes right to it. Use 4- or 6-foot levels to scribe a line, and follow immediately with the chiseling. Use a straight bar chisel for jointing walls.

Orange Chalk

After you have the walls laid out and poured, again lay out the stairs and the landings on the walls. Don't mark them out in pencil, as it is hard to get the marking out. You only need a really light marking. Also, never use blue or red chalk. It's extremely difficult to get out, if not impossible. Use orange chalk because it doesn't stain and can be easily removed (Bobby Harris of the Decorative Concrete Institute in Atlanta showed me that trick.) Do the final layout on the actual wall, for the stair and landing configuration. Then start building the stairs.

Deep jointer finishes the wall joints after the chisel has made an initial cut into the wall.

Use a level to make sure joints are plumb and true.

Orange chalk lines are all we allow because red, blue, or black chalk lines are hard to remove. Pencil marks can be difficult to remove as well.

This drain grate rests at a diagonal deep joint intersection.

Lighting

There are some lighting people who will be happy to come out to the site to educate your clients, provide them with lighting choices, and make professional recommendations. The award-winning lighting company FX Luminaire will come out and stage lighting for you. You are already thinking about where to place the lights as you form your walls and steps. Lights can be placed either in the walls or steps or both, and often your deep joints go wherever the lights are set: The boxes interrupt the concrete's mass and generally become the weakened plane of the wall where cracks can easily develop; hence a deep joint at each of the lights may help to control the possible crack that will emanate from the light box housing. It is a critical part of layout and a predetermination for light placement.

Meandering steps and walls perform very well together at night.

With hillside concrete construction, as in most concrete construction, it is best to determine all you can in advance. Because the lighting boxes are usually square or rectangular, the corners are susceptible to cracking. Scoring joints from each corner would not look good, so you might choose to place only one joint in the middle of the box. Most of the time that works, and the cracks will make their permanent home in the predetermined joint.

Lighting for walls is critical for many reasons. Aesthetically, it is a beautiful feature. It's also a safety feature. It allows people to see where they are going on sets of steps. Also, walking off into adjacent landscape that is slippery and steep could be treacherous if you get off the path. Often hillsides are dark expanses and you need to properly light them. A landscaper may choose to use post lighting to shine down on the landscape and to use up-lighting to illuminate walls, stairs, and other landscape and pedestrian features.

Value your relationship with a good lighting designer. Hire someone you trust. Your lighting designer is part of your team and can help make the whole team look really good.

Try to find a lighting representative who is willing to go out at night to the site to determine where the lights should be and what kinds of lights will work best. In the case of stairs, for example, you could put lights on every single riser, but you don't need that many. Going out at night and laying out the plan is the best way to do it. Study lighting and how it relates to the hardscape, softscape, and the big picture.

Flags were set at night to mark lighting placement for stairs after walls were poured and wall lights were on. A bare minimum of lighting needs to be considered for safely navigating your landscape after dark.

Another photo from the camera of Tom Ralston, who assisted with placement of flags for lighting determination at night.

Louver-lit stairs and round bird-beak brass covers on walls at night.

The formwork has stairs marked out so that lighting placement is laid out accurately.

Holes in walls are made for small, round, bird-beak light covers while flexible tubing is laid out for step lights.

Standard 6" stair risers require narrower step lighting, hence a custom light was developed by TRC to accommodate the bullnose with a light. The upper stair shows the custom light.

If you install great lighting, you will most certainly get a lot of "wow" when the project is finished. Pictures of our jobs at night, all lit up, have a certain magic to them.

Once in a while, we will use our Lumi Lumi balls to light our pathways or Lumi louvers to light our steps. Lumi Lumi is a phosphoric aggregate that we use in our concrete or in our fashioned concrete balls that become pathfinders. The Lumi lights are solar-powered and require no batteries. Just 10 minutes of sun will provide 10 hours of glow. (Visit www.lumilumiballs.com to learn more about them.)

Recently, we were seemingly thwarted by a situation where there were no step lights that seemed to work for our small 5 ½-inch riser. All of the frames for the step lights were too wide. Since "necessity is the mother of invention," we designed lights that would work and had them made up. We are now considering selling these unique light boxes for steps and walls. We are also working on various lighting for walls and columns, driveways and patios.

Light fixture fastening
to riser below
custom-built bullnose.

Custom light fixture
with "smurf" tube
conduit for low
voltage hook-up.

Upper patio with
wall lights and
city lights in the
background.

Finishing stairs
around the custom
lighting.

Using the Lumi Lumi louvers as an alternative to electrical lights. The Lumi aggregate does not need batteries to light up, only direct or indirect sun. These lights are fastened by screws and epoxy to retrofit lighting for the stairs.

The Lumi Lumi louvers on steps at night

The Lumi Lumi balls on a slight hillside during the day.

The Lumi Lumi balls lit up at night on that hillside.

Wall Caps and Copings

Wall caps are much like bullnose stairs. In fact, the profiles we use on walls always match the stairs we do and the pool coping. Most of the time we use the same color and texture as well so the different components look harmonious. If we have a wall cap that stands on its own suspended above the ground we will construct a double bullnose wall cap. These will run an additional five dollars a linear foot because of the additional bullnose foam, labor to form-set, and labor to finish. If it is a wall cap that dives into the dirt that the wall is retaining, then we will only have the front side finished with a bullnose.

Wall caps that work with the other elements are a wonderful way to make a statement aesthetically. Seat wall caps also function as a nice, broad expanse of concrete that is comfortable to sit on and consistent in color, texture, and profile with other concrete elements of design.

Copings can be aesthetically used in the same way as a wall cap or step. We take great care to level the pool or spa coping because most of them will ride on a grade beam of gunnite and most of the time they are not perfectly level. We will shoot the highest point of the spa's grade beam or the pool's grade beam, and fill in the low spots with nonshrink grout. This is because we would rather fill in the low spots than grind down high spots. This way the tile can lay level directly below the coping. If you do not use nonshrink grout to level the beam and the concrete bonds to the lower points behind the tile, there will be a tendency for the tile to crack with the movement of the earth.

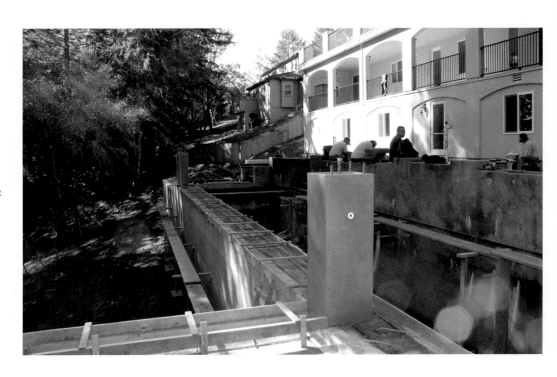

Hand-built wooden scaffolding for hillside coping and for the wall cap at the pool wall.

Finishing column cap; making sure it is flat by using a 4' level.

Finishing wall caps with plastic safety tape to provide a good polish on the fresh concrete radius.

Ganging up on a short stretch of wall cap. Notice the finisher is stepping on a small piece of plywood to avoid making a footprint on the newly finished stair tread.

Pouring a coping on a hillside on top of hand-built scaffolding.

Finishing inside spa coping with color hardener stucco technique.

Drainage Systems

For a retaining wall, the drainage system is extremely important. A good drainage system will negate or reduce the hydrostatic pressure that a hillside has on a retaining wall. The weight of soil increases exponentially when saturated with water, and thus the pressure against a concrete retaining wall will increase exponentially as well. A drainage system significantly reduces that pressure and allows the water to pass into a designated drain location.

An intentional space should be left behind the wall for a drain system during construction. First, bring filter fabric, then place a 4-inch perforated drain line, add drain rock into the fabric, and then wrap it (like a burrito). This will allow the water to pass through easily. If you were to backfill with dirt, the dirt would press against the wall. I have seen walls fail because they did not adequately relieve the pressure from the hillside with a drain system. This system takes the weight off the wall and allows any water that comes into the hillside to pass through, like a sieve.

Excavation here included the footings, wall, and the drainage system behind the wall.

You can also have a drain system to capture water on top of the backfill at the same time, creating a swale to capture surface water. We build percolation pits, or "perc pits," that are sometimes 4-feet wide by 4-feet long x 4-feet deep. We place filter fabric into the hole, add ¾-inch drain rock, cover the rock with an additional length of fabric, and then cover it all with topsoil or native soil. Different soils or civil engineers will specify different percolation pits. Sometimes we have two or three of these pits on a site, and sometimes they are deeper. Water goes into these pits and then drains down into the soil.

At other times we have what is called a dissipation pit, which basically does the same as a percolation pit, but it is designed to slow down rushing water coming through the drain line or lines. These pits are usually longer and shallower. At the end of the drain line is a perpendicular perforated drain line that becomes fashioned like a T. The top of the pit is open with rock, and the water will perc up out of the perforated pipe and then out of the dissipation pit.

A dissipation pit or a diversion pit, as they are sometimes called, is something that a civil engineer will specify to slow down the speed of the water so that you don't have lots of erosion where the water egresses. If you have copious amounts of water coming down a hillside, and you are running it through a drain line, you will have the potential for erosion. Civil engineers often run a drain line through different stations or pits. When the water reaches a dissipation pit at the end of the pipe, it hits a T and shoots out to the left and the right to further slow the water and mitigate its force.

Another consideration for a retaining wall is waterproofing. If the back of a wall is not waterproofed (the hillside of the wall), water can migrate through the wall (remember concrete is extremely porous) and stain the finished/exposed concrete wall. The staining

Cementitious waterproofing applied on the lower half of a hillside retaining wall prior to adding the drainage system.

Class II Permeable gravel installed behind hillside wall.

Installing filter fabric to wrap drain rock and drain line, which will prevent dirt and other contaminants from entering into the drain system.

Color hardener has been applied 2 feet below top of wall to provide the finished vertical face of a seat wall. A 4-inch perforated pipe with filter fabric is ready for drain rock.

Color hardener has been applied on the patio side of the wall to prepare for the drain system.

is usually white because of the salts that migrate through the water. Applying two coats of a cementitious waterproofing will usually prevent this type of staining or efflorescence from occurring. For flat work, drainage systems require preplanning and a modicum of skill. Drain stations should intersect into a joint grid pattern. Concrete typically shrink-wraps around anything in its way; if a drain grate is incorporated, concrete is typically going to shrink around that grate. Determine where the grate will be by laying out the flat work's grid pattern, and then make sure the drain grate covers line up perfectly with the grid, so that each corner of the grate lines up perfectly with a deep joint.

Lay out deep joints for the homeowner on the rock base and ask them first if they like the layout and the grid configuration. At that point, with the owner's approval, determine where the drainage stations will be located.

Drain grates cost between $20 and $200, and come in everything from plastic to bronze, brass, or nickel. There are some very beautiful grates available online and at plumbing supply houses. It's another little detail in the world of decorative concrete contractors. Get your homeowner to pick what he or she wants in advance. The more you can determine and specify before the job starts, the better off you'll be as the job unfolds. This is especially true if what you need has to be shipped or special-ordered.

A dissipater T pipe waits for filter fabric and clean drain rock to finish the dissipater pit.

Compacting baserock adjacent to the drain system. Note that color hardener is applied wherever the wall is exposed and below is the grey waterproofing to help prevent efflorescence.

Orange nylon strings with the grid layout configuration will determine the layout for drain grate stations.

A pool deck grid system and joint layout shown with marking paint (usually we will lay out with paint for owner's approval and then we will begin excavation for grates).

Mifab nickel bronze grate installed exactly on the apex of gridline intersection. *Photo by Mickey Rebecchi*

A second example of a bronze grate placed onto a concrete deck.

Sealing Dos and Don'ts

Seal every facet of concrete work that you do on as soon as you can to protect your new concrete work. Most often, you will use solvent-based sealers. Sealing with protect flat surfaces from foot traffic, landscapers trampling fertilizer, dog droppings, and tannic acid from trees. The number one concern is tannic acid. Redwood trees are notorious for tannic acid, as are oak trees. Once the tannic acid gets inside concrete, it can be difficult to remove. If you seal the concrete before the trees have a chance to bleed onto it, the sealant will protect the concrete somewhat from the resultant staining. Of course, the tannic acid will eventually win, unless you power-wash it off at least bimonthly.

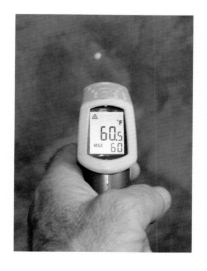

A Fluke 62 mini thermometer shows a reading of 60 degrees, which is the minimum temperature for sealing concrete.

Seal within seven to 10 days. One of the risks of sealing too early is that you get white spots when moisture comes up through the concrete and whitens the sealer. However, an early seal can be a distinct advantage for the concrete as it cures. The best cured concrete is set under water. In order to allow concrete to grow to its greatest strength, keep it hydrated. One way to cure concrete is to cover it with wet burlap sacks or plastic sheeting. However, if you hydrated your colored walls, slabs, or stairs with burlap or plastic, it would hideously destroy the effects you worked so hard to create. So, by sealing within a day or two, you help the concrete stay more hydrated. This will not be possible in cooler months if the temperature of the concrete drops well below the 60 degrees recommended for most sealers. Use an infrared temperature gauge (we use the Fluke 62 mini thermometer) to helps determine if you are at the 60 degree mark or not. If you are not, then do not seal. Do temperature tests at various spots on the hardscape to get good information that will help you make sound sealing decisions.

Concrete needs to hydrate to get to its highest PSI strength. Fronds within the concrete continue to grow when kept moist, and they start to entwine. That's the way a chemist described it to me. The more they can entwine by keeping moist, the stronger the bond will be. Concrete actually hydrates for 50 years. It's a long, long, long process. The first 28 days are the most critical. This is the benchmark everyone uses for the hydration process. Sealing concrete can help lock in the moisture to promote good hydration; however, many times it is not worth the risk of having the sealer fail. Cures can be used, but I have found that many of the cures easily whiten and can discolor the concrete, so for architectural/decorative concrete I tend to shy away from them.

Sealing a stamped patio using our Graco.

Sealing can also enhance the color of concrete. This is especially true if it is a lacquer-based sealer. Sealing can really promote the "wow" factor of a project, especially when you are acid staining. Acid staining has become extremely popular in the last 15 years. If you acid stain or color a project and don't seal it, you are not going to get anywhere near the value of color you will get if it is sealed. Again, color value enhances dramatically when you seal concrete, and most of the time it is desired.

There are different gradations of sealers: high-gloss, low-gloss, satin, and what is called natural impregnator, which does not change the concrete's color or impart any kind of sheen. Typically, we only use the gloss. A lot of people use the impregnating sealers on stone.

Most manufacturers say you should wait at least 28 days before you seal concrete. What I am recommending flies in the face of that and could potentially backfire on a contractor. We realize that it is risky to seal before 28 days. We also know that if you use these light acrylic, solvent-based sealers, you can strip them pretty easily with lacquer thinner or zylene. Lately we have been cutting our sealer with a chemical called EEP (Ethyl3-Ethoxypropionate).

It needs to be built into the bid that you have this potential for failure. You have to try to prepare for that risk. That's why your prices should be more expensive than less, always. When you bid against a lot of these other contractors, they are not taking into account the risks and the call-backs, and perhaps they will not even include sealing because it is so risky. On 20 or 30 percent of our jobs, there is some kind of a call-back. That's one of the disadvantages of working in decorative concrete. Sealers are the biggest culprit, at the top of the list for call-backs. Sealers have cost our company serious money. Sealers are almost a necessary evil.

We've been wrestling with sealer application for more than two decades. If there are no trees around, and if the concrete is not on the wet and shady side of the property, there is less risk. If you can wait for 28 days, that's what you should do. But, typically, we don't have that luxury.

Climates that have lots of inclement weather are going to have limited opportunities for sealing. It is a major consideration.

A homeowner and a contractor should understand that these products are going to have to be maintained. What happens to a lot of these sealers is they can whiten and look unsightly over time. They may have to be stripped. Sometimes you can get away with just applying a light spray of EEP or Zylene. This process will re-emulsify the sealer, and it can actually look pretty good. But, the sealants are so broken down, the only way you can repair them is to strip them completely off and reseal. You can use soda blasters to strip them, or you can strip them with Soy Gel, or use some of the methylene chloride strippers like Jasco. We typically start with acetone, lacquer thinner, or Zylene, and then use rags to clean up the mess.

Sealing the stucco on a large, outdoor Rumford fireplace with our Graco airless sprayer.

When you start sealing flat surfaces, it becomes slippery. It is not a big deal on vertical surfaces, but on horizontal surfaces, you have to be aware that you have protected it and enhanced it, but also made it a slippery surface. We put in pulverized glass, which increases the traction and makes it a little bit more slip-resistant. But don't ever use the expression "anti-slip" because you can never guarantee that no one is going to slip. Some of the higher trafficked areas will wear away the sealer. It is just one more risk to contend with in the decorative concrete realm.

As I have already mentioned, we like a blend of pulverized glass that is part amber and part fern green. That combination gives a nice, subtle, and muted hue. Glasses come in 30 to 40 different colors, so we can also do custom blends when we want to. There is also a commercial product called Shark Skin that people can use and work with. Typically, we prefer to use an airless sprayer (we use the Graco model 230 ES).

Stains from an oak tree will haunt a decorative concrete contractor, especially in the winter.

These walls indicate that sealer failure is beginning; the sealant will need to be removed with a lacquer or acetone wipe.

Hand-stripping a sealer that failed with Zylene, a green scouring pad, and rags.

A rectangular firepit under construction, prior to pour.

Close-up picture of rectangular firepit that shows gas line with shut-off valve and riser for fire ring.

Firepits and Fireplaces

Firepits are really hot in the marketplace right now, no pun intended. There's nothing quite like a firepit to promote a sense of community and familial spirit.

We love building firepits and have created specific dimensions for our firepits and their benches. They can come in all shapes and sizes: elliptical, round, oval, or square. We've built them all.

Today's firepits typically run with natural gas. They can be propane, but it's a different setup. You have to have a little more caution with propane as you run greater risks for explosion. Or fire pits can just be wood, which takes a lot more effort. A gas firepit is fuss-free and does not emit carbon dioxide gasses.

A firepit can only fit into a hillside environment when you have an upper patio or a lower terrace.

There are probably fifty different colors of glass now for firepits. We use lava rock, and prefer the black lava. We use big chips of glass; we use little jelly bean glass and small aggregates of glass that are ¼- to 1 ½-inch sizes. That's like frosting on the cake. Seeing these firepits with blue and white glass, tangerine, pineapple—it's like having a fruit salad inside your firepit. It's dramatic. To see flame coming out of colored glass is even more of a treat—or to see flames that shoot right out of sand.

The cost for our firepits starts at about $3,900.

The newly completed rectangular firepit by day and night.

Hillside Gallery

TRC used a platinum gray color hardener made by Alcantar for these intermediate bullnose profile wall caps with matching bullnose steps. This staircase was designed to fit into an existing segmented wall constructed by the owner. Adjacent walks and landings incorporated a light Italian slate stamp texture.

A small meditation spot with a seat overlooks steps that meander to a pool area; when there is no fog, there's a beautiful view of the city. *Photo by Bud Ralston.*

This overhead view show stairs that lead from a lawn area to a side yard; note the delicious colors chosen by both the landscape contractor and homeowner.

This stout wall has deadmen, piers, and grade beams heavily laden with rebar cages and dowels. At the top is a beautiful patio and barbecue area. Small stone tiles that match the grays in the concrete enhance the wall below the arbor. This tile work wraps into the backsplash and countertop of the outdoor kitchen. The same treatment lines the firepit base.

Note the stainless-steel railings on this decorative structural wall, which are also used for backrests. This project won a national award for TRC in 2009 for "best decorative structural project." Woodwork was by David Hooks Construction Services of Santa Cruz, California.

A closer look at the intricate outdoor kitchen cabinets, nooks, and crannies that were all fashioned with poured-in-place concrete and then highlighted with stone.

This hillside patio and staircase were built so that the owners of the Summit Market could add to their dining area. They chose an Alcantar sandstone color hardener and Scofield weathered sage release color. A light Italian slate was used on the vertical and horizontal patios and stairs.

An elegantly styled wrought-iron fence was fabricated for the new dining area at the market.

This hillside project features a harmonious blend of colors, textures, and shapes. The smooth countertop, walls, and deck of the lower patio take their color pallette from the rock walls above.

Wall and step lights switch on at dusk. The landscape design and plant choices add colors and textures that enhance the creative concrete design.

Colorful, full gardens add interest to this stairway as it works its way down the hillside with capstone bullnose profiles from the Stagmire Corporation.

A center landing area provides a resting spot. The project features weathered sage walls, cappuccino stairs, and sandstone flatwork. The stairs have an Italian slate texture. This spot is also where a water feature begins.

Colorful plants soften and enhance the beautiful concrete
work. Note the wall caps at the start of the steep staircase.

These simple stairs zigzag back and forth like mini switchbacks, creating an aesthetically pleasing descent to the pool area.

An overhead view of the zigzagging steps poured with a warm French gray manufactured by Matcrete.

Bali rainforest tile creates a colorful pattern in these acid stained concrete countertops.

A view to the water feature from the lower patio, which features the colorful acid stained countertops. The solid roof is arched; the owner planned to add a grass shack roof at a later date.

Notice the white boxes in the firepit patio walls. They are Bose speakers, adding to the "stairway to heaven" ambience of this hilltop patio.

An overview of the project featured on the preceeding pages with the upper patio, resting spot, and lower outdoor kitchen area. The large oval firepit is lined with multi-colored glass. Seat walls incorporate radiant heated tubing for staying warm on cooler evenings. Gas heaters provide additonal warmth. Note how the drain grates are centered on the apex of the jointing. This helps to control cracking.

A upper firepit area features a a nice ocean view.

This hillside stream was created for visual interest and also for the calming sound of water running over variously sized rocks.

Pops of color, including crystal clear blue water in the pool and crystal blue glass in the firepit and fire bowls, make for a dramatic setting. Note the ipe, or Brazilian walnut, deck and bench seats.

The same stream from above with a view of the pool, deck, fireplace, and cabana.

This view shows how the flair of the bullnosed stairs met with the resting area.

Stairs and hardscape flanked by colors, colors, and more colors.

This photo shows off the cappuccino-colored stairs that had the capstone profile and also shows well this color and texture play off the weathered sage hard troweled walls.

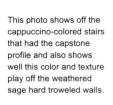

The same stairs and patio lit up at night.

The arch of the dome roof, with its pumpkinlike color, looks pleasing next to the curve of the path that leads up to the firepit patio.

This straight, side staircase is a handsome and well-lit express way.

The same stairway photographed from above shows the structure that houses the outdoor kitchen area.

Warm pendant lighting highlights the colorful acid stained concrete and stone countertops.

This challenging wall required about three weeks of work, including laser levels, grading, excavation, form-setting, and rebar.

Directly above the structural wall is the Shangri-La that now is enjoyed by homeowners and their guests.

A good perspective of the amphitheater-like, beige cream, semicircular steps in this hillside project designed by Michael McKay. The photo shows the project in its the final stages of completion and illustrates the inherent beauty of work on hillsides.

The morning sun peeks through the trees, creating a reflection on the water of this peaceful swimming pool with its endless edge and trough.

A shot of the fireplace surrounded by yellowstone stucco and a cantilevered concrete bench made with 4000 psi concrete, an oyster white color hardener, and a sand-washed finish.

Lounge chairs beckon visitors to enjoy the swimming pool, the surrounds, and the ocean view that will materialize when the fog clears.

Another view from above shows the organic vegetable garden flanked by flagstone steps and terraces, as well as the epi woodwork by West Builders of Santa Cruz, California.

A close-up of the serpentine hillside stairs with the Stagmire intermediate bullnose along with Matcrete's limestone color hardener and a sand-wash texture.
Photo by Bud Ralston

The same staircase elegantly lit up to create an artful setting that will immediately engage any visitor.

A winding, sloped path of three river flagstones broken up by bands of brown Mexican pebbles turned on edge to resemble dorsal fins. The firepit and bench seats are made of concrete and flagstone; the area can seat 12 people.

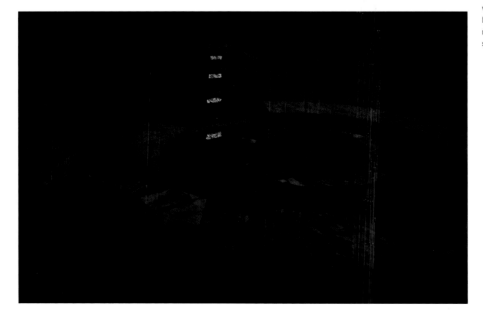

Copious amounts of three river flagstones surround well aged and worn concrete with sandstone color hardener; note the Lumi louvers on the steps. They have been retrofitted and only need 10 minutes of sunlight to provide 10 hours of glow.

A treacherously dark pathway along a slight hillside leading to the three river flagstone firepit is lined with Lumi Lumi balls to provide guidance at night. It is dusk and they are just beginning to glow.

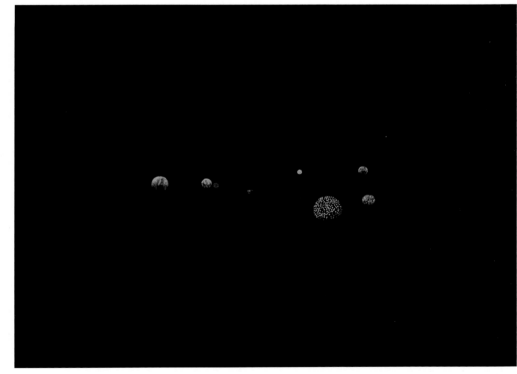

The lit Lumi Lumi balls are both dramatic and useful pathfinders to the home below.

A lit firepit provides a warm glow while the Lumi louvers add some pretty, safety lighting. The louvers were placed into these steps in 2011.

These concrete medallions are set in concrete and Lumi aggregates of various colors. The upper medallion has a 6' diameter and is called "Milky Way," the lower medallion is similar but is 9' in diameter and is called "The Big Bang."

This photo was taken during a full moon and shows the spectacular glow of the Lumi.

A late-night fire dances behind "The Big Bang" design on the pool deck's patio.

A Lumi ball was given as a gift to the owner of this new sculpted hillside and pool renovation. He says it is an almost eerie feeling to see it glow when all else around it is dark. The author has just lit the firepit in the distance.

Here the author stares at the rising moon while the Lumi ball looms large behind him.

Fire, lighting, sculptures, and plants create an artistic play of shadow and light. To the right is a glimpse of the "in the water bar" ready to be of service to any swimmers who are ready for libations.

A close-up of the cantilever stairs with clean and crisp edges, They were produced with a ¼" edger and top cover. The Scoffield classic gray color on the step riser and treads works nicely as it transitions from a charcoal-like hardscape to a soft, green lawn.

Corner steps lead from the pool to the small concrete countertop above the refrigerator and storage cabinet. The column caps, steps, and countertops all have the same Scoffield classic gray color and a hard trowel. There are three countertops on this project, and they are were polished by using a hand-polisher and various diamond pads. *Photo by Ryan Huebe*

Custom step lights were designed by TRC and fabricated by Roy Johnson Studios of Santa Cruz to fit within the tight riser faces. Copper frames with rectangular grid patterns hold the amber glass that produces a golden hue.

This day-lit hillside pool deck was a candidate for our first Lumi pool deck; the aggregates were more heavily seeded on the pool coping and sparser on the pool deck.

At night, when the stars are out in the mountains of Santa Cruz, the sky and the pool deck mirror each other with their scattered lights against inky backdrops.

This award-winning shot was taken above the serpentine staircase that leads from an oval upper patio to a pool and a firepit. Note how the city lights on the horizon compliment the multitude of lights in this vast hardscape.

Taken from a bird's-eye vantage point, this photo shows the curvature of the seat wall that surrounds the Rumford fireplace. It also shows the furniture added for entertaining guests.

A "beachside platform" is featured in this pool, which is surrounded by a cappuccino-colored pool deck with a nutmeg-colored coping. Flagstone steps on the left lead to a play area and garden.

Up-lighting shows off trees, plants, and the wall cap. The walls were troweled to produce a Monet-like effect by using small trowels and mists of water while finishing.

This pool and patio were designed by architect Michael McKay, originally from Los Gatos and now working in New Zealand. TRC fashioned quite a bit of decorative concrete into this hillside, which took many pours to complete. The circular steps have a kind of amphitheater feel and were poured with a beige cream color.

An overview of the new addition of slide, pool, and water seats in the pool near the endless edge. The various curvatures of the hardscape and pool play nicely off of the straighter and more geometric lines of the house, roof, and fireplace.

This oval hillside patio features a 3' 6" grid pattern and is flanked by an 18" high seat wall. Note the Matcrete limestone color.

When the sun goes down, the city lights make for a great view from the patio bathed in golden color.

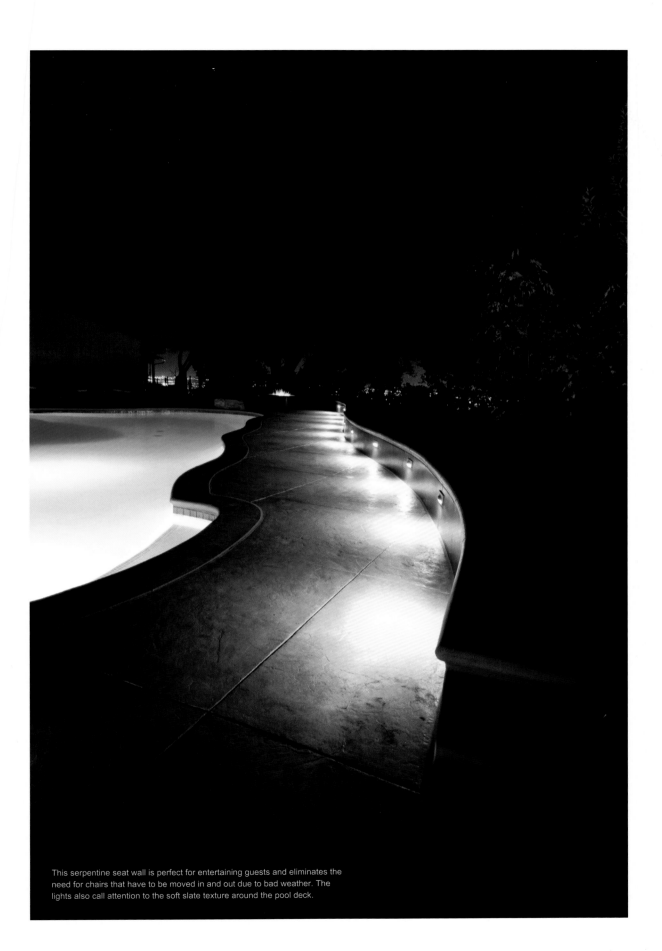

This serpentine seat wall is perfect for entertaining guests and eliminates the need for chairs that have to be moved in and out due to bad weather. The lights also call attention to the soft slate texture around the pool deck.

Fire and light create dramatic effects on this hillside pool deck. The picture illustrates the potential hillsides have to produce breathtaking results.

This homeowner chose to purchase a portable firepit for this space. The concrete seat wall creates an intimate setting around the firepit. The back of the wall is more than 5' tall; the seat is 18" high and has a 4" cantilever.

Great lighting like this cannot be underestimated, and it requires a good deal of preplanning. Lighting mock-ups can be staged prior to pouring concrete and are extremely valuable. The soft limestone color on the pool deck is brought out by these lights and so is the contrasting nutmeg color of the walls. *Photo by Ryan Heubel*

This taupe cast-in-place colored concrete bench was hard
troweled and has a seat cap made with a precast Verona stone.

Fire and lighting highlight the upper and lower paver patios. They are separated with bands and columns of colored concrete and precast Verona stone.

The back of the seats are out of plumb 5" within 18" from bottom to top of the backrest to provide very comfortable sitting, especially on these thick cushions. The multicolored blue glass of the fire pit matches the cushions.

When we first saw this photo, my associate Bill Goff said this is like looking at Las Vegas West, and so we began calling it that. The blue water has an intense and electric look, which was accomplished by the tile work and lighting provided from Royal Pools of San Jose. *Photo by Jeffrey Luhn*

Ipe bench tops constructed by West Builders warm the platinum gray concrete benches. This is a good view of the the stamped sandstone deck.

The pool's tile work is nicely highlighted in this evening photo.
Photo by Jeffrey Luhn

A setting like this could be titled "when concrete becomes art." The geometry and color of the new hardscape interact beautifully with the forest in the background.

Enthusiastic homeowner Todd Turowski offered some wine and cheese for the photoshoot. *Photo by Jeffrey Luh*

A full-view photo of the Turowski residence hillside pool deck. This image shows the wrought-iron fences, the column, and part of the gate. Also partially shown are the removable pool covers that house the automatic pool cover itself.

Another shot of a bench that attaches to a sierra sunrise flagstone that lies under a nutmeg cantilever bench with an intermediate Stagmire bullnose.

A close-up of this bench shows the multiple curvatures: horizontal, vertical, and a concave seat back that adds comfort. TRC designed this bench with owners Larry and Lisa Pott.

A limestone rock façade rests atop a concrete bench that had removable concrete lids that could be used for planting, as shown. Notice how the bench seat cantilever is echoed in the design of the firepit. Note also the multicolored glass in the firepit and the stone grey patio, with a platinum gray release textured with an Italian slate stamp.

A great view of the outdoor kitchen, water feature, firepit, and bench seat. In the backgroud is the stainless-steel rail made by Ralph Royer of RCR Fabrication and woodwork by David Hooks Construction Services, both of Santa Cruz, California.

Looking down on a cantilevered concrete bar with a concrete foot rest and colored concrete caps. A stone backsplash with matching countertop edges harmonize well with light stamped stucco.